D0882707

BREVERTON'S NAUTICAL CURIOSITIES

A Book *of the* Sea

BREVERTON'S NAUTICAL CURIOSITIES

A Book *of the* Sea

Terry Breverton

LYONS PRESS
Guilford, Connecticut
An imprint of Globe Pequot Press

CONTENTS

INTRODUCTION

'When beholding the tranquil beauty and brilliancy of the ocean's skin, one forgets the tiger heart that pants beneath it.'

Herman Melville, *Moby-Dick*

There is something elemental about the sea that draws us in and instils a sense of awe, adventure and fascination. With its unpredictable weather systems, astonishing diversity of life forms and its far-reaching impact on climate and the environment, there is so much about our oceans to intrigue and amaze us – not to mention the vast amount that remains unknown about the great waters that cover two-thirds of the planet.

This maritime miscellany is a response to that compelling attraction, offering an eclectic, informative and affectionate celebration of all things nautical. The collection of quirky and fantastic facts, figures, histories and stories gathered here reflects the weird and wonderful diversity that contributes to the sea's endless allure – from maritime slang and sayings to sea conditions and life at sea; from types of ships to famous naval battles; from great heroes to infamous villains; and from the ocean ecosystem and its amazing fauna to the sea's vital (and threatened) importance to the preservation of all life on Earth.

How many times have you heard such phrases as 'steer clear of', 'hit the deck', 'don't rock the boat', 'to harbour a grudge', but given little thought to them? In this book, you will learn the origin and meaning of hundreds of slang terms which remain in common usage to this day, such as 'born with a silver spoon', 'feel blue', 'get into a flap', 'hunky dory', 'over a barrel', 'pull your finger out', 'many ways to skin a cat' and 'wipe the slate clean'. The sea has had a truly remarkable effect upon our language, and the Royal and US Navies have given us some of the most colourful slang terms imaginable, especially for food and drink. As you read, you will discover that a 'one-eyed steak' is, in fact, a kipper and you may be tempted by such tantalizing delights as 'flightdeck buzzard' (chicken), washed down with some 'Nelson's blood' (rum) or a 'cup of Joe' (coffee).

The pages of this book also focus attention on some of the remarkable men and women – pirates, explorers, admirals, inventors and navigators – who have shaped our world. As well as including such famous maritime characters as Admiral Nelson, there are intriguing entries on lesser-known but equally significant figures. If Admiral William Brown had not released Garibaldi after defeating him in a battle on the River Paraná, for instance, modern Italy might not exist, and had it not been for the barely known genius John Ericsson, who designed the ironclad warship *Monitor*, the Confederacy might have won the American Civil War.

Among the villains of the seas, 'Black Bart' Roberts is shown to be history's most successful (and heroic) pirate of all time and piracy's only known teetotaller! His crew included the real-life version of *Treasure Island*'s Israel Hands, commonly thought to have died in poverty, but in fact (as this book reveals) tarred and hung in chains after being found guilty at the greatest pirate trial of all time.

Aside from tales of maritime heroism and treachery, and of human endeavour at sea, one of the greatest fascinations of the ocean lies beneath the waves. Even today we know more about the surface of the Moon than we do about the unexplored depths of our oceans, and wonderfully strange life forms continue to be discovered there. In the 'Animals of the Seas' section you will encounter some of the extraordinary diversity of the marine environment from 'walking plants' to the coelacanth (the world's oldest fish, which predates the dinosaurs), or shrimps that emit a noise louder than a gunshot and the hugely mysterious giant squid. You will also learn about the ocean's apex predators – creatures such as the sperm whale, leopard seal, great white shark or the North Pacific giant octopus – and

their incredible importance in the maintenance of the health of the seas. These animals exist at the top of their respective food chains but now most of them are endangered by man's activities. If they are lost, life in the oceans will change adversely.

Without the seas there would be no life as we know it. They are even more important than the rainforests because they dictate both the pattern of our weather and the world's water supply. I began writing this book initially to provide a sourcebook of interesting and amusing nautical facts, but quickly came to realize that our oceans and the life that they support urgently need protection. The rate of destruction of coral reefs, sea beds, mangrove swamps, fish and crustacean stocks, as well as of the top predators, is killing the ocean environment. When these effects are combined with man's contribution to severe oceanic acidification and other maritime pollution, we find ourselves approaching a tipping point after which the seas may never recover in the lifetime of humankind: inexcusable treatment of a natural resource that has brought us so much excitement, incredible riches and breathtaking beauty.

There are far too many fascinating men and women, astonishing animals, remarkable ships, nautical sayings, ports and places for me to be able to describe them exhaustively in this single volume, but I hope that the selection of entries included will encourage readers to learn more about the great waters that cover two-thirds of our planet and, above all, to appreciate the urgent need to protect them and preserve their integrity.

CHAPTER I

An A–Z
of Sea Slang

ABOVE BOARD One origin of this phrase is that pirates hid *'below board'* if they were sneaking up on an unsuspecting merchantman. Pirate ships carried up to 12 times the crew of an equivalent merchant ship. If all the crew were above board, all was fair and square. Also, early trading ships hid illegal cargo below the ship's deck. Legal cargo could be placed in plain view on the deck, or above the boards of the deck. Thus anything illegal was below board.

AHOY This naval term seems, to this author, to stem from the 'hoy', a common 16th-century coastal vessel, although no dictionary confirms this derivation. One source states that 'Ahoy' was a Viking battle cry. However, according to Smith in 1627, a ship was hailed thus *'Hoa the ship?'* or just *'Hoa!'* – asking where it was bound. The answer was *'Hoa!'* *'Holloa'* was also used for hailing ships. The inventor of the telephone, Alexander Graham Bell, used *'ahoy'* when making a call, and the recognized answer in the early days of phones was 'hoy'.

ALOOF, KEEP ALOOF On a lee shore, the order *'keep aloof'* meant to keep the ship's head nearer to the wind to prevent the vessel from being driven on to the shore. Hence the modern expression to 'stay aloof' means to 'keep away from', or 'keep your distance'.

ANCHOR, TO BRING ONE'S ARSE TO AN To sit down.

ANT'S BOLLOCK ON A BEACH Naval slang for something that is extremely difficult to locate.

APRICOT Cockney rhyming slang for beach, from 'apricot and peach'.

AT LOOSE ENDS We are *'at a loose end'* if there is little to be done. The ends of rigging ropes at sea became easily unravelled, forming 'loose ends'. They had to be tightly bound to keep them from unravelling, so when there was little work to do, the captain might order the crew to check the ropes for loose ends and repair them.

BEAM ENDS *'Nearly on one's beam ends'* means that the ship is keeling over and about to sink, with the deck beams almost perpendicular to the sea's surface. Now *'to be on one's beam ends'* means to be without money, a job or prospects, i.e. in a hopeless position.

BEAR UP A sailing expression meaning to bear the tiller up to windward in order to keep the vessel's head away from the wind. It is in common use with the metaphorical meaning of 'Keep your spirits up!'

BERTH, GIVE A WIDE BERTH The station at which a ship rides at anchor, either singly or as part of a fleet, is called the berth. To give a wide berth is to keep well clear of another ship.

BILGE WATER Because bilge water was so offensive, giving off noxious fumes and full of all sorts of unpleasant waste, to say that someone was *'talking bilge water'*, or just *'talking bilge'*, meant they were spouting rubbish.

BITE THE BULLET Men suffering flogging with a cat-o'-nine-tails were often given a bullet to bite on to stop them screaming in pain. If the unfortunate sailors did *'sing out'*, they were cruelly dubbed a *'nightingale'*.

(REACH THE) BITTER END, AT THE END OF ONE'S ROPE, IN DEEP WATER These expressions refer to last part of the anchor cable that remains within the ship when the ship is at anchor. The anchor rope (now called a line) on old sailing ships was secured to an oak post called the *'bitt'*, which was fastened by *'partners'* to the deck. Securing turns were held around the bitt, as the anchor was paid out into the sea. The 'bitter end' was the last part of the rope or cable, nearest the bitt. Thus to let a chain or rope out *'to reach the bitter end'* means that it has all been paid out and there is nothing left to release. It was hard work paying out the anchor. You were also physically *'at the end of your rope'* when you had reached the bitter end. If you came to the end of your rope without the anchor securing purchase on the sea bed, you were *'in deep water'* because there was no possible solution to the problem and the anchor was in danger of being lost.

BLACK-LIST A record of a person's misdemeanours kept by some officers for their private use, not abolished until the 19th century.

BLUE MONDAY, THE BLUES Traditionally the day for handing out the brutal punishments in the Royal Navy. There was a superstition that bad luck would befall the ship if this treatment was not delivered on Mondays. Nathaniel

Boteler noted in 1685 that *'the idleness of ships' boys is paid out by the boatswain with a rod – and commonly this execution is done on Monday mornings.'*

BOMBED, BOMBARDED, TANKED UP This used to be a fashionable slang phrase for being drunk. A *'bombard'* was a leather jug or pitcher which held 4 or 8 pints (2.25 or 4.5 l) of ale. We must remember that ale was far stronger in past centuries, until beer was taxed on its strength during the First World War to stop munitions workers becoming slapdash after overindulging. Thus anyone who drank a full container was definitely *'bombarded'* or *'bombed'*. The phrase *'tanked up'* has a similar derivation, from a tankard.

BOOM AND MIZZEN Cockney rhyming slang for prison, from words denoting masts on a ship.

BORN WITH A SILVER SPOON This term was applied to those officers in the Royal Navy who entered the service without taking examinations on the strength of their family connections. They were said to have joined the navy *'through the cabin windows'*. Those *'born with a wooden ladle'* were officers who attained their posts by merit, and they were deemed to have entered the navy *'through the hawseholes'*, i.e. the apertures through which the anchor passes.

BOTTLE FISHING A slang term for the practice of transporting liquor into the United States during the Prohibition Era in the 1920s. This trade was easier, safer and much more profitable than fishing on the dangerous Grand Banks southeast of Newfoundland.

BRACE OF SHAKES *'I'll be with you in a brace of shakes'* literally means *'I'll be with you before the sail has time to shake twice'*, in other words I'll be with you almost straight away.

BREAD HOOKS Hands or fingers when used in the ship's mess.

BRIDPORT DAGGER This Dorset town was renowned for the quality of its ropes, and was the preferred supplier to the Royal Navy. A *'Bridport dagger'* was slang for a hangman's noose.

CASTOFFS These were originally *'landsmen's clothes'* that the sailor would leave behind when he went to sea. Also some mooring ropes were left on land – the *'cast-offs'*.

CATGUT SCRAPER Any of the fiddlers in the ship's band.

CHOCK-A-BLOCK When two tackle blocks are so close to one another that

there can be no movement in the sails. The sails could be pulled in tight so that the ship sailed *'as close to the wind'* as possible. To *'chock'* is to secure goods tightly on deck, when the vessel is rolling in high seas. Also known as *'two blocks'*. The modern term – *'the room is chockers'* – meaning full, comes from chock-a-block.

CLEAN SLATE (WIPE THE SLATE CLEAN) Courses, distances travelled and tacks were at one time recorded on a log slate. On most ships, the first watch would record its observations on the slate. These would be carefully transcribed into a logbook before the next watch arrived. If there had been no problems, the new watch would disregard the old record and *'start a clean slate'*.

Brought up short

If we say a person is brought up short, he is forced to a standstill by a sudden reversal of fortune. In the days of fighting ships a vessel underway could be brought to an emergency standstill or 'brought up short' by dropping the anchors. As the anchor bit into the seabed, the ship shuddered to a standstill, accompanied by tremendous noise and clattering of masts and rigging. This action was sometimes due to a shot having been fired across a vessel's bows as a warning. If she failed

to stop, the next shot would be fired 'true', i.e. directly at her. Thus after a *'warning shot across the bows'* it was hoped that the intended prize vessel would immediately drop anchor and *'be brought up short'*, or *'brought up all standing'*.

COLOURS 'TIED TO THE MAST'

This meant that a ship would not surrender, and that a fight could be expected – there was no going back. The act of tying the flag meant that it could not be hauled down as a signal of surrender.

CRACK ON

A common term nowadays for *'let's get on with it'*. The former meaning was to carry sail to the full limit of the ship's masts, yards and tackles. When the ship was *'cracking on'*, the straining sails and sheets (ropes) would make cracking noises.

CRAMP ONE'S STYLE

This was originally *'crab one's style'* – when a rower *'caught a crab'* (missed a stroke with the oar and fell backwards) it would ruin the style of the rowing.

CRANK, CRANKY

A ship that was difficult to sail and unstable. The modern adjective *'cranky'*, meaning eccentric, awkward or difficult to understand, comes from the saying that *'this ship's too cranky'*.

CRAP, CRAPPY

This noun and adjective, in increasingly common usage as mild swear words in the media, come from the typically British attitude to its continental near-neighbours. To a sailor, a Frenchman was General Crapaud, pronounced *crappo*. (Crapaud is French for a toad.) The aforesaid gentleman spoke crappo, gibberish, instead of the Queen's English. In fact everything a Frenchman said was crappo, rubbish. Sometimes it was a *'load of crappo'*.

CUT AND RUN

This term comes to us from the days of sail. A hemp cable was cut with an axe, leaving the anchor stranded on the ocean floor, in order to make an emergency getaway. Square-rigged ships were often anchored in an open *'road'*, with their sails furled and held by ropeyarns. These small ropes would be slashed with knives and the sails dropped ready for action. Other terms from this action are *'cut loose'*, *'cut the ties (that bind)'* and *'break out'*. The *'ties'* are thin lines holding the sails furled. Unfettered sails are said to have been *'broken out'*.

CUT OF HER JIB

French and Spanish ships which frequented the notoriously stormy Bay of Biscay had their foresails cut thin, so that they could not be blown off the wind when pointing. A British ship might see a large three-decker and, if it had a thin foresail, *'not like the cut of her jib'*, knowing it to be an enemy ship. The French often carried two jibs when other ships only had one, and French jibs were cut much shorter on the luff than English jibs, showing a more acute angle.

CUT TO THE CHASE

The *'chase'* was both the ship being pursued (the target), and also the process of chasing it. If a ship was anchored and saw a ship *'in the offing'*, it could take up to an hour to raise its anchor, so its hemp cable would be cut to speed things up. The sails would be furled and secured by ties and rigging. These might also be slashed to allow the sails to drop and fill out so that the chase could begin immediately – thus *'cut to the chase'*.

CUTS NO ICE

Something that *'cuts no ice'* means that it has made little or no impression. The phrase comes from the days of exploration when ships sometimes struggled to make progress in polar pack ice.

DANCE THE HEMPEN JIG To be
hanging. The hangman's rope was usually made of hemp fibres. Before the invention of the trap door and the *'long drop'* which was meant to break the victim's neck, hanging caused death by slow asphyxiation, with the victim's feet possibly only inches from the floor. In their struggles to touch the floor, the hanged prisoner's feet might be seen to constantly move for up to 20 minutes or more. Sometimes friends of the dying man would attempt to pull his legs sharply to end the torment more quickly.

DECK CARGO
Naval slang for breasts.

(I'M GOING TO) DECK (YOU)
This threat is a declaration that you are going to knock your opponent to the deck. On ships any such behaviour is not tolerated, so the account would be settled when the two protagonists were next in port.

DEEP SIX This is water deeper than the
six fathoms (36 ft/11 m) that the traditional leadline can measure. When the sailor taking soundings called out *'By the deep: six!'* the captain knew there was plenty of water under the keel. The phrase also means to throw overboard or discard, when there is more than six fathoms of depth. One might say, *'Just because your watch was slow, you did not have to give it the deep six.'* The custom was also to ensure that any dead body

was only committed to the sea if the water was six fathoms deep or more. Thus to *'deep six'* someone means to dispose of him or her.

DEVIL TO PAY The first plank of the
outer keel of a wooden ship was called the garboard, but it was known universally by seamen as the *'devil'*, because it was the most awkward to get at during careening (when a ship is turned over on one side for cleaning or repairing). It was the longest seam in the vessel. It was almost impossible to keep the devil above water while trying to *'pay'* oakum into its seam, hammer it home and cover it with hot pitch to seal it. *'The devil to pay, and no hot pitch'* was a desperate situation where seamen could see no means of solving a problem. *'Between the devil and the deep blue sea'* also comes from a ship's devil, meaning that there is only the thickness of the ship's hull plank between the garboard seam and the ocean depths.

DONKEY WALLOPERS Royal
Marine slang for members of mounted cavalry regiments.

DON'T SPOIL THE SHIP FOR A
HA'PORTH OF TAR Leaving a job half-done by not properly using hot tar to fill in the planks when careening. Ships would leak if too little was applied, so a small extra effort would be worth it. *'Ha'porth'* is an abbreviation for *'halfpenny's worth'*.

Down the Hatch

We say this as a toast when raising glasses to drink alcohol, but its origins are maritime as the ship appears to consume cargo as it passes down through the hatch into the hold.

DOWN A PEG (OR TWO)

Humbled. An admiral flew his personal standard at the highest point of the mast, attached by rope to one of a series of pegs at its base. If a more senior admiral came aboard, the original standard would be taken down a peg or two to make room for the new flag.

DRESSING DOWN

Canvas sails could easily become waterlogged, which made the ship hard to handle and caused rot and tears. Thus they had to be treated with heated preservatives and oils to repel water. This could only be done when the sails were rigged, rather than rolled up. To *'dress down'* both sides of a sail, hanging off ropes, while the sail was flapping and snapping in one's face, was an unpleasant but necessary experience.

EAT MY HAT

Sailors kept their chewing tobacco in their hats, the linings of which became soaked in sweat and tobacco juice. If they ran out of tobacco, they would take out the linings of their hats and chew them.

FAG END

To *'fag'* meant to tease out or separate the single strands of a rope. The tips of the strands were known as *'fag ends'*, and the usage passed on to signify the last part of a cigarette, the butt.

A rope that has not been maintained and has a fag end is said to be *'fagged out'*.

FAIRWAY

The origin of this golfing term was the word for the channel of a narrow bay, river or haven through which ships usually navigate up or down.

FEELING BLUE

This may refer to the dread of *'Blue Monday'* (q.v.) with its harsh punishments. However, it is more likely to derive from the fact that any sailing ship that lost its captain or any officer at sea flew a blue flag, or painted a blue band across its hull, when returning to port.

FLAKE OUT

It was important to keep the anchor chain in good condition, and it was regularly laid out along the deck – *'flaked'* – to check for weak links. The anchor was also often *'flaked out'* on deck in preparation for anchoring. It was laid out in such a way so that it did not *'foul up'* when the anchor was dropped. Lying down in the sun on deck became known as *'flaking out'*.

FOOTLOOSE

The bottom of the sail is its *foot*, and when it is not tied to a boom, it is loose-footed, dancing freely in the wind with no restrictions.

FOUL UP If an anchor becomes entangled with its cable, it is *'fouled up'*. A *'foul berth'* is caused by another vessel anchoring too closely, where there could be a collision. A *'foul bottom'* means that it is difficult to secure anchors in the sea bed. *'Fall foul of'* is a nautical term for becoming impeded. From foul we get today's acronym SNAFU *(Situation Normal, All Fouled Up)*. More recent slang includes FUMTU *(Fouled Up More than Usual)* and FUBAR *(Fouled Up Beyond All Recognition)*.

FREEZE THE BALLS OFF A BRASS MONKEY (COLD ENOUGH TO) The monkey was a small brass tray which held a pile of iron cannon balls next to the guns. In extreme cold, the different coefficients of expansion of brass and iron meant that sometimes the neatly piled cannon balls would move and roll out of the tray.

GET INTO A FLAP Sails do not flap, they *'flog'*, but flags *'flap'*. Warships used to signal to each other with flags, and when there was a huge flurry of flagging, as when the fleet prepared for battle or manoeuvres, there was *'a bit of a flap on'*.

GET SPLICED, GET HITCHED To get married, as when two ropes are joined together.

GILT, KNOCK THE GILT OFF THE GINGERBREAD This means to spoil the best part of a thing or story. At German fairs gingerbread was often decorated with gilt to make its appearance more attractive. From this custom, the gilding and painted carvings at the bows, stern and entrance ports of sailing ships of war came to be known as *'gingerbread work'*. To *'knock the gilt off the gingerbread'* was therefore to incur the wrath of the captain by damaging the appearance of the vessel.

GODDAM MANNOWARRI In the Comoros Islands and Madagascar, any steamship is known as a *'mannowarri'*, from the days when large naval ships were known as men-of-war. A foreign seaman is known as a *'goddami'* because 'God damn' and its derivatives were the words most commonly heard spoken by British seamen who visited. In Swahili, on Madagascar, a 'goddam mannowari' means a sailor from a foreign ship.

GOING LIKE THE CLAPPERS To *'clap on'* more sail meant that the ship sailed faster, and it seems that this is the origin of the term.

GOOSE WITHOUT GRAVY When a man was hurt badly without any blood to be seen.

GRANNY'S KNOT The origin of the term *'granny knot'*, which is a reef knot tied the wrong way. According to W.H. Smyth, writing in the days before sex equality legislation: *'It is the natural knot tied by women and landsmen, and derided by seamen because it cannot be untied when it is jammed.'*

GRASS COMBERS Term of derision for men in the navy who came from farming backgrounds.

HALF-SLEWED When the yards which carry the sails are not properly braced to deflect the wind, they are said to be half-slewed, faltering and swaying ineffectively. Hence the synonym for affected by alcohol.

HAPPY AS A SANDBOY The Ostrich Inn, on the site of the original harbour of Bristol, stood next to the Redcliffe Caves, which used to be a major source of sand. Landlords used to send little boys *(sandboys)* into the caves to collect sand to spread on the floor of the tavern to soak up the beer spillages. They were paid in beer.

HAVEN'T A CLEW (CLUE) The sails are attached at their corners by brass rings (cringles) sewn into the clews (the lower corner of a square sail or aftermost corner of a fore-and-aft sail). If the clew should become undone, and the vessel *'has no clew'*, it will not sail anywhere until it is *'clewed up'* again. Clew lines are lines running from the corner of the sail to the yardarm and down to the deck. To clew is to haul a square sail up to a yard, before furling, by means of clew lines.

HIT THE DECK At close quarters, if a swivel gun or murderer was about to be fired, seamen would dive to the deck to try to avoid being hit. These guns were designed to sweep the deck killing men, rather than to incapacitate the rigging or damage the ship.

HONESTY AMONGST THIEVES The sea thieves, pirates, exacted such severe punishments for stealing from the 'commonwealth' booty, or one another, that there was very little theft among their company.

HUNKY DORY Meaning good or satisfactory, this term derived from Honki-Dori, a street in the port of Yokohama, Japan, where many a pleasure awaited visiting sailors.

IRISH HORSE This was the seaman's term for extremely tough salt beef (later, corned beef also earned the epithet). It was thought that the poor Irish worked their horses longer and harder than the English, which made them tough to eat.

JIBES, GYBES Swinging a boom *(gybing)* when changing course on a sailing vessel can lead to someone being hurt, or damage to sails or rigging. Gybes came to mean unwelcome actions, and are the origin of today's jibes.

(A FINE) KETTLE OF FISH Fish were boiled in huge pots or kettles at sea. If the results sometimes tasted foul, the contents were referred to sarcastically as a *'fine kettle of fish'*, which no man would eat. The term has come to mean a messy situation, which is difficult to solve.

KICK THE BUCKET In the absence of a scaffold, men were sometimes hanged standing on a bucket or cask. To drop them quickly, the bucket was simply kicked away.

KNOCK DOWN Ships had to carry a cooper, as all food and drink at sea was stored in wooden casks. Space was at such a premium in the cramped quarters and storerooms that the casks were usually knocked down (disassembled using a mallet) and the staves stacked and stored neatly when the contents were disposed of. The casks would then be made up again when new provisions were taken on.

KNOCK OFF Galleys used to be rowed to the rhythm of a hammer hitting a wooden block. When the hammer or

Know the Ropes

If sailors aboard a sailing ship did not know all the functions of the hundred of ropes that made up the rigging, and were not experts at dozens of knots, their ship could neither catch another vessel nor escape from superior forces. The rigging could comprise more than

10 miles (16 km) of ropes and cordage in the largest vessels, and the individual ropes had hundreds of different names and functions. The ropes were usually the same thickness and colour, and so could only be told apart from the precise position in which they were secured.

mallet ceased striking, the galley slaves could rest. Even today people *'knock off'* from work.

LANDMARK This is a point on the landscape from which a ship takes reference – so a *landmark decision* meant that the captain was sure of what he was going to do because of the lie of the land that he could see.

LAP-CLAP Copulation. To 'get a lap-clap' was to become pregnant.

LEEWAY The distance a ship is forced to leeward away from the wind, i.e. the lateral drift of a vessel. The ship may be blown off course, or be affected by currents. It is measured in degrees of compass and is dependent on the following conditions:

• the state of the sea
• the strength of the wind
• the ship's speed through the water
• the hull and sail areas that are presented to the wind
• the angle of the fore-and-aft line of the boat, and the direction of the wind
• the underwater hull shape of the boat

Different boats will make different leeway, and the steersman learns to know the amount his boat will give in varying conditions. Leeway is defined by the angle between the boat's fore-and-aft line and her line of wake.

LIMEYS, LIMEJUICERS From 1795, British warships were required to carry lime juice to prevent the onset of scurvy – a disease caused by vitamin C deficiency. American sailors still call British sailors *limeys*. British sailing ships were known across the world as *'lime juicers'*.

LOOK AROUND FOR LOOSE ENDS If a ship had to flee in an emergency without setting its sails properly, once it had escaped to safety, this was the instruction to sort out the pieces of rope, tie up things securely and to get the vessel ship-shape again.

LOOSE CANNON An unsecured cannon in a storm could do untold damage to men and the ship as it rolled about. The term now means an unorthodox person who can cause potential damage.

THE MAD HOUSE Naval slang for the offices of the Admiralty in London.

TO MAKE BOTH ENDS MEET Dating from at least the 17th century, this describes the habit of splicing two pieces of rope to make a longer piece, and thus not necessitating the purchase of a completely new rope.

MAN Strangely, although ships are usually 'female', as in *'Steady as she goes'*, many ships have been given male nomenclatures, e.g. man-of-war, merchantman, Guineaman, Indiaman, Greenlandman. A man-of-war is still female to her crew.

MARK TWAIN! The shouted report from a US seaman taking soundings at the bow of the boat indicating the depth of the water under the keel. This is Mississippi riverboat dialect, a shortening of the phrase *'Markin' on the twine'*, which would be followed by the water depth in fathoms. Samuel Langhorne Clemens (1835–1910) was a Mississippi riverboat pilot during the mid-19th century who took the term as his pen name when he became a writer in the 1860s.

MAYDAY The universal radio distress call for help, indicating that there is immediate danger of loss of life. From the French *'m'aidez'* meaning *'help me'*. It is always spoken three times to alert all radio operators.

MONEY FOR OLD ROPE Older, unneeded and frayed old rope would be sold on shore to local traders, and the money shared out amongst the crew. This old rope was often sold back to ships to be used as caulking material between a ship's planks.

NAIL ONE'S COLOURS TO THE MAST A ship's flags were known as its 'colours'. In battle the combatants tried to seize the colours flown on the opposing ship. To nail colours to the mast made them difficult to seize and signalled a resolve not to submit.

NANTUCKET SLEIGH RIDE When a harpooned whale raced off towing a dory full of seamen, the crew were said to be on a Nantucket sleigh ride. This reference is to the great whaling port of Nantucket, Massachusetts.

NO GREAT SHAKES As food barrels and other casks were emptied, they were 'shaken' apart to gain extra storage space. The pieces of timber came to be called *'shakes'*. Little value was attached to shakes, so something or someone of little value came to be termed *'no great shakes'*.

OCEAN DEVIL The Chinese name for foreigners.

OK There are many theories about the origin of this term, but one of the more likely seems to be from the French *'au quai'* meaning in port and safe. Another French derivation is from the Haitian harbour of *Aux Cayes*, famous for its superb rum.

ON THE FIDDLE This phrase has a nautical origin. Dining tables on HMS *Victory* and other ships were edged with a fixed or hinged rim, called a *'fiddle'*, to stop platters and jugs from sliding off.

Not only did the fiddle keep food on the plate, but it marked the limit of how big a helping a sailor was entitled to. If his helping touched or was on the fiddle a sailor was said to be 'fiddling', depriving another sailor of his share of food, which was an offence punishable by flogging.

OVER A BARREL

If you have someone *'over a barrel'*, they are in a position where they have little influence over their fate. Before the development of modern resuscitation techniques, a near-drowned person was placed face down over a barrel, which was then rolled vigorously back and forth in an attempt to revive him by draining the water from his lungs.

THE PARROT MUST HAVE A NUT

From the Elizabethan catchphrase, *'The parrot must have an almond'*, referring to the need to bribe certain officials and governors to turn a blind eye to pirates trading in their territories.

PAYING ON THE NAIL

Paying on the nail is a phrase signifying cash payment rather than credit payment. The Four Nails stand on the pavement outside the Corn Exchange in Corn Street, Bristol. These round-topped pedestals were used by merchants when closing a deal. Money was placed on the surface of a Nail, indicating that the bargain had been struck.

PICKLED

This synonym for being totally drunk may come from the fact that Admiral Nelson's body was preserved in alcohol after his death at Trafalgar – he was *'well and truly pickled'*.

PIPE DOWN

The routine naval order for silence on the mess-decks and *'Lights out'* at the end of the day. Freely used either to denote the end of any occupation or to mean *'Shut your mouth'* or *'Be silent'* (replacing the old order to *'Stash it'*, synonymous with *'Stow it'*).

PIPING HOT

Meaning very hot, the term comes from the days of sailing ships. A boatswain would pipe a signal when meals were served.

HE PISSES MORE THAN HE DRINKS

A mariner who boasts.

PISS-POT

A slang name for a *'saw-bones'*, or ship's doctor.

PITCHER-BAWD

A worn-out prostitute, only good enough to carry pitchers of beer to a tavern's customers. Pitchers were leather jugs, treated with tar pitch to help them hold their shape. Glass was too expensive and fragile for common use.

POSH

Before air-conditioning, cabins on the side of ocean liners facing the sun became unbearably hot. Thus richer passengers paid a premium to have their tickets on the P&O Line from England to India stamped *'Port Out – Starboard Home'*. So p.o.s.h. became a synonym for someone who was upper class.

PULL YOUR FINGER OUT

When cannon were loaded, a small amount of powder was poured into the ignition hole. To keep the powder secure before firing, a crew member pushed a finger into the hole. When the time came for firing the gun, he was told to pull his finger out.

PUT A NEW SLANT ON THINGS
Consider from a different perspective. *Slant* is the position of the wind relative to the ship, so a change in the wind would require a change of position. The angle of sail was altered to compensate for changing wind conditions.

PUT THROUGH THE HOOP
Undergo an ordeal; rigorously test. Prior to battle hammocks were rolled tightly and lashed to a ship's rails to provide protection against shot and splinters. Sailors were required to pass their rolled hammocks through a regulation size hoop gauge to check them for tightness, and therefore effectiveness.

ROSE COTTAGE
In all large naval ships there was a mess for contagious disease cases, known as Rose Cottage. Syphilis was prevalent and treated with mercury, giving rise to the saying *'One night with Venus and a lifetime with*

Mercury'. Cases of venereal disease were running at 104 per 1500 men in the Royal Navy in 1863.

SAND
This was kept at sea for holystoning (scouring) the decks. It was also used in violent rain so that men on deck could keep their footing and, with sawdust, to soak up blood in battle.

SCRAPING THE BOTTOM OF THE BARREL
Removing the last of the hardened pork fat from a cask, to put towards a *slush fund* (q.v.).

SEWN UP, ALL SEWN UP, ALL STITCHED UP
To be *'all sewn up'* means that everything is finished. A sailor who died at sea was sewn inside his hammock with a cannon ball at his feet, before being despatched to the deep in a burial at sea. Traditionally, the last stitch was placed through the nose to ensure that the man was really dead. It also

Rates

Warships in the Royal Navy fell into six classifications according to the number of guns they carried. First, second and third rate ships were 'ships of the line' with enough firepower to be included in a 'line of battle'. At Trafalgar in 1805, the ratings were: first rate = 100 guns or more; second rate = 90–100 guns; third rate = 70–90 guns; fourth rate = 50–70 guns; fifth rate = 32–50 guns; and sixth rate = up to 32 guns. From these terms we use *first rate* to mean excellent, and *fifth rate* to mean mediocre.

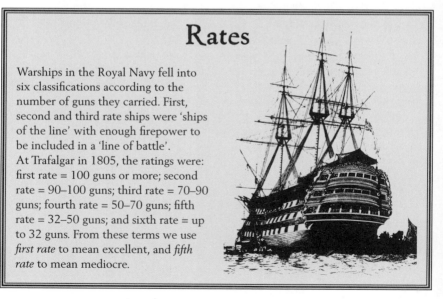

thwarted his ghost from appearing on the ship's decks after burial. The custom is said to have originated when a sailmaker accidentally put his needle through the nose of a '*corpse*', and the shock made the cataleptic victim revive and sit up. Probably the phrase '*stitched up*' also comes from the practice of stitching dead seamen into their hammocks.

SHIP SHAPE AND BRISTOL FASHION
Bristol was a great port for the slave trade, and vast quantities of tobacco, sherry and chocolate were imported there. Slave ships not only stank, but also could carry disease, so the citizens of the prosperous port would not allow ships to dock until they were cleaned and '*made tidy*' in the way that the Bristol Channel tides are predictable and orderly. Before entering the harbour, the ships were inspected to ensure that they were '*ship shape and Bristol fashion*'.

SLING YOUR HOOK
Unpopular ship mates were told to go and sling their hammocks elsewhere. Space was at a premium on ships, and places to sleep difficult to find.

SLUSH FUND
The grease, or *slush*, from frying salt pork or beef on a long voyage or from '*scraping the sides of the barrel*' was saved by the cook and sold to tanneries and candlemakers. Thus the term '*scraping the barrel*' also comes from the days of sailing ships. It was also applied to the thick, salty scum of fat that formed when salt meat was boiled, which was cooled and added to the '*slush fund*'. In 1866 the US Government applied the term to a contingency fund in one of its operating budgets, and the phrase then passed into general usage.

SON OF A GUN
In the age of sail when the wives and mistresses of sailors were allowed to stay aboard in harbour (and sometimes also go to sea), they occasionally gave birth on board ship. There was little room for mothers in labour, except the gangways, which had to be kept clear at all time. The only space available was between the guns on the gun decks, and the newborn child was called a 'son of a gun', as often no-one knew its father.

SPLICED, TO GET
A seaman's term for getting married, referring to the permanent nature of splicing two pieces of rope together. Two ends of ropes are untwisted, then twisted together and fastened with string to make one continuous length of rope.

(AS) STRAIGHT AS THE CROW FLIES
British coastal vessels often carried a cage of crows. These birds hate large expanses of water, and head straight towards land when released at sea, something that is useful in fogs or when a helmsman was unsure of his bearings. The lookout perch on sailing vessels thus became known as the *crow's nest*.

SWING THE LEAD
Slang for 'taking it easy'. Near land, one job was to lower a lead weight on a line to assess the depth of the water near shore and to avoid shallows. It was the easiest job on ship, so anyone 'swinging the lead' was understood to be a slacker, not carrying out the normal arduous duties of his shipmates.

THERE ARE MANY WAYS TO SKIN A CAT

The full phrase is *'to skin a catfish'*. This refers to the act of removing the very tough skin from the delicate flesh of a catfish. In the creeks and shallow coastal waters of the Caribbean and eastern seaboard of the Americas, catfish were easily caught by pirates. There are many ways to skin a catfish and all were initially developed through trial and error, in an attempt to find the best way to remove the skin without tearing the edible flesh into smaller bits and chunks.

THREE SHEETS TO THE WIND

Almost totally drunk. A sheet is a line used for trimming a sail to the wind. There is only one sheet on fore-and aft sails, and there are just two on a square sail set on a yardarm. On a Bermuda-rigged vessel there are two sheets for the jib-foresail and one for the main sail. Thus a drunken man, even if he had three sheets to trim his sails and steer his course, would still be too unsteady to steer a straight course. When all three sheets were allowed to run free, they were said to be 'in the wind', and the ship would lurch and stagger. If the boat is *'three sheets to the wind'* the sails are not drawing wind and the ship will not make progress, but drift downwind. Stages of drunkenness were noted by sailors as being 'one sheet to the wind' for slightly inebriated, 'two sheets to the wind' for drunk, and 'three sheets to the wind' for being helpless.

TIDY

Derived from 'tide' meaning methodical, well-arranged, just as reliable as the tides.

TOUCH OF THE TARBRUSH

This derogatory term meaning a person of mixed ancestry has a more innocent derivation. It was applied to a seaman who worked his way up to the *quarterdeck* where only officers were allowed. Thus he was accepted as an officer, but was still thought to be a little 'common' by his fellow officers because he had been used to applying tar when an ordinary sailor. However, seamen meant it as a compliment, as the officer had not paid to get his rank. It only later came to describe someone of mixed race.

WEST COUNTRY SLANG

Many sailing terms have been shortened as a result of the influence of West countrymen at sea – *vittles, bos'n, cox'n, fo'c'sle, for-ud,* etc., etc. One of the best examples in spoken English is the Bristol slang *'Armchair they?'* enquiring the price of items. It is a vernacular way of asking *'How much are they?'*

CHAPTER 2

Sea Conditions *and* Weather

WIND AND RAIN

BAYAMO A violent storm of heavy rain and lightning that occurs around southern Cuba, especially in the Bight of Bayamo.

BLACK SQUALL A sudden and violent storm in the West Indies, responsible for the unexplained loss of many a privateer and pirate. The differential between very warm air near land and the onset of colder air off the sea sometimes generates spectacular electrical storms.

CALM IN THE EYE OF A STORM This phenomenon of a very still region of air at the centre of a hurricane has been recorded over centuries by sailors who have survived hurricanes, cyclones and typhoons.

CHOCOLATE GALE A brisk northwesterly wind common in the Spanish Main and West Indies.

CYCLONE This is an area of low pressure, around which winds blow anti-clockwise in the northern hemisphere. Also the term used for a hurricane in the Indian Ocean and in the western Pacific Ocean.

THE DOCTOR This is the name given by West Indians to a cooling trade wind. The *Harmattan*, a cooling easterly wind blowing from December to February (the dry season) on the west coast of Africa, is also known as the *doctor*. Perhaps slavers or slaves carried the terminology with them across the Atlantic to the Caribbean.

EL NIÑO AND LA NIÑA AND THE TRADE WINDS El Niño and La Niña are among the greatest causes of climate variability, apart from the seasons themselves. The El Niño event of 1997–8 caused over 2000 deaths, with the global bill for repair of damage estimated at around £20 billion. A rise in sea temperature of up to 9° F (5° C), between Ecuador and Peru usually indicates the start of an El Niño event. The east to west trade winds across the equatorial Pacific can change direction, with warm water being forced eastwards. Its evaporation when it reaches land precipitates drenching rains in South America, while Indonesia suffers a drought. With La Niña, the southeast trade winds grow stronger, and warmer water comes to the west Pacific, leading to excessive rains there but dryness in the east Pacific region. During La Niña, cold waters rise to the surface to cool the ocean and depress land surface temperatures. This can last for 12 months. La Niña generally makes dry areas drier and wet areas wetter. Historical data show that both events are linked to abnormal temperature, storms and rainfall across the world.

FAFF, FAFFING ABOUT This is when the wind blows in flaws (q.v.) – it is not consistent and is therefore *'faffing about'*, from which we get the current phrase for acting aimlessly.

FLAW A sudden and unexpected gust of wind. The modern word flaw, in the sense of an unexpected defect, may have the same origin.

FLUKE A wind irregularity. This has come to mean a chance happening which is not planned and which may be lucky or unlucky in its consequences.

GALE WARNING A gale is classified as a wind of 34–40 knots, force 8 on the Beaufort Scale. (A knot is a unit of speed equivalent to one nautical mile per hour.) A strong gale is 41–47 knots, force 9. A storm is classified as over 49–55 knots, force 10, and a violent storm is 55–63 knots, force 11. Hurricanes are over 63 knots. A *'gale warning'* is issued for forecasts of 34–47 knots.

HORSE LATITUDES AND 'THE CALMS' These are areas of variable winds on either side of the *Doldrums*, at around 30 degrees of latitude in each hemisphere, in both the Atlantic and Pacific Oceans. They are also known as *'the Calms of Cancer'* and *'the Calms of Capricorn.'* They may have been named from the Spanish habit of throwing horses overboard to save water when ships were becalmed.

HURRICANE This is a massive rotating storm forming over warm seas near the Equator, and is also known as a *'tropical cyclone'*. The winds blow at least 74 mph (119 kph), accompanied by low air pressure, an enormous downpour of rain, and thunder and lightning. The winds rotate anti-clockwise around a calm central eye of the storm. In the western Pacific Ocean, it is called a *'typhoon'*. When hurricanes move from the ocean on to land, there is almost inevitably extensive destruction, but as the storm moves over land it begins to weaken and dies down because the storm is caused by warm ocean water. There are around 100 tropical cyclones each year, with about 12 in the Atlantic Ocean, 15 in the eastern Pacific Ocean and the rest in other areas. Joshua Slocum (1844–1909) in *Sailing Round the World* wrote: *'I once knew a writer who, after saying beautiful things about the sea, passed through a Pacific hurricane, and he became a changed man.'*

HURRICANES ARE FEMALE A name is now given when a tropical depression is upgraded to a tropical storm. Previously there was no recognized system of nomenclature, e.g. Hurricane Santa Anna of 1825 was named after the saint's day, and the Galveston Hurricane of 1900 named after its place of landfall. Before the Second World War, to avoid confusion especially when more than one storm was in the same ocean basin, a letter designation was given to each hurricane, e.g. B-1066. The Australian forecaster Clement Wragge then began using letters from the Greek alphabet, characters from Greek and Roman mythology, and even the names of politicians he did not like. The naming convention took off when western North Pacific forecasters began naming storms after their wives and girlfriends, and from 1945 these hurricanes were officially given female names.

NORTHEAST TRADES As a general rule, the prevailing winds in the Atlantic blow from the northeast in the latitudes extending from about 5 to 30 degrees north of the equator.

SQUALL There is a traditional saying: *'When it squalls, a prudent sailor reefs his sails.'* A squall is a sudden increase in wind speed of at least 18 mph (29 kph) and rising to 25 mph (40 kph) lasting minutes rather than hours, which slackens as suddenly as it arises. It is usually associated with weather such as rain showers, thunderstorms or heavy snow. There is sometimes a temporary change in the wind direction.

TRADE WIND A regular and steady wind blowing in a certain direction – it can be either perpetual or seasonal. The main trade winds are caused by the Earth's motion and the action of the Sun on the atmosphere, and they occur between 30 degrees north and 30 degrees south of the equator. They were invaluable in the days of sail. Those south of the equator blow from the southeast, and those in the northern hemisphere come from the northeast. Thus the transatlantic crossing used different routes each way. They were known as the trade winds because they assisted merchant ships engaged in trading. The meeting of these particular trade winds, just north of the equator, creates the *'Doldrums'* where sailing ships were often becalmed for weeks waiting for a wind to carry them back into the Trades. Thus *'feeling down in the doldrums'* meant that sun-baked, listless crews became depressed at their lack of progress. The crews would often take to the rowing boats and try to tow the ship towards windier conditions. Surface winds known as westerlies flow from the Horse Latitudes (q.v.) towards the poles, but from the equator to 30 degrees north there are prevailing northeasterly winds, and from the equator to 30 degrees south there are prevailing southeasterly winds.

TYPHOON A typhoon is a violent tropical cyclonic storm in the Pacific, with winds blowing at over 74 mph (119 kph).

UPWIND The direction that faces towards where the wind is blowing from. To look downwind is to look in the direction in which the wind is blowing.

URUCANA The effects of both the strong wind and Gulf Steam flowing north through the Caribbean.

WATERSPOUT This is usually a funnel-shaped cloud, specifically referred to as a non-supercell tornado over water. A cyclonic vortex forces water upwards into the air.

WAVES NAMED ROSSBY AND KELVIN The ocean is full of waves, but the Rossby wave is quite unlike the waves you see on a beach. A tidal wave travels very quickly, with all the water moving in the same direction. In a Rossby wave, however the upper layer of the ocean, around 300 feet (91 m) or so, will slowly move one way while the lower part, from 300 feet down, will be slowly moving the other way. After a while they switch directions. Everything happens very slowly – 100 times slower than walking speed – and so it takes months or years for a Rossby wave to cross the oceans. These waves are huge, hundreds or thousands of miles in length (not height), and can hardly be identified on the surface. A Kelvin wave has some characteristics in common with Rossby waves, but is faster and only found within about 5 degrees of latitude around the equator. El Niños often start with a Kelvin wave propagating from the western Pacific towards South America, with sea level being a few inches higher than usual, moving along the equator from Australia to South America. When an El Niño gets established in the middle or eastern part of the Pacific, it creates Rossby waves that drift slowly towards southeast Asia. After several months of travelling, they finally approach the coast and then reflect back. The changes in interior ocean temperature that these waves can propagate compensate for the original temperature changes that caused the El Niño in the first place.

WHISTLE DOWN THE WIND (WHISTLE FOR THE WIND)

Whistling in a British warship was always discouraged, and even in 1910 it was a punishable offence in Training Establishments. The reason was twofold. Firstly, all orders were passed by means of a bosun's pipe (or whistle) and so casual whistling could lead to confusion. Secondly, many sailors feared that whistling was the Devil's music, and that it was possible to whistle up a storm. The 1960s *Naval Ratings Handbook* contains the advice that *'whistling is only music in the ears of the perpetrator'*. When becalmed in a sailing boat, an old sailor would sometimes stick his knife in the mast and whistle for the wind.

WIND DOG An incomplete rainbow signifying the approach of a storm.

WINDFALL This has come to mean an unexpected bonus, the phrase originated in the days of sail. It described a sudden unexpected rush of wind (falling) from a mountainous shore, which allowed a ship more leeway to steer away from it.

WIND WAVES These are wind-generated surface waves on the oceans, resulting from the wind blowing over a vast stretch of sea. Some waves in the oceans can travel for thousands of miles before reaching land. Wind waves range from ripples to massive rogue waves. When being generated and affected by local winds, a wind wave system is called a wind sea. After the local wind ceases, wind waves are called swell. Generally, a swell consists of wind-generated waves that are not affected by the local wind at the same moment. They have been generated elsewhere, or some time previously. Waves are characterized by wave height (trough to crest), wavelength (crest to crest), period (time interval between consecutive crests) and the direction of wave propagation.

WIND'S EYE The point from which the wind blows. If it blows from the north, it is a northerly wind.

SKIES AND SEAS

ANTARCTIC CIRCUMPOLAR CURRENT (WEST WIND DRIFT) – THE WORLD'S LARGEST CURRENT The ACC flows west to east around Antarctica and is the dominant circulation feature of the Southern Ocean. Because it prevents warm waters from reaching Antarctica, the continent can maintain its giant ice cap. Its strength has always been a major problem for sailing ships travelling westwards around Cape Horn. It circulates through the Atlantic (Southern), Pacific and Indian Oceans.

BLACK RIVER, BLACK STREAM – THE WORLD'S SECOND LARGEST CURRENT This is the Kuroshio (formerly Kuro-Siva) Ocean Current. It is darker blue in colour than surrounding waters which accounts for its name. Coming up the coast of China from the Philippines, it is 10–12° F (6–7° C) warmer than its surrounding waters. North of Japan, it meets a cold Arctic current, causing dense fogs similar to those found on the Grand Banks off Newfoundland. This is caused by the Arctic current dipping under the Black River. It then curves round to warm the coast of California, heading north as far as Alaska. It flows between 25 and 75 miles (40 and 120 km) a day, at around 2 mph (3.2 kph), and is around 3000 feet (915 m) deep.

BLUE WATER This is the term for deep or offshore seas, which are usually over 100 fathoms (600 ft/183 m) in depth. Ships suited to rivers and coastal waters are called *brown water* vessels as opposed to *blue water* ocean-going vessels.

CROSS SEA In a sudden wind change, as in a cyclone, each change of wind produces a different direction of the sea that can last for some hours after the wind has changed. The sea runs up in pyramids, making a ship difficult to sail until the storm abates.

DEAD WATER The eddy water that follows the stern of the ship. It does not flow away as quickly as the water on the ship's sides.

FETCH *'Fetch'* is the nautical term for the distance that wind and waves can travel towards land without being blocked. It is also the distance sailed to a location without the vessel having to tack (change course).

FLOGGING A DEAD HORSE
The *Horse Latitudes* are an area around the Atlantic's Canary Islands, named after the Spanish Golfo de las Yeguas (Gulf of the Mares), or perhaps because the Spanish threw horses overboard to save precious water when becalmed there. Sailors were paid a month in advance, and usually spent the money straight away or gave it

Currents and Climate

Ocean currents are like rivers of hot or cold water extending to a depth of 300 feet (91 m). Their direction and strength derives from forces such as the Earth's rotation, the gravitational pull of the Moon, winds, salinity, temperature (which affects density), depth contours, shorelines and other currents. The five major ocean currents are those of the North and South Atlantic, North and South Pacific and the southern Indian Ocean. When sea water enters polar regions, it cools or freezes, becoming saltier and denser and tending to sink. A global 'conveyor belt' is set in motion when this colder water (known as 'deep water') sinks in the North Atlantic, moves south, then circulates around Antarctica, finally moving northward again to the Indian, Pacific and Atlantic basins. It may take 1000 years for deep water from the North Atlantic to find its way into the North Pacific.

Surface currents are much quicker. Cold surface currents originate in polar and temperate latitudes, and tend to flow towards the equator. Like warm surface currents, which flow from the tropics towards the poles, cold currents are mainly driven by winds, as well as the Earth's rotation. These currents are an important factor in the redistribution of heat between the tropics and the polar regions, modifying the temperatures of coastal areas as far as 65 miles (105 km)

inland. As tropical airstreams move over these cold currents, 'advection fog' forms over the sea. The winds are stripped of most of their moisture, and onshore winds become dry. Cold currents therefore contribute to desert conditions. Conversely, warm currents bring unusually warm conditions to the higher latitudes and lands affected by them. The Gulf Stream surface current is what is known as a 'western boundary current', and is strong, warm, deep and fast. 'Eastern boundary currents' can be associated with 'upwelling'. This is the upward motion of dense, cold, nutrient-rich water to replace the warmer nutrient-depleted water on the surface. This attracts fish. The California Current is an eastern boundary current and is broad, cold, shallow and slow. Off Africa's eastern coast, the Somali Current is strange as it reverses direction twice a year, running north from May to September and south from November to March. When it flows northward, upwelling brings nutrients to the surface, supporting productive marine life, but such abundance falls when it moves south. 'Coriolis forces' cause currents to move clockwise in the northern hemisphere and anti-clockwise in the southern hemisphere, and deflect them about 45° from the wind direction. This movement creates distinctive currents called 'gyres', usually where currents meet.

to their families. It took around a month to cross the Atlantic from the Americas and reach the Horse Latitudes, and this was known as the *'dead horse month'* because the seamen could expect no pay. To mark its end, crews stuffed a canvas likeness of a horse with straw and marched it around the deck. It was then strung up from the yardarm and cut adrift to float away in the sea, as the crew chanted to the captain, *'Old man, your horse must die'*. Admiral William Smyth commented that it was difficult to get crews to work properly when they were not being paid in that first month, about as much use as trying *'to flog a dead horse into activity'*.

FOG AND 'THE PERFECT STORM'

Even great storms will not clear fog off Newfoundland. The *Mariner's Dictionary* tells us *'the warm water of the Gulf Stream penetrating high latitudes is productive of fog, especially in the vicinity of the Grand Banks where the cold waters of the Labrador Current makes the contrast in the temperatures of the adjacent waters most striking.'* This was the setting for the book and film, *The Perfect Storm*.

FOLLOWING SEA

This is the term for waves fetching in the same direction as the heading of a vessel, usually catching up with it and passing under the keel. A following sea gives the vessel a slow pitching action, and makes steering difficult since the seas counteract the normal function of the rudder, and can even cause a vessel to broach (turn broadside to the wind).

FOUL

'Foul' describes the ocean floor when it is unsuitable for anchoring because of sediment, slick mud, debris or rocks. It also describes stormy weather.

FREAK WAVE

Also called a 'rogue wave', this is an unpredictable, abnormally large wave which occurs on a seemingly random basis. It is a threat even to huge oil tankers and ocean liners. (It is not the same as a tsunami, being a localized event occurring far out to sea and not reaching land.) Oceanographers define a freak wave as one that is more than double the 'significant wave height' (SWH). They have been reported throughout history but their scientific validity was only confirmed as recently as 1 January 1995 by measurements taken at the Draupner Oil platform in the North Sea. Mid-ocean storm waves can commonly reach 23 feet (7 m) in height, and on extreme occasions 50 feet (15 m). For centuries there have been stories of 100-feet (30-m) waves, vertical walls of water following a deep trough, appearing without warning. They happened often in clear weather, against the prevailing current and wave conditions. Scientists dismissed the idea, stating that a wave of over 50 feet (15 m) was only likely to happen once in 10,000 years. Their basis for this conclusion was mathematical probability theory. Ocean-going ships are generally designed to survive storm waves of 50–65 feet (15–20 m), but a 100-foot (30-m) wave would mean a pressure of up to 100 tonnes per square metre exerted by the weight of water, and a ship could be smashed to pieces. They probably account for a high proportion of unexplained losses in deep water, as there is little time for the ship to radio for help.

Recently, satellite imaging has shown that such freak waves are far more common than the predictions of probability theory allow. They happen many times every year in all the world's oceans. Buoys in the Gulf of Mexico measured giant waves during *Hurricane Katrina*. In 2004, ocean-floor pressure sensors showed a freak wave during *Hurricane Ivan* which was over 90 feet (27 m) high and about 650 feet (200 m) long. There are several theories surrounding the origin of freak waves. They may be caused by 'diffractive focusing' caused by seabed or coast shape, when several smaller waves meet in phase and their crest heights combine.

FREAK WAVE CATEGORIES

- *'Walls of water'*, which travel up to 8 miles (13 km).
- *'Three sisters'*, groups of three waves.
- *'Single, giant storm waves'*, building up to four times a storm's wave height and collapsing after seconds.

Freak Wave Occurrences

Many ships have been sunk without trace over the centuries without records of freak waves being available. Losses of low-flying planes and rescue helicopters have also been attributed to them. Of authenticated rogue waves we can include the following:

- In 1903 RMS *Etruria* was in the Atlantic four hours out of New York when struck by a wave 50 feet (15 m) high which carried away part of the fore bridge.
- In 1933 the crew of the navy oiler USS *Ramapo* was hit by a 112-foot (34-m) wave in the North Pacific.
- In 1942 RMS *Queen Mary* was carrying 15,000 American troops in a gale 700 miles (1125 km) off Scotland. She was hit by a 92-foot (28-m) wave and listed to 52 degrees before righting herself.
- In 1966, the Italian liner *Michelangelo* lost a crewman and two passengers when a wave tore a hole in the superstructure, smashing glass 80 feet (24m) above her waterline.
- A 95-foot (29-m) 'near-vertical' wave smashed into the cruise liner *Queen Elizabeth 2* in 1995 in the North Atlantic. Her captain stated that the wave *'looked like the white cliffs of Dover'*.
- In the South Atlantic in 2001, the bridge windows of both the *Bremen* and the *Caledonian Star* were smashed by a 100-foot (30-m) wave, resulting in all power and instrumentation being lost. The latter's First Officer stated that it was *'just like a mountain, a wall of water coming against us'*.
- In 2005, *Norwegian Dawn* was hit by three freak waves in succession off Georgia, USA. The 70-foot (21-m) waves *'seemed to come out of thin air'*.
- MS *Prinsendam*, a cruise liner, was hit by a 66-foot (20-m) wave in the Antarctic in 2007.

'THE GRAVEYARD OF THE ATLANTIC'

Off the coast of Cape Hatteras, the warm northbound Gulf Stream meets very cold currents from the Arctic to form the treacherous and shifting *Diamond Shoals.* Hundreds of ships have been wrecked here.

GULF STREAM This huge, warm North Equatorial Current moves at up to 4 knots (4.6 mph/7.4 kph) from the Caribbean to the Gulf of Mexico, through the Florida Straits and across the Atlantic travelling around 80 miles (130 km) per day. It is the fastest ocean current, around 1200 feet (366 m) deep, and by the time it reaches Cape Hatteras (North Carolina) has grown to 78 miles (125 km) wide. Off South Carolina it meets an inshore Arctic current, and from aerial pictures one can compare the dull green water of this cold current to the blue of the Gulf Stream. Opposite New York the Gulf Stream curves east, with its main branch heading between Iceland and Northern Scotland. A smaller stream, Rennell's Current, curves into the Bay of Biscay, warming the shores of western Europe and the southern shores of Britain. The UK would have the same cold climate as Labrador in Canada (which lies on the same latitude) if it was not for the effects of the Gulf Stream. This author has bathed in the sea off the coasts of both Africa and south Wales in August, and the sea temperature has been far warmer in Wales.

HEAD SEA Waves coming from the direction in which a vessel is heading.

TO MAKE HEADWAY

The forward motion of a sailing ship.

HUMBOLDT'S CURRENT

Emerging from the Antarctic, this current splits at the foot of South America, with one stream heading into the Atlantic past the Falkland Islands. Another branch flows into the Pacific along the coast of Chile. The Chilean branch carries numerous icebergs, and these cool the temperature of southwestern South America. This huge sea river is wider than the Gulf Stream and three times as deep, being responsible for the cooling of the seas as far north as the Galapagos Islands, near the equator.

ICEBERG CLASSIFICATIONS

A *'growler'* is a piece of iceberg less than 3 feet (90 cm) high and less than 15 feet (4.6 m) long. A *'bergy bit'* is 3–13 feet (0.9–4 m) high and 15–46 feet (4.6–14 m) long. Larger sizes are categorized as small, medium, large and very large, the last being over 240 feet (73 m) high and over 670 feet (204 m) long. Their shapes are characterized as *dome, pinnacle, wedge, dry dock* and *block.* Ninety per cent of an iceberg is under water.

ICEBERGS The largest iceberg sighted was in the Southern Ocean in 1956. It measured 240 miles by 60 miles (386 by 97 km), about the size of Rhode Island. In 1958, the United States Coast Guard icebreaker *East Wind* measured the world's tallest known iceberg off western Greenland. At 551 feet (168 m) above sea level, it was only 5 feet 6 inches (1.7 m) shorter than the Washington Monument in Washington, D.C.

ICEBERGS – OF THE STRIPED VARIETY

Icebergs in the Antarctic sometimes have stripes, formed by layers of snow which react to different ambient

Heave

There are many meanings for this nautical term:

- Waves *heave* up and down in rough seas, so a wave can heave a boat onto a reef by lifting it.
- To *heave* a line can mean either to throw a line or to take the strain and haul in on a line.
- To *heave the lead, heave the log* is to throw or to cast something.
- To *heave a cable short* means to raise it from the bottom of the sea until the vessel is almost directly above the anchor.
- To *heave a ship ahead (astern)* is to warp her ahead when not under sail, by means of cables, or to cause her to move, forcing her from or to a particular position.
- To *heave a ship down* is to throw or lay her on her side for careening.
- To *heave about* is to suddenly put the ship about.
- To *heave in* is to shorten lengths of ropes or cables.
- To *heave in stays* is to put the ship on another tack.
- To *heave out* a sail is to unfurl it.

- To *heave taut* is to turn a rope.
- To *heave to* is to turn into the wind and set sails to stop or gain control in heavy weather.
- To raise or haul up by means of a rope, line or cable, as in the order: *'Hove the anchor up and set sail'*.
- To move a vessel in a certain direction or to a specified position: the frigate *hove alongside*.
- To pull at or haul a rope or cable: the brig is *heaving around* on the anchor.
- To push at a capstan bar or lever.
- To *heave into sight* (or view) is used for a ship that rises or seems to rise over the horizon into view.
- A *heaving line* is a rope with a heavy knot on the end light enough for a seaman to throw to a dock or to another vessel. The 'bitter end' of the heaving line is secured to the end of a heavier dockline or towing line, so that it can then be hauled over.

conditions. Blue stripes can be created when a crevice in the ice sheet fills up with meltwater, and freezes so quickly that no bubbles form. When an iceberg falls into the sea, a layer of salty seawater can freeze to its underside. If this is rich in algae, it can form a green stripe in the ice. Brown, black and yellow lines are caused by sediment, picked up when the

glacial ice sheet grinds slowly downhill towards the sea.

LABRADOR CURRENT This is the cold ocean current flowing from the Arctic to Labrador on the east coast of Canada, where it meets the Gulf Stream which it diverts across the Atlantic, so warming the waters of Europe.

LAMB'S-WOOL SKY A collection of white orbs of cloud.

NORTHEAST PASSAGE The route between the Atlantic and Pacific Oceans running eastwards above northern Europe and Russia. The first passage was made in 1878–9 by the Swede Nils Nordenskjold. The Northern Sea Route has been navigable since the 1930s for mainly Russian ships, made navigable by Russian icebreakers. It halves the time of passage between Russian Atlantic and Pacific ports. It is likely that in the next few years it will be used more by ships of all nationalities as the sea warms, thus avoiding the need to use the Suez Canal to get to the Far East, and so enabling the use of larger ships for this journey.

NORTHWEST PASSAGE The route between the Atlantic and Pacific Oceans running westward above Canada and Alaska. Many expeditions failed to find and navigate it over the centuries until Roald Amundsen succeeded in *Gjoa* in 1903–6. In 1969 the *Manhattan* was the first commercial ship to use the passage. It appears that global warming will make it far more feasible for large ships to use the waterway in the future, so shipping can avoid using the Panama Canal.

THE NORTH POLE AS AN ISLAND In August 2008, NASA satellite pictures showed that melting ice had totally cleared the Northwest and Northeast Passages. It was the first time in 125,000 years that the two shortcuts linking the Atlantic and Pacific had been ice-free at the same time. In 2005 the Northeast Passage across the top of Russia opened, while the Northwest Passage remained closed. In 2007 the position

was reversed. The Northeast Passage cuts 4600 miles (7400 km) off the voyage from Germany to Japan, and the Beluga group will send its first ship through it in 2010. Some experts now believe that the North Pole will be ice-free clear water all year round by 2030. Others say that it will be ice-free between mid-July and mid-September by 2013. Professor Mark Sereze of the US National Snow and Ice Data Center predicts that the Arctic ice-cap had entered a 'death spiral'. In 2008, tourists had to be evacuated from Baffin Island's Auyuittuq National Park because of flooding from thawed glaciers. *Auyuittuq* means *'land that never melts'*.

SAINT ELMO'S FIRE These are luminous electrical discharges seen on mastheads, yardarms and rigging that may be observed during heavy rain, thunder and lightning. It was a good omen for sailors as St Elmo was one of the patron saints of seamen, and this natural

phenomenon showed that the saint was protecting their ship. The phenomenon generally occurs as the ship is passing out of the storm, which is probably why the superstition arose. The balls of electrical fire were also known as *Castor and Pollux, Corpo Santo* and *compasant*.

SEA SMOKE A very cold wind can cause vapour to rise from the sea. The phenomenon is also known as *water smoke, warm water fog, steam-fog* and *frost-smoke*.

SEA STATE A summary description of the height, period, direction and fetch of the ocean surface waves at a given time and place.

SEAS OF ALL SORTS A heavy sea is full of large waves. A great sea means that the whole ocean is agitated. A head sea means that the waves are coming from ahead. A long sea has a steady motion of long extensive waves. A short sea is when waves are running irregularly, broken and interrupted. A hollow sea is when there is shoaling water or a current setting against the waves. In this, the line from crest to trough makes a sharp angle, so the sea is very dangerous.

SILVER THAW The name given when large flakes of ice fall off the sails and rigging during a thaw.

SNEAKER WAVES A 'sneaker wave' is a disproportionately large coastal wave which can appear in a 'wave train' (sequence of waves) without warning. If you stand on a rock on the seashore with the tide coming in, you should notice that several more or less equal waves are followed by a larger one. Folklore says that every seventh wave is bigger than the

previous six, and there is some statistical evidence to back this up. Faster waves catch up slower ones and combine to make a bigger wave.

SPINDRIFT The fine mist of water swept from the tops of waves by the action of high winds.

TIDES The highest tides on Earth are found in the Bay of Fundy east of New Brunswick, Canada. The channelling effect of the bay is responsible for the amazing difference between high tide and low tide, which, during spring tides, can reach 53.5 feet (16.3 m). This is almost as tall as a four-storey building. The second highest rise and fall in the world is in the Bristol Channel (Severn Sea) between England and Wales, at 47 feet (14.3 m).

TIDES (CAUSES) Tides are periodic rises and falls of large bodies of water, caused by gravitational interaction between the Earth and the Moon. The gravitational attraction of the Moon causes the oceans to bulge out in its direction. Strangely enough, another bulge occurs on the opposite side of the Earth since the Earth is also being pulled towards the Moon (and thus away from the water on the far side). The Earth is rotating while this is happening, so two tides occur each day, as first scientifically explained by Sir Isaac Newton (1643– 1727). Spring tides are especially strong tides, occurring when the Sun, Moon and Earth are in alignment, and the gravitational forces of the Moon and the Sun are both contributing to the tides, and thus making them higher than usual. They happen during the full moon and new moon, and are nothing to do with the season of Spring. Neap tides are much

Wave Codes

Wave Code	Description	Height from trough to crest (feet)
0	Glassy calm	0
1	Calm, ripples	0–1
2	Smooth, wavelets	1–2
3	Slight	2–4
4	Moderate	4–8
5	Rough	8–13
6	Very rough	13–20
7	High	20–30
8	Very high	30–45
9	Phenomenal	Over 45, the centre of a hurricane

weaker tides. They occur when the gravitational forces of the Moon and the Sun are perpendicular to one another (with respect to the Earth). They occur during 'quarter moons'.

WAVES (CAUSES) The wind causes waves on the surface of the ocean, as it transfers some of its energy to the water through friction between the air molecules and the water molecules. Stronger winds cause larger waves, when we may experience 'storm surges'. A wave does not represent a flow of water, as waves of water do not move horizontally, they only move up and down. On a windless day one can watch a floating buoy bob up and down with a wave – it does not move horizontally with the wave from its position.

WAVES (HIGHEST) The highest (non-tsunami) wave was recorded in 1933 during a hurricane by crew on the USS *Ramapo*. It measured 112 feet (34 m) from trough to crest. The highest

recorded tsunami wave was at Lituya Bay in Alaska in 1958. Three small fishing boats encountered it. Two rode the waves and their fishermen survived. The other boat was lost. The coastline was unpopulated. The tsunami inundated approximately 5 square miles (13 km^2) of land along the shores of the bay, sending water as far as 3600 feet (1100 m) inland, and clearing millions of trees. To measure the height of the wave, scientists looked for the high water mark, the line where the water reached its highest point on land. Then they measured the elevation of the highest point on the high water mark to establish a measurement of 1720 feet (516 m) high – the biggest wave ever measured.

WHITECAPS This is broken water at the tops of waves, caused by winds of 12 knots (14 mph/22 kph) and over. They were also known as *'Neptune's sheep'* in days of sail. They often presage unexpected gusts of wind under cloudless skies known as *'white squalls'*.

UNDER THE WEATHER

Before radar, all ships had to keep watch for the approach of other vessels. The seaman standing watch on the weather side of the bow would become tired of the constant pitching of the ship, and the spray and wind blowing in his face. Boats pitch up and down more at the bow and stern, and he was also *'facing the weather'*, often in stormy conditions. Consequently, he was *'under the weather'*. This miserable job came to lend us the phrase that signifies we are feeling ill. Passengers aboard ships become seasick most frequently during times of rough seas and bad weather. Seasickness is caused by the constant rocking motion of the ship. Sick passengers go below deck, which provides shelter from the weather. On a ship the greatest swaying action is felt on deck, and the most stable point is down low in the ship towards its centre. This is another derivation for being 'under the weather', when passengers feeling poorly went below, away from the weather.

KEEP A WEATHER EYE OPEN

This is an old sailing term – trouble will generally come from the side of the ship where weather is developing.

MAKE HEAVY WEATHER

The weather is the wind, and to *'make heavy weather'* is to make unnecessary work sailing into it.

WEATHER BEATEN When a ship has been badly damaged by a storm.

THE WEATHER MAKER

The ocean determines climate and plays a critical role in Earth's habitability. Most of the solar energy that reaches the Earth is stored in the ocean and helps power oceanic and atmospheric circulation. In this manner, the ocean plays an important role in influencing the weather and climatic patterns of the Earth.

WEATHER QUARTER The quarter of a ship which is on the windward.

Tsunamis

A rogue wave is not the same as a tsunami. Tsunamis are mass displacement-generated waves which propagate at high speed. They are more or less unnoticeable in deep water. They only become dangerous as they approach the shoreline and do not present a threat to shipping unless it lies very near the coast. In the 2004 'Asian Tsunami', the only ships lost were in port. A tsunami can reach 100 feet (30 m) high as it nears land, having been triggered by a volcanic eruption, earthquake or landslide. The largest ever known was said to have occurred in 1737 off Siberia's Kamchatka Peninsula and was recorded as 210 feet (64 m) high. Another claimant for the largest recorded tsunami measured 190 feet (60 m) above sea level, travelling at hundreds of miles per hour, caused by an 8.9 magnitude earthquake in the Gulf of Alaska in 1899. A tsunami can travel at well over 600 mph (965 kph) in the open ocean – as fast as a modern jet aircraft – so it can take only a few hours for a tsunami to travel across an entire ocean. A wind-generated wave, however, travels at a maximum of about 55 mph (89 kph). Ninety per cent of tsunamis occur in the Pacific Ocean. Some of the world's largest tsunamis include:

65 million years ago Chicxulub crater at the tip of Mexico's Yucatán Peninsula. This crater was caused by a large meteoroid. Its impact and the subsequent tsunami may have triggered the mass extinction which wiped out the dinosaurs and many other species.

1490 BCE Greece (Aegean Sea). A tsunami was caused by the eruption/collapse of the volcanic island of Santorini. This tsunami may have caused the end of the Minoan civilization in Crete.

26 January 1700 Japan (Pacific Ocean). A tsunami caused by an earthquake of magnitude 9.0 off the western coast of Vancouver Island, Canada.

26 August 1883 Indonesia. A tsunami caused by the eruption/collapse of the volcano Krakatoa. Almost 40,000 people died.

15 June 1896 Honshu, Japan. 28,000 people killed.

18 November 1929 Grand Banks, Canada (Atlantic Ocean). Tsunami caused by an offshore earthquake of magnitude 7.2. Twenty-seven people died.

1 April 1946 Aleutian Islands, Alaska (Pacific Ocean). Tsunami caused by an earthquake of magnitude 7.8 in the Aleutian Islands of Alaska. More than 170 people died.

4 November 1952 Kamchatka Peninsula, Russia (Pacific Ocean). Tsunami caused by an earthquake of magnitude 8.2 off the coast of the Kamchatka Peninsula (Russia). No lives lost.

9 March 1957 Aleutian Islands, Alaska (Pacific Ocean). Tsunami caused by an earthquake of magnitude 8.3 that occurred south of the Andreanof Islands (in the Aleutian Islands off Alaska). No lives lost.

9 July 1958 Lituya Bay, Alaska. Tsunami caused by a landslide. The massive initial wave was over 1700 feet (500 m) high travelling at 100 mph (160 kph).

22 May 1960 Chile (Pacific Ocean). Tsunami caused by an earthquake of magnitude 8.3 that occurred off the coast of south central Chile. Up to 2290 people died (due to the combined effect of the earthquake and tsunami).

28 March 1964 Prince William Sound, Alaska (Pacific Ocean). Tsunami

caused by an earthquake of magnitude 8.4 in Prince William Sound. 122 people died.

17 September 1992 Nicaragua (Pacific Ocean). Tsunami caused by an offshore earthquake of magnitude 7.0. About 200 people killed.

17 July 1998 Papua-New Guinea. Tsunami caused by an underwater landslide that was triggered by an earthquake. Many thousands of people killed.

23 June 2001 – Southern Peru (Pacific Ocean). Tsunami caused by an earthquake off the coast.

26 December 2004 Indonesia, Thailand, Sri Lanka, SE India (Indian Ocean). Tsunami caused by an earthquake of magnitude 9.0 in the southern Indian Ocean. Its epicentre was off the coast of Sumatra. About 230,000 people died.

CHAPTER 3

Life *at* Sea

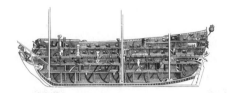

THE PARTS OF A SHIP

ANCHOR The name originates in the Greek word *'anklos'* meaning bend, and from which we also derive 'ankle' and 'angle'. Angling itself requires a bent hook. The largest anchor is known as the sheet anchor. The next in size are the bower anchors, hung in the bows of ships, and generally the smallest is the kedge anchor. Different types of anchors are required to hold the vessel to the seabed, depending on different seabed conditions.

ASTROLABE A navigational instrument to measure the altitude of the Sun and stars (Spanish *astrolabio*). It was developed by the Greeks and refined by the Arabs, and did not need a horizon. It was used until the 18th century, but any heavy seas made its use impractical on board ship.

AWNINGS These were pieces of sails supported like canopies on deck to provide sailors with shade in hot climates.

BACKSTAFF A navigational aid to measure the apparent height of a landmark of which the true height is known, e.g. a lighthouse. From this information, the distance of the ship to the landmark could be calculated. It was invented by the explorer John Davis around 1595, so it was also known as the *Davis quadrant*. It was a great improvement on the *cross staff*, as the user did not have to stare into the Sun to measure its altitude.

BAGGYWRINKLE The name given to old ropes used as *chafing gear*, which prevents damage to the ship from rubbing against other ships or moorings.

BALLAST This is from the Old German, and meant *'belly load'*. Weight has to be carried in the belly, or hold, of the ship to give her stability and keep her *'trim and shipshape'* in the water. Insufficiently ballasted boats will tend to tip, or heel, excessively in high winds, and possibly capsize. When sailing vessels carried cargo, it was at times necessary to sail to or from a port without the cargo load. In order to do this safely, enough ballast of little or no value, such as sand or stones, would be loaded to keep the vessel upright. This ballast would then be discarded when the cargo was loaded. Cardiff was once a great trading port, exporting huge amounts of coal. You can see non-local stone in many of its great Victorian and Edwardian buildings – this was originally brought to the port as ballast.

BARRICADE A strong wooden rail acting as a fence on the quarterdeck. In time of battle it was filled with rolled hammocks, rope-mats and old cable to intercept small shot.

BEAM The width of a vessel, and also a structural component. Both uses come from the Anglo-Saxon word beam, meaning tree.

BELOW Below decks, as in *'going below to F deck'*. A sailor never says 'going down to F deck', always using the term below. Perhaps saying 'down' was unlucky, with connotations of 'down to the bottom of the sea'.

BERMUDA RIG Also known as Marconi rig, using a triangular mainsail.

BILGE AND WASTERS *'The breadth of the place the ship rests on when she is aground'* – Captain John Smith, 1627. The bilge was also the filthy, stagnant, lowest part of the ship where rats could always be found. Rats were despised both for their urine smell, and because they fouled precious food. However, in times of scarcity, they were the only source of fresh meat on a vessel. Bilge water stank as it lay on the flat bottom of the ship, so could not be pumped out. Rubbish and waste gathered in it, in the *waist* or centre of the bottom of the ship, creating difficulties in steering. *'Waisters'* were older, unfit or forced seamen who were given the unpleasant job of trying to clear up the mess, and prevent the bilge water becoming too much of a problem. These were sailors who could not be trusted in the rigging, and who were given other menial tasks like *'swinging the lead'*, casting around to sound out the depth. Spelling over time changed to today's mispelt *'wasters'*, people who are a target for derision.

BILGE PUMP Sometimes three men had to man the bilge pump if a ship was experiencing *'green water'* on deck, and they had to be lashed in place or be swept away. A pump could extract up to a ton of water (*c.*1000 litres) a minute from belowdecks, and in storms had to be manned permanently. On HMS *Victory*, 150 men would work in relays around the clock in heavy seas, pumping 120 tons of water an hour out of the bilges.

BINNACLE The stand on which the ship's compass is mounted. Before the 18th century, the word was *bittacle*, which came from the French *habitacle* and the Latin *habitaculum*, meaning a place of habitation. Before compasses came into use, the name referred to a lantern stand.

BITTER A turn of a cable about the *bits*. The *bits* were the two huge square pieces of timber to which the cables were fastened when the ship lay at anchor.

BOARD, BOARDING PARTY, ON BOARD, UNDER BOARD, BOARDING CARD, ALL ABOVE BOARD Board is the side of a ship, as in: *'Put that by the board'* (over the side). If anything at sea went overboard it was *'by the board'*, with absolutely no chance of being recovered. To *'take aboard'* was to put all useful things on the deck, ready for immediate use. *'All above board'* meant that the planks, or boards, which make up the deck are visible to everyone, and nothing can be hidden. *'Above board'* meant having one's hands above the card table when gambling. Similarly, *'under board'* meant acting deviously. Thus today, when we take instructions *'on board'*, we will not forget anything. It also means to go onto a ship – today's *boarding card* or ticket for an airplane originally applied only to sailing ships.

Alphabet

The following sea shanty is called 'The Sailor's Alphabet':

A is the anchor that holds a brave ship,
B is the bowsprit that often does dip,
C is the capstan on which we do wind, and
D is the davits on which the jolly boat hangs.

Chorus:
O hi derry, hey derry, ho derry down,
Give sailors their grog and there's nothing goes wrong,
So merry, so merry, so merry are we,
No matter who's laughing at sailors at sea.

E is the ensign, the red, white and blue,
F is the fo'c'sle, holds the ship's crew,
G is the gangway on which the mate takes his stand,
H is the hawser that seldom does strand.

Chorus

I is the irons where the stuns'l boom sits,
J is the jib-boom that often does dip,
K are the keelsons of which you've told, and
L are the lanyards that always will hold.

Chorus

M is the main mast, so stout and so strong,
N is the north point that never points wrong,
O are the orders of which we must beware,
P are the pumps that cause sailors to swear.

Chorus

Q is the quadrant, the sun for to take,
R is the riggin' that always does shake,
S is the starboard of our bold ship, and
T are the topmasts that often do split.

Chorus

U is the ugliest old Captain of all,
V are the vapours that come with the squall,
W is the windlass on which we do wind, and
X, Y and Z, well, I can't put in rhyme!

Chorus

Board can mean to attack or inspect a vessel without its master's permission, as in: *'Heave to! We are going to board you!'* A *boarding party* is a group of people organized to go on board a vessel to attack or inspect it, usually bearing arms.

BONNET This is an addition to another sail, and the order to fasten it on is *'lace on the bonnet'*. To take it off is to *'shake off the bonnet'*. Bonnets were used only on the mizzen, main, fore and sprit sails, and if they were in place, each sail was called a *course*. Thus it was a *main course and bonnet*, not *mainsail and bonnet*. Bonnets were added to the sail in moderate weather to catch more wind.

BOOMS There are several definitions: fenders to which sails are fixed to control its position; spars on which the foot of a triangular sail is bent; spars that swing out from a derrick or mast to provide a purchase for lifting cargo or boats over the side; and floating dams used to contain oil spills.

BOW, BOWS From the Old English *'bog'*, meaning bough, the front of the ship, the pointed end to most landlubbers.

BOWER ANCHORS These are used almost constantly. The *best bower anchor* is that on the starboard bow, and the *small bower anchor* is the same size, on the port bow.

BOWSPRIT (SPREET) The spar sticking forward over the bows of the ship, above any figurehead, carrying the headstay as far forward as possible.

BRACES These are ropes, two to each yard, and they are used to hold, square or traverse the sails.

BRIDGE The control or command centre of any power vessel. The term arose in the mid-19th century, when the *bridge* was an athwartships structure very much like a footbridge, stretched across the vessel between or immediately in front of the paddle wheels.

BRIG This became naval slang for the ship's prison, because during the Napoleonic Wars Admiral Nelson placed his French and Spanish prisoners in ships called brigs. It is still the term used in the US Navy.

BRIGHTWORK This originally applied to polished metal objects, and came to refer to the bright painted woodwork which was kept scrubbed on the topside of a boat. There is an old saying *'Bright it should be, and work it is.'*

BULKHEAD This is a transverse, or fore-and-aft, partition or wall in a vessel which gives rigidity of structure, creates compartments for rooms and storage spaces, and helps control the spread of fire. They were often knocked out by pirates to lighten the ship and accommodate more men and weapons. It comes from the Old Norse *balker*, meaning *'partition'*.

BULWARK A solid rail or wall extending along the ship's sides above the deck. From Old English and Norse, it now means in non-nautical speech someone who is regarded as extremely reliable.

BURTHEN A ship's tonnage or carrying capacity, based on the number of *tuns* of wine that could be carried in the holds, the total number giving the burthen (burden).

BUTTOCKS The breadth of a ship, which *'has a narrow or broad buttock'*, according to Captain Smith (*A Sea Grammar*, 1627).

CABLE A very heavy rope, measuring more than 10 inches (25 cm) in circumference. Also now a large and very strong wire rope used on machinery to lift heavy cargo, or to tow nets and trawls.

CABOOSE In 1769, William Falconer referred to this as a sort of box. It was a very small galley for cooking on the open deck of naval ships. It was originally a wooden deck structure housing the ship's galley in the 18th century. The word derives from the Dutch *'kombuis'*. The term could also mean a cooking stove and forge sometimes located on the gun deck.

CANVAS All sails and hammocks were originally made from strong-fibred hemp which was obtained from the plant *Cannabis sativa*. It developed into heavy, tightly-woven material made of flax, cotton and sometimes hemp. Although modern sails are made of oil-derived

materials, they are still named after a semi-legal drug. It is also used as a collective noun meaning all the sails of a ship, as in: *'Let's stow the canvas'* or *'She is carrying a lot of canvas'*.

CAPSTAN A bollard-shaped drum which rotates, and around which a hauling line is wrapped several times to get a purchase, to lift heavy weights, such as the anchor. A capstan chantey (shanty) was a rhythmic sea song with a short repetitive answering chorus, sung by the crew as they trod around the capstan, pushing on the bars to raise the anchor. The rhythm helped them to act in unison. All anchors and cables and other heavy rigging before the advent of steam propulsion were worked by hand-operated capstans of massive size. In HMS *Victory*, for example, the main capstan was 'handraulic' to the extent that 280 men, 140 of them on each of two decks, manned the capstan bars. A fiddler used to sit on top of the capstan playing tunes to which the men sang.

CHAIN LOCKER A forward compartment below deck where the anchor chain is stowed. The cramped and somewhat unhygienic conditions led to certain bars in harbour pubs and hotels being known as 'The Chain Locker'.

CLINKER-BUILT The construction of a hull with the lower edge of each plank overlapping the upper edge of the plank below it. This style is also known as *lapstrake*. *Carvel-built* vessels have the edges of the planks meeting flush giving a smooth appearance to the hull. From the 15th century all warships were carvel-built. The use of cannon at sea meant that carving gunports in a clinker-built ship compromised the integrity of its structure.

CLOSE QUARTERS A small wooden fortress or barricade erected on the deck of a merchant ship when attacks by pirates were expected. Small openings – loopholes – enabled sailors to fire weapons while enjoying some protection. Wooden partitions in the quarters below decks also had loopholes pierced in them to allow defenders to thrust pikes and cutlasses through and fight off boarders – i.e. to *'fight at close quarters'*.

COMPANIONWAY Any stepped passageway used to go from one deck to another. The term is more used in US ships today, whereas the British traditionally use the term ladders.

CROSS STAFF Also called a *fore-staff* and a *Jacob staff*, it was introduced around 1515 to enable the determination of latitude. A calibrated wooden stick was used to measure the distance between a star and the horizon.

CROW'S NEST A resting platform on a mast for sailors working the yardarms, it was also used as a look-out point. Crows or ravens were carried on board to help early navigators determine where the closest land lay, when the weather prevented sighting the shore visually.

In cases of poor visibility, a crow was released and the navigator plotted a course that corresponded with the crow's as it invariably headed straight toward land, *'as the crow flies'*. If the crow returned, it could not find land. The crow's cage (nest) was situated high on the mainmast where the lookout also stood his watch. Thus, he shared this lofty perch with a crow or two, as the crows' cages were kept there. The Spanish lookout at the crow's nest spotted the West Indies, the New World, before Christopher Columbus.

DAVITS A pair of cranes used for hoisting and lowering a ship's boats. The word came into use in the early 17th century and at that time was spelled *'davids'*, possibly a reference to their unknown inventor.

DEADWEIGHT TONNAGE 'DWT' is the number of tons of cargo, stores and bunker fuel that a ship can transport.

DEADWOOD Heavy longitudinal timbers fastened over the keelson, to which are attached the timbers of the bow and stern. The term now is used for people who are *'along for the ride'* in the terms of being a waste of space, and dragging everyone else down.

DECK What one walks on aboard ship, never the floor. Originally from the Middle Dutch *dec*, meaning roof.

DEGAUSSING GEAR A countermeasure to the threat of magnetic mines, whereby electrical cables are passed around a ship's hull and a measured electrical current hopefully cancels out the ship's magnetic field.

DEVIL BOLTS The use of *'devil bolts'* was a corrupt practice adopted by shipbuilders to save money. The 64-gun warship *York* foundered in the North Sea in 1804 because copper bolts were not used to hold the ship's timbers together at key points. Instead, the bolts had been faked by inserting copper heads and tails in appropriate positions, connected by hidden wooden dowels. *Devil bolts* with too short shanks, fitted when repairing the *Blenheim*, were also blamed for the loss of Admiral Thomas Troubridge's flagship in 1807.

DOGHOUSE A part of the belowdecks cabin which is raised above the deck level to provide additional headroom below. It is unsure whether the term *'in the doghouse'* originates here or refers to the kennel of a dog.

DOLPHIN STRIKER A short downward spar under the bowsprit, its function is to spread the stays and counteract the upward pull of the rigging. If a dolphin were to leap out of the water below the bowsprit, it had a good chance of hitting this spar.

DROGUE Francis Drake used an improvised drogue to deliberately slow his ship down when chasing the Spanish ship *Nostra Señora de la Concepcion*. It was a conically shaped bag which trailed behind the ship, its mouth open to the water. The Spaniard was racing away as night fell and thought herself secure. However, at night Drake cut the drogue and quickly caught up and surprised the Spanish prize.

DUTCHMAN'S LOG, LOG This was a buoyant object (formerly a log), usually attached to a rope, thrown overboard from the bow of a ship. The time was measured for it to pass the stern. Knowing the ship's length, and the time taken to move that distance, the ship's speed could be measured. Records were then kept (logged) to estimate how far the ship had travelled each day.

ECDIS Electronic Chart Display and Information System. Modern ships employ a database of nautical charts issued by the National Hydrographical Authority. Appropriate charts can be displayed on computer screens on the bridge, and used for navigation. ECDIS also displays safety information, position, depth and other system readings to aid the watch.

EYES The eyes of a ship are the extreme bows. The name comes from the ancient custom (still maintained in some parts of the world) of painting eyes on each side of the bow so that the ship could see where she was going.

FIFE RAIL In 1800 there was an order introducing high bulwarks to replace the old 'drift and fife rails' in line-of-battle ships. The term had been applied to a rail

around the lower part of a ship's mast to which the belaying pins for the rigging were secured. It is believed the name may come from a man playing the fife who sat on it while men hauled on the ropes in time to his tune.

FIGHTING TOPS These were platforms or baskets around the tops of the masts from where marksmen could shoot down on the enemy.

FIGUREHEAD There is no practical purpose to the figureheads on sailing ships. They were ornamental devices to show the owner's wealth or taste and to inspire the crew. The fashion for topless women as figureheads came from the belief that bare-bosomed ladies could calm the stormy seas. Their origin was the *'nostrum'*, or beak, of galleys that were used to ram other vessels. These beaks were sometimes surmounted by figureheads representing religious or national emblems.

FLY BY NIGHT When sailing downwind at night, a large, single, *fly-by-night* sail was used to do the job of several smaller sails. Requiring less

Fluke

This is the end of the anchor which digs into the seabed. A ploughshare pulled across land will try to bury itself, and so will an anchor, which is designed to both turn and bury itself.

Different types are used for different seabed conditions. The one most of us are familiar with is called the *'fisherman's anchor'*, with a crown in its centre and two arms with a fluke at each end.

attention, it could only be used downwind, so was very rarely seen.

FORE-AND-AFT RIGGED The inside (luff) edge of a sail is attached to a mast, and the lower edge to a boom. The boom can then be moved from one side of the ship to another to direct the ship or react to changing winds. The sails run parallel to the keel, whereas on a square-rigger they are set perpendicular to the keel, crosswise the ship.

FORECASTLE, FO'C'S'LE Formerly a raised deck at the front of the ship, from where fire was directed at the enemy – it served the function of a castle tower. Over the years its height was lowered to make boats more manoeuvrable, and to enable the captain on the poop deck to see what was happening. Thus the forecastle (pronounced *folks'l*) came to mean the front decking. In medieval ships there were also *'aftercastles'* for the knights and soldiers on board fighting ships. These structures made them unwieldy and unseaworthy.

FRAMES The 'ribs' of a vessel, from the Old Italian *fram*, meaning frame.

FUNNEL The smokestack of a steamship. Many transatlantic liners, such as the *Titanic*, had a dummy funnel, both for aesthetic reasons and because passengers equated more funnels with more power and a speedier crossing.

FUTTOCK A curved piece of timber composing the frame of the ship, referred to by location, e.g. first futtock, second futtock and so on.

GALLEY The ship's kitchen where food is prepared. The origin is uncertain but may have arisen because the ship's cook and helpers thought of themselves as *'galley slaves'*. (A galley was originally a fighting ship propelled by oars, from the Latin *galea*.)

GANGWAY! This is the portable ramp used for moving goods or people to and from a pier or dockside, from the Old English *'gangweg'* or passageway/pathway. Any crewman struggling through with a heavy load would shout this warning to ensure that others moved out of the way. Other shipboard passageways are also called gangways.

GENOA, GENNY The biggest jib-sail on a ship.

GOLLYWOBBLER We have a phrase today, *'I have the collywobbles'*, meaning to be afraid. There may be a connection with this name for the large square staysail hoisted between the masts of a schooner in a reaching wind to increase its speed.

GPS The Global Positioning System that allows sailors to determine their dimensional position, velocity and time, anywhere in the world at any time. The system uses data from 24 satellites in six circular orbits.

HALYARDS The ropes or tackles by which sails are hoisted, e.g. the jib halyards, topsail halyards, etc. Part of the running rigging, they are used to haul the yards, hence 'haulyards' which eventually became halyards.

HAMMOCK, HAMAC Columbus noted that the Carib Indians slung a *'hamorca'* between trees, and he then introduced it into European ships. Their swinging action counteracted the swell of the waves, and made for a more

Gun Walls, Gun Wales, Gunn'ls

In the 15th century, these were called *'gonne walles'*, the upper edge of a ship's side, which prevented guns and other deck items from falling over the side. They had openings to let sea water wash from the deck, and to let the guns fire. The saying *'awash to the gunn'ls'* means that the sea is coming over the deck. From the same source comes *'packed to the gunn'ls'* or *'full to the gun wales'*. This meant that the lower decks were crammed full of cargo and men, and so was the top deck, so that the ship could take no

more plunder. A *wale* was any of the strakes on the side of a vessel, from the Old English *'walen'*, or ridge. Like many nautical terms gun wale is always shortened and pronounced gunn'l or gunnel.

comfortable sleep than in a bunk or on deck. However, the original invention of this swinging bed at sea was in ancient Greece by Alcibiades around 450 BCE. Hammocks on Royal Naval vessels were first authorized in 1597.

HEAD Roman galleys had elaborate heads on the bow, which were fitted with bronze *beaks*, and used for ramming. As sailing ships developed, the *'beakhead'* became a term applied to a structure projecting from the stem and the bowsprit. This was usually a work platform, decked with grating and open to the sea below. Waves washing through the grating made a constant flushing action and thus an ideal lavatory. *Heads* is the naval name for latrines, as they were originally sited in the extreme bow (head) of the ship. The rating responsible for their general cleanliness is the 'Captain of the Heads'.

HELM From *The Gentleman's Dictionary* by Georges Guillet de Saint-Georges, 1705, we read: *'HELM, or Tiller, of a Ship; is that Piece of timber which is fastened into the Rudder, and so comes forward into the Steerage, or Place where he at the Helm Steers the Ship, by holding the Whipstaff in his Hand. Some Ships have a Wheel, like those in Cranes, placed between the Quarter-Deck and Coach; which has several Advantages, to what the Common Methods have.'* Wheels started to become common in the 1730s, replacing the tiller, as they required considerably less effort to control.

HOLD The part between the keelson and the lower deck where all goods, stores and victuals are carried.

HOUSE FLAG Each merchant shipping line had their own house flag and a distinctive colour pattern painted on their funnels.

Jackstaff, Union Jack

JACKSTAFF, UNION JACK

In 1603 James VI of Scotland became James I of England, Wales and Scotland, uniting the three countries. The English St George's flag (red cross on white) was combined with the Scottish St Andrew's flag (white saltire on blue) to make the *Union Flag*. James instructed it to be flown on all his ships. A small new mast was added to the bowsprit of all ships of the Royal Navy in 1606 to fly this new Union Flag. King James used the Latin version of his name when signing orders and official letters, *Jacobus Rex*, but used *Jac* for personal letters. Thus the new mast became known as a Jackstaff. Modern warships no longer have bowsprits, but the jackstaff is still used to fly the Union Flag at the bows. Only when it is flown from a ship in this way should it be called the Union Jack. At all other times, when flown from buildings or flagpoles, it is the Union Flag, never the Union Jack. Naval ships did not have to pay port taxes and harbour dues in Britain, as the ports were owned by the Crown. Thus merchantmen began to add jackstaffs and fly the Union Jack to save money. Therefore in 1634 a law was passed whereby only Royal Navy ships can fly the Union Jack, only on the jackstaff, and only when stationary in port. Only the monarch's vessel can fly the Union Jack while sailing.

JIB A triangular sail set on the boom which runs out from the bowsprit.

JIB OF JIBS According to Admiral Smyth in *The Sailor's Word-Book*, only *'flying-kite-men'* knew this sail, it being the sixth jib on the bowsprit, the sequence being storm jib, inner jib, outer jib, flying jib, spindle jib, jib of jibs.

JOLLY BOAT A light, general purpose boat carried at the stern of the ship, and deployed when it was more able to manoeuvre near land. Probably the word originated from the Danish *'jol'* or yawl.

KEEL The first step in constructing a ship such as a galleon was to lay the keel (from the Spanish *quilla*). This principal timber ran fore and aft for the whole length of the ship, supporting the *frame* just like a backbone. In larger ships they were often made of elm, because oak was not long enough, while the other timbers used for the frame would be oak. To the frame was fixed the *boards* (planks).

KITES The highest and lightest sails, set above the *royals*, and including *skysails* (see *skyscrapers*), *moonsails* and *stargazers*.

They were also referred to as *royal studding* and *topgallant studding* sails.

LADDER On shipboard, all stairs are called ladders, except for literal staircases found aboard passenger liners. Most *stairs* on a ship are narrow and nearly vertical, hence the use of the term ladder.

LARBOARD The port or left side of any ship when facing the bow, from the Old English *'laddebord'* or the Norse *'hlada bord'* (loading side), the opposite of starboard.

LATEEN The dominant rig on sailing boats in the Mediterranean and Indian Ocean. It was unsuitable for the rougher conditions of the Atlantic. A triangular sail is set on a long yard and attached to a short mast.

LIFELINE Ropes were left trailing from sailing ships in case someone fell overboard from the rigging or was washed over in heavy seas. However, to *grab a lifeline* was to be very lucky indeed.

LINE Any small rope aboard ship, such as buntlines, cluelines, bowlines, ratlines, marlines etc.

LOG-BOOK The written record of a ship's progress, coming from the daily practice of throwing a log overboard (attached to a line) to estimate the speed of a ship. The time for the log to 'fall away' from the ship up to the measured length of the line was measured by a half-minute sand-glass, and the speed of the ship computed using the time elapsed and length of line used.

LOOPHOLE A small opening, often in the bulkheads, through which arms could be employed to fire at the enemy.

MAGAZINE A secure room in the hold where ammunition was kept and guarded. It was lit by candles in the 'light-room' adjoining it, but no candles or lanterns were allowed in the magazine.

MAINSTAY The supporting timber framework of the mainmast, this has come to mean the *chief support* of any person or organization. The term also applies to the chief ropes securing the mainmast in position.

MARINE DIESEL ENGINES

The world's largest marine diesel engine, and also the first 14-cylinder low-speed engine, entered service in September 2006 in a large container ship. The Wärtsilä Corporation's RT-flex96C is the world's most powerful engine with an output of 108,920 bhp (80,080 kW) at 102 rpm. It is a breakthrough for ship propulsion, as low-speed marine engines have traditionally been built with a maximum of 12 cylinders.

MASK PAINTING In the Napoleonic Wars, ships' hulls were painted black, with red, white or yellow stripes signifying the gundecks, and the gunport covers were painted black. Merchant ships copied this pattern, with black dummy gunport covers, to discourage pirates and privateers from attacking them because they looked like naval warships. The camouflage was also known as *'painted ports'*, when alternate black and white rectangles were painted on the hulls of merchant ships to simulate the appearance of gunport covers.

MIZZEN (MIZEN) MAST The rear mast on a ship, the third or aftermost mast of a square-rigged sailing ship. To *mizzen* is to fit the mizzen sail and to *change the mizzen* means to bring the yard to the other side of the mast.

MOONRAKER An evocative name for a small sail, also called a *moonsail*, set in light winds above a skysail.

NETTING This was used to secure hammocks and sails. *Boarding netting* was spread across the rigging to stop boarders jumping onto the deck in battle. It stretched to a height of about 12 feet (3.7 m) above the quarterdeck, and also helped protect the crew from falling objects and the debris of battle.

OAK Some 5750 mature oak trees were required to build a 100-gun line-of-battle ship. Because of shipbuilding Britain's oak forests were decimated from the Middle Ages onwards, such was the need to build merchant vessels and warships. Cheaper, more available woods decayed faster and splintered more easily in action. Splinter wounds from other woods, especially from teak, tended to turn septic. Another huge advantage was the sheer compression resilience of oak timber. After the 1816 bombardment of Algiers, the 98-gun HMS *Impregnable* was found to have 233 items of heavy shot embedded in her hull.

OCTANT A navigational instrument, not particularly accurate, but vital before it evolved into the sextant in the late 18th century. It was invented by John Hadley in 1731 and thus is also known as *Hadley's quadrant*. Easy to use, it involved two mirrors taking measurements of up to 90 degrees from the deck of a ship.

ORLOP The deck above the holds in old ships, which would now be called the platform deck, was known as the orlop deck. It is a contraction of *'overlap'*, a word of Dutch origin meaning *'that which runs over the hold'*. In HMS *Victory* the orlop deck was painted – the wounded were taken there to be tended by the ship's surgeon. On this first deck below the waterline the injured and their attendants were safer, and blood was not so noticeable against the red paint. Marines sometimes shared quarters with midshipmen in the *orlop*, and the term orlop is still in use in merchant ships.

OVERHEAD The ceiling aboard ship, and always referred to as such, just as the floor is always a deck, and stairways are always ladders. Ceiling on a vessel refers to the interior planking or plates affixed to the ship's frames.

PARTNERS The stout wooden framework necessary to hold a mast, pump, capstan or bitt to the deck. Without partners, none of these would hold tight. This seems to be the origin of the business term of partners.

PLIMSOLL MARKS *'Load lines'* painted on the middle of both sides of a ship, indicating the maximum depths to which a ship can safely be loaded. Samuel Plimsoll's bill to make the marking of load lines compulsory was ratified in 1876, ensuring that ships were no longer overloaded when they went to sea.

POOP DECK The raised weather deck at the stern of a sailing ship, usually above the captain's quarters. It was usually the highest deck, from where the captain directed battles. Thus if the ship has two decks above the main deck aft, the poop deck is above the quarterdeck. The name came from the Middle English *'poupe'*, itself from the Latin *'puppim'*, meaning the rear section of a ship. In Latin, *'puppis'* meant a doll or small image. The Romans and other ancient seafaring peoples had a small sacred idol or image affixed to the stern, where the deity it represented could watch over the vessel. *Puppis* then altered to *puppim* over time, in this context giving a new word representing the stern.

PORTHOLES Porthole comes from the French *'porte'* and Latin *'porta'* (door). It referred to a cover which can be opened to allow cannon to be stationed within the ship, not just on deck whereby a ship could become top-heavy.

QUARTERDECK That part of the upper deck, usually extending from the mainmast to the stern, used by officers only. It was usually the location for ceremonial functions and for disciplinary hearings. By tradition the starboard side of the quarterdeck belonged to the captain, although it could be used by any officer as long as the captain was not on deck. It is less necessary now, but in the days of small vessels on long voyages, the officers needed a space to walk, and even now captains or officers-of-the-watch can be seen pacing the quarterdeck. Presumably the starboard side became the captain's choice because it was furthest from the noise and turmoil of loading the ship which happened on the port side.

QUARTERS This refers to the officers' accommodation, that were situated on the starboard or port quarters.

RATLINES, RATLINGS The small ropes fastened to the shrouds, by which men go aloft to trim the sails. They are pronounced ratt-lins, just as the bowline is pronounced boe-lin.

Rigging

The two basic ways to rig sails are:

- Square-rigged, in which the sails are bent to the yards, carried athwart the mast and trimmed with braces. Being sturdy, square-rigged sails catch a lot of wind.

- Fore-and-aft rigged, in which the sails are not attached to the yards but are bent to gaffs, and set on the mast or on stays in the midship line of the ship, giving increased manoeuvrability to the vessel.

Rigging referred to all the ropes or chains needed to support the masts, and arrange the sails according to the wind direction. In docks, riggers fitted the ships with standing and running rigging before they were sent to sea.

RIG The rig of a ship comprises her masts, spars, stays (or rigging) and sails, and how they are arranged. The modern term of *rig* meaning clothing, and the term *'well rigged out'*, meaning well furnished with equipment and clothing, come from the days of sailing ships.

RIGGING – RUNNING AND STANDING *Running rigging* is the term used for the lines (ropes) used in raising, lowering and controlling sails. On old sailing vessels it was easily recognized because, for flexibility, it was not coated with tar and therefore of a lighter colour than the standing rigging. A square-rigged ship requires a huge amount of running rigging, including bowlines, braces, brails, buntlines, clewlines, halyards, leechlines, sheets and tacks. *Standing rigging* supported the masts and other spars. It was heavily tarred for protection from weather and therefore darker than running rigging, or even black in colour. It refers to the lines (usually heavier-duty than those used in running rigging) which are more or less fixed in position when the boat is at sea, compared to running rigging which is often being altered when under sail. Standing rigging (such as stays and shrouds) is put under tension to keep various spars, such as masts and bowsprits, securely in position and adequately braced, to handle the huge loads generated by sails. Early sailing vessels used rope of hemp or other fibres for rigging. This later gave way to wire ropes of various types.

ROSTRUM This was the Latin for the *beak* of the war galleys, used for ramming other vessels. The rostra (plural of rostrum) of captured ships were taken to Rome to display in triumph. They were laid out in front of the speakers' platform at the Forum, and over the years the dais there became known as the rostrum.

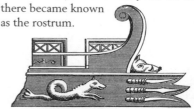

SAINTE BARBE (French), SANTA BARBARA (Spanish) A term used in the 17th century for a powder room or magazine. St Barbara was tortured and killed by her heathen father for being a Christian, and he met divine retribution when he was disintegrated by a thunderflash. She thus became the patron saint of those working with explosives, and her image was often hung up outside a powder room on ships.

SAND-GLASS The only way that mariners in earlier centuries could tell the time. Like egg-timers, sand-glasses consisted of two glass globes with a narrow neck, and they were turned when the sand ran out of the top globe. They were usually calibrated in half-minute, half-hour, hour and four-hour sizes. The half-minute was used to judge a ship's speed, by allowing a computation based on how much line would run out from a ship in half a minute. The half-hour glass measured time, with a bell or drum being sounded at every turn of the sand-glass.

SCUPPERS AND 'DOWN THE DRAIN' These are holes in the bulwarks to free the decks of seawater. Today seamen take the word to generally mean the whole of the waterways round the deck. Anything *'scuppered'* has in effect *'gone down the drain'*.

Sails in the Age of Sail

As ships grew larger as trade increased, and as nations competed by building bigger warships, the strains imposed on ropes and sails meant that a few large sails could no longer cope, without them breaking or tearing. They also required more men to manage them because of their weight. Thus smaller sails in greater numbers were used to catch every piece of wind to drive the ship without the constant threat of breakage. To be most efficient on larger ships, they were square-rigged, i.e. square to the hull. Specialist sailors handled different sails. The younger, more nimble men might be assigned up the masts to the 'tops', while hardened old salts might reef mainsails from the decks. Smaller sails meant that small teams could control them. An added benefit was that a cannonball hit could cause a large sail to tear and so affect the ship's speed and handling. Having many small sails hedged the bet of being hit in battle – several sails might be shot away but the ship could still operate effectively. Even with dozens of sails being used, larger warships could only manage 8–10 knots (9–11 mph/14–18 kph), but small fast clippers could make around 17 knots (20 mph/32 kph). Developments towards the end of the days of sail, such as geared winches, better fittings and fewer, better quality ropes, meant that the size of the sailing crew could be reduced.

Sails were given names which indicated their position on the mast – the lowest square sail was the *course*, the next sail up the mast was called the *topsail*, the next the *topgallant* sail, and the fourth sail, above the other three, was called the *royal*. Thus if the royal was attached to the mizzenmast, it was the *mizzen royal*. For even extra wind coverage, a ship might put out *studding sails* which would be fixed outboard of the sail, on both sides of it, so we might have *mizzen royal studding sails*. From the mid-19th century, the topsails and topgallants were each split into upper and lower sails. This again allowed smaller crews to manipulate the sails, and gave captains extra options in choosing which sails to set. These sails themselves were not square in shape, as 'square' referred to them being set square to the ship. They were trapezoidal, being longer in the *'foot'* (lower edge of the sail) than in the *'head'* (top of the sail). A sail is also not flat in use but three-dimensional, as its *'belly'* (its curve in the wind) means that its foot does not follow a straight line but curves with wind pressure. The sail is fixed to a *'yard'* (spar at right angles from the mast) along its head, and its *'clews'* (bottom corners) are controlled by the *'sheets'*. Sheets are the lines and ropes used to hold the sail, often running through blocks to secure and shorten or lengthen them.

SCUTTLE This term is an Anglicized form of the Old French *'escoutilles'*, and refers to a small hole cut in a hatch cover, or in the side of a ship, to let in light and air. This latter is commonly called a porthole by a landlubber but is referred to as a scuttle by an old seaman.

SEA COCK A sea valve which opens to the sea, to admit or discharge water.

SHEET ANCHOR A large emergency anchor, a resource that a seaman relies on in the face of danger, e.g. if a ship is being dragged onto rocks.

SHROUD, SHROUDS Permanently installed lines or cables that lead from the masthead to chainplates on the hull amidships, and which can be made taut to support the mast. They are part of the standing rigging of a sailing vessel. The large horizontal ropes are not just fixed to the masts, but latticed with the vertical *'ratlines'* that sailors scrambled up to furl and unfurl sails.

SKYLIGHT A framework on the deck which allowed light vertically down into the cabin and gunroom below.

SKYSAIL A light sail set above the royal on square-rigged ships, used in light winds when the ship needs to catch every breath of wind.

SKYSCRAPER The 18th-century origin of this architectural term was a small, triangular sail set above the skysail on the old square-riggers to try and catch more wind in areas of calm air – to *'scrape the sky'*. It was later used to describe a tall person, and then for the first time in the 1880s a tall building. Other names for the very highest sails used on ships were *moonrakers* (or *moonsails*), *angel's foot*

stools and *star gazers*, all used in times of dead calm. They were never used in strong winds as they would rip away.

SMOKING LAMP (LANTERN) During the 16th century, sailors began smoking aboard ship. The smoking lamp was devised as a safety measure, to keep the hazard of fire away from the combustible tarred woodwork of the ship. Thus smoking was restricted to a certain area of a vessel, with a smoking lamp located in the forecastle or next to the galley. It was an oil lamp safely mounted in a place where sailors could get a light for their pipes. The smoking lamp was put out whenever smoking was forbidden. Even today the officer of the deck in the Royal Navy says *'the smoking lamp is out'*, which is the order to cease smoking before drills, refuelling or taking ammunition. A symbolic smoking lamp is still used on some modern ships to signify times when it is permitted to smoke in designated safe areas.

SONAR Called ASDIC in Britain, it was one of the greatest inventions of the Second World War. Sonar was first installed on British destroyers in November 1941, and was a form of 'searchlight' beam that hunted for submarines. If a target U-boat fell within the search beam, it reflected the *'ping'* of a transducer back to the destroyer. Based on the amount of time needed to return the ping, the sonar could calculate the submarine's range. Sonar worked best at slow speeds, making the searching ships easier targets. Once the target was passed over, contact was lost. Early sonar also could not determine depth, which was needed for setting pressure fuses on depth charges. A final shortcoming was that it had to be aimed below the surface to prevent waves and surface noise distorting the beam. Surfaced U-boats could not be detected until surface radar was developed.

SPANKER On a schooner, the spanker is the aftermast together with its sail. On a square-rigger it is a quadrilateral fore-and-aft sail set on the mizzenmast or aftermast.

SPAR The general term for any of the above deck timbers to which sails are bent, such as the masts, booms, gaffs, yards and sprits. Today's term *'sparring'* comes from sailors playing (and sometimes fighting) with spars, trying to keep from being hit.

SPINNAKER A large triangular sail set on a spar that swings out opposite the mainsail, used on yachts when running before the wind. In 1866 this type of sail was first used on the English cutter *Sphinx*. Because of its massive size, it was known as *'Sphinx's acre'*, from which we get the word spinnaker.

STACK The ship's funnel on an engine-powered vessel. The origin is probably naval slang, and ships were known as three-stackers, four-stackers etc. To *blow the stacks* was to force compressed air through to clean them, from which we get the term *'blowing one's stack'* meaning losing one's temper.

STATEROOM An officer's or passenger's cabin aboard a merchant ship, or the cabin of an officer, other than the captain, aboard a naval ship. The term may be derived from the fact that in the 16th and 17th centuries, ships often had a cabin reserved for royal or noble passengers.

STARBOARD Until the 13th century in Northern Europe, steering a ship was carried out by means of a huge oar, lashed to the right *(steer-board)* side of a ship. The boat then always had to be berthed on the left-hand side, i.e. it was secured to the harbour walls of the port. Thus the left of a boat became known as the port side (or larboard), and the right as the starboard. The great problem was that a wind blowing on the starboard beam might push the ship away from the vertical, lifting the steer-board out of the water. Steering was then impossible. A violent wind on the port side could roll the ship so badly that the steer-board could be broken off. Only the innovation of the centreline rudder, brought back to Europe by Crusaders, solved the problem and made the steer-board obsolete. *Starboard tack* means sailing with the wind blowing from the starboard side.

STAYS These are the heavy ropes on sailing vessels that run from the masts to the hull, usually fore-and-aft along the centreline of the vessel. They prevent the masts from *springing* (coming away from the deck), when the ship is *'sending'* (pitching downwards into the hollow between two large waves). The stays attached to the mainmast are *mainstays*. The stay that runs aft is called a *backstay* and the stay that runs forward is called a *forestay* or just a stay. Lines running from the mast to the side of the ship are usually called *shrouds*. Iron wire rope was introduced to replace rope in the 1860s for the standing rigging of all ships, whether sail or steam. Later, iron wire rope was succeeded by steel wire rope, then galvanized steel wire while the latest yachts use stainless steel wire, rods and composite fibres.

STEERAGE Originally the junior officers' quarters in a naval vessel, the term refers to the fact that the ship's tiller often projected into the 'steerage compartment', located far aft. In the 19th century the term came to mean the cheapest passenger (and emigrant) quarters aboard a liner, again often near the ship's stern where the noise of the ship's screws and engines was unrelenting.

Steel Ships

For a given weight of material, steel is stronger than iron, but it is also more expensive. Though the technique of making steel had been known since before the birth of Christ, its use in the western world seems to have started in Damascus round about 1000 CE. The art then was lost, but by 1700 its use was again recorded in Britain. However, it could only be made in small quantities. As the Industrial Revolution developed, the main material used in large quantities for construction was therefore iron, and it was not until the Bessemer Process for making steel in quantity was introduced in 1855 that engineers could contemplate using it for large structures. Bessemer steel was unreliable in quality, however, until the Siemens' open hearth process made it a viable material. Steel was thus not introduced into shipbuilding until 1876, when a small steel paddle vessel was built for river work in Burma (now Myanmar). The Admiralty built two fast despatch vessels, *Iris* and *Mercury*, of steel in 1877. Iron vessels had a reputation for the durability of their structural members and plating, and iron was far cheaper, so it took some time for steel to be generally accepted. Wrought iron is very corrosion-resistant, which is why many old iron ships have enjoyed long lives as hulks (e.g. Brunel's *Great Britain* now on display at Bristol, and HMS *Warrior* at Portsmouth).

Later called 3rd-Class, there was little light or ventilation in this cheapest accommodation, and steerage passengers only had access to a restricted area of the top deck. The SS *Great Britain* had its steerage passengers divided into *'messes'* of around eight people, who took turns at being mess leader. The leader had to fetch food from the ship's pantry, take it to the communal galley for cooking, collect and distribute the meal, and tidy up after the passengers had eaten.

STEERING WHEEL Not in common usage until the early 18th century, it replaced the whipstaff (q.v.). This spoked wheel on the steering shaft allows a good purchase, and a mechanical advantage which enables the helmsman to turn and steer the vessel more easily. Very few people make the connection, when driving, that this term is nautical. We also see the word in *'steer clear'* and *'steering committee'*.

STERN The rear end of a ship, deriving from the Old Norse *'stjorn'*, the steering oar set at the back of the older ships.

STORM BOTTLES Used from the 1750s at sea, these were hermetically sealed glass tubes, containing water, alcohol and camphor. Crystals fell to the bottom when weather conditions were improving, and floated to the top if things were getting worse.

STRAKE This is a longitudinal plank. Strakes make up the sides of a boat. The thick strake or plank which is the highest ridge is the gunwale.

SUIT, SUIT OF SAILS Term from the early 1600s meaning the ship's complete outfit of sails.

SWAB The swab was a kind of large mop made of old rope, on a long handle, used to clean the ship's decks (from the Dutch *'zwabberen'*, 'to mop'). Someone who was told to clean the decks was referred to as a *'swab'* or *'swabbie'*. As it was the lowest form of duty on a ship, to call someone a *'scurvy swab'* was to call him a diseased, worthless person.

TACKLE Traditionally pronounced *'tay-kle'*, it refers to gear on deck in general or, specifically, to blocks and their associated lines – as in *'block-and-tackle'*. The word comes from the Middle Dutch *taekel*, and this is the source from which the unusual pronunciation was derived. In the 18th century, *tackling* was the term for the bits and pieces essential to catch a fish – hooks, bait, lines etc. – and it was later truncated to *fishing tackle*.

TILLER This is a long hand lever attached to the top of the rudder that is used to steer the vessel. The term is derived from the handle of a plough used to till the soil.

TOPGALLANT SAIL The very top sail on a mast – changing this in a Force 9 gale was not a job to volunteer for.

TOPSIDES The visible outside of the hull, i.e. the outside face of the hull between the water and the deck.

WALES The reinforcing pieces of strong timber that go around a ship, a little above her waterline.

WARDROOM The mess and lounge area for commissioned officers. Before about 1700 each officer lived and 'messed' in his own quarters, cramped as they were. The captain's cabin, on the other hand, was known as the *Great Cabin*. Under it was the *'wardrobe'*, a locker often used to stow articles of value taken from prizes. When not in use for that purpose, the officers used it to hang their spare uniforms. It is first spoken of as being used as a general officers' mess in about 1750, at which time it was of much greater size than a locker, and was renamed the wardroom.

WHIPSTAFF In the earliest days of sailing, the officer gave an order such as *'hard-a-starboard'*, meaning *'push the tiller or steering oar as far as you can to starboard'*, whereby the ship turned hard in the opposite direction, to port. From around 1450, however, a new form of steering was used. Ships had added 'castles' to the main deck, so the steersman had to be lifted to a higher level. The deck had become so high above the rudder that the helmsman needed a remote way of turning the tiller, if he was to be

on the deck and see the sails. The whipstaff was devised to solve the problem. It was a strong piece of timber which passed through a hole in the deck to a pivot, and from there to the end of the tiller. A mechanical advantage of about 4:1 was obtained, at the cost of a more limited rudder movement. The helmsman stood with the whipstaff roughly vertical in front of, or beside, him. The whipstaff was pushed in the direction in which the ship was to turn. By the early 18th century, the ship's wheel was being introduced on larger ships. As ship size had continued to increase, ships had become more difficult to control. The new *steering wheel* was connected to the tiller by block and tackle, which provided a smoother and less limited rudder operation with less effort.

THE WHOLE NINE YARDS
Yards are the timber spars running at right angles to the masts, supporting square sails. (On either side of the mast, the yard is called a *yardarm*). A fully-rigged three-masted ship generally had three major sails upon each mast. If all nine sails were being used, the *'whole nine yards'* were working – she was at maximum capacity.

WINDLASS A lifting device, usually set in the forecastle and hand operated. It is a horizontal cylinder, turned by a crank, on which a rope winds, and was often used instead of a capstan for the purpose of raising the anchor.

YARD Any spar horizontal to a mast, used for suspending sails – the yardarm was the yard on either side of the mast, which was the easiest place from which to hang any miscreant.

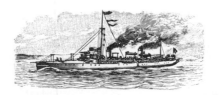

TYPES OF SHIP AND BOAT

AVISO A small, very fast boat carrying dispatches between Spain and its warships and colonies.

BALTIMORE CLIPPER A fast and manoeuvrable topsail schooner developed in Chesapeake Bay from the late 18th century, 70 to 90 feet (21 to 27 m) in length, with fine lines and raked masts. Their sleek design has influenced the lines of racing yachts.

BARCO DE AVISO A Spanish *packet-boat*, or mail-ship, sent every year between the King of Spain and his *flota* or *treasure fleet* captains. It usually held vital intelligence upon the movements and timings of the treasure galleons. The captains of these packet boats *('navios de aviso')* swore to the King to destroy or sink any letters rather than let them fall into enemy or pirate hands.

BARQUE, BARK A smallish, fast-sailing ship with three masts. The foremast and following mast were rigged square and the aftermast (mizzenmast) was rigged fore-and-aft. It could hold 90 men, and had a shallow draught. Before the 1700s, the term was applied to any small sailing vessel.

BARQUENTINE, BARKENTINE A small three-masted ship, square-rigged on the foremast only, and fore-and-aft rigged on the other two masts.

BATHYSCAPHE A relatively small, manoeuvrable submersible vessel, specially constructed to withstand enormous pressure and used to explore the deep ocean floor.

BATHYSPHERE A hollow sphere built of steel alloy and designed to withstand underwater pressure, used to carry observers to the deep ocean floors. The bathysphere, which was lowered on a cable and could not manoeuvre, has been largely replaced by the bathyscaphe for deep ocean exploration.

BATTLECRUISER A large warship carrying heavy armament, which is smaller, faster and more manoeuvrable than a battleship. Modern cruisers can carry aircraft and are armed with missiles.

BATTLESHIP The largest and most heavily armed of the classes of warships, its name derives from 'line-of-battle' ships. They are generally considered outdated in modern naval warfare, thought to serve political rather than military purposes, and have been replaced by aircraft carriers as the greatest symbol of might in modern navies. The largest battleships were the *Yamato* and *Musashi* of the Imperial Japanese Navy which fought in the Second World War. Both displaced 71,700 tons and were 863 feet (263 m) in length.

BLACK SHIP An East-India Company trading ship, built from Indian teak and therefore of a dark appearance.

BOAT Any small craft, as opposed to a ship – a ship carries boats. However, submariners and naval aviators refer to their respective vessels, submarines and aircraft carriers, as 'boats'. Boat is derived from the Middle English *'boot'* and the Old Norse *'beit'*.

BRIG From about 1700, a popular two-masted sailing ship. Both masts are square-rigged, and on the mainmast (the stern mast) these is also a gaff-rigged sail. It was formerly an abbreviation of brigantine, but came to mean a brigantine with greater sail-power. The brig was used in large numbers around 1790, both as a merchant vessel and as a naval ship. She was rigged for speed, carrying both topgallant sails and royals. They were used across the world for scouting and reconnaissance duties, tracking down enemy ships. In 1814 the Royal Navy had 71 brigs of various types carrying 10 to 16 guns, each with a length of 110 feet (33.5 m) and a crew of 100–120 men.

BRIGANTINE A twin-masted workhorse of a ship, favoured by pirates for its manoeuvrability. Both masts are usually fully square-rigged, with a fore-and-aft sail on the lower part of the mainmast. They could hold 100 crew and many cannon. A standard ship might measure 100 tons, be 80 feet (24 m) long and mount 10 cannon. The availability of various combinations of square or fore-and-aft sails made her extremely versatile in different sea conditions, so it was a good choice for battle or combat rather than quick, *hit and run* piracy.

BRÛLOT French for fireship, this was a ship loaded with explosives and set alight to drift into the enemy's fleet, which was especially successful if the fleet was anchored in port.

BUMBOAT Derived from the Dutch *'boom-boat'*, this was a broad-beamed small boat which carried provisions to ships, and also removed their rubbish. The door-to-door salesman of the harbour, the bumboat skipper sold tobacco, beer, fresh vegetables, ice, meat, books, cordage, fishing gear and other goods that were difficult to get hold of at sea. Many crew were not allowed ashore for fear of desertion, so they would purchase their needs from a bumboat. Also, until the advent of locks and stone docks, most large ships had to anchor offshore, so needed these supply boats for provisioning.

CARAVEL Portuguese and Spanish *(carabela)* ships used for ocean voyages as well as coastal trade, with two or three *masts*. They were large and narrow, with no lookout stations on their masts. With a single deck, a pointed prow and a flat stern, they had lateen sails.

CARGO BOATS These must be built for cheapness, great hold capacity and a certain steady speed. The speed of cargo boats, from the tramp steamer of Victorian times to today's container ship, has not risen in line with the increase in speed of other means of transport. The technical means of driving modern tankers, bulk-carriers (for such cargoes as iron ore and coal) and container ships at speeds of around 30 knots (35 mph/ 56 kph) exist, but are totally uneconomic. This is one reason why steam turbines, gas turbines, and nuclear propulsion have never been actively developed for powering freight shipping.

CARRACK A huge ship weighing up to 1200 tons, it was used by the Spanish and Portuguese for trading with India, China and the Americas. With high fore-and-aft castles and enormous firepower, pirates could only take them by stealth. They were three-masted, with square sails on the fore and mainmasts, and lateen-rigged on the mizzen. Popular from the 14th to 16th centuries, she was succeeded by the galleon, which had finer lines and lay lower in the water.

CHARIOT SUBMARINES These *Human Torpedoes* appeared in the Royal Navy in 1942, and were similar to German and Italian devices. They carried one 700-lb (318-kg) charge on their bows, which had to be fixed to the target. The crew consisted of two men wearing shallow-water diving suits, sitting astride the craft. With electric motors (run off batteries) these craft were transported close to their targets in special containers welded to the outsides of conventional submarines. The submarines would surface out of range of the target and the chariots were deployed. Chariots were used in the Mediterranean and Far East theatres. Their first successful employment was the sinking of the Italian cruiser *Ulpio Traiano* in Palermo harbour, 3 January 1943.

Clipper Ships

Clippers were fast, slender ships, multiple-masted with a large sail area, possibly so named because they *'clipped'* off the normal time taken to carry cargo. Another theory is that the term comes from falconry, where to *'clip'* is to move swiftly. They were succeeded in the late 1800s by square-riggers and steamships, which were designed to take much larger cargoes, although at slower speeds. Sailing ship owners suffered from competition from the new steamships, so ways had to be found to make sailing vessels cheaper and quicker to operate. The longer a ship was, the faster it would sail, so by piling on as much sail as possible a very fast ship was created. These ships, especially the high speed clippers such as *Cutty Sark* and *Thermopylae*, were best on long runs, where steamships could not compete because of the need for frequent re-coaling. The voyage to England to deliver the first of the year's tea crop led to exciting races between ships, with people betting on the outcomes.

COFFIN BRIGS These brigs carried the mail between England and the United States, and were built for speed rather than safety across the North Atlantic. '*Coffin ship*' came to be used as a derogatory term for ships which were thought to be unseaworthy.

COG In the mid-13th century this replaced the *knorr* as the main trading ship in northern Europe. She was bigger, and used a stern rudder instead of a steering board or oar, so the stern was no longer pointed. There was an enclosed deck, and the forecastle and aftercastle were enlarged, making them suitable for fighting when manned with more crew and soldiers.

COLLIER BRIG Owners of coal mines in the Tyneside area of northern England could only get their coal to London by sea. Ships were required which were cheap to build and operate, such as the collier brig. At the mouth of the Tyne, they were loaded by keel boats that had brought the coal from the pits upriver. Carrying *black gold*, they were subject to attacks from pirates from the 16th century onward, which forced them to travel in convoy, sometimes with an escort. This Tyneside fleet became the biggest single group of co-ordinated shipping ever seen in Britain, and consequently their experienced crews were a target for press gangs. Around 1680, collier brigs were on average 77 feet (23.5 m) in length, displacing 180 tons and carrying a crew of 10-25 men.

CONFEDERATE RAIDERS Twenty Confederate ships destroyed 257 Union ships during the American Civil War, disrupting trade and almost destroying the US merchant marine. CSS ships of the Confederate Navy also challenged USS ships of the Union Navy for control of shipping routes.

CORVETTE Originally an armed sailing ship smaller than a frigate, it was used for patrols and scouting. Now it is a fast, highly manoeuvrable warship, smaller than a destroyer, and a class of anti-submarine escort vessels.

CROMSTER, CROMPSTER, CRUMSTER Most of Henry Morgan's privateering fleets were made up of *cromsters*, a merchant ship which looked like a small galleon. They were quite fast, but not as manoeuvrable as a sloop. She had a foremast, a mainmast and also a rear mast supporting a lateen (triangular) sail (or sometimes a gaff sail). Her advantages over the sloop were that she could hold more treasure, carry more cannons and have three or four times as many crew. Up to 16 guns could be carried on a gun deck, with additional guns lashed to the top deck.

CUNARD LINE The most famous shipping line, founded in 1840 as a scheduled North Atlantic service, its ships included the *Lusitania*, *Mauretania*, *Aquitania*, *Queen Mary* and *Queen Elizabeth*. It merged with the *White Star Line* in 1934 at the British government's request, in return for loans to build the latter two liners. It has been a division of *Carnival Cruise Lines* since 1998.

CUTTER A one-masted ship favoured by smugglers over the years. Larger ships such as galleons were too slow, and were useless after they had been ransacked. Usually cutters had a mainsail, at least two headsails, a forestaysail and a jib. They later came to be used as pilot vessels and by the revenue services and coastguards to prevent smuggling. The origin of the name is that they could 'cut' the time taken to make any voyage.

DERELICT A ship that has been abandoned at sea, from the Latin *derelinquere*, to forsake, it has come to mean a tramp or vagrant.

DESTROYER High-speed warship used with strike forces, in support of amphibious operations and in convoys. It was the most effective anti-submarine vessel in both world wars.

DHOW Lateen-rigged coastal trading ship common in the Indian Ocean, Arabian Gulf and Red Sea.

DINGHY A vessel used for rowing or sailing, from the Hindi *'dingi'*, meaning small boat.

DOGGER, DOGFISH A *dogger* is a two-masted type of ketch with a blunt prow, and is remembered today in the European weather forecasts for Dogger Bank. This large shoal area 60 miles (100 km) off northeast England was noted for its huge cod, herring and dogfish catches. *Doggers* became the favoured trawler in the North Sea, crewed by *doggermen* and catching *doggerfish*, the origin of today's *dogfish*.

DREADNOUGHT Name given to the class of heavy battleships, built following the launch of HMS *Dreadnought* in 1906.

DROGER A coastal trade ship in the West Indies.

DUCK Nickname for the DUKW, the American six-wheeled amphibious truck first used in the Sicily invasion in 1943. One was until the 1990s used by the monks at Caldey Island, off Tenby, Wales, to ferry visitors and supplies off boats and onto the beach there.

E-BOAT Measuring 106 feet (32 m), these Second World War German motor torpedo boats (MTBs) carried two torpedo tubes and anti-aircraft guns and had a top speed of almost 40 knots (46 mph/74 kph).

FASTER SAILING SHIPS By the early 19th century, *Yankee Clippers* reigned supreme on the trading routes, making life difficult for English shipping. Americans built smaller, faster vessels, requiring smaller crews. Their ships were also much cheaper to manufacture, owing to the quantity and quality of available woods. American merchant and naval officers were often also better seamen than their English competitors, who generally secured their positions by nepotism. American captains usually owned a share of their ships, so they tried to make every voyage efficient and profitable. At this time a New York draughtsman, John Willis Griffiths, stated that he could build even better American ships, redesigning the round bows of American clippers and making them knife-like to cut through water more efficiently. Instead of the widest part of the ship (the *beam*) being forward, he placed it amidships. There was terrific opposition from established owners and builders, and it took him until 1843 to get a contract to build a 750-ton ship. When *Rainbow* was launched in 1845, his critics gathered, expecting to see her turn turtle. She had a longer length to beam ratio than normal, and far more rigging than other clippers. In February she sailed to China, breaking all records to return in September, earning her owners $90,000, twice the costs of building her. Her master recounted, *'We met no ship, American or foreign, that doesn't know the look of her heels. The vessel will never be built to beat her.'* She again left for China in October, taking just 92 days against the monsoon (the prevalent wind in the eastern seas), and returning in 88 days. These times (and profits) were unprecedented, and she inaugurated a new type of ship.

The first was the *Sea Witch*, 100 tons heavier, which set an incredible sailing record from China to New York of 77 days. The *Sea Witch* was also hugely influential in fast ship design. There was now a race to produce such profitable ships, and two new designs of clippers were launched only 60 days after their keels had been laid. The average time around Cape Horn from New York to California had been between 180 and 270 days, but Griffiths' *Waterwitch* made it in 97 days. Donald McKay was another famous American ship designer, and his *Flying Cloud* sailed an amazing 374 nautical miles (430 miles/693 km) in one day. Griffiths' *Sovereign of the Seas* was possibly the fastest of all, on one voyage laden with sperm oil she sailed 396, 311, 411 and 360 nautical miles (456, 358, 473 and 414 miles/734, 576, 761 and 666 km) on four consecutive days, an average of 15.5 knots (18 mph/ 29 kph).

Donald McKay's *Lightning* later achieved 436 nautical miles (502 miles/808 km) in a day, averaging over 18 knots (21 mph/ 33 kph). By 1860, the USA owned a total of 5,290,000 tons of shipping against Britain's 5,710,000. However, the British now fought back with their own improvements, including the famous *Aberdeen Clippers*. There were also problems because the Americans were using soft woods to make their ships. Their huge spread of sails made American ships leak badly as their frames spread, so often tons of tea in the cargo could be ruined. British ships were of sounder construction, and began combining speed with this strength, so regained popularity with merchants and skippers.

FELUCCA A small lateen-rigged sailing vessel with a narrow beam, capable of a surprising turn of speed. They are common in the Mediterranean.

FIRESHIP These were used against the Spanish Armada, and by Henry Morgan against the Spanish to escape Lake Maracaibo. The preferred option was to use grappling irons to attach the fireship against an enemy vessel, and then the attacking crew would light a slow *'match'* (fuse) and escape in a small boat. Captain Smith in 1627 describes their use: *'Now between two Navies they use often, especially in a Harbour or Road where they lie at Anchor, to fill old Barks with Pitch, Tar, Train-oyl, Lynseed-oyl, Brimstone, Rozin, Reeds, with dry Wood, and such Combustible things. Sometimes they link three or four together in the night, and put them adrift as they find occasion.'*

FLAGSHIP The ship that carries the admiral (and his flag), or in a merchant

First Rater

The English first-rate ship of the line of the 1750s onwards was probably the finest warship of the *Age of Sail*. Because of the sheer size of the 100-gun ship, 800–850 men were needed to work the guns and man her. They were around 210 feet (64 m) in length, displacing 2000 tons. A first rate was also the *flagship* of any squadron that she sailed in, so had to carry the admiral and his staff. She cost about £67,000 to build in 1760 (over £95 million now, using the Average Earnings Index), and because of the difficulty of getting sufficient quantities of wood, rope and guns (as well as the cost), they were a rarity among the world's fleets. During the 18th century, the British fleet had only around five or six first rates in service, a number which sometimes rose to 11. They might last 50–70 years or even more, undergoing many redesigns and re-riggings. The *Victory* was over 40 years old when she fought at the Battle of Trafalgar and had been rebuilt twice.

fleet, its most important ship. The term has passed into the language as denoting the best store in a chain, the best car in a range and so on.

FLOTAS and GALEONES This was the Spanish treasure fleet that usually made its way once a year towards Spain, carrying plate from the gold and silver mines of South and Central America. Its captains took an oath to burn, sink or destroy their ships, rather than let them fall into enemy hands and so enrich their foes. Thus pirates and privateers preferred to take such ships by stealth, or extremely quickly. Henry Swinburne, in *Travels in Spain* (1779) wrote *'The flota is a fleet of large ships which carry the goods of Europe to the ports of America, and bring back the produce of Mexico, Peru, and other kingdoms of the New World.'*

FLUTE, FLEUT, DUTCH FLUTE An early 17th-century ship, cheap to build, with a large hold, but easy prey for pirates. She was about 300 tons and 80 feet (24 m) long, and needed only a dozen seamen to man her. With a flat bottom, broad beams and a round stern, flutes became a favourite cargo carrier, with about 150 per cent of the capacity of similar ships. Remember that docks did not exist at that time, so their flat bottoms allowed these ships to come inshore, and/or settle on the seabed when the tide was out. However they were slower and less wieldy than the normal merchant ship, so were more easily taken.

FLYBOAT From the Spanish *'filibote'* – a vessel with a capacity of around 100 tons. Used for passenger and cargo traffic in fairly sheltered waters.

Types of Ships

15th-century Spanish caravel

Henry VIII's flagship Great Harry *c.1514*

Ship of the line, Sovereign of the Seas, *c.1637*

The Ho Nam *paddlewheel steamer,* 1882

Inman & International Co's screw liner SS City of Paris *c.*1891

German battleship Kaiser Wilhelm II *c.*1902

FREIGHTER A ship designed and employed principally to carry dry cargo or freight, unlike, say, an oil tanker.

FRIGATE This three-masted warship weighed around 360 tons and was 110 feet (33.5 m) long, carrying 195 men and 26 guns. It was fast, but not big enough to be a *'ship of the line'*, and was often used for independent action, such as against pirates. As a modern warship, a frigate is smaller than a destroyer, being used for anti-submarine, patrol and escort duties.

FULL-RIGGED SHIP A fully square-rigged ship, with three or more masts, also known as a square-rigger.

GALIOT A long, sleek ship with a flush deck, carrying from two to ten small cannon. Used by the Barbary Corsairs, powered by oars, she carried from 50 to 130 men.

GALIZABRA A fast Spanish frigate, heavily armed, used in the 17th and 18th centuries. She could bring treasure back to Seville from the Spanish Main by herself, rather than wait for the escorted convoy of treasure galleons known as the *'Flota'* to set sail.

GALLEY Formerly a ship that could be rowed, often with a lateen sail, the term came to mean, in late 17th-century England, an armed merchantman with one or more flush decks. Earlier, in the 16th century, a typical galley had one or more masts fitted with lateen sails. There were around 30 oars, each manned by up

Galleon

Used both for trade and war, these huge ships had three or four masts, square-rigged on the foremast and mainmast and lateen-rigged on the after-mast(s). A galleon on the transatlantic route might vary between 400 and 1000 tons, with 400 tons being far more common. Sailing qualities varied, with speeds of 4–8 knots (5–10 mph/8–16 kph), and they could carry 20–76 guns of varying calibre. If used as a man-of-war, there were 36 guns mounted on each side, with two remaining guns mounted aft, making 74 cannon, plus numerous swing guns mounted along the rails to repel boarders. They were usually terribly overcrowded, often carrying

an infantry company of at least 100 troops under an army captain. There was a *'split command'*, whereas on Dutch and English ships the naval captain also commanded the soldiers. Because of its high sides and even higher poop deck, the galleon was easily rocked by the sea, and it pitched and rolled more than other ships.

to six rowers, usually prisoners who were chained to their benches. They were far more nimble than fully rigged sailing ships, and could keep out of their angle of fire, being used to great effect by the Barbary Corsairs (often using free pirates rather than slaves as crew), and were popular until the late 18th century in the Mediterranean. They were not suited to Atlantic conditions, however. A galley could also mean a single-banked six-oared pulling boat, otherwise known as a ship's *gig* in the 18th and early 19th centuries.

THE GRAND FLEET The name given to the home-based Royal Navy fleet in the Napoleonic Wars and during the First World War.

GREAT CANOE The Rama Indians of the Caribbean Miskito Coast gave this name to any European ship from across the *'Great Water'* (Atlantic).

GREAT WHITE FLEET President Theodore Roosevelt sent this fleet of 16 new white battleships around the world in 1907–9, calling at 20 ports on six continents, as a sign of America's growing naval power and as a preemptive warning to Japan, which had just won the Russo-Japanese War.

GUARDACOSTA – COSTA GARDA Private revenue cutters used by the Spanish to enforce their Caribbean trading monopoly. They were commissioned by local governors, fitted out in Spanish or colonial ports and earned their money by the prizes that they took.

HERMAPHRODITE BRIG, HALF BRIG A two-masted ship equipped with the foremast of a brig and the mainmast of a schooner.

HERRING BUSS From the Tudor era onwards, the fishing fleets of Northern Europe increased in size, generally favouring this 65-foot (20-m) ship. When fishing and bringing in the catch, the mainmast and the foremast were lowered, so that the standing rigging could be cleared out of the way. Thus almost the entire length of the ship could be used to work the nets. Many of the busses were flush-decked, with only limited accommodation for the crew.

HOGBOAT, HAGBOAT, HECK BOAT Hagboat describes a type of Swedish ship with a certain type of hull that had a beaked prow and a single gun deck, closely resembling the hull of a frigate. Hagboats resembled warships, though they were primarily used as merchantmen on the European sea routes. In the 17th and 18th centuries these large square-rigged pinks were used both as merchantmen and warships. Black Bart Roberts's *Royal Rover* was classified as a hogboat. *The Weekly Journal* reported in 1720 on his attack on the Portuguese treasure fleet: *'The Lisbon Fleet from the Bay of All Saints, Brazil, has arrived. But one vessel of 36 guns was taken by a pyrate ship (formerly an English hog-boat) and two others plundered.'*

HOG-IN-ARMOUR A dismissive description of an ironclad ship. The first ironclads were protected by a covering of iron over their wooden hulls.

HOOKER Often called a *howker* in England, to the French she was a *houcre* or *hourque*, and Dutch called her a *hoecker*. She was a small merchant vessel used in the coastal waters of Northern Europe. Some hookers had pole masts, while others had the more usual separate mainmast and topmast, with tops, shrouds etc. All hookers had bluff rounded bows and sterns, with a high rudder and tiller fitted over the bulwarks. In 1770 they averaged 87 feet (26.5 m) in length, displacing 120 tons.

HOY A small, heavy coasting-vessel for goods and passengers that plied its trade close to the coast, from the Dutch *'heude'* and *'heu'*. The English hoy, or work-sloop, dated from around the end of the 17th to the start of the 18th century, and was square-rigged with a gaff sail. They were often used for smuggling and piracy, taking six to ten cannons on the top deck, with swivel guns fore and aft, and a crew of 30 men. Hoys were hit-and-run ships, used for night attacks near the coast, not for long voyages.

INDIAMAN Sometimes applied to any ship engaged in the East India trade, but strictly an armed large ship of the Honorable East India Company.

IRONCLAD In 1819 the French General Paixhaus invented an exploding shell and a gun to fire it. The 24-bore cannon was introduced into naval service, and at the Battle of Sinope in 1853 a Russian fleet armed with this new device defeated a larger Turkish fleet. The wooden ships were destroyed by gunnery. The solution was to cover or 'clad' the hull in iron as defence against this new shellfire, hence the term *'ironclad'*. Wooden warships were now sheathed in iron armour and driven by both steam and sail. Next, the French laid down the first proper ironclad ship. She carried 4.5-in (11.4-cm) armour, which was considered to be sufficient to keep out

a projectile from a 68-pounder gun. A two-decked 91-gun ship, the *Napoleon*, the finest vessel in the French Navy in 1857, was converted by removing the two upper decks, lengthened by 23 feet (7 m) and armoured from stem to stern. She was renamed *Gloire* and sailed in 1858. The British had to react to this development, and in 1859 HMS *Warrior* was laid down. She was bigger and faster than the *Gloire* but difficult to handle. The development of the exploding shell thus caused fundamental changes in all warship design.

JUNK, CHINESE JUNK From the Javanese *'djong'*, the Portuguese used the word *'junco'* to describe these flat-bottomed boats of the Far East. With no keel, a flat bow and a high poop (stern), her width is about a third of her length and her rudder can be lowered or raised. She has two or three masts with full-battened square sails formerly made from bamboo, rattan or grass. The foremost mast is typically raked forward over the bow. She is an easy to steer, seaworthy vessel, both used and captured by Far Eastern pirates over the centuries.

KETCH A strongly built two-masted sailing rig with the mainmast mounted somewhat forward of the beam, and a mizzenmast mounted forward of the rudder post. The aftermast is thus shorter than the foremast.

KETTLE-BOTTOM Description of a ship with a flat bottom.

KNORR Based on the Viking longship, this was the standard trading ship in northern Europe from the eighth century until the development of the cog in the mid-13th century. She was pointed at bow and stern, open-decked and clinker-built (overlapping planks formed the hull). She was single-masted with a square sail, and a steering oar for a rudder. Later, raised platforms were added at each end to give shelter and act as 'fighting platforms' for defence.

LIBERTY SHIP This vessel was at the heart of the biggest ship-building programme in history, with the US Maritime Commission mass-producing cargo ships to make up for losses to submarines in the Second World War. Around 2750 were built between 1941 and 1945, each 442 feet (138 m) long and capable of 11 knots (13 mph/20 kph). Known as *'ugly ducklings'*, their slow speed led to great losses from U-boats and to the development of the improved *Victory Ship*.

LIFEBOAT This was said to have been invented by Admiral Samuel Graves, who died in 1787. The Royal National Lifeboat Institution (RNLI), a registered charity, operates all UK lifeboats, and they are manned by volunteers. It was founded by Sir William Hilary in 1824 and by 1849 had saved 6716 lives.

LIGHTER A flat-bottomed boat used for transporting cargo between a ship and the shore.

LIGHTSHIPS, LIGHTVESSELS These served as floating lighthouses in the USA from 1820 onwards, on sites too deep or unsuitable for lighthouses. The first in Britain was established on the Nore Sandbanks in the Thames Estuary in 1732. All in the USA have now been replaced by towers, platforms or buoys. The last decommissioned lightship in the USA was on Nantucket Shoals, in 1985. There are just eight unmanned lightships remaining around the UK.

LONDON WAGGON The tender which carried impressed men from near the Tower of London to the receiving ships of the fleet at the Nore, an anchorage near the mouth of the Thames.

LONGBOAT Towed behind a ship, a longboat could hold up to 60 or 70 men, and was normally propelled by oars, although a movable mast and sail might also be used. They were needed in the days before quays were routinely built to get stores and transport men ashore.

LONGLINER This fishing vessel uses lines up to 80 miles (130 km) long, with branch lines containing thousands of baited hooks. Longlines are the most efficient method of catching large, high quality, high value fish, such as bluefin and yellowfin tuna, swordfish and Patagonian toothfish. In the 1980s, following the global ban on lethal drift nets, longlining became increasingly popular. An estimated 1 billion hooks are set annually by longline fleets. There is a terrible by-catch ratio, however, which includes endangered albatrosses and turtles. In 2006, the Hawaiian longline swordfish fishing season was closed because of excessive loggerhead turtle by-catch, but usually there is little inspection and enforcement across the world's oceans. Longliners are contributing to the rapid extinction of all species of albatross and turtle.

LUGGER A small, fast three-masted coastal ship.

MANILA GALLEONS For over 200 years, these huge, heavily armed Spanish treasure ships voyaged from Manila in the Philippines to Acapulco, Mexico and back.

MIDGET SUBMARINES The X3 midget sub for the Royal Navy was first launched in 1942. It was about 50 feet (15 m) long and 6 feet (1.8 m) in beam. It had a quiet electric motor and carried four crew and was armed with a 2-ton releasable amatol charge (its 'side-cargo') carried either side of outer casing. These submarines had to be towed by, or attached to, a larger submarine to get within striking distance of the target. X.6 and X.7 carried out a successful attack on the German battleship *Tirpitz* in Altenfjord on 22 September 1943, under the command of Lieutenant Cameron and Lieutenant Place, both of whom were awarded the Victoria Cross. XE.3 carried out a successful attack on the Japanese cruiser *Takao* at Singapore on 31 July 1945, and Lieutenant Fraser and Leading Seaman Magennis were also awarded the VC for this action.

NAVAL CUTTER Cutters were used as scouts and dispatch boats, depending upon speed to get them out of trouble. Conditions were very cramped for the crew, and their 14 small guns were more

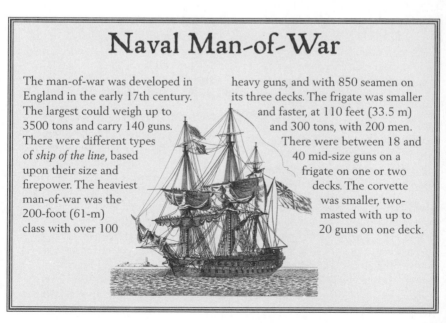

Naval Man-of-War

The man-of-war was developed in England in the early 17th century. The largest could weigh up to 3500 tons and carry 140 guns. There were different types of *ship of the line*, based upon their size and firepower. The heaviest man-of-war was the 200-foot (61-m) class with over 100 heavy guns, and with 850 seamen on its three decks. The frigate was smaller and faster, at 110 feet (33.5 m) and 300 tons, with 200 men. There were between 18 and 40 mid-size guns on a frigate on one or two decks. The corvette was smaller, two-masted with up to 20 guns on one deck.

for defiance than for serious resistance. They appeared to be carrying sails that were too big but, because of their deep draught, these large sails were needed to drive the ship through the water at speed. In the early 18th century, the Royal Navy usually had about 20 cutters. A typical vessel was just 65 feet (20 m) in length, broad-beamed at 20 feet (6 m), and displaced 115 tons.

NAVAL SLOOP Bigger and more heavily armed than a standard sloop, this craft was developed in the early 18th century as a pirate-hunting ship, with a crew of 70 men. She displaced around 113 tons, was 65 feet (20 m) in length, and was *'sharpened'* to allow for faster attacking. She was also fitted with seven pairs of oars to extend through the gunports in order to chase pirates and smugglers in windless conditions. Her crew could fire each of her twelve 9-pound cannons every 90 seconds.

NAVAL SNOW Comparable to a brigantine, with a crew of 90 and eight mounted 6-pounder cannon. Just 60 foot (18 m) long, she was distinguished by her fore-and-aft trysails. She managed well in a light quartering wind, and became the common patrol ship when the Royal Navy operated to eradicate piracy in the 19th century.

PACKET A fast ship in a regularly scheduled mail, cargo or passenger service. The first transatlantic packet service was introduced by the *Black Ball Line* in 1818.

PIG BOAT US Navy slang for a submarine, because of the smell their unwashed crews used to give off when coming ashore.

PINK There were two types of pink. The small Mediterranean cargo ship with a flat bottom and a narrow stern was the Italian *pinco*. In the Atlantic, it was any vessel with a very narrow stern, derived from the Dutch *pincke*.

PINNACE In the 18th century, a small, fast boat that could be rowed or sailed. The term was also used to describe the ship's longboat that ferried men to the shore. In the 16th and 17th centuries, pinnaces were larger, from 20–60 tons.

PIRAGUA, PIROGUE, PIRAGAYA A native dugout, a sea-going canoe used by natives in Central and South America. The term comes from the Carib language. Also sometimes in the West Indies it referred to a plank-built boat with one sail and a flat bottom. Many pirates started their careers using a pirogue, which could not be chased around the shallow waters of the Caribbean cays, and could land on any beach.

POCKET BATTLESHIP After the 1919 Treaty of Versailles, the German navy was forbidden to build battleships, so it developed this class, which was bigger than a cruiser but smaller and faster than a battleship. The Germans designated them as an armoured ship (*'Panzerschiff'*) and the three built were named *Admiral Graf Spee*, *Deutschland* and *Admiral Scheer*.

PT BOAT A fast 'patrol torpedo' boat used in the Second World War by the US Navy. Capable of up to 45 knots (52 mph/ 83 kph), 800 were built. In 1943, J.F. Kennedy was captaining *PT-109* when it was cut in two by a Japanese destroyer in the Solomon Islands. He later became President of the United States.

Q-SHIP, DECOY SHIP A naval ship camouflaged as a merchant ship during the First World War to counter the threat of U-boats. Also employed at the beginning of the Second World War by the US Navy and Royal Navy, but abandoned as ineffective.

RATE The classification of naval warship according to how many guns it possessed. This is the origin of the term *'first rate'*, *'second rate'*, etc. In 1610, the HMS *Resolution* was described as a first rate of 80 guns, but with better technology, bigger ships with more guns came to be classified as 'first rates'. In the 1700s, a first rate man-of-war carried over 100 guns, a second rate 84–100, a third rate 70–84, a fourth rate 50–70, a fifth rate 32–50, and sixth rate ships carried up to 32 guns. In 1810, there was another change, with first rates now having more than 110 guns, second more than 90, third more than 80, fourth more than 60 and fifth rates more than 50 guns. Only the first three rates were used in the *'line of battle'* in a main battle fleet. There were few fourth rates, and they were only used in the *'line of battle'* in smaller fleets. Fifth and sixth rates were usually known as *frigates*. The sixth rates were known as *sloops* if commanded by a commander rather than a captain.

RIVA Italian company founded in 1842 which makes the beautiful, sleek mahogany motorboats seen on the waterways of Venice.

SCHOONER An easily handled, fast, two-masted ship, with all lower sails rigged fore-and-aft. With a shallow draught, she could carry up to 75 crew, mounting eight cannon and four swivel guns. Less than 100 tons, she was popular with pirates in the Caribbean and Atlantic in the 18th century, and could reach up to 11 knots (13 mph/20 kph). She had all the best features required for a pirate vessel. Her very narrow hull and shallow draught made her ideal for the Caribbean and North American coast, as she was small enough to navigate the shoal waters and hide in remote places. She was quick and sturdy, so ideal for privateering. The chief advantage of her fore-and-aft rig was that it was very economical with manpower. Some very large schooners were built , the largest being the *Thomas W. Lawson*, with seven masts which were all the same height, and with gear and sails that were more or less interchangeable.

SHALLOP Similar to a skiff, she was a smaller boat than the longboat – vessels used to transfer men and supplies on and off the ship when moored. These small boats had a mast, sail and rudder, and often also a tarpaulin to keep goods dry. The term is also loosely applied to a small boat for one or two rowers or a sloop.

SHEBEC A narrow ship with one mast with a lateen mainsail and a small foresail on the bowsprit. She also carried 15 oars on each side. They were favoured by the Barbary Corsairs in the Mediterranean as they were fast and manoeuvrable.

SHIP A general term for any large, ocean-going vessel (as opposed to a boat). Originally it referred specifically to a vessel with three or more masts, all square-rigged. The origins of the word are lost, though it is recognizable in all languages descended from the various old Nordic tongues.

SHIP OF THE LINE Usually a major warship with at least two gundecks, being classified as a first-, second- or third-rate ship, powerful enough to engage in a line of battle.

SLOOP A single-masted ship of up to 100 tons with a long bowsprit, almost as long as the hull, she was rigged fore-and-aft. The fastest boat of her day, she was liked by pirates and smugglers because she was easy to handle and had a shallow draught, so could escape in shallow waters. She drew only 8 feet (2.4 m) of water and was easy to manoeuvre. From the 18th century the term was used for a small vessel with one to three masts carrying four to 12 guns on the upper deck. Capable of around 11 knots speed with the aid of its square topsail, she could take up to 75 crew and mounted 14 cannon. In general, the one-masted sloop was smaller than a two-masted schooner, then proportionately bigger were a two-masted corvette, a three-masted snow, a three-masted frigate and a three-masted ship of the line.

SMACK A small sloop-rigged boat used for fishing and small coastal trading.

SNOW Like a brigantine, but smaller, with a main and foremast, and a supplementary sail rigged close behind the mainmast.

SQUARE RIGGER Any ship with sails set on yards at right angles to the vessel's hull. They can be trimmed to about 30 degrees from the centreline on each side.

STEAM SHIPS *'Engines and machinery are liable to many accidents, may fail at any moment, and there is no greater fallacy than to suppose that ships can be navigated*

on long voyages without masts and sails, or safely commanded by officers who have not a sound knowledge of seamanship.' Proving that officers and textbooks are often wrong, this extract was in the preface to *Seamanship* by Commander G.S. Nares, 1865.

Tall Ship

The term for a deepwater ship since the 16th century, now applied to large, traditionally rigged ships used in sail training. John Masefield (1878–1967) penned the following well-known lines in his poem 'Sea Fever':

'I must down to the seas again, to the lonely sea and the sky,
And all I ask is a tall ship and a star to steer her by,
And the wheel's kick and the wind's song and the white sail's shaking,
And a grey mist on the sea's face and a grey dawn breaking.'

SUPERTANKER These are the largest oil tankers. When the Suez Canal closed between 1967–75, larger supertankers were developed, first VLCCs (Very Large Crude Carriers) and then ULCCs (Ultra Large Crude Carriers).

TAR BARGE What other sailors condescendingly call crude oil carriers. They effectively make every other trip in ballast, and act as a pipeline between the oilfield and refinery.

TIN CAN US slang for the thinly armoured destroyers of the Second World War, which relied on speed and manoeuvrability to avoid destruction by larger warships or torpedoes.

TONNAGE Tonnage, as a maritime unit of ship measurement, usually has nothing to do with weight. It is a measure of volume, and thus of a ship's cargo-carrying capacity. It probably derives from the number of tuns (wine barrels of a certain size) that a medieval merchant ship could carry. French wine was carried in '*tonneaux*', wooden casks standardized at 2240 pounds (1016 kg). Ships were assessed on how many tonneaux (tons, or tuns) they could carry. Before 1824, the tun/ton was defined as having a volume of 68,800 cubic inches or 252 gallons. Until recently one ton (shipping or measurement tonnage) was 100 cubic feet. There are several complicated definitions of tonnage since metrication and containerization.

TRAMP (STEAMER) Ship that usually transports low-value commodities, such as coal or scrap iron, operating not on scheduled routes but as and when required by customers.

TUGBOAT A small, powerful watercraft designed to perform a variety of functions, especially to tow or push barges and large ships. In 1736 Jonathan Hulls of Gloucestershire patented a boat to be powered by a Newcomen steam engine, to move large vessels in and out of harbours. The first tugboat actually built was the *Charlotte Dundas*, powered by a Watt engine and paddle wheel and seen by famous American marine engineer Robert Fulton, aka *Quicksilver Bob*.

ULCC Ultra Large Crude Carrier, developed in the 1970s and usually more than 300,000 deadweight tonnage.

VICTORY SHIP A faster and improved design of the Second World War Liberty Ship, capable of over 15 knots (17 mph/ 28 kph). A total of 531 Victory Ships were built in 1944–5.

WINDJAMMER Derogatory term among steamship crew for any square-rigged sailing ship. John Masefield wrote of them: '*They mark our passage as a race of men, / Earth will not see such ships as those again.*'

Wooden Ships

Modern films cannot really convey the conditions on a sailing ship of the 16th–19th centuries. They were damp, dark, cheerless places, reeking with the stench of bilge water and rotten meat. They always leaked and were difficult to get dry, so seamen often suffered from illnesses brought on by damp conditions and the absence of dry clothes, especially in the Atlantic. On a pirate ship, it was even worse. Their ships often carried up to five times the crew of a merchant ship, with men packed in like sardines. As well as carrying loot and more guns and munitions than the average boat, more people were needed to carry the day in a fight. Pirates were known to try and keep the decks clean by washing them down with brandy, and all crews fumigated below decks by burning pitch and brimstone. The ships were plagued by disease, cockroaches, fleas and rats. However, rats were often used to supplement the diet of salt beef or pork (often crawling with maggots) and mouldy, slimy bread. Water rapidly turned fetid in all oceans, so men could easily suffer from the cramps and agonies of dehydration, especially as the only available alternative to water, alcohol, is itself a renowned diuretic.

X-CRAFT British midget submarines introduced into service in 1943.

XEBEC Shallow draught ship with three masts, popular amongst 18th-century corsairs in the Mediterranean.

YACHT In the 17th century a *'jachtship'* was defined as *'a ship for chasing, a light sailing vessel, a fast piratical ship.'* There were many spellings, but the origin was the Dutch *'jaghen'*, to hunt. The United Provinces of the Netherlands used yachts, small, flat-sterned naval pinnaces to escort their *fluits* (Dutch flutes) and herring *busses* and prevent their being attacked. One of these fast yachts was made to high specifications and presented to King Charles II by the Dutch, and so the word came to symbolize a pleasure-craft.

YAWL Boat with two masts, a taller mainmast and a smaller mizzenmast aft.

SHIPS OF SPECIAL SIGNIFICANCE

AARON MANBY This paddle wheeler, launched in 1821 in England, was the world's first steamship to be built of iron.

ABCD SHIPS The cruisers *Atlanta*, *Boston* and *Chicago*, and the dispatch boat *Dolphin*, were the US Navy's first steel ships, launched in 1883.

ADMIRAL POPOV – THE ROUND SHIP This Russian battleship was circular in design. With sister ship *Novgorod*, she was launched in 1875. These unusual vessels were designed to fire their 12-inch guns in any seas, but were difficult to steer.

ARGO AND THE GOLDEN FLEECE In Greek mythology, Jason and the Argonauts sailed on the *Argo* to find the Golden Fleece. She was built by Argus, helped by the goddess Athena, and the goddess Hera protected her crew. After her successful voyage, she was consecrated to the sea god Poseidon at Corinth, and then turned into the constellation of Argo Navis. The Argonauts seem to be symbols of the first Greek mariners who discovered that the Black Sea was not an open sea. The voyage has been traced to Lemnos, Samothrace, through the Hellespont to Kyzikos and Colchis on the Black Sea, then along the Danube, Po and Rhone rivers, to Libya and Crete in the Mediterranean. A 'replica' of the *Argo*, a 50-oar galley carrying a crew from all 27 EU member states, sailed from the Corinth Canal in 2008. The intention was to sail and row from Iolkos (near Volos) to the ancient Black Sea kingdom of Colchis in modern Georgia. However, Turkish authorities could not guarantee a safe passage, so the *Argo* travelled 1200 nautical miles (1380 miles/2223 km) from Volos to Venice.

AURORA AND THE RUSSIAN REVOLUTION On 25 October 1917, the Russian cruiser *Aurora* fired a round of blanks when anchored on the River Neva. It signalled the storming of the Winter Palace in Saint Petersburg, and the start of the Bolshevik Revolution. The *Aurora* is today a floating museum in Saint Petersburg.

BEAGLE The 90-feet (27-m) bark which carried Charles Darwin, as a medical officer and naturalist, around the world between 1831 and 1836. Darwin's discoveries were allied with those of the great naturalist Alfred Wallace to lay the foundations of the theory of evolution.

HMS *BELFAST* This is the last surviving battlecruiser from the Second World War, which can now be visited in the Pool of London. It is incredible how many famous naval vessels have been scrapped for peanuts rather than being taken into care as heritage centres and tourist sites.

BLACK PANTHER The nickname given to U-1105, one of ten U-boats coated with an experimental rubber-tiled skin as a countermeasure to sonar/asdic. It was commissioned too late in the war (June 1944) to have any major effect, sinking only one small warship, and at sea the rubber coating began to peel off. However, it might have been immensely successful if used earlier in the war.

HMY *BRITANNIA* The Royal Yacht *Britannia* last sailed in 1997, before being retired after 40 years of service. She is now open to the public in Edinburgh's port of Leith. The crew dived daily to check her hull and the seabed when she was in any harbour. All gangplanks were checked to never be steeper than 12 degrees. The teak decks were scrubbed in silence, and all duties had to be completed noiselessly before 8a.m. when the royal family woke. If a member of the crew met a member of the royal family, he had to stand as still as a statue and pretend that the royal personage was not there. Men were selected for the 240-strong crew who saw perfection as their personal goal.

CUTTY SARK – THE WORLD'S ONLY SURVIVING TEA CLIPPER One of the fastest clippers, launched in 1869, with a top speed of 17 knots (20 mph/31 kph). She is displayed in a dry dock in Greenwich, London, but was badly damaged by fire in 2007. Captain John Willis, a shipowner, asked Hercules Linton to design the fastest ship in the world to prove that sail was superior to what he disparagingly called '*steam kettles*'. Her first captain, George Moodie, said '*I never sailed a faster ship. At 10 or 12 knots she did not disturb the water at all. She was the fastest ship of her day, a grand ship, and a ship that will last forever*'. She was built to rival the fastest clipper of her day, the *Thermopylae*, which still holds the record for a 60-day crossing to Melbourne.

DOVER BRONZE AGE BOAT This was made from six oak timbers, and moss appears to have been used to caulk the planking. Only 31 feet (9.5 m) of hull was recovered, half of the original boat, which was capable of being rowed to France around 3550 years ago.

EARTHRACE – SAIL IS QUICKER THAN POWER! This 75-feet (23-m) carbon fibre trimaran attempted in 2008 to beat the world circumnavigation record of 74 days 25 hours and 53 minutes set by the *British Cable and Wireless Adventurer* in 1998. It was built to 'pierce' waves, rather than skim over them, with air intakes at the top of its 'wings' which remained above the water when the boat was submerged. Its range was 2000 nautical miles (2300 miles/3700 km) at 25 knots (29 mph/ 46 kph) and the planned journey time was 65 days, but it took only 60 days, a world record for a powered boat. Its top speed was 40 knots (46 mph/74 kph). The course was dictated by detours to fuel stops on land, so sailboats are actually quicker in circumnavigation. Bruno Peyron (French) in January–March

2005, made the fastest circumnavigation in 50 days 16 hours 20 minutes 4 seconds in a maxi-catamaran, ten days faster than *Earthrace* would later achieve. Adrienne Cahalan (Australian) in February–March 2004 became the fastest woman to complete a circumnavigation (with the crew of *Cheyenne*) in 58 days 9 hours 32 minutes 45 seconds. Ellen MacArthur (English) in 2004–5 made the fastest single-handed circumnavigation in 71 days 14 hours 18 minutes 33 seconds.

EAST INDIAMEN These were magnificent armed merchant ships, owned and operated by the East India companies for trading with India, the East Indies (Borneo, Celebes, Java and Sumatra) and the Far East. They were the largest ships of their day, and the captain, passengers and officers enjoyed relatively excellent accommodation. About 300 tons and 160 feet (49 m) long, they carried a maximum crew of 300, but the top gun capacity of 54 cannon was often undercut to make more room for cargo.

EXXON VALDEZ This VLCC grounded in Prince William Sound, Alaska in 1989 polluting 3200 miles (5150 km) of shoreline in America's worst oil spill. Some 215,000 barrels of oil (7,525,000 gallons/34 million litres) were lost in eight hours.

SS GREAT BRITAIN Brunel's ship was the first ocean-going iron steamship, and the first ship driven by a screw propeller. The largest (302 feet/92 m long) and most powerful ship in the world, she was launched in 1843. She served as a transatlantic liner, an emigrant ship to Australia, a troop carrier in the Crimean War and was converted to a

sailing ship and then used for storage in the Falklands. She is now a wonderful museum in dry dock in Bristol, where she was built.

SS GREAT EASTERN Launched in 1858, Brunel's ship was a huge paddle wheeler, 700 feet (213 m) long with five funnels. Her purpose was to serve the England to India route, avoiding coaling several times during the voyage, but she was sold at a loss before she made her maiden voyage. The *Great Eastern* sailed the Atlantic from 1860–4, and laid transoceanic cables from 1866–74, being broken up in 1888.

GREAT REPUBLIC 353 feet (108 m) long, this four-masted US bark was the largest clipper ever built when launched in 1853. Renamed the *Denmark*, she sank in a North Atlantic storm in 1872.

SS GREAT WESTERN Brunel launched his 236-feet (72-m) wooden paddle-wheeler steamship in Bristol in 1837, as an extension of his Great Western Railway, to carry passengers by train from London to Bristol and then on to New York. On her maiden voyage she took 16 days to cross to New York. In 1837 a race was held between her and the *Sirius*, which sailed out of Cobh, near Cork. The *Great Western* crossed in 15 days and 5 hours, winning by more than three days.

HMS HERMES In 1913 the light cruiser *Hermes* was provided with a hanger that could carry three seaplanes, a launching platform, and cranes to retrieve the seaplanes after they had landed alongside the ship. In 1914 she was joined by HMS *Ark Royal*, the first ship to be completed as a seaplane carrier. Seaplanes were launched by being lowered to the water and then taking off as normal. Eventually her deck was used to launch land and seaplanes. A second HMS *Hermes* was the first warship to be designed and built as an aircraft carrier. She was designed in 1917, completed in 1924 and could carry 24 planes for take-off and landing from her deck.

HOLLAND I She was the Royal Navy's first submarine, launched in 1901, but capable of sailing only 60 miles (97 km) before the battery went flat or the air ran out. The measurement of toxic gases was carried out by a crew of three white mice – if they keeled over, it was time to surface. Admiral Sir Arthur Wilson, First Sea Lord 1909–12, stated *'The crews of all*

The 'Holy Grail' of Lost Ships

In 1780, the 226-ton HMS *Ontario*, with 22 cannon, two 80-feet (24-m) masts, and a huge hull with cargo space for 1000 barrels, defended Montreal from Yankee militias, which were threatening to sail across Lake Ontario and seize Montreal. However, she sank in a squall that year with around 120 men, women and children on board and was never seen again, the worst-ever disaster recorded on Lake Ontario. She was found in 2008 and has been filmed, using a remotely operated submersible. At 500 feet (152 m) deep, and in pitch-black water, the *Ontario* leans on a 45-degree angle, her masts still projecting straight up from her decks where several guns lie upside-down. Zebra mussels cover much of the woodwork, but a brass bell, brass cleats and the stern lantern are visible. Seven big windows across the stern still have glass in them. *'This is the only Revolutionary Era vessel in such perfect shape,'* said author Arthur Britton Smith. *'To have a Revolutionary War vessel*

that's practically intact is unbelievable. It's an archaeological miracle.' A rare feature that helped to identify the ship were the two crow's nests on each mast. There are an estimated 4700 shipwrecks in the Great Lakes, including about 500 in Lake Ontario. The sloop *Ontario* is the oldest vessel to be discovered on the floor of the Great Lakes and hopefully can be recovered, but is being treated as a war grave in an undisclosed location. The cold, fresh water combined with a lack of light and oxygen have slowed the process of decomposition and account for the ship being found largely intact.

submarines captured should be treated as pirates and hanged'. Thus the submarine service adopted a flag bearing the skull and crossbones, after that genius retired.

MS *INDEPENDENCE OF THE SEAS*

The biggest cruise ship in the world, she made her maiden voyage in May 2008, having been built in Finland. The 160,000-ton Royal Caribbean International liner boasts a climbing wall, 308 slot machines, a miniature golf course, 19 gaming tables, a 440-yard (400-m) jogging track, water fun zone, ice rink, 1350-seat theatre, surf simulator, and the highest point on the ship is the 'Skylight Chapel'. Up to 4375 guests are cared for by 1360 crew, including 400 waiters serving up to 50,000 meals a day. There are 15 passenger decks with 15 lifts, and she measures 1112 feet (339 m) in length.

LIGHTNING

Built in 1854 at East Boston, USA, for Liverpool's Black Ball Line, this clipper set an incredible speed record of sailing 436 miles in 24 hours (averaging 18.2 mph/29.2 kph). It is known that the *Cutty Sark* could temporarily achieve 17 knots (19.6 mph/31.5 kph), but it appears that the incomparable *Lightning* may have been the fastest sailing ship of all time over a sustained period.

USS *LONGBEACH*

The first nuclear-powered surface warship, she is a cruiser completed in 1961. The nuclear-powered aircraft carrier USS *Enterprise* and the frigate USS *Bainbridge* were subsequently launched in 1964. They circumnavigated the globe without needing to stop to replenish their nuclear fuel supplies.

RMS *LUSITANIA*

The sinking of this liner by a U-boat in 1915 drew the USA into the First World War, as 128 of the 1198 dead were Americans. Germany claimed that the passenger liner was a legitimate target as she was carrying munitions, a claim denied by Britain. The British accused the 'Pirate Hun' of slaughtering civilians, and Americans were falsely told that German schoolchildren had been given a day off school to celebrate the sinking. She was the fastest liner in the North Atlantic, and Germany said she was being used to break its blockade of Britain. In 2008, 8 miles (13 km) off the south coast of Ireland, around 4 million rounds of US-manufactured Remington .303 cartridges were found on the wreck. This possibly explains why she sank in just 18 minutes, with such a loss of life. Some of the 764 survivors reported a second explosion, which was probably munitions exploding, as only one torpedo was fired at the ship.

MANHATTAN

This US supertanker was the first commercial vessel to pass through the Northwest Passage in 1969. However, the venture was abandoned at that time as being uneconomic. With recent global warming causing a diminution of the Arctic ice cover, there is a new focus upon commercial vessels possibly regularly using the passage.

MARY CELESTE This American brigantine was en route from New York to Genoa in 1872, and found underway near the Azores. Nothing seemed to be wrong but there was no-one on board and her cargo of alcohol was intact. Captain Briggs, his wife, daughter and eight crewmen had vanished. One theory is that the mould named ergot may have contaminated the ship's rye bread and its effects might have driven everyone mad and caused them to jump overboard.

MAYFLOWER The 90-feet (27-m) galleon carried 102 settlers to found the Plymouth colony in Massachusetts in 1620. A faithful replica, *Mayflower II*, sailed the same route in 1957 to mark the founding of the Jamestown colony and this is preserved in Plymouth, Massachusetts. She crossed the Atlantic in 55 days, 11 days fewer than the Pilgrim Fathers took.

MEDWAY QUEEN – THE HEROINE OF DUNKIRK A 1924 paddle steamer, built for leisure excursions, she was used to evacuate youngsters from London before being fitted as a minesweeper. At Dunkirk, she shuttled back and forth on seven trips saving 7000 soldiers, only pausing to refuel. On her last trip, she was badly damaged and assumed lost, but managed to limp home with one paddle. When she arrived at Dover the whole fleet saluted her. She is being restored as the last estuary paddle steamer in Britain.

THE *MIGHTY SERVANT* – THE STRONGEST SHIP IN THE WORLD She carries huge structures such as oil rigs across the seas. Her cargo deck measures almost 500 feet by 160 feet (152 m by 49 m), and she can carry cargo up to 45,000 tonnes. It is impossible for cranes to shift this weight aboard the ship, so she sinks into position by opening her seacocks and filling her ballast tanks with 70,000 tonnes of seawater. Only the bridge and accommodation structure remain above the waves, and the cargo deck is stabilized at 70 feet (21 m) below sea level. The rig is manoeuvred and held in place by tugs over the cargo deck. The ballast is then pumped out and the *Mighty Servant* rises to accept her cargo.

NEWPORT MEDIEVAL SHIP
In July 2002 the well-preserved remains of a medieval ship were discovered during excavation on the banks of the River Usk in Newport, Wales. Unusually, the hull remained largely intact, and it is estimated to have been 82 feet (25 m) in length with a 26 feet (8 m) beam. The central section of the ship and bow section (but unfortunately not the stern) has now been conserved. The Newport Ship is dated to before 1468, as the wooden cradle that held her for repairs is of that date. She demonstrates an evolutionary step between Viking longships and the later trading vessels known as cogs or caravels. Many great trading ports feature vessels of this type on their seals, and it is of international interest, being typical of the North European vessels upon which the commerce of the time relied. It is also the type of ship in which voyagers explored the Americas, and is the only surviving example of an armed merchantman of this period. It had apparently recently returned from Portugal, on the evidence of the pottery and large lumps of cork bark in the bilges.

It has decking and superstructure still visible. It predates Francis Drake by over 100 years, and the *Mary Rose* by 50. The sailors on such ships would have been armed, to protect against piracy, and in war would have provided the second-rate ships of the embryonic Royal Navy. It may have belonged to 'Warwick the Kingmaker', and appears to have been abandoned during the Wars of the Roses. Finds recovered from within the vessel include 15th-century coins, Portuguese pottery, cork, stone cannon balls and engraved brass straps. Nearby, in 1994, a smaller medieval boat dating from 1240 was found at Magor Pill and its remains have been preserved. Clinker-built, it was carrying iron ore and foundered.

NIMITZ CLASS – THE LARGEST CAPITAL SHIPS EVER BUILT

These ten nuclear-powered US aircraft carriers are the largest capital ships ever built, and are named, in order of construction, USS *Nimitz (CVN-68)* commissioned in 1975, *Dwight D. Eisenhower, Carl Vinson, Theodore Roosevelt, Abraham Lincoln, George Washington, John C. Stennis, Harry S. Truman, Ronald Reagan* and *George H. W. Bush*, which came into service in 2008.

POTEMKIN She was a battleship in the Black Sea Fleet, commissioned in 1904, named after Prince Potemkin, the commander-in-chief of the Black Sea Fleet under whom the naval officer John Paul Jones served in 1788. She was the scene, in June 1905, of a famous mutiny, one reason for it being poor morale after Russia's humiliating defeat in the Russo-Japanese War. Another reason was bad meat brought on board, which the men refused to eat. The ship's

commander considered that this amounted to mutiny and, acting in accordance with an old Russian naval custom, ordered that a number of men should be selected at random, covered with a tarpaulin, and shot. The men selected to kill their fellow sailors refused to fire. This account was later denied by officers of the ship who survived the mutiny, but one rating was undoubtedly shot by the captain, whereupon the captain, the chaplain, and four other officers were killed by the crew. When the *Potemkin* returned to Odessa, the sailor's body was exhibited to the crowd ashore and rioting followed, some 5000–6000 people losing their lives mainly during the famous charge of mounted Cossacks down the Richelieu Steps (now known as the Odessa Steps). After wandering around the Black Sea in search of support, the battleship was scuttled, but was later raised and refitted. The mutiny is the subject of Eistenstein's wonderful film *The Battleship Potemkin* (1925). The ending, showing the Russian fleet rallying to the Potemkin's leadership, is fiction or propaganda – take your pick.

RMS QUEEN ELIZABETH

This Cunard transatlantic liner was the world's largest ship (83,673 gross tons) when launched in 1940, and served as a troopship during the war, sailing singly as she was too fast to travel in convoy. She ended passenger services in 1968 and was purchased and renamed the Seawise University before being destroyed by a fire in 1972 in Hong Kong Harbour.

RMS QUEEN ELIZABETH 2

QE2 was for 30 years the Cunard flagship, making her maiden voyage in 1969. She is one of the largest liners at

Queen Anne's Revenge

This British ship, the *Concord*, was launched in 1710 during the War of Spanish Succession (Queen Anne's War), but in 1711 was captured by the French and renamed *Concorde*. She was captured by the pirate Ben Hornigold while en route from West Africa to Martinique laden with gold, silver, jewels and slaves. In 1717, Blackbeard, one of Hornigold's crew, took over the *Concorde*, renamed her *Queen Anne's Revenge*, and placed another 20 cannon on her. Six months later she was lost on the Outer Banks of North Carolina. She was found in 1996 off Beaufort Inlet and 18 cannon, wine bottles, pewter plates and other valuable items have been so far salvaged from Blackbeard's flagship.

963 feet (294 m) long, 70,327 tons, and has a top speed of 32.5 knots (37 mph/ 60 kph). She was sold to Dubai but has not been converted, as the 2008–9 financial crisis has hurt that country's economy more than many others.

RMS *QUEEN MARY* From 1938–52 this Cunard liner was the fastest ship in the world, capable of 32 knots (37 mph/ 59 kph), and making 1001 scheduled Atlantic crossings, plus 72 troopship crossings and assorted pleasure cruises. She still holds the record for the most people transported at sea, 16,683 in 1943. She was sold to Long Beach city in California in 1967 where she is displayed as a hotel and tourist attraction.

RAINBOW WARRIOR The plucky Greenpeace vessel protested against French nuclear testing in the Pacific, and was sunk by the French Secret Service in Auckland Harbour, New Zealand in 1985. Two bombs exploded, two minutes apart.

A Greenpeace cameraman, Fernando Pereira, was drowned. The French denied all responsibility, but there was overwhelming evidence of the complicity of French agents. Eventually, in a plea bargain which ensured no details would reach the public domain, two French operatives (out of a much larger team) served less than two years in comparative luxury in a French 'prison'.

ROSKILDE LONGSHIP Found in Roskilde Harbour, 25 miles (40 km) from Copenhagen in 1997, this Viking longship was a massive 114 feet (35 m) in length, the longest ever found, and dates from the time of Canute the Great, around 1025. The Vikings came from Norway, Sweden, Finland and Denmark, and the 'Viking Age' when they were at the peak of their power lasted from the late eighth to the late 11th century. To build their ships, oak planks were overlapped and nailed together, and the spaces between the planks were made watertight by being stuffed tightly with tarred wool or other animal hair. They had a shallow draught so could be used in shallow water and on rivers and lakes. There was one square sail, probably made of wool, criss-crossed with leather to reinforce it and keep its shape when wet. The length of the oars varied, depending where they were used, and the oarsmen sat on their storage chests rather than seats. A *steerboard* – a steering plank – was fastened to the right-hand side of the ship at its stern. The deck stretched the entire length of the ship, with ports cut for the oars along its length.

NS *SAVANNAH* The first nuclear-powered merchant ship was launched in 1959, but was a commercial failure. She left service in 1972 and was exhibited at Charleston and then mothballed in Virginia's James River.

SS *SAVANNAH* This paddle steamer was built in New York and sailed from Savannah to Liverpool in 25 days in 1819. Although she sailed most of the

way instead of relying on her wood-fuelled boilers and detachable paddles, her success inaugurated steam travel. After this voyage she was converted to a sailing ship but sank in 1821.

SOVEREIGN OF THE SEAS

She was built in 1638 by Phineas Pett at the insistence of King Charles I, who wanted an impressive and technically advanced '*Great Ship*'. She was to be the largest ship ever, a 100-gun vessel, and the first ship ever to carry royals among her sails. The design of the carvings, which were all finished in gold leaf, was by Anthony Van Dyck. She was supposedly known to the Dutch Navy as the '*Golden Devil*' and was to be avoided wherever possible because of the weight of artillery that could be brought to bear. She was rebuilt at least twice, and eventually she was renamed *Royal Sovereign* before being accidentally burned and destroyed in 1696. Her build cost was £65,586, as against the average cost of £6080 for a 40-gun ship. This is around £105 million in today's terms. Measuring 212 feet (65 m) in length, she

displaced 1605 tons, and her wartime complement was 813 men.

SUTTON HOO BURIAL SHIP

In 1939, the burial ship of one of the earliest English kings, Raedwald of East Anglia (ruled 600–624), was discovered under one of 20 earthen mounds in a field near the River Deben, at the harbour of Woodbridge in southeast Suffolk. The wood had perished, but plank marks in the soil showed that she was made of nine oak planks on each side, being 88.5 feet (27 m) long, 15 feet (4.5 m) wide and 5 feet (1.5 m) high amidships. She would have required 20 rowers per side and had no mast. No body was found, but the burial treasures put the discovery on a par with Stonehenge, and they are now in the British Museum. Other graves included a chamber-grave of another man buried with a ship (but looted), and of a man buried with a horse.

THERMOPYLAE This 212-feet (65-m) tea clipper was the greatest rival of the *Cutty Sark*, and on its maiden voyage set a still unbeaten record of 63 days from London to Melbourne.

THOMAS W. LAWSON A steel schooner, launched in 1902 at Quincy, Massachusetts, she was the largest schooner and the only seven-masted schooner ever built. Her fore to aft masts were: fore, main, mizzen, jigger, driver, pusher and spanker.

TORREY CANYON At the time in March 1967, this ship caused the world's greatest oil spill, when the total cargo of 17,340 barrels of oil (607,000 gallons/2.75 million litres) was discharged into the English Channel, polluting the West Country, Channel Isles and Brittany.

THE TREASURED SHIP

This was the remarkable flagship of the Chinese explorer Zheng He, whose *'sails, anchors and rudders cannot be moved without 200 or 300 people'*. Built in the early 15th century, she was said to be 490 feet (149 m) long by 204 feet (62 m) in the beam (more than twice the length of the first transatlantic steamer of four centries later), and had nine masts.

HM FRIGATES *UNICORN* AND *TRINCOMALEE*

His Majesty's Frigate *Unicorn*, of 46 guns, was the last intact warship from the days of sail to remain in service. She was one of the *Leda* class of frigate which included the *Shannon*, *Chesapeake* and *Trincomalee*. She served in the Royal Navy for 145 years, only being decommissioned in 1968 and now is open to the public at Victoria Dock, Dundee. She was built in Chatham's royal dockyard, and was launched in 1824. She is the world's most original wooden warship, with 90 per cent of her original timbers, and needed less restoration than the *Trincomalee*. At Hartlepool, the HMS *Trincomalee*, built in Bombay for the Admiralty in 1817, has been restored and is the oldest ship afloat in the UK, and the last of the commissioned frigates of the Nelson era.

SS *UNITED STATES*

She was the fastest ocean liner, averaging 35.6 knots (41 mph/66 kph) eastbound and 33.9 knots (39 mph/63 kph) westbound on the transatlantic route on her 1952 maiden voyage. This is also the name of one of the six original frigates constructed for the US Navy as a result of the Navy Act of 1794. The others were named *President, Congress, Constitution, Constellation* and *Chesapeake*.

HMS *Warrior* – The End of the Wooden Walls

The most technically advanced ship of her day and the first fully ironclad warship, she was 418 feet (127 m) long and was launched in 1860. She was designed in an urgent response to the French building *La Gloire*, a wooden warship covered in iron armour and driven by steam and sail. Because the *Warrior* was made of teak between iron plates, she could be made longer than wooden men-of-war (the inner iron cladding was an inch (2.5 cm) thick, with 18 inches (46 cm) thickness of teak and then 4 inches (10 cm) of wrought iron as the outer layer). Whereas the French clad their wooden hulls of ships in 5 inches (12.7 cm) of iron above the waterline, *Warrior* also covered its guns, boilers and engine in iron 'boxes'. She could choose between propulsion by steam or sail, and Napoleon III called her *'a black snake among rabbits'*. She outgunned any other ship of the day, had watertight bulkheads, and could make up to 16 knots (18.5 mph/30 kph). As she was so long, guns could be mounted on a single deck, rather than on two or three, which made the ship more stable. Her guns were thus twice the size of that of any other ship, and she carried six 68-pounders and ten 110-pounders. When under sail, to reduce drag, the 10-ton single-screw propeller was lifted out of the water by 600 men manning tackles. Her launching made all wooden men-of-war obsolete. She is now on display at Portsmouth Historic Dockyard, England.

VASA Sunk in Stockholm 1628, she was raised in 1961, the only preserved 17th-century ship in the world. This popular vessel is displayed in Scandinavia's most visited museum. The reason that *Vasa* sank was because Sweden's King Gustavus Adolphus interfered with the design. She thus had so shallow a draught that not enough ballast could be added to compensate for the top-heaviness caused by cannon. The king and his court saw her founder on her maiden voyage.

PS *WAVERLEY* Built in 1946, she is Europe's last sea-going paddle steamer and operates in the United Kingdom on the Clyde and the Bristol Channel each summer, run by a preservation society.

WORLD'S OLDEST LIFEBOAT

The *Zetland* was a rowing (pulling) lifeboat, built at South Shields in 1802 for Redcar. Crewed by local fishermen, it was in service until 1880, saving 502 lives, and is on display on Redcar seafront.

WHO DID WHAT AND WHO DOES WHAT AT SEA?

AB The 'able-bodied' seaman in the merchant marine is the rank between 'ordinary seaman' and 'petty officer'.

ADMIRAL The highest ranking naval officer, in charge of a squadron or fleet at sea. The buccaneer Henry Morgan was Jamaica's 'admiral' in charge of dozens of privateering vessels. Admiral comes from the Arabic term *amir-al-bahr* meaning commander of the seas. Edward I appointed the first English admiral in 1297 when he named William de Leyburn *'Admiral of the sea of the King of England.'* Later the title became Lord High Admiral and the holder was concerned with administering naval affairs from the Admiralty, rather than commanding at sea, until the 16th to 17th centuries. When he commanded the fleet an admiral would either be in the lead or the middle portion of the fleet. When an admiral commanded from the middle portion of the fleet, his deputy, the vice-admiral, would be in the leading portion or van. The vice-admiral is the admiral's deputy or lieutenant and serves in the admiral's place when he is absent. The British vice-admiral also had a deputy at the rear of the fleet called the rear-admiral.

ADMIRALTY Edward III was fighting both the French and Spanish when he established the Court of Admiralty of England in 1360, a body responsible for administering the king's ships. Originally a 'one-man band' in 1297, there are now five 'Sea Lords' and thousands of staff.

BEACH MASTER In the 19th century, this was the officer in charge of disembarkation when landing, and who usually led an attack on the land-based defenders. He could shoot anyone on his own side if he thought them to be cowardly. The Labour Chancellor of the Exchequer Dennis Healey was a beach master at the Salerno and Anzio landings during the Second World War. However, he referred to himself, then a major, as a Military Landing Officer, 'Beach Master' now being an American title.

BOATSWAIN The *bosun* was in charge of the rigging, sails, cables and anchors, making sure they all work efficiently. He was also usually in charge of stores, and replacement of provisions. In charge of all the work on deck, he translated the captain's orders into operations by the crew. Interestingly, the names of the lower ranks on board – boatswain, coxswain and seaman – are all derived from the people's language, Anglo-Saxon. The names of the officers – admiral, captain and lieutenant – are all derived from the language of the court in medieval times, French. The Spanish equivalent of the boatswain was the *'contramaestre'*, superior in rank to all sailors except the *'piloto'*. The *piloto* was the equivalent of the British ship's master.

CAPTAIN and MASTER In medieval times in Britain, the captain was a courtier or army officer who embarked in the ship with his soldiers to do the fighting. The *master* and *boatswain*, with a naval crew, handled the ship. However, in Elizabethan times, longer sea voyages became more common, so the captain had to have practical knowledge of the ship as well as of fighting. Commanding officers of ships of the first six 'rates' were ranked as captains. Lesser ships had commanders or lieutenants in command, who were called captain while at sea. In the merchant navy, the old title of master still exists, as he is concerned with ship handling and not with fighting.

CARPENTERS These were vital for not only ship repairs and careening. Because of their sharp saws, they also used to amputate limbs rather than the ship's surgeon. Often the carpenter would have separate quarters combined with a workshop. He repaired battle damage to masts, yards, hatches and the hull, and also kept leaks out with wooden plugs and oakum fibres. As 'sea artists' they were needed by pirate crews, especially for stripping prizes to convert them to pirate ships.

CHIEF MATE, CHIEF OFFICER
Also known as the *'first mate'* or 'first officer' he is second-in-command to the master or captain on a merchant ship, taking over in the master's absence or incapacity. He usually has qualified for a master's ticket. The chief mate is customarily a watchstander and is in charge of the ship's cargo and deck crew. He is responsible to the captain for the safety and security of the ship.

COAST GUARD Because of high duties on silks, tobacco and spirits, smuggling flourished across Britain, even during the Napoleonic Wars, usually abetted by local lords who took their cut. Elizabeth I had instituted a system of *'vice-admirals'* to prevent the vice of smuggling. However, even her half-brother, Vice-Admiral Sir John Perrot, dealt with smugglers and pirates. Customs officers were not powerful enough, and were usually by-passed, until the end of the Napoleonic Wars. In the 1820s there was a surplus of manpower, and the Coast Guard Service was formed. It built cottages at watch points near all coastal landing places, and smuggling was virtually halted.

COCK UP CREW In port, the merchant ship's *'cock up crew'* had to slew the (horizontal) yard arms inboard, and brace them neatly so that they did not interfere with another ship's rigging, or any dock equipment. This had to be done before the crew was allowed ashore. The yards were neatly turned up (*cocked up* or *cockbilled*) so that they lay at an upward angle to the masts However, yards are said to be *scandalized* (Latin *scandalum*, a cause of offence) when they are *cocked up*. Yards were cocked up in a mark of respect to a dead crew member.

COOK The ship's cook was often a disabled seaman, especially in the merchant service. Cooking presented its own dangers on wooden ships at sea, and the ovens were placed on a bed of bricks to heat kettles and pots.

COOPER These were needed on larger ships, as at sea everything not in a tarred canvas bag was kept in a wooden cask. The cooper made casks to keep gunpowder dry, food pest-free, and to stop spirits leaking. With imperfect storage, the casks needed constant maintenance to keep them intact. Casks were 'knocked down' when they were empty, to save storage space and make way for new cargo, and reused time after time.

COXSWAIN, COCKSWAIN

Originally the *'swain'* or boy in charge of the cockboat. The cockboat was used to row the ship's captain ashore. In time the coxswain became the helmsman of any boat, regardless of size or whether it was driven by oars, sail or power. The term dates from at least 1463 and is pronounced cox'n.

CREWS Especially on merchant ships, these were usually a very mixed bag, with many being press-ganged into service. For Woodes Rogers' privateering circumnavigation he gathered a crew of 333 in 1708, of whom only about 20 per cent were sailors. He described them thus

in *A Cruzing Voyage Round the World*:
'... above one third were foreigners from most nations; several of her Majesty's Subjects on board were Tinkers, Taylors, Hay-Makers, Pedlers, Fidlers &c. one Negro, and about ten boys. With this mix'd Gang we hop'd to be well mann'd, as soon as they had learnt the Use of Arms, and got their Sea-legs, which we doubted not soon to teach 'em, and bring them to Discipline.'

CRUSHER The 'Regulating Petty Officer' is the equivalent of a policeman in the navy. Prior to 1914 they were known as 'ship's corporals'. They justified their time by looking for, and 'crushing', incidences of crime rather than trying to prevent its occurrence.

DOGWATCH In the navy, these are 'half-watches' of two hours each, from 4 to 6 and 6 to 8 p.m. The term dates from at least 1700. Dogwatch may be a corruption of *'dodge watch'* as it is only two hours long. Another reason may be that it enabled sailors to dodge having the same watch every night, as the dog watch permits a shift in the order of the watch, with rotas altering by two hours every day. It could also be a reference to the fitful sleep known to sailors as *'dog sleep'*, because it is a stressful watch, as dusk falls.

The watches aboard ships are:
Noon – 4 p.m. Afternoon Watch
4 – 6 p.m. First Dogwatch
6 – 8 p.m. Second Dogwatch
8 – Midnight First Night Watch
Midnight – 4 a.m. Middle or Mid-Watch
4 – 8 a.m. Morning Watch
8 – Noon Forenoon Watch.

FIRST MATE In most ships, this was the captain's right-hand man, who would take over if the captain was killed or incapacitated in battle. However, the rank was the equivalent of the hated lieutenant's role in the Royal Navy, so nearly all pirate ships chose the title of *quartermaster* rather than first mate.

FIRST SEA LORD The operational head of the Royal Navy, a far more exotic title than that of his American counterpart, who is known as the Chief of Navy Operations.

GREASER The Merchant Navy's usual term for the man who lubricated the engine was a *'greaser'*, which was also frequently used as a derogatory term for all engine-room personnel.

GROMMETS, GROMETS Ship's boys or apprentices used for menial tasks, from the Spanish *'grumete'* meaning novice seaman, or Teutonic *'grom'*

meaning youth. The term was originally applied to boys from the Cinque Ports who looked after a ship in harbour.

HANDS Sailors on board are usually referred to as *'the hands'*, and in the singular as *'one hand'*. This is said to come from the expression *'One hand for yourself and one for the King'* used by men working aloft in the days of sail.

IDLER William Falconer, in his 1789 *Universal Dictionary of the Marine* described an idler as a member of the crew who worked all through the day, and thus was not required to keep the night watch unless there was an emergency – 'artists' like carpenters, cooks, sailmakers and the surgeon were therefore exempt. They were thus *'idle'* and off-duty at night, and called *'idlers'*. The name has come to be used in the derogatory sense of being a *shirker*, but that was not the original meaning.

Gunner

The gunner led the groups of men manning the cannon. His greatest skill was in aiming from a rolling and pitching ship at another rolling and pitching ship, and he would train and oversee each group of four to six men who were responsible for loading, aiming, firing, resetting and swabbing for the next 'load and fire'. He would also check that guns were not dangerously over-heating (when they could burst their barrels) or recoiling excessively

(a grave danger on the gun deck). He would coordinate timing, especially for broadsides. By 1700, cannon were available which could fairly accurately hit a target from 700 to 1000 yards (640 to 910 m) away.

JAUNTY, JONTY The traditional nickname for the master-at-arms, the chief of the ship's police. The name *'master-at-arms'* first appears in about 1860. The name *'jaunty'* is said to be a corruption of the French *gendarme*, which, Anglicized, became *John Damme*. The adjective jaunty comes from the seaman's swagger of a master-at-arms when he is on shore.

LODEMAN This was a ship's pilot. *The Black Book of the Admiralty*, the list of maritime law, custom and usage, was codified from the *Laws of Oleron* in 1336. These *Laws of Oleron* were introduced into England by Richard the Lionheart in 1189, copied from his mother Eleanor's legislation in 1152 in Aquitaine. The tenor of these laws survived through the years in the Royal Navy. The following quote from the *Laws of Oleron* is priceless *'If a ship is lost by default of the lodeman, the maryners may bring the lodeman to the windlass or any other place and cut off his head.'*

MARINER In the 17th century a mariner was the equivalent of an able-bodied seaman, and a sailor the equivalent of an ordinary seaman. A *'master mariner'* is now the shipmaster or captain of a merchant vessel.

MASTER The ship's master was also sometimes called its pilot. He was responsible for sailing the ship, a specialist in navigation and pilotage, who directed the ship's course. The *'sailing master'* was in charge of navigation. Charts were inaccurate or non-existent, so it was a difficult job, and many were forced into pirate service. Today the master is the highest officer aboard a merchant ship, and is also known as the captain.

MATE This was said to come from the term *'meat'* as the original boucaniers used to share each other's meat, but more likely came from *'matelotage'*, the living and sharing together of buccaneers in Tortuga and Hispaniola. The ship's mate is responsible for overseeing the sailors, ensuring that the captain's orders are carried out, for stowing cargo and organizing the crew's work. There are different categories of mate on today's larger ships, first mate, second mate etc.

MIDSHIPMEN The oldest slang name for a midshipman, *'reefer'*, has died out but *'snotty'* remains. The latter name is said to have originated about 1870, from the story that the three buttons on the cuffs of midshipmen's jackets were put there to prevent them from wiping their noses on their sleeves. This story seems unlikely because buttons were standard on the cuffs of all naval officers' jackets before this period. Buttons were actually being removed from the cuffs of working jackets around this time. Midshipmen have been defined within the Royal Navy as *'the lowest form of life'* and as *'a medium of abuse between officers of unequal seniority'*. They are also commonly known as *'middies'*.

Life On Board Ships

Sailors furling the mainsail on an 18th-century sailing ship

The gun deck on an 18th-century British man-of-war

Sailors turning the capstan on the deck of an American line-of-battle ship c.1856

Sailors swabbing the deck of a wooden ship

Helmsman turning the ship's wheel

Stokers fuelling the boiler with coal on a steam ship c.1880

MUSICIANS On a pirate ship, their prime function was to play extremely loudly, if pirates were forced to attack. Pirates preferred to take ships peacefully, to capture the ship, cargo, crew and any passengers, but in an attack the black or red flag was raised and as much noise was made as possible, a cacophony to frighten the victim's crew. The Royal Navy had a ship's trumpeter. Black Bart Roberts allowed his musicians to rest on a Sunday, but at all other times, night or day, they were supposed to answer a bored crew's calls for entertainment.

NIPPERS The hands whose job it was to 'nip' a sailing ship's anchor cable to the capstan, when the anchor was being weighed, were always the smallest and youngest men on board. Hence the word *'nipper'* has come to mean a youngster. The anchor cable in large sailing ships was too large to bend around a capstan on the quayside. Smaller lines *(messengers)* were used to heave the cables, and these were *'nipped'* to the cable by dextrous small boys, who became known as *nippers*.

PETTY OFFICERS In the Age of Sail these were the officers that occupied a position between the commissioned and warrant officers and the sailors. Two types of petty officer, the midshipman and master's mate, had a little more power. Master's mates evolved into sub-lieutenants, and midshipmen evolved into naval cadets. It is thought that their being sticklers for the rules led to them being referred to by the term 'petty'.

POWDER MONKEY The term was used in the Royal Navy for the younger men and boys who made up most of the gun crews in the 17th century. They could move more quickly between the low decks than fully grown men. Poorly treated, ill-paid, and with no chance of promotion to a less dangerous job, they were always keen to desert if possible and join a pirate crew. Often mere children, they carried small buckets of powder from the ship's magazine to the guns, thus minimizing the chance of major explosions. Royal Marines were stationed near the ladders during battles to prevent children or frightened crew members from hiding.

PURSER, PUSSER The clerical officer aboard a passenger or merchant ship. He is in charge of the vessel's accounts, documents, and payroll, and on most ships provides a safe for the passengers' valuables. In the early navy, the purser was a low-ranking officer in charge of all of the ship's stores. The word comes from the Latin *bursariar*, the person in charge of expenditure. On naval ships the supply officer disbursed goods, and the name 'bursar' for the person in charge of finances at a public school comes from *'disburser'*. In the Royal Navy, the term became 'purser' for the person in charge of money and stores. The slang for purser in the Royal Navy is *'pusser'*, possibly deriving from a West Country pronunciation of the word.

QUARTERMASTER The representative of the *'Interest of the Crew'* to a pirate captain, and democratically elected by pirate crews, he was literally in charge of the operations of the ship when not in action. The virtual equal of the captain, when a prize was captured, the quartermaster often took it over. He kept order, judged disputes and disbursed food

Promotion

During the Napoleonic Wars, because of the rapid expansion of the Royal Navy, it became possible for men to rise from the lower deck to become captains on merit. The usual system was for the upper classes to buy their sons officers' commissions. At the end of the wars in 1815, the acceptance of merit and personal qualifications for entry to the officer class was abandoned, and His Majesty's ships were once more commanded by those with more money than experience. There was also a huge rise in maritime unemployment, leading to a surge in piracy. There were few jobs, no welfare state, and seamen were forced by penury into crime. The Battle of the Glorious First of June in 1794 had been effectively won by James Bowen, Master of the Fleet and in charge of Admiral Howe's flagship. A former merchant mariner, he held senior warrant rank and could not progress to becoming an officer. Lord Howe asked what he could do to reward Bowen's services in securing the victory, and Bowen asked for a junior lieutenant's commission, which he was granted, eventually becoming an admiral. Advancement of this type was extremely rare, and after 1815 the situation deteriorated even more. The Lord Commissioner of the Admiralty, Admiral Milne, wrote in 1859 *'As regards promotion from the forecastle to the quarterdeck, I have no desire to see anyone but a gentleman of birth decorated in a Post Captain's uniform.'* Winston Churchill was First Lord of the Admiralty from 1939–40 (having previously held the post from 1911–15), and immediately he became concerned with the iniquities of the naval appointments system. In 1940 Churchill overturned an Interview Board decision on Dartmouth College entry which had failed three officer candidates. The grounds for their failure had been that one applicant had a slight Cockney accent, and the other two were sons of a chief petty officer and a merchant navy engineer.

and cash. Because he was second-in-command, he usually received a larger share of plunder than other crew members. He often was given a prize vessel when it was taken, and became captain himself. Usually, only the quartermaster could flog a seaman, and then only after a vote by the crew. In the US Navy, the quartermaster has a role in navigation of the ship.

RANKS Officer rankings in the Royal Navy of the 19th century were as follows: Admirals of the Fleet, Admirals, Vice-Admirals, Rear-Admirals, Captains of the Fleet, Commodores, Captains of above three years, Captains of fewer than three years, Commanders, Lieutenants of eight years, Lieutenants of fewer than eight years, Sub-Lieutenants and Midshipmen – no less than 13 layers.

ROYAL MARINES

The Royal Navy not only carried marines for shore raids, but marines were also used to keep the impressed sailors under control and stop them deserting, or hiding during battle. The control of captains over their own (mainly pressed) men could be difficult to exercise in war, as a large proportion of their badly treated sailors did not want to be at sea. The marines were first raised in the 17th century as soldiers who were trained for marine warfare. In 1759 the marines were designated a light infantry corps, and a marine artillery division was formed later. A typical ship's detachment was then one to three infantrymen and two to three artillerymen. The marines consisted of around 18,000 volunteers who were sworn in for seven to ten years service, and who underwent barracks training before going to sea. Until the 1923 amalgamation into one corps, the Royal Marine Artillery and the Royal Marines Light Infantry were known as the *Blue Marines* and the *Red Marines*. For centuries the marines in a ship lived between the officers and the men, probably to insulate any threat of mutiny. After the Nore Mutiny in 1797, Admiral St Vincent had the marines moved further aft, and ships' small-arms were moved with them. The *marines' mess* is even now called the *marines' barracks*.

SAILOR The word's origin was a person who was a *'sailer'*.

SBS The Royal Navy's Special Boat Service (SBS) is the sister unit of the British Army's Special Air Service (SAS) regiment. Based in Poole, Dorset, the SBS specializes in special operations at sea, along coastlines and on river networks. The SBS also has a team on standby for maritime counter-terrorism operations. The SBS thus specializes in water-borne action, but its members are also highly skilled on land. Recent operations have taken place in the mountains of Afghanistan and the deserts of Iraq. Previously known as the *Special Boat Squadron* and exclusively drawn from the Royal Marines, membership of the SBS is now open to members of other UK regiments and forces.

STEWARD – THE KEEPER OF THE PIGS A general term for any member of a ship's crew involved with commissary duties or personal services to passengers and/or crew. The term comes from an old Anglo-Saxon term: *Styweard* or *Sty-warden*, the keeper of the pigs.

STOKER *'Stoker'* was the Royal Navy's name for the man who shovelled the coal into the furnaces under the boiler(s). In the Merchant Marine, the name was 'fireman', or 'fireman and trimmer', as the stokers also had to trim the balance of the coal in the stoke-holds.

SURGEON (Chirurgeon) These were formerly known as *'barber-surgeons'* – barbers became surgeons because they had the sharpest implements for cutting. Surgeons *('sawbones')* were in huge demand upon pirate ships, although it was rare for them to be trained as doctors. They were bone-setters, who could also extract bullets, treat venereal disease, staunch wounds and amputate limbs to prevent gangrene.

'THREE BADGER' A sailor or marine of low rank but great experience, as shown by the three chevrons worn, good conduct badges each denoting years of loyal service.

VICE-ADMIRAL From 1525 onwards, these worthies were appointed to stop the 'vice' of smuggling and piracy prevalent in Tudor England, Wales and Ireland, being responsible for law enforcement along portions of the coast. Many vice-admirals, like Peter Carew in Cornwall, and Sir John Perrot in Pembroke, collaborated actively with pirates and made considerable personal gains from the *vice*. The first effective laws against piracy date from 1700, with a new system of vice-admiralty courts established in all the English colonies, which allowed panels of naval officers and harbour officials to try pirates and summarily sentence them without trial by jury. Allied with the rise in British sea power, piracy was thereafter doomed.

WARRANT OFFICER The warrant officer occupied a position half-way between a rating and a commissioned officer. He had invariably started out as an ordinary seaman and worked his way up. He was generally a man of vast experience, and was respected by his subordinates and superiors alike. Often, he would have been relatively uneducated, or (and they frequently were) self-educated as the post-holder had to be literate. In military terms he would have been the equivalent of a sergeant-major. Warrant officers were phased out in the Royal Navy but the rank has been recreated. Warrant officers in the US Navy are technical specialists.

WOMEN AT SEA In the merchant navy, captains sometimes carried their wives and families aboard. In the Royal Navy, women sometimes acted as 'powder monkeys' bringing charges from the ship's magazine. Other women masqueraded as men for years without being found out. Apart from their first month's pay, sailors' were only paid when they returned from sea, to discourage desertion, so their wives ashore were destitute, many resorting to prostitution or begging to earn money. Many men had been 'pressed' into service, and their wives were smuggled aboard, appearing only when out to sea and then having to share a hammock with their man in the crowded lower decks. Because of the length of the voyages, there were many births at sea, supposedly bringing luck to the ship.

Ship's Officers

Captain John Smith's *A Sea Grammar* of 1627 describes those in charge in a naval ship:

The Captain's Charge is to command all, and tell the Master to what Port he will go, or to what height. In a Fight, he is to give Direction for the managing thereof, and the master is to see the cunning (conning) of the Ship, and Trimming of the Sails.

The Master and his Mates are to direct the course, command all the Sailers, for Steering, Trimming and Sailing the Ship; his Mates are only his Seconds, allowed sometimes for the two Mid-Ships-Men, that ought to take charge of the first prize.

The Pilot when they make land doth take the charge of the Ship till he brings her to Harbour.

The Chirurgion (Surgeon) is to be exempted from all duty, but to attend the Sick, and cure the Wounded: and good care would be had he have a Certificate from the Barber-Chirurgions Hall of his sufficiency, and also that his Chest be well furnish both for Physic and for Chirurgery, and so near as may be proper for that clime you go for, which neglect hath been the loss of many a man's life.

The Cap Merchant or *Purser* hath the charge of all the Carragasoun (Cargo) or Merchandise, and doth keep an account of all that is received, or delivered, but a Man of War hath only a Purser.

The Master Gunner hath the charge of the Ordinance, and Shot, Powder, match, Ladles, Sprunges, Worms, Cartrages, Arms and Fire-Works; and the rest of the Gunners, or Quarter Gunners to receive their Charge from him according to directions, and to give an account of their stores.

The Carpenter and his Mate, is to have the Nails, Clinches, Roove and Clinch-Nailes, Pikes, Splates, Rudder-Irons, Pumpnails, Skupper nails, and Leather, Sawes, Files, Hatchets and such like, and ever ready for caulking, breaming, stopping leaks, fishing, or splicing the masts or yards as occasion requireth, and to give account of his store.

The Boatswain is to have the charge of all the Cordage, Tackling, Sails, Fids and Marling-Spikes, Needles, Twine, Sail-Cloth, and Rigging for the Ship, his Mate the Command of the Long-Boat, for the setting forth of Anchors, weighing or fetching home an Anchor, Warping, Towing or Mooring, and to give an account of his Store.

The Trumpeter is always to attend the Captain's Command, and to (be) found either at his going ashore, or coming aboard, at the entertainment of Strangers, also when you hale a Ship, when you charge, board or enter; and the Poop is his place to stand or sit upon, if there be a noise they are to attend him, if there be not, everyone he doth teach to bear a part, the Captain is to encourage him, by increasing his

Shares, or pay, and give the Master Trumpeter a reward.

The Marshal is to punish Offenders, and to see Justice executed according to Directions; As Ducking at the Yard's Arm, Hauling under the keel, Bound to the Capstern (Capstan), or mainmast with a Basket of Shot about his Neck, Setting in the Bilboes, and to pay the Cobty or the Morjoune; but the Boys the Boatswain is to see every Monday at the Chest, to say their compass, and receive their punishment for all their week's offences, which done, they are to have a quarter can of beer, and a biskit of bread, but if the Boatswain eat or drink before he catch them, they are free.

The Corporal is to see the setting and relieving the Watch, and see all the Soldiers and sailers keep their arms clean, neat and yare, and to teach them their use.

The Steward is to deliver out the Victuals according to the captain's direction, and Mess them four, five or six, as there is occasion.

The Quarter-Masters have the Charge of the Howle (Hull), for Stowing, Romaging and Trimming the Ship in the hold, and of their Squadrons for the watch, and for Fishing to have a Seine (net), a Fishgig (trident), a Harpon-yron (Harpoon), and Fish-Hooks, for Porgos, Bonitos, Dolphins, or Dorados, and Rayling-lines for Mackerel.

The Cooper is to look to the Cask, Hoops and twigs, to Stave or repair the Buckets, Baricos, Cans, Steep-tubs, Runlets, Hogsheads, Pipes, Buts, etc. for Wine, Bear, Sider, Beverage, Fresh-water, or any Liquor.

The Coxwain is to have a choice Gang to attend the skiffe, to go to and again as occasion commandeth.

The Cook is to dress and deliver out the Victuals, he hath his Store of Quarter cans, Small cans, Platters, Spoons, Lanthornes (lanterns), &C. and is to give his Account of the remainder.

The Swabber is to wash and keep clean the Ship, and Maps.

The Liar is to hold his place but for a week, and he that is first taken with a lie, every Monday is so proclaimed at the main-Mast by a general cry, 'a Liar, a Liar, a Liar', he is under the Swabber, and only to keep clean the Beak-head, and Chains.

The Sailers are the ancient men for hoisting the Sails, getting the tacks aboard, haling the Bowling, and Steering the Ship.

The Younkers are the young men called fore-Mast-men, to take in the top sails, or Top and Yard, for furling the sails, Bousing or Tricing, and take their turns at the Helm.

The Lieutenant is to associate the Captain, and in his absence to execute his place, he is to see the Marshall and Corporal do their duties, assist them in instructing the soldiers, and in a fight the fore-castle is his place to make good, and the Captain doth the half-deck, and the Quarter-master, or Master's Mate, the Mid-ships, and in a Statesman of War, he is also allowed as necessary as a Lieutenant on Shore.

CLOTHING AT SEA

BANDANNA, BANDANA The word comes from the Hindi *bandhnu* or *badnu*, a dyeing technique. It is unknown whether seamen used these brightly coloured headbands, popularized in pirate films, but in cold weather they wore leather, woollen or cloth tight-fitting caps. The privateer William Williams in the 18th century wore a Scotch bonnet instead, similar to today's beret, which protected him from the Caribbean sun and was unlikely to blow away.

BELL BOTTOM TROUSERS

The uniform trousers of a sailor, about 5 feet 10 inches (1 m 78 cm) tall, measure a wide 25 inches (63.5 cm) round their bottoms. Seamen used to make and repair their own clothes, and found it easier and less wasteful to use the full width of material. A bolt of serge-cloth in Britain for many years measured 54 inches (137 cm) across. Allowing two turn-ins for stitching together, this gave exactly two trouser legs. Wide trouser legs were easier to roll up when scrubbing decks, but it seems that the original reason for this style was determined by the standard width of bolts of serge.

BIGWIG In the early years of the 20th century nearly all men in Europe wore hats, whether they were bald or not, old or young. In centuries before, the rich wore wigs rather than hats, and the richer the person, the more wigs he had. Louis XIV began the practice of wearing really long and tall wigs, and all of Europe's royalty copied him. In England, the length of the wig that a man wore depended on his importance, so many people, including naval captains and admirals, began to wear these full-length wigs. W.H. Smyth in his *The Sailor's Word-Book* described *bigwigs* as *'the term applying to high-ranking naval officers.'* Admiral Sir Henry Morgan wore a full-length black wig, and Captain Chaloner Ogle, who killed Black Bart, wore a white one. As a result of their becoming 'too common', a law was passed declaring that only nobility, judges, and bishops could wear full-length wigs. They thus became the real *bigwigs*, the truly important people to whom lesser citizens had to pay obeisance. Incidentally, *'to pull the wool over the eyes'* refers to the wool in these wigs. Street robbers would pull the wig down over the victim's eyes to confuse him and make their getaway.

BLAZER In the Royal Navy, captains were permitted to deck their crews out in uniforms of their choice, if they bought the clothes. Crews did not generally have uniforms, but on ceremonial occasions, some of the richer captains tried to better others with the smartness of their crews. The boat's crew of HMS *Harlequin* were dressed in *Harlequin* costumes, and HMS *Caledonia's* wore tartan. However, the poor crew of HMS *Tulip* were forced to dress in green suits with a flower in their caps. By common consent, the most admired of these uniforms were those of HMS *Blazer*, whose captain chose navy blue jackets, and blue and white striped jerseys. The 'blazer' is now a semi-formal casual jacket, formerly always navy-blue and often with brass or silver buttons, and the style comes from this captain's choice of uniform for his crew. Over the years navy blue became standardized for crews and officers in the English navy.

'BRASS-BOUND MAN' Until the 19th century, the only seamen wearing 'regulation uniform' were the commissioned officers of the Royal Navy (whose uniform was introduced in 1748). Their 'dress uniform' was decorated with gold lace and brass buttons (gilt buttons for the richer officers). Other seamen dressed as suited them. The Royal Navy introduced uniforms for its ratings in 1857, and 1st class petty officers and chief petty officers now wore uniforms with a brass-buttoned navy reefer jacket. These were copied by the more prestigious commercial shipping lines, like the Cunard and P&O, and gradually the brass-buttoned reefer jacket came to be generally accepted as the mark of the maritime officer.

DUNGAREES Worn by sailors since the 18th century, from the Hindi *'dungri'*, a type of cotton cloth.

DUNGAREE DUCK The name for a blue or striped cotton cloth worn by Indian seamen. Also it is the former name for *Bombay Duck*, the small spiced fish served in Bombay and now at Indian restaurants worldwide.

EARRINGS The wearing of earrings by sailors possibly comes from an eastern custom of wearing amulets as charms and insignia of rank. In England they appear to date from the time of Elizabeth I, because of a maritime superstition that pierced ears would improve eyesight. Early blindness was common for lookout men who squinted into the Sun for hours at a time. However, it seems that the real reason for the wearing of an earring by nautical men was that it would pay for their funeral if they died on land. The occasional gold earring is still seen in the merchant navy, worn usually on the left ear lobe only.

EYE-PATCH The most common cause for wearing this amongst sea-dogs was not sword-play but staring into the Sun. Before John Davis invented the *backstaff* in 1595, navigators had to use *sighting-sticks* to measure the Sun's height above the horizon, by looking directly into its glare to find latitude. In a few years, the sight of the eye was usually ruined.

GALLIGASKINS, PETTICOAT TROUSERS, SHIPMAN'S HOSE

The wide breeches formerly worn by seamen.

KNOCKED INTO A COCKED HAT

Ships' officers wore cocked hats for centuries. In these early days of sailing, the ship's position was charted by marking three plotting lines on a map.

Within sight of shore, a series of bearings on known features could be taken, and turned into back bearings to give the ship's position on a navigation chart. At least three points are needed for a good 'fix', but the ship's motion, weather conditions, compass accuracy and other variables usually meant that the lines did not meet at a fixed point. The ship should be at the junction of all three, but due to these inaccuracies it was often placed in a small triangle. The triangle was known as a cocked hat after the common three-cornered hat worn by ships' officers. Thus the ship was known to be in the 'cocked hat' somewhere.

LANYARD Many privateers wore crossed sashes, to hold pistols, daggers, knives and so on, to prevent these being lost overboard. A lanyard was a short line of rope, often tied to these sashes, used for making anything fast, and all seamen had recourse to using them. Items were fastened by lanyards to their sashes, belts and boots. In the Royal Navy, the original use of a lanyard was to hang the seaman's knife in front of his body. It was of such a length that a man aloft could open the knife with one arm outstretched, the other holding onto the rigging. It was worn under the collar for comfort, appearance and to prevent strangulation should the lanyard be grasped or caught below its Turk's Head knot.

LONG CLOTHES, LONG TOGS

Clothes which were loose and could be worn ashore. On board a merchant ship, baggy pants and coats could get caught in the rigging, so clothes were generally tight-fitting. If men had 'bell bottom' trousers, they were rolled up for work on the deck or in the rigging.

LOUSY Pressed men often had head lice (were 'lousy') and were shorn as a routine, so a pigtail denoted that you were an experienced seaman. The 'lousy' newcomers were sometimes not very good at sea if they were impressed non-maritime men, and their uselessness equated with 'being lousy'.

MONKEY JACKET A short red jacket worn by midshipmen in the Royal Navy. Other sailors also wore these coats in different colours, which were cut short to enable seamen to climb the rigging more easily. The origin of *'donkey jacket'*, a short navy jacket worn by workmen, may come by association from monkey jacket. Maritime monkeys can climb rigging, landlubber donkeys cannot.

MONMOUTH CAP A very popular 18th-century sailor's hat, a sort of big woollen beret with a bobble on top, made in Monmouth, Gwent, and worn on the back of the head. It kept one warm, protected the wearer from the Sun, and would not blow off.

PETTICOAT BREECHES

These baggy trousers, widening out and ending at mid-calf, were ideal for barefoot mariners scrambling up the rigging.

QUEUE A *'tail'* (from the French) or pigtail, affected by many seamen who stiffened it with a mixture of flour and water, and tied the end with a ribbon.

REEFER JACKETS These were warm, and *'short-style'* to avoid getting tangled in the shrouds or rigging. Midshipmen were known as *'reefers'* as they had to attend to the tops when taking in reefs. Their dress included these short jackets, *reefer-jackets* and hence *reef-jackets* or *reefers*.

Pigtails

PIGTAILS Even more popular in the 18th and 19th centuries than today amongst art teachers, advertising executives and balding rock stars, pigtails were *'tarred'* at sea, which may be the origin of the phrase *'Jack Tar'*, the popular name for a seaman. However, it is more likely that seamen were called *tars* because their hands were always covered with tar from the ropes and ship's timbers. In *The Shipping News* we read: *'Sailors once wore their hair in queues worked two ways, laid up into rattails, or plaited in four-strand square sinnets. The final touch called for a pickled eelskin chosen from the brine cask. The sailor carefully rolled the eelskin back (as a condom is rolled), then worked it up over his queue and seized it. For dress occasions he finished it off with a red ribbon tied in a bow.'* Long hair could easily get caught in the ship's equipment when working onboard. To prevent this from happening sailors would tar (or tallow) their pigtails. Officers were excused from this hair care and sometimes wore powdered wigs. Pigtails were fashionable for crew from about 1785–1825, but naval crewmen were still allowed long hair (tied into pigtails and tallowed/tarred) up until the early 20th century.

SCOTCH BONNET A sailor's hat, so close-fitting that it could not be blown away and lost. It was sometimes known as a 'Scotch Tam', woven in one piece without a seam or binding. It was a comfortable and larger type of beret to protect the seaman's head against the Sun, sometimes with a red tail hanging down the back.

THE 'SILK' The sailor's black silk 'handkerchief', worn round the throat, is popularly thought of as a sign of mourning for Lord Nelson, but its origin is far older. Originally it was worn in action either around the brow to prevent sweat running into the eyes, or as a general purpose sweat rag, or as a pad to cushion the body against hard knocks or chafing on the beams of decks.

SLOPS This is the naval name for any article of ready-made clothing which can be purchased from the ship's clothing store. Slops were introduced into the Navy in 1623. The compartment in a ship where slops are kept and issued is called the *Slop Room*.

SLOP CHEST The supply of clothes (and also knives, tobacco etc.) which the crew could buy on board ship. The amount was totalled and taken off their pay when it was time to settle up at the end of the voyage.

SLOPPY A *'sloppe'* was a loose-fitting garment, and it is mentioned by the poet Chaucer. In 1632, because its crews were dressed in tatters, the Royal Navy ordered that *slops* should be carried aboard ships, kept in a *slop chest*, and issued to the men at sea. As they were all one size, usually damp and musty, the adjective *sloppy* was born, meaning something untidy or slovenly (as in *'sloppy dresser'*). Very basic slops were provided in the Royal Navy in the 17th century, but civilian tradesmen, 'slop-sellers', were more readily patronized than naval stores. To ensure that his men had sufficient clothing to protect them against all weather, a captain could order a man to purchase items of up to two months' pay in value.

TARPAULIN, TARPAWLING

Seamen wore canvas hats that had been coated with tar to waterproof them. They were known as *'tarpaulins'*. They also had capes of tarpaulin to cover them in bad weather. Many sailors painted their clothes with tar to keep out the wind and rain, and their trousers were known in the north of England as *'tarry-breeks'* (tar covered trousers or britches). The first use of the word is seen in 1605, and the origin is tar-pall, or tar-palling. To pall was to glut or satiate, so palling was the process of saturating canvas or fabric with tar. The ship's longboat also usually carried a tarpaulin to protect against the ingress of rainwater.

TATTOOS Like hooped earrings, these were not generally worn by mariners, despite popular stereotypes. The first record of a sailor being tattooed is one of Captain Cook's men in Tahiti in 1764. Tattooing of seamen began among Roman Catholic sailors, the decoration usually in the form of a crucifix, as a means of identification for their bodies so they would be assured of the proper religious rites and burial. Admiral Smyth tells us in 1867 that *'the Burmese, South Sea Islanders, and others, puncture the skin until it bleeds, and then rub in fine soot and other colouring matter. The practice has become common among sailors.'* One particular design which was considered a seaman's charm was that of a pig, which used to be on the foot but later moved to just above the kneecap.

Uniform

George II (1683–1760) was so attracted by a dark blue riding costume with brass buttons, worn by the Duchess of Bedford, that he is said to have ordered the colour scheme for naval officers' uniform. The most popular colour in the English and foreign navies had previously been red. The Admiralty order promulgating the British uniform regulations in 1748 began: *'Whereas we judge it necessary, in order the better to distinguish the Rank of Sea Officers, to establish a Military uniform cloathing for Admirals, Captains, Commanders and Lieutenants, and judging it also necessary to distinguish their class to be in the Rank of Gentlemen, and give them better credit and figure in executing the commands of their superior officers; you are hereby required and directed to conform yourself to the said Establishment by wearing cloathing accordingly at all proper times; and to take care that such of the aforesaid officers and midshipmen who may be from time to time under your command do the like.'*

In 1760, as other navies had uniforms, English officers petitioned the Admiralty for a uniform instead of 'slops' for their men, but no guidance was given. The unofficial uniform at that time was described as *'a little low cocked hat, pea jacket, canvas petticoat trousers not unlike a kilt, tight stockings and shoes with pinchbeck buckles'*.

The cocked hat for men was later replaced by a shiny black tarpaulin hat, with the name of the ship emblazoned on a broad black ribbon. The dress regulations of 1847 stated that men's caps were to be like the officers' but without a peak, which is the origin of today's sailors' cap. There were many variations of this basic uniform. Some sailors wore coloured *'comforters'* for warmth, and knitted waistcoats. Captains of ships still used to dress their ships' crews, how they saw fit, as is described in the entry on *Blazer* (q.v.). By 1800 the unofficial uniform was a blue jacket with white stripes (or white thread) down the seams, and a striped or checked shirt. (Striped jerseys are still worn in the French and Dutch navies.) The white trousers were either long or bell-bottomed to be easily rolled up, or short to show the stockings. Today's British naval uniform was not authorized until 1857. It was decided that the collar, which was used as protection from the tallow or tar that was worn on the pigtail, was to have three white tapes rather than the former two.

MARINE ENTERTAINMENTS

Vice-Admiral Henry Fleet remembered the entertainment aboard naval ships when he was a midshipman on the frigate *Constance* in the 19th century: *'Generally in the evenings at sea and very often in harbour the men sang. We had quite a melodious crowd and some of the songs were excellently rendered. It was before the days of music hall and many of the favourite ones were written by Dibdin, the sailor's poet. Jack was sentimentally inclined and most of the songs were of that class – of Mother and Home. In harbour with other ships present a regular concert would take place, each man giving a turn in rotation, the ditty rendered receiving so much applause as the audience considered it merited, and they were impartial critics. The effect on a fine, still night was most pleasing. Sometimes in harbour the hands were piped to "dance and skylark". Then – if in the mood – the men would dance and play games such as Sling the Monkey, Baste the Bear or Able Whackets. A favourite was Follow the leader, when all sorts of pranks were indulged in and some daring feats performed on the masts and yards.'* The game *Baste the Bear* involved the 'bear' having a piece of rope tied around his waist while his 'keeper' held the other end and had to protect him from a circle of sailors who aimed blows at him, using knotted handkerchiefs or pieces of rope. In *Sling the Monkey*, the unfortunate

'monkey' was slightly better off in that he was given a knotted handkerchief or rope with which to defend himself. The drawback was that he was usually suspended by a rope around his shoulders and swung from a yardarm, back and forth amidst his assailants. Able-whackets was *'a popular sea-game with cards, in which the loser is beaten over the palms of the hands with a handkerchief tightly twisted like a rope. Very popular with horny-fisted sailors.'* (W.H. Smyth, *The Sailor's Word-Book*, 1867). *King Caesar* was another game, now known as *British Bulldogs*. One man is placed in the centre of the deck and the other men try to get past him. Whoever he brings down has to help him when the crew come back the other way. Eventually every member playing has to stop the sole survivor from getting through the line of men across the deck.

BILLIARDS Several taverns such as the George and the Feathers in 17th-century Port Royal had billiard rooms, which were usually situated in the yard, or away from the main bars, to prevent fights occurring.

CAPTAIN'S MISTRESS On his three major voyages of discovery, Captain James Cook spent so many hours in his cabin, poring over this game's stratagems, that his crew joked he had a mistress aboard – hence its name. It is a sophisticated version of 'four-in-a-row' for two people. Taking turns, each player tries to be first to position four 'rounds' (wooden balls) in a row, horizontally, vertically or diagonally in the 'chutes', while his opponent tries to prevent him.

CARDS With dice, cards were the most important way of passing the time on board a ship, or when pirates were holed up hiding somewhere. Many pirates lost all their booty this way, and were thus condemned to a life of perpetual piracy. Arguments over cards were very common, and arguments among pirates and privateers were settled by a duel, or by the ship's quartermaster.

DICE Dice games were the most popular pursuit among Black Bart Robert's crew, and the frequent quarrels caused by gambling on his ship forced him to get his pirates to abandon them, except on land. *Shut the Box, 'Batten down the Hatches' or Canoga* is an old dice gambling game played at sea, as is *Crown and Anchor* – the classic nautical dice game played with special dice. *Going to Boston* is a fast gambling game, and in *Yacht* players try to make special patterns using five conventional dice.

EYE TO THE MAIN CHANCE
It may be that this phrase originated in the possibility of making vast sums of

The Drunken Sailor

A traditional heaving shanty or chantey, asking the question *'What shall we do with a drunken sailor?'* There are many different versions of the lyrics. Note that *'early'* is often pronounced as *'earl-eye.'*

What shall we do with a drunken sailor, (three times) Early in the morning?

Chorus

Heave-ho and up she rises, (three times) Early in the morning.

Other verses, with the line repeated three times include: *Stick him in a bag and beat him senseless; Put him in the longboat till he's sober; Put him in bed with the captain's daughter; Pull out the* plug and wet him all over; Give 'im the hair of the dog that bit him; Put him in the scuppers with a hosepipe on him; Take 'im and shake 'im and try an' wake 'im; Give 'im a dose of salt and water; Give 'im a taste of the bosun's rope-end; Stick on 'is back a mustard plaster; Soak 'im in oil till he sprouts a flipper; Heave him by the leg in a running bowline; Tie him to the taffrail when she's yardarm under; Shave his belly with a rusty razor; and so on.*

The eventual outro is:

That's what we'll do with a drunken sailor, (three times) Early in the morning. (followed by a long Amen) money privateering in the Spanish Main. More likely it came from the dice game of *Hazard*, in which players throw twice. The first throw is the main throw, and the second is the *'chance'* throw.

FACE (OR BRAG) IT OUT WITH A CARD OF TEN To set upon the enemy, with none too sure an opinion of the outcome. In a card game, a card of ten spots is useful, but not sure to win. This assumption of a bold front would be better with a *'sure card'*, another saying of the time.

FIRESHIP 17th-century maritime slang for a prostitute with venereal disease.

FISHMONGER *'Fishmonger'* meant whore, probably derived from *'fleshmonger'*, and *'fishmonger's daughter'* also came to mean a harlot, from the late 16th century.

THE FOLLY INN The Royal Yacht Squadron has its headquartes in Cowes Castle on the Solent, overlooking the entrance to the River Medina. Just above it on the Medina in the mid-18th century the hull of the deserted *Folly* was pulled up on the foreshore. It was frequented by young rakes for gambling and drinking after they cut a door into its sides. The inn was later built over the hull, but the ship's hull could still be seen through the dining-room floor until 1979.

FRENCH GOODS, FRENCH GOUT Seamen often suffered from this, syphilis. To be *'Frenchified'* was to suffer from venereal disease. *'Frenchman'* was the epithet applied to any foreigner, so anything 'bad' was French. The prevalence of venereal diseases was often the main reason for wanting a doctor on

board, and sometimes ships were taken by pirates just for the contents of their medical chests to treat the illness. Even in recent times VD has been a problem among sailors. The first female MP, Lady Astor, was elected in 1919. She then proposed in Parliament that merchant seamen should wear a yellow armband to identify themselves as potential carriers of venereal disease.

GOOSEY GOOSEY GANDER AND GOOSEBITE Southwark on the Thames in London was where many sailors spent their money in taverns and brothels. Pubs and brothels in many English ports were created by Henry II (reigned 1154–89) to raise revenues for the Crown. By the 16th century, Southwark's biggest brothels were owned by the Bishop of Winchester, who gave discounts to priests. During the Reformation of the 1530s, Henry VIII took over the wealth of the cathedrals and abbeys and church lands, and also the brothels on crown property in his major ports. Prostitutes at the time were known as *'geese'* as they could give you a nasty *'goosebite'*. Goosebite was the term used for any venereal disease. Henry VIII closed down the brothels, so the 'geese' had to ply their trade elsewhere, often in their clients' homes. Thus we get the nursery rhyme:

'Goosey goosey gander
Whither shall I wander?
Upstairs and downstairs
And in my lady's chamber.'

HAZARD, HAZZARD Wildly popular in the Middle Ages and up to the 19th century at sea, this is an old English game played with two dice.

It is mentioned in Chaucer's 14th-century *Canterbury Tales*. The name *'hazard'* derives from the Arabic word *az-zahr*, the plural of dice. Although its rules were complicated, hazard was so popular in the past that it was often played for money. The phrase 'to hazard' can be synonymous with 'to dice', in the sense of taking a chance. In the 19th century, the game *'Craps'* developed from hazard through a simplification of the rules.

HOOKERS This term may have come from the prostitutes who used to frequent that great entrepot of European trading, the Hook of Holland. The most common ship there at one time was the *hooker* (see ship types). Also, in the 19th century, some ships were known as *'old hookers'* by their crews, presumably because they were female and traded for money. Much earlier, in the 16th century, *hookers* were thieves who used a hook to gaff the possessions of their victims in the streets, and ran away with the loot. Perhaps some of these hookers were female.

HORNPIPE This small reeded wind instrument traditionally accompanied sailors' songs and dances, and came to give its name to a sailor's dance, usually in 4/4 time, vigorously performed by a single person. It was popular at sea because of its compact size and ease of playing. Usually arms were kept still, to avoid someone getting shoved overboard. Captain Cook encouraged his men to dance the hornpipe, usually accompanied by a fiddle (rather than a hornpipe), as it kept them fit and also kept boredom at bay on long voyages.

KEEP MUM From the dice game *Mumchance*, similar to *Hazard*, but which had to be played in complete silence. The saying was probably originally *'keep mumchance'*, i.e to keep quiet.

KING ARTHUR A game played in warm climates. A seaman impersonated King Arthur, and he was drenched with buckets of water until he could make one of his tormentors smile, who then exchanged places with him.

Pilot Verses

PILOT VERSES These were sailing directions sung to popular tunes, to memorize navigational information. *'Wadham's Song'* dates from 1756, was sung to the tune of *'I'll Tell Me Ma'*, and was considered the best guide to Newfoundland waters at this time:

From Bonavista to the Cabot Isles
The course is north full 40 miles
When you must steer away nor'-east
Till Cape Freals, Gull Isle, bears west-
*   nor'-west*
Then nor'-nor'-west 33 miles
Three leagues offshore lies Wadham's
*   Isles*
Where of a rock you must beware
Two miles sou'-sou'-east from off
*   isle bear.*

MIND YOUR P's and Q's Sailors received credit at quayside taverns until they were eventually paid. In these blissful pre-metrification days, beer was sold in pints and quarts. The innkeeper kept a record of p's and q's for each debtor, and ensured that they were entered on his account. Some tavern owners would put extra ticks in the pints and quarts columns if they thought the seaman was drunk and would not notice. Thus it was important to be mindful of how many drinks – *p's and q's* – you actually owed.

PROSTITUTES Nowadays called 'sex workers' by the politically correct, these ladies (and sometimes men) were more numerous in ports than elsewhere, waiting for the return of sailors from the sea with full wage-packets. Tiger Bay in Cardiff was known across the world as a hotbed of pubs and brothels. In London the Ratcliffe Highway area included Wapping, Shadwell, Limehouse and St George and was notorious for filthy boarding houses, opium dens, brothels and taverns. So many Orientals settled in Limehouse that it became known as Chinatown. In Jamaica, visitors complained that Port Royal's punch-houses were swarming with *'vile strumpets and common prostitutes'*. In the 17th century, John Starr's brothel there contained 21 white and two black women. The most famous was the 'German Princess', Mary Carleton, who had been convicted of theft and bigamy and transported to Jamaica in 1671. She was returned to London in 1673 to be hanged at Tyburn. Born in Canterbury around 1634, she was a teenage criminal before appearing on the London stage,

where a play, *The German Princess*, was written especially for her. Her two years as a prostitute in Port Royal made some impact – she was described as being *'as common as a barber's chair: no sooner was one out, but another was in. Cunning, crafty, subtle, and hot in the pursuit of her intended designs.'* Ordinary sailors in both the merchant navy and Royal Navy, a huge proportion of them 'impressed' men, were not allowed ashore as they would almost certainly desert their terrible life at sea. Thus the more generous captains allowed their ships to be met by supply boats full of local prostitutes – sometimes 400 coming on board at a time.

RATTLE THE BONES Play dice.

RUM, BUM AND BACCY This was the layman's description of life in the lower decks, where alcohol, homosexuality and tobacco were all said to be popular ways of passing the time.

RUN UP A TAB In dockside taverns, credit would be chalked up *'on the slate'*. 'Tablet' was another word for the writing slate, so unsecured credit was *'chalked up on the tab'*, and the term to have something *'on tick'* or *'on the tab'* also comes from this custom. The loans had then to be paid off to talley-men or to the inn.

SCRIMSHAW Men on whalers passed their time by decoratively carving the teeth of sperm whales, and figuring baleen (whalebone), engraving ornate pictures as presents for their wives and girlfriends. The designs were meticulously scratched into the surface of the bone, then rubbed with ink or stain to make the design stand out. The peak of this type of engraving occurred around 1830–50.

Sea Shanty, Chantey

A song with a definite rhythm, a working song to help men co-ordinate their efforts in pulling ropes and lines. They were also known as *chanteys*, so the origin is probably the word chant. A chanteyman would usually lead the singing, and the crew or work party would join in. Traditional shanties are grouped into different types. 'Short Haul Shanties' were used for tasks requiring quick pulls over a short period of time. 'Halyard Shanties' were used for heavier work with more set-up time between pulls.

'Capstan Shanties' were used for long, repetitive tasks requiring a sustained rhythm, but not involving working the lines. Often merchantmen were undermanned, and singing shanties helped maximize efficiency.

SHOW A LEG, SHAKE A LEG!

The origin of this term, meaning 'get out of bed' or 'stir yourself', is intriguing. In the Royal Navy, the crew were forbidden to leave the ship when in home port for fear they would desert the stinking conditions. As a result their women or *'wives'* were allowed to come on board in the port, and to sleep with the men in their hammocks. The boatswain's mates called the men on deck every morning, and if they saw a hammock with a body still in it shouted *'show a leg!'* If the leg was hairy, the offending crewman was chased to his duties. If it was relatively hairless, the mates allowed the *'wife'* to sleep on. Not until 1840 were women prohibited from sleeping aboard when His Majesty's ships were in their home harbours. The original phrase was *'Shake a leg or else a purser's stocking'*. Thus a naval man would be wearing a stocking, or it would be his mistress/wife.

SKYLARKING

Having fun, or mucking about. During rest periods, sailors raced up and down the rigging. They were often encouraged by the officers as this strenuous activity kept the crew fit. They raced among the skysails, perhaps 100 feet (30 m) above the deck, playing around and showing off their surefooted agility.

SQUEE-JEE BAND

A ship's band for entertainment purposes in the late 19th–early 20th century, mostly made up of concertinas. If you had no-one who could play such an instrument, you might have a *'phoo-phoo band'*, made up of jews' harps.

STEWS

The raucous area of narrow alleyways, gambling dens, taverns and brothels frequented by sailors in port.

ILLNESS AND INJURY AT SEA

AMPUTATION AND A BUCKET OF LIMBS The surgeon usually anaesthetized the patient with rum, and warmed his instruments in a brazier, both to lessen the shock and to sterilize the wound and surgical instruments. Opium was rarely available. John Woodall in *The Surgeon's Mate* (1617) wrote: *'It is no small presumption to dismember the image of God'*. The amputee had to give his consent and he was then held down by at least two men. The dismembering saws were kept wrapped in oil-cloths so as not to be rusty. John Ballet, the surgeon on one of William Dampier's circumnavigations of the globe, *'with a steady hand and good speed, cut off Flesh, Sinewes and all to the Bone.'* Leaving flaps of skin, he sawed through the bone, sewed the flaps together, staunched the bleeding with cotton and propped the stump high on a pillow. Limbs were placed in a bucket for throwing overboard. Samuel Leech recorded a bitter fight between HMS *Macedonian* and USS *United States* in 1812 – *'The surgeon and his mate were seared in blood from head to foot. They looked more like butchers than doctors. Having so many patients, they removed them to the ward-room, and the long table, around which the officers had sat over many a merry feast, was soon covered with the bleeding forms of maimed and mutilated seamen.'*

BLOODY FLUX Common on ships and apt to spread like wildfire, this was dysentery accompanied by a bloody discharge. Diseases spread quickly on ships even today. In the 17th and 18th centuries the various 'prescriptions' recommended for the bloody flux included anise or quinces, grated nutmeg, laudanum or sitting on hot bricks. Blood-letting was also practised.

CAISSON DISEASE – THE BENDS This medical condition was first diagnosed when it was contracted by divers during the construction of caissons (foundations) for the Brooklyn Bridge between 1869 and 1893. It later came to be known as 'decompression sickness', more popularly *'the bends'*.

DROPSY Old naval term for oedema, internal swelling with water retention. Most common around the feet and ankles, it can affect the whole body.

SEASICKNESS, MAL DE MER It is believed that 80 per cent of the world's population is susceptible to seasickness. Most will overcome the symptoms after spending several days at sea.

SHIP FEVER This was typhus or other forms of infectious disease, especially those transmitted by fleas, lice or mites. Patients suffered from severe headache, sustained high fever, depression, delirium

Scurvy – The Scourge of the Sea

In 1593, Captain Richard Hawkins noted that sour oranges and lemons were the best treatment for scurvy (scorbutum), but not until 1795 did Royal Navy vessels routinely carry lemon juice to combat this disease. Later far cheaper lime juice replaced lemon, from which the American slang *'limey'* for British immigrants or visitors derived. With no fresh fruit or vegetables, scurvy had been endemic on long voyages. It also caused shipwrecks because crews were made so weak by lack of vitamin C that they sunk into a dull lethargy from which they could not be shaken. Symptoms began with swollen gums, then loss of teeth, a weakened heart and black blotches beneath the skin, before a sailor sank into a final exhausted torpor with glazed eyes and swollen addomen and legs. Wounds would not heal, and there was the pain of spontaneous haemorrhaging into muscles and joints. Gasping for breath like floundered fish, the blood vessels around a victim's brain eventually ruptured and he died. In 1636, John Woodall wrote in *The Surgeon's Mate* that daily orange juice was the antidote. During Admiral George

Anson's round-the-world expedition of 1740–4, 1051 of his 1955 men died of scurvy. In 1747 Dr James Lind re-established the fact that vitamin C prevented scurvy. In 1779 some 2400 seamen were admitted into shore hospitals suffering from scurvy after the Channel Fleet had been on a ten-week cruise. An estimated 800,000 British seamen needlessly died from scurvy before the Royal Navy began carrying citrus juice in 1795. Merchant vessels, unbelievably, only adopted the practice in 1854.

and the eruption of red skin rashes. Also known as *'gaol fever'* (as it was endemic in overcrowded, squalid prisons), it was often brought on ship by men who had been impressed from prisons. Combined with *'the bloody flux'* it was often deadly.

SMALLPOX This disease exterminated whole tribes of Africans, Native North Americans and South American Indians when introduced by the white man. A terrible epidemic in Boston in 1721 affected half of its 10,000 population,

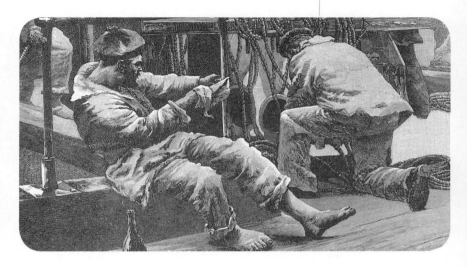

and the preacher Cotton Mather recounted how the Africans dealt with the disease in their homelands. Their remedy was to cut open a healthy person's skin and put some of the pus from the disease into this wound. On 26 June 1721, Dr Zabdiel Boylston inoculated his small son and two of his slaves with smallpox, to the horror of the city elders. The treatment was a success. Around the same time smallpox was rife in London and Lady Mary Wortley Montagu convinced the Princess of Wales to support inoculation experiments. She asked the king to pardon six convicts if they would submit to inoculation, and they were treated on 9 August by Dr Charles Maitland. The treatment worked. Not until 1796 did Dr Edward Jenner inoculate with a cowpox lesion and the disease become preventable.

SYPHILIS This was known as *'the great pox'* in the 15th century, and the variola virus was called *'the small pox'* to differentiate it. It was called the 'French disease' in England, Italy and Germany, and the 'Italian disease' in France. The Dutch called it the 'Spanish disease', and the Russians called it the 'Polish disease'. The Turks called it the 'Christian disease' and the Tahitians the 'British disease'. The national names are indicative of the fact that the disease was often spread by foreign sailors during unprotected sexual contact with local prostitutes. In its early stages, the great pox produced a rash similar to smallpox but smallpox was a far more deadly disease.

YELLOW JACK, YELLOW FLAG
Tropical fever or yellow fever, which turned the victims yellow with jaundice and made them spew up black vomit. The *'Yellow Jack'* was therefore a flag flown by ships to indicate that there was disease aboard. *'Yellow Jack'* was also a particularly nasty term of abuse hurled at someone a seaman did not like. Sometimes a ship might hoist the yellow jack to pretend there was serious illness aboard to ward off an attack.

FOOD AT SEA

ADMIRALTY HAM A term for any canned meat.

BANYAN DAYS Queen Elizabeth I introduced this cost-saving measure in her navy – meatless days where fish or cheese were served instead. The slang name came from the custom of Hindu seamen refusing to eat meat.

BELLY TIMBER This is a term for food, especially meat. *'There can be no adventure without belly timber'* was a saying of the 18th century.

BREADFRUIT A tropical fruit in the Pacific Islands. The pulp is starchy and edible, which may possibly be mistaken for the taste of bread.

BULLY BEEF Meat such as pork and beef was packed into barrels and covered with salt to preserve it at sea. Salt beef was sometimes boiled to make it edible, and the French *'boeuf bouillé'* became *'bully beef'*. Sometimes the meat was too tough to eat, and seamen made snuff boxes or ornaments out of it to pass the

time. It was in the interest of the ship's cook to boil meat extremely well, as all the accumulated fat and grease could be used by the cook to sell for making tallow or candles, a perk of his job.

BURGOO Oatmeal, boiled and seasoned with butter, sugar and salt – a gruel similar to porridge. It was easy for anyone to prepare this in the ship's galley, even in the roughest seas, and it had enough sustenance to help with the hard work aboard ship. Mariners uniformly hated it. It was first mentioned in 1656 by Edward Cox in *Adventures by Sea*. Burgoo could also be a mixture of crushed hard tack and molasses.

CACKLING FART, CACKLE FRUIT An egg. A 'cackling cheat' was any type of fowl. A 'cackler' was a blabber who gave away secrets.

CANKY A standard native meal for the men serving on the Guinea Coast. It was Indian meal and water or palm-wine, baked to make bread and cakes, or boiled to make cakes.

CANTEEN MEDALS Naval name for stains down the front of jumper, jacket or coat caused by dropped food or drink.

CORNISH DUCK Comic slang for pilchard, so common off Cornwall.

CRACKERJACK A combination of preserved meat and broken biscuits served at sea. *'Dandyfunk'* was another dish, which was composed of broken biscuits and molasses.

DOGSBODY Meals made from passengers' leftovers mixed with ship's biscuits were known as dogsbody. This poor-quality food was fed to people of the lowest status onboard, who then became known as dogsbodies. Another form of dogsbody was sea biscuits, or hard tack, soaked in water to a pulp, with added sugar.

DOUGHBOYS Hard dumplings made of a quarter-pound of flour and boiled in seawater, described in William Dampier's *Voyages* of 1697. They were still standard fare in the Royal Navy in 1897.

FISH AND BROCCOLI AND CANCER
Tuna and halibut contain selenium, the mineral which raises levels of the cancer-fighting enzyme, thioredoxin reductase. Broccoli contains the compound sulforaphane which has the same effect. The Institute of Food Research in Norwich has shown that when combined, fish and broccoli are 13 times more effective at slowing the growth of cancer cells than when eaten individually. If broccoli is not available, Brussels sprouts, cauliflower, kale and cabbage also contain quantities of sulforaphane, but a meal consisting of sprouts, cabbage and fish is not a particularly appetizing ensemble, unfortunately.

HARDTACK Biscuits baked without salt in a hot oven, also called sea biscuits, which were taken on long voyages as they resisted spoilage.

HARNESS CASK The tub in which salt meat was soaked before being cooked, in order to extract the brine in which the meat had been pickled; also known as the *'steep tub'*. The name is said to have been introduced by cynical mariners either because they felt the harness was the only part of the horse not in the tub, or else from the leathery nature of the meat.

HORSE BEANS *'Horse beans'* were fed to slaves on the *'Middle Passage'* from Africa to the Americas. Very large beans, they were used as animal fodder in Europe, and to make them semi-edible for humans, they were pulped then covered with *'slabber sauce'*, made from palm oil, flour, water and red pepper. William Williams, the author of *The Journal of Penrose, Seaman*, was fed horse beans when he was a prisoner of the Spanish at Havana.

HOTCHPOTCH, HOTCHPOT, HODGEPODGE This expression has been corrupted to 'hodgepodge' over the years. In Anglo-French, it was used to describe a dish made in a single pot in which many ingredients were mixed. It was usually a mutton broth or stew, with vegetables. The origin appears to have been from the Old French *'hocher'* (to shake) and *pot*. Thus ingredients were mixed or shaken up in a large cooking pot. During the 13th century, it came to refer to the process of gathering and sharing equally cargo that had been damaged and strewn about after the collision of two ships. (Both ships were to blame, so the salvage was shared jointly between the owners). The remaining goods were, by the process of *hotchpot*, divided equally between the owners of the two vessels, based on the premise that both ships contributed to the loss. The term is now synonymous with confusion and disorder, a jumble.

HUMBLE PIE The origin of this term is that *'umble'* was the intestines of deer. The master ate pie made with venison – muscle meat – while the servants ate *'umble pie'*.

JERKY What Americans call today *'beef jerky'* were strips of meat called *'viande boucanée'* and what English buccaneers called 'jerked meat' after the American-Spanish *'charqui'*. Hard and dry as a board after being slowly smoked in the *'boucanes'*, they were sold by the Tortuga boucaniers in bundles of a hundred, for six pieces of eight. They were essential for crew in the tropics.

JUNK Salt beef or *'salt horse'* was extremely stringy, coming from poor and tough cuts of meat. Junk was a type of bulrush from which rope was made. Thus salt horse also was known as *junk*, something of poor quality, from which we get the modern meaning.

KETCHUP This thick spicy tomato sauce may take its name from the Malay word *kēchap*, and possibly also a similar word in Cantonese. *Kēchap* was a sauce, but one without tomatoes, containing fish brine, herbs, and spices. Sailors seem to have brought the sauce to Europe, where it was made with locally available ingredients, such as the juice of

mushrooms or walnuts. At some time, when the juice of tomatoes was first used, ketchup as we know it was born. In the 18th and 19th centuries ketchup was a generic term for sauces whose only common ingredient was vinegar. The word is first recorded in English in 1690 in the form *catchup*, in 1711 in the form *ketchup*, and in 1730 in the form *catsup*.

LAVER BREAD The seaweed called laver or purple laver is also known as black butter, purple sea-vegetable, or sloke, and its Latin name is *Porphyra umbilicalis*. In Chinese it is jee choy; in Gaelic it is sleabchan, sleabhach, or sleadai; in Swedish it is veckad purpurtang. However it is best known, culinarily, as nori, the dried sheets of seaweed used to wrap maki-type sushi. It is harvested in winter at low tide, and is found attached to vertical surfaces, such as rocks or piers. Laver is prepared in the UK by slow simmering, for as long as five hours, to form a thick gelatinous purée, and is available in cans or loose from south Wales markets. Known as *Bara Lawr* in Wales, is usually served with bacon and/or cockles, the bacon being from the back, not the side of the pig.

LOBLOLLY Porridge, pottage or gruel, another word for burgoo.

LOBSCOUSE, 'SCOUSE A stew of small bits of salt meat, broken ship's biscuits, potatoes, onions and spices. Because of the poverty of Liverpool, something similar was a common dish in the city, and the modern slang for a Liverpudlian, 'scouser', comes from this dish. The origin of the word is the Welsh *'lobscaws'*, and many poor Welsh families settled there, looking for work.

Food Slang in the Navy

For some of this, you will need a *'can spanner'* (tin opener). Food is often referred to as *'scran'*, which you eat in the galley or mess. *'Horlicks'* is not the popular bedtime drink, but a major cock-up or mess, probably a linguistic softening of 'bollocks', which itself sounds like a nasty disease. The quality of naval food and drink depends on the *pusser* (purser), the *'jam bosun'* (victualling officer) and the *'custard bosun'* (chief cook). The wardroom steward is a *'soup jockey'*. A hungry Royal Marine could *'eat a horse between two hammocks'* or alternatively *'a cow between two bread vans'*. To eat, Marines use *'gobbling rods'* (cutlery), known to others at sea as *'eating irons'*, *'scran spanners'*, *'port and starboard oars'*, *'KFS'* (knife, fork, spoon), *'yaffling irons'* and *'fighting gear'*. An old term for the mouth was *'grub-trap'*. Common food terms are, and were, as follows:

365 or 'Marines' Breakfast' – bacon and eggs, available every day of the year.

Acting rabbit – baked meat pie.

Adam and Eve on a raft – two fried eggs on toast.

Arrigones – tinned Italian tomatoes, from the brand of an early supplier of the cans.

Awning – pastry pie crust.

Babies' heads – tinned, individual steak and kidney pudding or dumplings.

Ballerina shit – pink blancmange.

Banjo – sandwich made from a French loaf. An 'egg banjo' includes a fried egg.

Barney Clark (US) – burger topped with a fried egg, named after the first man to receive an artificial heart.

Bathing beauty – blancmange, because it shivers and has lovely curves.

Beagle balls – rissoles (when the Second World War started, the pack of beagles at Dartmouth Naval College was put down, and there were rissoles on the menu that night).

Beetle bait – treacle or jam.

BITS – beans in tomato sauce.

Black-coated workers – stewed prunes, possibly because in appearance they resemble cockroaches.

Bonsai trees – broccoli spears.

Brown neutralizer – HP brown sauce twinned with tomato sauce.

Bully beef – corned beef.

Bunny food, bunny grub – lettuce or green salad ingredients.

Burgoo – porridge.

Cackleberries – boiled hens' eggs.

Cannon balls (US) – baked, candied apples served to midshipmen at the Naval Academy on special occasions.

Chow (US) – food. Chow down – eat.

Car smash – tomato sauce or tinned tomatoes with bacon, resembling blood and body bits.

Cardiff virgin – Welsh rarebit.

Cheese possessed – Royal Marine term for 'processed cheese' found in their 'rat packs' (ration packs).

Cheese 'ush – cheese and onion quiche, the edge pastry being known as 'guardrails'.

Cheesy hammy eggy topsides – cheese, ham and an egg on toast.

Chinese wedding cake – rice pudding with currants or raisins in it.

Chinky nosh – Chinese food.

Clacker – the pastry crust on a pie.

Comanche bollocks – tinned plum tomatoes.

Corn, corned dog – corned beef.

Cow pie – steak pie, from the comic book character Desperate Dan's favourite meal, with the horns sticking out from the dish cover.

Cowboy meal – bacon and tomatoes.

Crowdie – cold mixed oatmeal and milk, or oatmeal and boiled water with treacle, butter or sugar.

Crunchy pasty – not eaten these days, but a turtle or tortoise.

Curry mush – shin beef, much used disguised in curries.

Deep sea steak – kipper.

Dog's body – pease pudding in the Royal Navy, dried peas boiled in a cloth.

Doughboys – from dough-balls, hard dumplings boiled in salt water.

Duff – pudding, so figgy duff is the slang for fig pudding, plummy duff is plum pudding etc.

Dynamited chicken (US) – chicken à la King or chicken cacciatore.

Elephant's footprints – spam fritters covered with batter and then deep fried for breakfast.

Figgie-dowdie – West Country pudding made with raisins, and also plum-pudding made with figs and dough.

Fishes' eyes – tapioca.

Fartleberries – baked beans.

Flightdeck buzzard (US) – chicken.

Floaters in the snow – sausage on mashed potatoes.

Flummery – a dish made from oatmeal, or soured oats.

Frog in a bog – toad in the hole.

Forty fathom duff – very stodgy steamed suet pudding.

Fu-fu – a well-known dish in the merchant navy which consisted of barley and treacle.

Gammies – raisins.

Geedunk (US) – candy.

Glitter – marmalade or jam.

Grease – butter or margarine.

Grenade – Scotch egg.

Growler – pork pie.

Gyppos or Jippers – gravy.

Harbour cotters – fish steaks in batter.

Hasty pudding – a batter made with flour or oatmeal stirred in boiling water, eaten with treacle or sugar.

Herrings in – as HITS.

HITS – herrings in tomato sauce.

Hockey pucks (US) – Swedish meatballs. Also known as 'trail markers', 'porcupines' or 'road apples'.

Horse potatoes – old name for yams.

Italian teabags – ravioli.

Jam wedge – jam sandwich (not sarnie).

Jockanese cackleberries – Scotch eggs.

Joe, cup of Joe (US) – a cup of coffee. Josephus Daniels (1862–1948), Woodrow Wilson's Secretary of the Navy, abolished the officers' wine mess in 1914, so the strongest drink aboard Navy ships could only be coffee.

Landmine – a hard bun.

Mad dog's vomit, MDV – mixed vegetable salad or sandwich spread.

Manchester slut – derived from Manchester tart, a pastry covered with jam, then a layer of lemon curd custard and then sprinkled with desiccated coconut powder.

Musical veg – baked beans and/or peas.

Mousetrap – basic Cheddar cheese.

Mrs B – named after Mrs Beeton, tinned duff or sponge pudding.

Mungy – naval slang for food, perhaps from the French *'manger'*, to eat.

Mystery meat (US) – term given to chicken, pork or beef (and sometimes fish) when completely unidentifiable by sight or taste.

Nelson's dandruff – salt.

Nuts, Midshipman's nuts – broken bits of ship's biscuits, eaten to round off a meal, so called because they were as small as a boy's testicles.

Nuts and bolts – lamb stew, because there were always pieces of bone in it.

Nuts and bolts with an awning – old description of steak and kidney pie cooked on ship rather than opened from a tin.

Nutty – chocolate, whether it contains nuts or not.

One-eyed steak – kipper.

Oosh, hoosh, hush, open air pie – well-spiced dish of diced meat, onions and vegetables, cooked in an oven. If there is a pastry cover, it becomes 'oosh with an awning'.

Pea-do – pea soup.

Pigskin pie – a fatty bacon roll.

Pink lint – Spam or any other luncheon meat.

Pipes – macaroni.

PITS – pilchards in tomato sauce.

PLM – Spam (plastic luncheon meat).

Pot mess – nourishing stew kept continually cooking, to which vegetables and other ingredients are constantly being added. A 'mess of pottage' has the same origin.

Pozzie – old sailor's slang for marmalade or jam.

Ratpack – tinned rations, ration packs in the Marines. An 'Arctic ratpack' is for freezing conditions and contains dehydrated and foil-wrapped rations.

RBG – rich brown gravy.

Red lead, Red – canned tomatoes or tomato sauce.

Ring stinger – extremely hot vindaloo or fal curry.

Roller (US) – hot dog, also known as 'tube steak' or 'dangling sirloin'.

Rudolph (US) – reindeer meat, which was also known as 'radioactive Rudolph' when it was brought onboard in Scandinavian ports soon after the Chernobyl meltdown.

Salad gear – the bunny grub, celery, tomatoes etc. that make up a salad.

Sarnie – probably of Liverpudlian provenance, a sandwich.

Schooner on the rocks – a piece of roast meat surrounded by potatoes.

Seggies – grapefruit segments.

Snake and pigmy – steak and kidney pie.

Shithouse flap valves – hamburgers.

Sinker – suet dumpling.

Slide – butter or margarine.

Sliders (US) – hamburgers, so named for their high grease content.

Slingers and gyppo – sausages served with gravy.

Smeggers – semolina pudding.

Soft Tommy, soft tack – old name for bread when it was given out instead of biscuits or hard tack.

Spithead pheasant – kipper.

Spring-loaded chicken – rabbit.

Tiddy oggy – Cornish pasty, also traditionally the term for a seaman born in Devonport.

TITS – tomatoes in tomato sauce.

Torbay steaks – to submariners, these are faggots, after the exploits of a notable homosexual on HMS *Torbay*.

Train smash – as car smash, but adding sausages.

Trelawney – old dish of barley-meal, water and salt.

Tum-tum – West Indian dish of boiled plantain cooked into a paste and fried.

Whales – sardines.

Worms in red lead – tinned spaghetti in tomato sauce.

Yellow peas – sweet corn.

Yellow peril – smoked haddock.

MARINE APHRODISIACS

An aphrodisiac causes the arousal of sexual desire. The word derives from the Greek goddess of love Aphrodite. Items from the seas and shorelines with such a reputation include the sea holly *(Eryngium maritimum)*, clams, hagfish, mudskipper and oysters. It is possible that diets in the past were nutritionally deficient in zinc, but people would eat zinc-rich oysters and their overall health would improve, leading to an increased sex drive. Turtle eggs, eaten raw with salt and lime juice, are also said to be an aphrodisiac, leading to the poaching of many turtles, which are cut up to extract their eggs. Caviar is the eggs of sturgeon which contain a lot of beneficial vitamins. Being rich in phosphorus, caviar is very nourishing to nerve cells, and again is supposed to be an aphrodisiac.

MESS From the Anglo-Saxon *mese*, table, the space where the crew ate and slept. A mess means a quantity of food for a table, or the provision of food, from which the ship's mess possibly gets its name. It is applied to a part of the ship's company that eats together, (such as the officers' mess) and, by extension, the place where they eat. On passenger liners, the passengers may still eat in dining rooms, but the crew eats in the mess.

NELSON'S SEAMEN'S DIET

Victualling yards in Portsmouth, Plymouth, Great Yarmouth and Deptford (London) supplied the fleet. A typical breakfast was 'burgoo' – boiled oatmeal seasoned with salt, sugar and butter, along with 'Scots coffee' – hard-baked ship's biscuits burnt to a charcoal, then crushed and mixed with hot water. Lunch was stew with salt beef, pork or fish, and whatever vegetables were available – some dried and reconstituted. In the evening there were ship's biscuits (full of weevils which were banged out by hungry sailors) with butter and cheese. Sailors also had tots of rum, and around eight pints of beer a day.

PASSENGER MENUS For those passengers with money, food at sea in the early part of the 20th century was of a reasonable standard. There were several courses, and it is interesting how 'cauliflower cheese' sounds much better when described as *'choux-fleurs en branches au fromage'*. The following is a dinner menu from the Orient Line's SS *Otranto* on a cruise to the Norwegian fjords, 1 August 1927:

Consommé vert-pre or Potage crème d'argenteuil

Barbe sauce aux crevettes

Cotelettes de chevreuil à la milanaise or Choux-fleurs en branches au fromage

Melon sorbet

Poached chicken

Blackcurrant pudding or Baked vanilla custards or Arctic chocolates

Sardine and tomato croutes

Cold Sideboard
Cumberland ham and roast sirloin of beef and salad

In the SS *Great Britain*, a cow was given a cabin on deck as she was needed to provide milk for the passengers' tea. In 1864, a passenger made a note of the other animals that the ship carried.

The list included three bullocks, 150 sheep, 30 pigs, 500 chickens, 400 ducks, 100 geese, 50 turkeys, and enough hay, root vegetables and cattle feed to keep them fed until needed for the table. The icehouse only kept meat fresh for a few days after leaving port. The law required that the crew and steerage passengers must be fed a basic ration of staple foods such as oats, dried peas, ship's biscuits and bread. However, a passenger travelling first-class could expect far better. In 1852 one wrote: *'I have had two meals, breakfast which was very nice, coffee, meat, eggs and dinner which was first-rate, quite such as you would get at the best hotels: soup, grouse, pigeon and veal pies, pork, ham and other meat dishes, sundry puddings and tarts and jelly, blancmange, cheese, celery and after all a dessert.'*

Provisions for a Liner

Victualling a transatlantic liner was a mammoth logistical exercise. For a single voyage, the RMS *Oceanic*, cruising for the White Star line between 1899 and 1914, needed the following provisions: 200 barrels (17.5 tons) of flour for making bread and pastry; 50,000 lb (22,680 kg) of fresh beef and mutton (requiring the slaughter of 66 bullocks and 283 sheep); 12,000 lb (5450 kg) of lamb, pork and veal; four tons of poultry and game; two tons of smoked and dried meat; 5000 lb (2268 kg) butter; 2000 eggs; 3000 quarts of milk and cream; 3000 quarts of ice cream; 10,000 lb (4536 kg) of sugar; 2500 lb (1134 kg) oatmeal; 46 tons potatoes; and tons of other vegetables and fruit. There were also drinks, crockery, cutlery, towels, table linen etc. to bring on board, and 20 men were kept constantly in service washing and drying the finer china and silver. In 1703, at Kinsale, Captain William Dampier had the *St George*

provisioned with the staple diet of bread, meat, cheese and a gallon of beer a day for the men. Beer was brewed far stronger, to keep better at sea. Rum, arak, brandy and claret were also loaded on board. Water was only used for cooking, and acted as ballast in the lower tier of casks in the hold. There were also casks of butter, and of Suffolk cheese. This hard cheese was made from skimmed milk and was supposed to last six months without spoiling. Beef and pork were salted twice, and crammed into casks. The casks were then topped up with *'bloody pickle'*, made by boiling, de-scumming and clarifying the meat juices. Live bullocks, geese, ducks, hens, pigs and goats were loaded on board to provide fresh meat, and their faeces covered the decks. Dampier carried cats on board to keep down the rats, and dogs for hunting when they were on land. There was also rice, oatmeal, biscuits, dried peas and currants, but no greens or citrus fruits.

RED HOUSE BISCUITS King Henry III chose Deptford-on-Thames as the Royal Navy's dockyard, and many famous warships were built there. The Red House was rebuilt in 1685, along with other huge Thames-side store-houses, and it became the Navy's official victualling yard in 1742. The hard *'Red House Biscuits'*, 'hard tack', became the staple diet of sailors.

SALAMAGUNDY, SALMAGUNDI This food was the last dish Black Bart was eating, with a captured merchant captain, before the Royal Navy attacked him. Its name could reflect the French *'salemine'*, meaning highly salted or seasoned. The basic variety consisted of *'Poor John'* (salt fish) boiled with onions. It could also include chopped meat, eggs and anchovies – whatever was available, in fact. The most luxurious version had meat, turtle, fish and shellfish marinated in spices, herbs, garlic, palm hearts, spiced wine and oil, and was served with cabbage, grapes, olives, pickled onions and hard-boiled eggs. The term seems to have come from the French *'salmigondis'*, a communal meat stew to which any available vegetables were added.

SALT HORSE, SALT JUNK Slang for the salt beef carried in casks of brine water. The meat was usually too tough to recognize as beef, so sailors believed that anything might have been thrown in the casks. Because it was kept in a barrel called a *'harness cask'* sailors had the idea of a 'horse' in its harness.

SCOTCH COFFEE Also known as *'lobscouse'*, this was the ubiquitous salt beef, boiled up with ship's biscuits, potatoes, onions and some vinegar.

SEA DUST American slang for salt.

SEA PIE Ship's biscuits between layers of meat or fish and vegetables, hearty fare for rough, cold weather. The number of crusts allow it to be designated a two or three-decker.

SEA TURTLES These were captured and kept on deck in the Caribbean and elsewhere, turned on their backs and shaded from the sun. They provided a useful source of fresh meat. The ready availability of green turtles in the West Indies in effect helped the spread of piracy, as they could be kept for weeks on deck until ready to be eaten. However, the leatherback turtle was inedible, and the hawksbill turtle unpleasant to taste. Green turtles were the only vegetarian turtle, and made a superb soup when laced with sherry (see also page 338).

SHIP'S BISCUITS (HARD TACK) Bread would not keep on long voyages, so biscuits were made with flour and the minimum of water or milk, moulded into flat cakes and packed tightly into canvas bags. The technique of making hard tack gave us the expression *'that really takes the biscuit'*. Hard tack should last for up to a year after being baked. The biscuits quickly became infested with a type of black-headed weevil (called *'bargemen'* for some reason). As a result, before any sailor ate a biscuit, he tapped it as a precaution on the table to knock the weevils out of it. Leavened bread was referred to as *'soft tack'*.

SKILLYGOLEE, SKILLY, SKILLYGALLEE When salt meat was boiled to make it edible, the water was then mixed with oatmeal to make a savoury broth or thick soup. It was served to naval prisoners, and prisoners-of-war kept in hulks. Skillygolee, or skillygallee, later became the name for an oatmeal drink sweetened with sugar (in place of cocoa) consumed by seamen during the Napoleonic Wars (1803–15).

SPOTTED DOG In 1805, Admiral Nelson wrote from HMS *Minotaur* to the purser on HMS *Ajax*, a week before the Battle of Trafalgar. He wanted more raisins and suet, probably to make a hearty meal of spotted dick, then known as spotted dog as it had the appearance of a Dalmatian's skin when cooked. Others say that the name of this steamed suet pudding with raisins comes from spotted dough. Suet is the raw fat from beef or mutton, and thus full of calories needed for energy. Some say that spotted dick has raisins throughout the pudding while spotted dog has raisins just on the outside.

SQUARE MEAL Meals were served on square wooden platters, which could be more easily and securely stowed in a rack than round dishes. When weather conditions were poor, sailors were constantly working, eating food from their pockets, being *'lucky to get a square meal'*. These wooden platters were often not filled, as food ran short, but those who had been working especially hard were given a *'square meal'* filling the dish as a reward. It seems that *'fair and square'* also had this nautical origin, when all the crew had a fair meal, with the platters being filled to their corners. *'Clean your plate before you have your dessert'* comes from the use of square plates. The meat course was wiped off with bread, and the platter turned over for the sweet, if there was any.

(THREE) SQUARE MEALS A DAY Living conditions aboard British warships in the 1700s and 1800s were poor. A sailor's breakfast and lunch were sparse meals usually only consisting of bread and a beverage. However, the third meal of the day contained meat and was served on a square dish. Hence the *'square meal'* was the most substantial meal served. Therefore if one has three square meals a day, one is considered to be eating very well.

STAR-GAZY PIE The tiny harbour of Mousehole in Cornwall was battered by storms so badly that no boat could get out and its people were starving. Legend has it that local resident Tom Bawcock went out in the huge storm and brought back seven species of fish. Tom Bawcock's Eve is celebrated every 23 December with a famous dish commemorating the event. A dish is served with a pastry crust, out of which peer the heads of seven different types of fish. Often it is made with only pilchards, but there are dozens of different recipes.

SWEET FANNY ADAMS – CANNED MUTTON This dates from 1867, when a little eight-year-old girl named Fanny Adams was found dismembered and mutilated. Her murderer, Frederick Baker, cut her up and left the pieces of her body in a field in Alton, Hampshire. At this time the Royal Navy was first issued with canned mutton, and it became staple diet aboard its ships. Of poor quality, it came to be known as Fanny Adams, and then mockingly as *'sweet Fanny Adams'*. Her grave can still be seen in Alton. *'Fanny'* also became slang for a cooking pot.

DRINK AND THE MARINER

ARRACK, ARAK A very potent liquor brewed from rice, sugar and coconut juice. The home-made hooch, arrack, made from coconuts in the West Indies, was particularly strong. In modern Lebanon, the strong alcohol arak has an aniseed taste.

BAWDY HOUSE BOTTLE A term for a very small-sized bottle of alcohol. This probably derives from the brothels (bawdy houses) making excessive money on selling alcohol.

BEER Before brandy or rum was drunk by sailors, beer was the accepted ration drink provided. In their days the celebrated English navigators Hawkins and Frobisher said that they could cruise as long as the beer lasted. However, the beer was often poor. William Thompson addressed an *'appeal to the public to prevent the Navy being supplied with pernicious provisions'* (1761). The beer *'stands as abominably as the foul stagnant water which is pumped out of many cellars in London at the midnight hour and the sailors were under the necessity of shutting their eyes and stopping their breath by holding their noses before they could conquer their aversion so as to prevail upon themselves in their extreme necessities to drink it.'*

BLACK FOOD Guinness, also known as *'African lager'* because of its strong sales in Nigeria as a supposed alternative to Viagra as an aphrodisiac.

BLACK STRAP A lethal combination of rum, molasses and chowder beer, reported to be the favourite tipple of Black Bart Roberts's crew. The quaintly named member of his 'House of Lords', Valentine Ashplant, was in charge of making alcohol on Bart's pirate ships. Later in the 18th century it was the pejorative term for thick, sweet port, also known as *'black stripe'*. Bad quality port, served to invalids, was also known as *black strap*, as were any rough, dark Mediterranean wines.

BOULEPONGUES A 17th-century drink which was supposed to have killed many Europeans in India, made from arrack, sugar, lemon juice and *'muscadine'*. The word may be a corruption of 'bowl of punch'.

BUMBOO, BOMBO Along with rumfustian, the favoured alcoholic beverage on the pirate base of New Providence, it was a mix of rum, water, nutmeg and sugar. Because all the ingredients were readily available, it was quick to make, and undeniably effective, becoming the common drink of Caribbean sailors.

CRACKING A BOTTLE

This familiar modern slang, as in 'let's crack a bottle of wine', stems from the days when pirates captured ships containing alcohol. In their eagerness to drink, corkscrews were not necessary as the heads of the bottles were cracked off against the nearest hard surface, or sliced off with the blade of a cutlass.

THE ETIQUETTE OF DRINKING

PORT In the Royal Navy, the port or Madeira decanters are unstoppered, passed always to the left, and then stoppered, before the Loyal Toast is drunk. This practice suggests that the wine is served only for that purpose. The origin of the custom of passing the port always to the left is uncertain. It may be symbolic of the movement of the Earth in turning towards the Sun which ripens the grape.

FLIP A strong pirate 'cocktail' of small beer, brandy and sugar, heated with a red-hot iron, popular from the 17th century onwards. *'Small beer'* was a light or watered beer, and *flip* seems to have been derived from the name Philip. However, others believe that it was introduced by Admiral Cloudesley Shovel. The pirate captain, Henry Every, was described as *'lolling at Madagascar with some drunken sunburnt whore, over a can of flip'*.

GROG Alcohol, usually Jamaica rum. We still say we are *'feeling groggy'* today if we are not very well – this refers to the frequency of hangovers in the 17th and 18th centuries when privateers and pirates used to carouse between and during voyages *'on the account'*. In the Royal Navy, rum replaced brandy as the daily ration because of its cheap and plentiful availability from newly conquered Jamaica. However, in 1740 Admiral Vernon directed that the rum should be diluted with water, because of drunkenness in the fleet. The daily pint of rum was replaced by adding two pints of water (a quart), and the grog was dispensed twice during the day instead of just at one time. As the rum in those days could easily be 60 per cent proof and more, it is no wonder that some crews were incapable of action if they drank a pint quickly. The origin of the name *'grog'* was that Admiral Vernon was known as *'Old Grog'* as he habitually wore overcoats made of grogram. Grogram was a coarse fabric of silk mixed with wool or mohair, often stiffened with gum. The rum mix was further weakened to three parts water to one part rum later. Drunken sailors were punished until the early 20th century by having *'six water grog'*, their allowance diluted with six parts water instead of three parts. Grog (in decreasing quantities) was served in the Royal Navy until the last *'grog ration'* – one part rum to three parts water – issued twice a day to sailors in half-pint measures, was drunk on 30 July 1970

HOGSHEAD A large cask (barrel) used generally for shipping wine and spirits, as well as tobacco, sugar and molasses. As a measure for beer or cider it is 54 gallons (245 litres). A statute of King Richard III in 1483 fixed a hogshead of wine at 63 wine-gallons, or 52.5 Imperial gallons (239 litres). The word seems to derive from the Dutch *oxehoved* or the Old Swedish *oxhooft*, meaning ox's head, and it was corrupted to hogshead over time.

Drink Slang in the Navy

Terms for drink include:

Abu Dhabi, Hadji (US) – refers to any product labelled in Arabic aboard a ship, particularly cans of drink.

Acey-Deucey Club (US) – facility serving alcohol for first and second class petty officers.

Adam's ale – drinking water.

Apple Jack (US) – slang for 21-day wine made out of bug juice (q.v.), sugar and yeast. Applejack(ed) means extremely intoxicated.

Apples – rough cider, scrumpy.

Beer day (US) – on many ships, all hands are given two beers if they are underway without a port call for a given period of time, generally 45 days. Both beers are opened when they are given to the crewmember to prevent them from being hoarded.

Bilge juice (US) – illegal alcoholic beverage created while on long deployments by fermenting yeast, water and sugar.

Black strap – cheap Mediterranean wine.

Brew – the urn from which a 'wet of tea' is poured.

Bubbly – rum.

Bug juice (US) – Kool-Aid-like beverage in dispensers on the mess deck. Also the nickname given to the powdered drink served with MREs (meals-ready-to-eat).

Car smash – brandy and champagne mixed in a cocktail.

Dead steam – water.

Electric lemonade – very strong lager.

Fogram – any poor quality wine, spirit or ale. Too much fogram would make one *'foggy'* or drunk.

Geo-graffy – an old drink made of burnt ship's biscuits boiled in water.

Gimlette – gin and lime juice. The navy surgeon Thomas Gimlette concocted this to try to encourage mariners to drink fruit juice and thus avoid scurvy.

Goffas – fizzy drink.

Gorilla snot – Bailey's Irish Cream liqueur and 'sticky greens' (crème de menthe) mixed.

Glop – any alcohol.

Gnats' piss – any weak liquid, e.g. weak tea or coffee, low alcohol beer or wine.

Grog – rum.

Hanky-panky – a mix of brandy or whisky and ginger wine, good for colds.

Hipsy – an old drink compounded of brandy, wine and water.

Horse's neck – brandy and ginger ale. If rum is used instead of brandy, the name is 'lion's neck'. The old name for this drink was warrant officer's champagne.

Irish light ale – Guinness.

Kye – hot cocoa.

Limers – soft drink issued to sailors in tropical zones.

Loopy or looney juice – any very strong alcohol which will send you *'round the loop'*.

Messdeck champagne – poor Maltese wine disguised by 7-Up.

Neaters – undiluted rum.

Nelson's blood – rum.

Nigerian lager – Guinness.

Norwester – drink comprised of equal parts of rum and water.

Plew – old slang for tea.

Prairie oyster – hangover cure of the yolk of an egg in a glass, covered with brandy and Worcester sauce, and swallowed whole. Another recipe is port wine, Worcester sauce, red pepper, mustard and again the unbroken yolk of an egg.

Pusser's – the Royal Navy's favourite brand of rum.

Pusser's dust – cheap instant coffee.

Reindeer juice – strong alcohol (you might end up on the roof).

Rocket fuel – strong alcohol, especially a mix of brandy and Benedictine.

Rosy dawn – hangover cure of a red tonic medicine mixed with Alka-Seltzer and aspirin and served fizzing.

Screech – an odd alcoholic drink. In Malta it was Coca-Cola and wine, to disguise the taste of the wine.

Scrumpy royal – triple vintage cider, traditionally drunk on payday. Cider is popular amongst seamen, especially as so many come from the West Country, and the great ports of Plymouth, Portsmouth and Bristol are found there.

Sherbert – beer or alcohol.

Snakebite – half lager and half cider, a drink that is more than the sum of its parts, alcoholically, often topped with blackcurrant cordial.

Stagger juice – strong alcohol, especially rum.

Starboard light – crème de menthe.

Sticky greens – drinks with a crème de menthe base.

Suds – beer.

Toddy – rum or whisky with hot water and lemon.

Tutti Frutti – half rough cider, half sweet cider, topped up with blackcurrant cordial.

Vino collapso – strong drink.

Wallop – beer.

Yellow peril, smoked haddock – Pernod with lemonade or water.

KIDLEYWINK, KIDDLEYWINK, KIDDLYWINK According to Admiral Smyth in 1867, this was: *'A low beershop in our western ports'*. Kiddlywink is an old name for a Cornish beer house, which became popular after the 1830 Beer Act. They were licensed to sell beer or cider by the Customs and Excise rather than by the Magistrate's Licence which was required by traditional taverns. Reputedly used by smugglers, they often had an unmarked bottle of spirits hidden under the counter. The Kettle 'n Wink bar of the Western Hotel in St Ives, Cornwall, is known as the Kidleywink.

KILL-COBBLER Gin, in the 17th century. There is now a 'gin cobbler' cocktail, but possibly the best of the slang names for gin over the last 300 years was *'meat-drink-washing-and-lodging'*, suggesting that gin provided everything one could possibly want. Other synonyms for gin, the drink of the masses, were: *mother's ruin, kill-grief, comfort, bit of tape, blue tape, blue ribbon, light blue, sky blue, white tape, white satin, white wool, white ribbon, stark-naked, strip-me-naked, bunter's tea, south sea, cock-my-cap, wind, poverty, apricock-water, diddle* and *roll-me-in-the-kennel*. Cockney rhyming slang is *needle and pin, nose and chin* and *Vera Lynn*.

KILL-DEVIL The most popular drink in the pirate haven of Port Royal. Governor Modyford described this strong rum punch: *'the Spaniards wondered much about the sickness of our people, until they knew the strength of their drinks, but then wondered more that they were not all dead.'* The Dutch equivalent, *'kilduijvel'*, seems to be the forerunner of kill-devil. By the 19th century, it was *'new rum'*, just distilled, with pernicious effects.

KILL GRIEF Strong drink, usually rum but sometimes gin.

KING OF SPAIN'S DAUGHTER A privateering term for looted wine. A tun of wine was 252 gallons (1146 litres), so a 72-tun ship could carry 72 x 252 gallons of wine. A quantity of 126 gallons (573 litres) was called a *pipe* of wine. Wine was stored in lead *'pipes'* in the West Indies, giving the seasoned alcoholic illnesses such as the *'dry gripes'*.

LEATHER TANKARDS, BLACKJACKS These were used at sea for centuries as they did not break, and several were found in the wreck of the *Mary Rose*. The originals were probably lined with bees' wax or tree resin. In dockside taverns they were coated with tar and known as *blackjacks*.

LIQUOR *'Good liquor is to sailors preferable to warm clothing'* – Woodes Rogers, c.1718. Wearing damp clothing while sailing in the Atlantic day and night and subsisting on small portions of awful food, sailors found that alcohol provided much-needed calories to keep their body temperature up. A daily liquor ration was a contractual obligation in both the merchant marine and Royal Navy. Until the 19th century, water was a carrier of all types of disease-causing organisms, so everyone drank cider, beer or wine for preference, on land or at sea. From the 17th century, Caribbean rum became more popular than beer at sea, because beer went sour quickly.

MUM A 17th-century strong ale made from wheat and oats, and flavoured with herbs. From the German *'mumme'* in Brunswick, where it originated; the Dutch equivalent is *'mom'*.

The Loyal Toast and Remaining Seated

The privilege accorded to the Royal Navy of remaining seated while drinking the sovereign's health is traditional, but obscure in origin. There are three popular theories: (a) that King Charles II when on board the *Royal Charles* bumped his head on rising to reply to the toast; (b) that King George IV when Regent and dining on board one of HM ships said, as the officers rose to drink the King's health, '*Gentlemen, pray be seated, your loyalty is above suspicion*'; (c) that King William IV while Duke of Clarence (Lord High Admiral) bumped his head as he stood up at dinner in one of HM ships. On many wooden ships it was almost impossible to stand upright between decks except between the deck-beams. Also, in ships having a pronounced '*tumble-home*' (i.e. steeply sloping sides), anyone seated close to the ship's side would find it difficult to stand at all. This privilege of remaining seated does not extend to naval messes on shore. The following are the routine toasts drunk after dinner in wardrooms in Nelson's time: Sunday – *Absent friends*; Monday – *Our ships at sea*; Tuesday – *Our men*; Wednesday – *Ourselves* (as no one else is likely to concern themselves with our welfare); Thursday – *A bloody war or a sickly season*; Friday – *A willing foe and sea room*; Saturday – *Sweethearts and wives*.

Thursday's toast is a reference to promotion, in the past most easily obtained by stepping into dead men's shoes. Friday's toast refers to success in battle, thus giving a share of the bounty to the officers. The mess president gives the toast and then calls on the youngest member of the mess present to reply to the toast.

NELSON'S BLOOD Nickname for rum among mariners. They believed that Nelson's body had been returned to England after Trafalgar preserved in a barrel of rum, but in fact it was in a barrel of brandy and spirits of wine.

PUNCH To distilled alcohol or wine, various elements were added, such as tea, fruit juice, sugar, spices and lime juice. Men often drank from a ladle out of the bowl. Taverns of ill repute were often referred to as punch houses.

PUNCH HOUSE Common term for a brothel, where alcohol was sold – a visitor to Port Royal wrote that its punch houses contained '*such a crew of vile strumpets and common prostitutes that 'tis almost impossible to civilize*' the town.

PUSSER'S ROYAL NAVY RUM

Rum was first introduced for crews in the tropics in 1655, and it soon became standard issue across the Royal Navy. The daily ration was controlled by the purser (pusser), and only ceased to be distributed in 1970. Pusser's Blue Label bottles are a strong 54.5 per cent abv, and it is recommended 'on the rocks' or as 'grog' diluted with four parts of water.

RUMBULLION This is the demon offspring of rumfustian (see below), described by Burl when Black Bart Robert's crew distilled it at Damana Bay, Hispaniola, in February 1721: *'For that catastrophic brew two huge vats were rowed ashore and filled with molasses, skimmings of overripe fruit, a minimum of water and a liberal splashing of sulphuric acid. The liquid fermented for 8 days while a still was constructed. A complicated system of pipes arranged vertically in a trough of water led from a capacious copper vessel over a fire to a spiral tube under a cooling waterfall that continually dribbled over it. A pewter tankard was set under the spiral and drop by paralytic drop the rumbullion filled it. Only the most foolhardy drank more than one mug.'*

RUMFUSTIAN A popular privateers' hot drink blended from raw eggs, sugar, sherry, beer and gin.

RUMMER A glass for drinking rum cocktails. Seamen in the West Indies usually used pewter mugs or coconut shells as rummers.

RUM PUNCH This great Caribbean cocktail is a mixture of lime juice (plus Angosturas bitters if required); sugar syrup (or pineapple or orange juice); plenty of rum and water or more juice to dilute. It stems from the easy availability of limes, rum and sugar syrup, and the ingredients and proportions are remembered thus, as one becomes more and more inebriated: *'One of sour, two of sweet, three of strong and four of weak'.*

SALTY DOG Take a glass and moisten the rim – at sea saliva will do. Invert onto a saucer of salt. Turn back upright and add a measure of gin (or vodka, rum or whisky) and top up with grapefruit juice (or orange juice, apple juice or other alcohol – whatever is left in the locker). Drink what is known as a cocktail.

SIR CLOUDESLEY Drink of small beer and brandy, with spices, sweeteners and lemon juice, named after Sir Cloudesley Shovell (1650–1707).

SPANISH This is *'sack'* – Canary wine. Also slang for Spanish gold or coins.

SOUTH WIND This is a possible response in a messroom to *'How's your glass?'* You might answer *'There's a south wind in it'* meaning it is empty. Perhaps as a south wind is normally a warming wind, it meant that the drink had 'evaporated'. If you ask for a *nor'wester*, it is half spirit and half water. A *north wind* is neat spirits, in other words a bitter wind.

SUCKBOTTLE A pirate who was always drunk – to *suck* was slang for drinking alcohol.

SUCKING THE MONKEY In the War of American Independence (1775–82), England was blockading the United States, and a large fleet was stationed in the West Indies. For years the officers could not understand why their crews of impressed men were often too drunk to stand up. They even stopped the grog

Rum, 'Kill-devil', 'Demon Water'

Fresh water, even in casks, would not keep for long on board ship and from early times wine or beer was substituted. The usual ration was a gallon per day per man. Brandy was in use from 1650 to 1687, until it was replaced by rum after the capture of Jamaica. Shortage of stowage space for beer led to the introduction of brandy at sea, then rum in the 18th century. This was issued twice a day, at lunch and at supper, the daily ration being a pint of rum for a man and half a pint for a boy. In 1824 when the use of tea became common in the navy, the suppertime ration was cancelled. Rum also was dished out regularly upon pirate ships, following the Royal Navy tradition. Rum was cheap and plentiful in the Caribbean because it was easily made from sugar cane and was distilled from the 1640s onwards. Sugar growers cured sugar in clay pots, and as it crystallized, a brown liquid called molasses drained out of the remaining sucrose. This was recycled by natural fermentation, and then by distillation to give a clear liquid, which darkened as it matured in wooden casks. The French called it '*tafia*', and the English *rum-bullion*, shortened to rum. Perhaps the term originated because it was '*rum*' (odd) to get precious booty (bullion or alcohol) out of waste products. Later,

the name *rumbullion* was transferred to another drink. On the other hand, fresh water was usually taken from a river near a port, or from a polluted river, and was only of any use for cooking. Barrels of water quickly became slimy, and were simply not potable. Pirates were often drunk because there was little alternative liquid to drink. '*Rum*', in the sense of '*odd*', or '*different*' was used as a prefix in much 17th- and 18th-century slang. A '*rum beak*' was a justice of the peace, a '*rum bite*' a swindle, a '*rum blower*' was a pretty woman, a '*rum bluffer*' or '*rum dropper*' was an inn-keeper, a '*rum bob*' was an apprentice, '*rum booze*' was good wine (later becoming an egg 'flip' containing rum, port, egg yolks, sugar and nutmeg), a '*rum bubber*' stole tankards from taverns, a '*rum buffer*' was a good-looking dog, a '*rum chunk*' was a gold or silver tankard, a '*rum clout*' or '*rum wiper*' was a silk handkerchief, a '*rum cod*' was a full purse of money, '*rum cole*' was newly minted money, a '*rum cove*' was a clever rogue, a '*rum cull*' was a rich fool, a '*rum doxy*' was both a beautiful woman and a pretty whore, and so on and so on. Other terms seamen would have used are '*rum slum*' for punch, and '*rum quids*' for a great share of booty or captured goods.

supplies for a time, with no improvement in their condition. Native women boarded the warships to sell fruit and coconuts. Many men had persuaded the women to replace the coconut milk with rum, and they stored and hid up to a dozen coconuts, wherever they could. When *'sucking the monkey'* they were secretly drinking rum. When a seaman was sucking rum, the end of the nut resembled a monkey's face. The term was later applied to illicitly using a straw to suck rum or sprits from a cask, which became known as a *monkey*. The straw or clay pipe-stem used for surreptitiously sucking the cask's contents was known as a *'monkey pump'*.

SUCKY This means drunk, as a *'suckbottle'* was a drunkard. *'Suck'* was strong alcohol, and *'rum suck'* was very good quality rum. To *'suck one's face'* was to drink heavily.

SUN IS OVER THE YARDARM, SUN OVER THE FOREYARDARM

A reasonable excuse for imbibing alcohol. In the northern latitudes it was assumed that the sun would show above the foreyard of a ship by 11a.m., which was approximately the time in many ships for the forenoon *stand-easy*. This was when many officers would take their first drink of the day. Thus the original phrase was

'The sun is over the foreyardarm' (meaning it is late in the forenoon). At a time when naval officers indulged in heavy drinking, the Admiralty directed that no officer was to partake of liquor until the sun was over the foreyardarm.

SYLLABUBS These were drinks or dishes sold in Port Royal taverns, made by curdling cream or milk with a mixture of wine, cider or anything alcoholic, producing a soft curd which was then whipped with gelatine, then sweetened or flavoured.

TOASTING The custom is said to have begun with the ancient Greeks. The host took the first sip of wine to show his guest that it was not poisoned. At a mess dinner it is generally forbidden to propose a toast before the Loyal Toast to the Sovereign, although foreign heads of state are toasted first if foreign guests are present. In civilian circles it is permissible to drink toasts in water rather than alcohol, but naval superstition presupposes death by drowning for the personage toasted. Likewise a glass that rings tolls the death of a sailor. One must stop the ring and the devil will take two soldiers in lieu of a sailor. This explains why naval officers never clink glasses when drinking a toast.

TODDY Today we drink a 'hot toddy' especially in the depths of winter. Its original 17th–18th-century meaning was a drink of liquor and water mixed with sugar and spices and served hot.

WET Liquor, as in *'let's have a wet'*. As an adjective it meant that someone was under the influence of alcohol, or prone to drinking too much.

PUNISHMENT AT SEA

BILBOES These were long iron bars fastened onto prisoners' legs stretching them apart and making it difficult to escape. The sliding shackles meant that usually prisoners could only sit and not stand. Bilboes were also humorously known as *'garters'*. They were almost the nautical equivalent of the village stocks. The word derives from Bilboa, which was supposed to make the best steel for fine swords in Europe. A *'bilbo'* was also a rapier bought from the Bilboa region.

CAPSTAN The *'capstan'* was a punishment popular in the navy through the 17th century until the early 18th century, whereby the arms were outstretched on a capstan bar and a heavy weight suspended from the neck.

CAT-O'-NINE-TAILS A short stick with nine knotted ropes used to flog seamen. The 1801 *British Mariner's Vocabulary* tells us that a 'cat-o'-nine-tails' is *'nine cords about half a yard long fixed upon a piece of thick rope for a handle, having three knots on each at small intervals, nearest one end.'* One lash could take the skin off the back, and six would make the back raw. Punishments of over a hundred lashes meant that the miscreant died in agony. From this implement of torture, we get today's phrase *'there's no room to swing a cat'* – the deck was sometimes too full of onlookers and

cannons etc. to draw back an arm properly to inflict the lashing. As the gun decks had only 4 feet 6 inches (137 cm) of headroom, the punishment had to be carried out on the main deck where there was more room to use the 'cat'. The punisher 'combed the cat' after each lash, drawing each of the bloody ropes apart. If this was not done, the coagulated tails would stick together. In the Royal Navy, the prisoner was forced to make the cat, and tie knots in the each of the nine tails. Later, they were standard ready-made issue obtained from military stores. The cat largely replaced keel-hauling as a method of punishment in the Royal Navy, where there was a theoretical maximum of 12 lashes that could be given. Vicious captains ignored this, and it was only ended as a form on punishment in 1879.

CAULK An unpleasant job, often given as a punishment, that involved driving strands of old rope or oakum into the ship's seams (between planking), then sealing it with pitch or resin to prevent leaking and to stop the oakum from rotting through contact with salt-water. Before this a shipwright used a *'beetle'* (heavy mallet) to drive *'reeming-irons'* (iron wedges) into the sides and decks to open a gap between the planks. The oakum was *'clinched'* in by pressing it with a knife or chisel into the seam, as a temporary measure if there was no time for proper caulking. It was necessary to leave a narrow seam between planks, which was sealed with oakum and pitch, as wood expands in water. As the planks take up the water, they compress the oakum and so help to make the ship more water-tight.

COLTS, STARTERS AND RATTAN CANES

Until suppressed in 1811 it was a common practice for boatswains' mates to carry and use on their men 'colts' or 'starters', small whips somewhat like knouts or knotted ropes, which they carried concealed in their hats. The boatswain's mark of authority was the bamboo cane or rattan he always carried, and with which he summarily executed punishment. A punishment awarded by mess-deck court martial for cooks who spoiled a meal was to be 'cobbed' and 'firked', that is beaten with stockings full of sand or bung staves of a cask. This practice was also officially disallowed after 1811. Other forms of punishment, in an attempt to make a punishment fit each crime, were usually harsh and often ingenious. In the 19th century it was ordered that 'cruel and unusual punishments are to be avoided'. Before that time, the following were commonly practised: ducking from the yardarm, placed in the bilboes (stocks to which painful pressure was applied), hanging by the arms in the rigging and the *Wooden Horse* (q.v.). Discontinued in the 17th century were 'gagging and

scraping' of the tongue for habitual swearing or blasphemy, and *boring the tongue* with a red hot iron for repeated or aggravated offences.

DRY DUCKING As in 'ducking at the yardarm', but the fall was abruptly stopped before the miscreant hit the water, often dislocating his arms.

DRY FLOGGING The victim kept his shirt on – because of poor hygiene, his back was then far more like to become infected and painful, with scraps of dirty cloth becoming embedded into the flesh.

DUCKING AT THE YARDARM

A punishment in the Royal Navy – a seaman was tied under his arms, around his waist and under his groin, hauled up on a rope to a spar and dropped violently into the sea several times. Some pirates amended the ducking so that the victim was dropped onto the deck. This was to encourage others to divulge the whereabouts of any loot before it was their turn for a *ducking*. Other punishments favoured at sea were being forced to eat live cockroaches, filling up someone's mouth with iron bolts, and knocking out teeth with metal bolts.

FELONY In the 18th century, all felonies were capital offences. However, for very minor offences, if a thief could prove he could read he might plead 'benefit of clergy' and escape by being branded 'T' for thief on his cheek. This punishment lasted until 1829. Some pirates managed to get away with the branding of the letter 'P'.

FLOGGING AND A 'FOUR-BAG'

Carried out with a cat-o'-nine-tails, even officers could be flogged in the Royal and

American navies when they were reduced to the ranks. The victim was spread-eagled to a hurdle, grating or ladder, or sometimes across a gun on deck. Under *The Articles of War Act* of 1653, English captains were limited to imposing a flogging of 48 lashes, with a court-martial being required to sanction more than 12, but very few captains observed the limit. A 'four-bag' was the term for four dozen lashes. The practice was finally stopped in 1850 by the United States and 1879 by the Royal Navy.

FLOGGING ROUND THE FLEET, GOING THROUGH THE FLEET

A court-martialled man was strapped across a grating on a boat and rowed alongside the ships of the fleet lying in harbour. He was given 12 strokes of the cat-o'-nine-tails at the first ship by the boatswain's mate, 12 at the second

and so on, up to his quota of lashes, sometimes up to 300 or 500 which meant certain and agonizing death. The crew of each ship was paraded on deck to watch the punishment.

HAZING

One of the reasons why seamen were reluctant to fight off pirates, and many willingly joined them, was this practice of making life at sea as bitter and miserable as possible for them. *Hazing* was the practice of giving seamen unpleasant, disagreeable jobs, often during their leisure time, by bullying ship's officers. It comes from the Old French *haser*, to punish by blows or scare. Punishments included picking oakum (q.v.) or being forced to stand for hours on end, although the exhausted sailors had done nothing wrong. A pirate in the novel *Treasure Island* shouts *'I'll be hanged if I'll be hazed by you, John Silver!'*

Gunner's Daughter

The gun to which boys serving in the Royal Navy were tied or *'married'* when being whipped. On some ships it was superstition that if the boys were not whipped on a Monday, there would be no good winds for the following week. To *'hug'* or *'kiss the gunner's daughter'* thus meant a whipping. When *'married to the gunner's daughter'* for a flogging, the miscreant was tied to the four deck rings which held each cannon in place. As the sailor was tied to the gun barrel, the saying *'you've got me over a barrel'* comes from this time. Sailors were

struck with a rope's end on the gun deck, where the ceilings were only a maximum of 4 feet 6 inches (137 cm) high. For more serious offences, requiring enough room to *swing a cat* (-o'-nine-tails), the punishment was carried out on the main deck.

HEMPEN HALTER The hangman's noose (rope was made from hemp).

HOLYSTONE The soft sandstone used in the navy to scrub the wooden decks of ships. It was either called holystone because it was full of holes, or more likely because sailors had to kneel, as in prayer, to use it. After wetting and sanding, decks were rubbed with holystones by rows of sailors until they were almost white. Such was the dislike of merchant and naval captains in seeing their crew *'idle'* that they sometimes gave the men pointless jobs, like holystoning a clean deck or cleaning the anchor cables.

In the days of sail, the *Philadelphia Catechism* was:

'Six days shalt thou labour and do all thou are able,

And on the seventh – holystone the decks and scrape the cable.'

I'LL NAIL YOU FOR THAT! This threat dates from the days when justice consisted of hanging or flogging. For other crimes one could be *'nailed'*. The miscreant was taken to the hangman's gibbet and *'nailed'* through the earlobes until night. Women were also nailed through the tongue for slander.

Impressment

The official act of taking men to serve in the army or navy, usually against their will. It is not generally known that many of Oliver Cromwell's *New Model Army* were impressed men. (Many of these *'redcoats'* ended up as buccaneers in the West Indies, serving in their faded red jackets under Captain Morgan.) Service in the navy was generally hated, so there was always a shortage of seamen, and thus *'press gangs'*, were used to impress unwilling men into the service. In 1536, Mary Tudor's government disallowed Thames watermen from exemption to being *'pressed'*, as all of London's taverns were then a fruitful source of recruitment. Elizabeth I gave *'protection'* (exemption) to mariners from being pressed for army service in 1563, but allowed any itinerant vagrant to be pressed in 1597. Queen Anne gave protection to apprentices under 18 years of age in 1703. In 1740 George II exempted men aged over 55, Thames watermen employed by fire insurance companies, and masters and mates of merchant ships. A proportion of seamen in colliers (coal ships) were given protection in 1774. The 1812 War between England and America broke out partially as a result of the British practice of forcibly impressing American sailors from boarded American ships, claiming that they were British subjects.

IRONS, IRON GARTERS Bilboes
were carried on all the Armada ships, and
were soon taken up by British ships as a
form of punishment. To *'iron'* a man, or
'clap him in irons' was to put him in
bilboes (q.v.).

KEEL-HAUL, KEEL-RAKE
To keel-rake was to drag the victim under
the length of the ship, a terrible
punishment. Possibly a Dutch invention,
this punishment soon caught on amongst
other navies in the 15th and 16th
centuries as a means of discipline. A rope
was attached to a high yardarm on the
starboard, passed under the ship, and
raised up to a port yardarm. A seaman,
sometimes with lead weights on his legs,
was dropped from the yardarm, dragged
under the keel of the boat and hauled up
on the other side to the other yardarm.
Apart from the 'near-drowning' effect,
the victim was severely banged against
the keel, and lacerated by encrusted
barnacles and keel splinters. Sometimes
this was done several times until the man
died from drowning, a broken neck or
shock. When hauled on deck, the victim
was given time to recover his breath, and
then the process was repeated. The
punishment went on until the victim had
suffered enough, or he had died. Often,
when under water, a *'great gun'* was fired,
causing more pain in his ears. The longer
the ship had been at sea, the more
encrusted the hull became, and the more
likely it was that the victim would not
survive. It was the standard Royal Navy
punishment until flogging with a
cat-o'-nine-tails took over around 1700.

KISS THE WOODEN LADY To be
forced to stand facing the mast with one's
arms encircling it and wrists lashed
together. It was a minor punishment, but
shipmates were encouraged to kick the
offender in the buttocks when passing.

LET THE CAT OUT OF THE
BAG A sailor found drunk on board was
ordered to fashion a cat-o'-nine-tails or
'make a rod for his own back', which
would then be kept in a leather bag.
When sailors *'let the cat out of the bag'*
they were in for misfortune, usually on
Blue Monday. The Royal Navy's cat-o'-
nine-tails was kept in a red baize bag, and
not removed until the offender was safely
secured to the gratings and there was no
possibility of reprieve, so *'the secret was
out'*. Beating of seamen with a birch cane,
which was even worse than a cat-o'-nine-
tails, with miscreants strapped to a
wooden frame, was not stopped until
1906. Authority to use the cat was not
removed from the Naval Discipline Act
until an Order-in-Council of 29 March
1949. The only form of corporal
punishment which remained until 1967
was a maximum of 12 cuts with a cane
for boy ratings. The French name for a
cat-o'-nine-tails was *'martinet'*, from the
17th-century disciplinarian colonel, the
Marquis de Martinet.

MAROONING To abandon a sailor or
prisoner on a desolate, deserted cay or
uninhabited island. He was usually given
a musket, some shot, a little gunpowder
and a bottle of water. It was a rare
punishment, leaving the seaman the
option of killing himself if he could not
survive or no rescuers arrived. A *'maroon
island'* was an uninhabited island.
Cimaroons, abbreviated to *'Maroons'*
were a West Indian community founded
by escaped Negro slaves who cohabited
with Amerindian women. Maroon is a

corruption of cimaroon, *'dweller in the mountains'* – a fugitive or lost person.

MASTHEADING One of the milder punishments, when a seaman was sent up to the masthead crosstrees until the captain allowed him to come down. He lashed himself in place to avoid falling asleep and crashing to the deck.

PICKING OAKUM Strands of old hemp rope or manila fibres were soaked in tar, and stuffed in between the planks of a hull to stop leaks. Unpicking old rope to force into these strands was a slow, tedious job which hurt the fingers and thumbs. *'Picking oakum'* was a regular punishment for minor misdemeanours. In the Royal Navy, each man in the ship's cells had to unpick a pound of oakum every day. The word comes from the Anglo-Saxon *'acumba'*, signifying the coarse part of flax.

PILLORY For minor offences ashore, many pirates had been punished in the pillory before they escaped to sea. A frame held a standing man, with his head and two arms protruding through three holes. The prisoner's ears were then nailed to the wooden frame, so he could not avert his face from missiles hurled at him by the crowd. Men and women died from this punishment, and blinding was common. The last use of the pillory was in 1814.

PIZZLE The dried penis of a bull was used as a whip for Arab galley slaves in the Mediterranean. The penis was cleaned, salted and dried. By stretching and sometimes twisting it during this process, it became a highly flexible, rod-like whip around 3 feet (91 cm) long (but it can be stretched much longer,

becoming increasingly thin). In 1624 an English poem recounted how Barbary pirates used pizzles to force Christian slaves to row harder. The Spanish copied this in their galleys in the 17th century, and it has been used all over the world for inflicting corporal punishment. It was used in France's Devil's Island prison, in Nazi concentration camps, and by General Franco's Guardia Civil for torture. Now pizzles are used as riding crops in the famous Palio horse race in Siena's main square. In 1736 an English merchant seaman, Andrew Andrewson complained of his captain beating him *'upon the head with an Elephant's dry'd Piz'l'*.

RUB SALT INTO THE WOUND After a flaying with the *'cat-o'-nine-tails'*, vindictive officers would order salt to be rubbed into the offender's raw flesh to make the punishment even more painful. However, it did serve to help the healing process if the victim lived long enough. Also Roman sailors were paid a quantity of salt as part of their *'salarium'* (salary, from the Roman *'sal'* for salt). The sailors thought that they were being doubly punished at losing part of their salary if they had to rub salt into their wounds after battle.

RUN THE GAUNTLET Risk being attacked or criticized from two or more sides. As a form of punishment it involved forcing a sailor to walk between two rows of men, each armed with a rope cosh with which to hit the offender. *'Gauntlet'* is a corruption of *'gantlope'*, which derives from the Swedish *'gata'* (lane) and *'lopp'* (running course).

SUN-DRIED Left hanging in an iron gibbet, after execution, as an example to other pirates or would-be mutineers. Sometimes the body was tarred to preserve it from falling to pieces, or being pecked to bits by birds, and the grisly remains could be seen at prominent viewpoints for months or even years.

TARRING AND FEATHERING This was ordered for theft at sea by King Richard I. The victim was stripped, smeared with tar and then flock and feathers, and towed to the shore.

THIEVES' CAT A cat-o'-nine-tails with knots in it to make the punishment worse. Only used as punishment for theft.

THREE SISTERS Three rattan canes bound together with waxed twine, used to hit the backs of seamen to make them 'start' or move more quickly when working. Used randomly and frequently by the boatswain's mate in the 17th and 18th centuries, the practice was nevertheless illegal. It was not prohibited until 1809, but was still in use long after that time in the Royal Navy. The emblem is still seen as the badge of office worn by today's master-at-arms.

TOEING THE LINE When a ship's crew was lined up for inspection or orders, their toes would be aligned along a seam in the deck's planking. The seam was packed with oakum, then sealed with a mixture of pitch and tar. These lines between planks were about 6 inches (15 cm) apart. A common punishment for youngsters for any indiscipline required them to 'toe the line' for a designated length of time, in fair or foul weather.

TRICING The process of tying someone to the rigging to administer 'a taste of the rope's end', a flogging.

WOODEN HORSE Described by William Williams, the privateer, in the 18th century, the wooden horse was a form of punishment and torture used in the military for dereliction of duty and drunkenness. Two planks about 8 feet (2.4 m) long were nailed together at a sharp angle to make an uncomfortable 'horse's back'. Four pieces of wood were nailed to make the horses legs, and the horse was placed on a stand on truckles, so it could move. A *head and tail* were added. The miscreant was forced to sit on the horse's back, his hands tied behind him and sometimes weighted to make the pain worse. Weights, often 8-pound (3.6-kg) muskets, were also attached to each of his legs, to 'stop the horse kicking him off'.

YARDARM EXECUTION The last official yardarm execution by hanging in the Royal Navy took place at Talienwan Bay, China, during the Second Chinese War in 1860, and was witnessed by General Sir Alexander Tulloch. The culprit was a marine charged with attempting to murder his captain, and the execution was also witnessed by troops specially paraded on shore.

SLAVES AND SLAVERY

AMAZING GRACE AND THE SLAVER CAPTAIN

John Henry Newton (1725–1807) had gone to sea with his father at the age of 11, but in 1743 he was forcibly pressed into naval service, becoming a midshipman aboard HMS *Harwich*. After attempting to desert, Newton was put in irons and court-martialled. In front of 350 members of the crew, the 19-year-old Newton was stripped to the waist, tied to a grating, received a flogging of 96 lashes, and was reduced to the rank of a common seaman. Newton then became the servant of a slave captain bound for the coast of Sierra Leone who badly abused him. Early in 1748 he was rescued by a captain, who had been asked by Newton's father to search for him on his next voyage. Sailing back to England aboard the slave ship *Greyhound*, the ship almost sank. Newton believed that God had saved him. He then became first mate on the Liverpool slaver *Brownlow*, bound from Liverpool to the West Indies via the coast of Guinea. He made three further voyages as captain of slave-trading ships, only stopping slave-trading activities in 1754 after a serious illness. In 1755 Newton became tide surveyor of Liverpool, and after lay preaching he was ordained into the Church of England in 1764. When he became an Evangelical minister, he looked back at his early life: '*I once was lost, but now am found,*' he wrote in his hymn '*Amazing Grace*'. In addition to powerful abolitionist preaching, Newton helped change attitudes towards slavery with an influential account of the *Middle Passage*, based on his personal experience. '*Let it be observed, that the poor creatures, thus cramped for want of room, are likewise in irons, for the most part both hands and feet, and two together, which makes it difficult for them to turn or move, to attempt either to rise or to lie down, without hurting themselves, or each other. Nor is the motion of the ship, especially her heeling, or stoop on one side, when under sail, to be omitted; for this, as they lie athwart, or cross the ship, adds to the uncomfortableness of their lodging, especially to those who lie on the leeward or leaning side of the vessel.*' Newton encouraged William Wilberforce, the MP for Hull, to stay in Parliament and '*serve God where he was*', rather than enter the ministry. Wilberforce listened to Newton's advice, and spent the next 20 years working for the abolition of the slave trade. Newton in Sierra Leone is named after him, and he was recognized for his hymns 175 years after his death when he was inducted into the Gospel Music Hall of Fame in the United States in 1982.

ASIENTO, TREATY OF This was a notorious part of the peace settlement negotiated, when Britain defeated Spain in the War of Spanish Succession (1702–13). Britain was given the monopoly for supplying Negro slaves to the Spanish West Indies for 30 years, at 4800 slaves a year. Many more slaves than this were smuggled by English slavers into the Spanish colonies, along with smuggled English goods. By 1739 continued conflict between British merchant ships and the Spanish *'garda costa'* led to *The War of Jenkins's Ear* in 1739.

BAGNO, BAGNIO These were North African slave prisons used by the Barbary Corsairs to hold their captives for ransom, or to serve as mine workers or slaves to man the galleys. Algiers' state bagnio held 3000 prisoners, and Tunis in the 17th century had eight such overcrowded and squalid prisons.

BLACKBIRDERS Slave ships. Crews were difficult to obtain for these vessels, as the mortality rate amongst crewmen probably rivalled that amongst the *'blackbirds'* (slaves) themselves. The evil trade was known as *'blackbirding'* or *'blackbird catching'* and many slave merchants made fortunes from it after the Treaty of Asiento.

MIDDLE PASSAGE From the 16th to 18th centuries, slave ships from England sailed to Africa's west coast with cargoes of rum, firearms and brass goods. These were bartered for slaves, who were then shipped (the 'middle passage') to the Spanish West Indies and later the southern states of the USA. Slaves were exchanged for rum and sugar in the Caribbean, and tobacco and cotton in

America, with the rum, sugar, cotton and tobacco returning by sea to Britain. Each of the three passages was fantastically profitable, bringing great wealth to Liverpool and Bristol. For the middle passage, the naked male slaves were pulled out of their dungeons in Africa and, chained together, were herded onto ships. They were prodded down a ladder to the upper hold, then pushed onto a long shelf and chained by the ankle and wrist to the shelf-board. Many slaves passed out in the stench and the suffocating heat. The hold on slave ships was usually 6–7 feet (1.8–2.1 m) high, and was divided half-way up by a platform to double the number of slaves that could be transported. Slaves were chained in pairs at the ankle. Up to 400 slaves could be pushed into the hold of the ship, each occupying a space 5–6 feet (1.5–1.8 m) long, 16–18 inches (41–46 cm) wide and 3–4 feet (0.9–1.2 m) high. A little air came in through the overhead gratings, and the only place for bodily wastes was to seep between the planks they were chained to, dripping onto chained slaves on the lower shelves. The slaves might wait in port for up to ten months in these conditions before sailing. Women and children were taken aboard separately to the men, and they were at the mercy of the whims of the captain and crew. Apart from measles, gonorrhoea, syphilis and smallpox contracted from the Europeans, the prisoners suffered from malaria, yellow fever and amoebic dysentery. The worst disease was *'the bloody flux'*, the symptoms being fever and a bloody running discharge of the bowels. It stunk so much that barrels of vinegar could not remove the stench. *'Blackbirders'* could be smelt up to a mile away, and candles could not be lit in the foetid air on the slave decks. The only time that the prisoners could move was when they were taken to the deck to eat or exercise, and be cleaned. If they refused to eat, they were whipped. If they continued to refuse, iron bars were lodged into their jaws and food jammed down their throats. One captain cut off the arms and legs of *'the most wilful'* protesters to *'terrify the rest'* into obeying his orders. Casualties were appalling, and up to 55 per cent of the slaves might die on the middle passage. It is estimated that 10–12 million Africans were shipped to the Americas and around 1.8 million died during this terrible journey.

NEGRO SEAMEN ACT 1822

South Carolina passed this act, requiring all black seamen to be jailed when their ships were in port, to prevent them from spreading ideas of freedom to local black slaves. Other states and colonies, such as North Carolina, Florida, Georgia, Alabama, Louisiana, Cuba and Puerto Rico, followed suit. The acts were not abolished until after the American Civil War of 1861–5.

SLAVE PROFITS From around the time that the pirate Howel Davis was trading with John Leadstone, commonly called *'Old Crackers'* on the Guinea coast of Africa, there exists a merchant captain's bill for dealing with traders. In 1721, the price for a male slave was eight guns, a wicker bottle, two cases of spirits and 28 sheets of cloth. A female cost nine gallons of brandy, six iron bars, two pistols, a bag of powder and two strings of beads. A boy cost seven large kettles, an iron bar, a length of cotton and five lengths of blue and white cloth. The merchant at the same time would have to pay the Royal Africa Company £15 for a man and £12 for a woman, so the company forts were always potentially full of money which attracted pirates. The sale price was £60 for a man and £48 for a woman in the West Indies, with a 25 per cent death rate on the Atlantic crossing being factored in to account for these prices. From this coast, the Royal Africa Company sold around 18,000 slaves a year, and the private traders around 75,000, but they still could not meet the insatiable demand. By 1820, Guinea slaves could be bought for a just few beads, or $30 at the most, and sold in the Americas for $700. American captains were said to make a million dollars from each voyage. Some idea in modern values of the worth of the slave market is that in 1766 the Liverpool slaver *Vine* carried slaves worth £1.3m from Guinea to Dominica and returned in seven months. In 1764 the *Africa* transported 268 slaves to Kingston, Jamaica, making a profit of almost £1m on the voyage. Between 1783 and 1793 slaves were worth about £50 each, or over £4600 in today's terms and in this period British ships carried around 304,000 slaves in 878 voyages, yielding around £1388 million in today's currency. Much of the investment capital to construct the superb buildings in the city of Bath came from the Bristol slave trade.

Slave Trade

In 1562, John Hawkins removed 300 slaves from a Portuguese vessel, and this event marks the beginning of the English slave trade. It was difficult to get crew for the *'blackbirders'* – as their life was generally short and disease-ridden. Sailors were sometimes treated incredibly badly on the slavers transporting men and women to the West Indies for work on the sugar plantations, and to America for the tobacco crops. The Royal African Company, with its monopoly on the slave trade and its royal patron, wished to transport only healthy slaves who would achieve top prices on the market. However, merchant captains had their profit assessed on the number of slaves that arrived alive, and therefore overcrowded their ships unknown to the Company. Any numbers left over from the official cargo made the captains extra money. Robert Falconbridge wrote *(An Account of the Slave Trade, 1788)* that between half and two-thirds of the transported slaves perished each year, and around 40,000 a year were being shipped in the late 18th century. Falconbridge describes the disgusting conditions where the slaves were packed on the decks and held in irons by the wrists and legs, lying in their own filth and urine: *'They are frequently stowed so close as to admit of no other disposition than lying on their sides, nor will the height between decks, unless directly under the grating, allow them to stand'*.

Brief daily exercise was allowed to keep them mobile, and each morning they were hosed with salt water and the dead thrown overboard. If they did not eat, they were tortured. A Captain Williams used the cat-o'-nine-tails to keep the slaves fit by making them dance. Williams also threw a live slave overboard, and had intercourse with the prettiest of the female slaves. If they refused him, they were flogged until they submitted. Williams also flogged his own crew until they were a *'gory mass of raw flesh'*, according to his surgeon James Arnold. The captain of the *Zong* in 1783 threw 133 sick slaves overboard, 'for the safety of the ship', on the pretext that there was no water for them. In this way the underwriters had to pay for the value of the cargo, rather than the owners of the ship lose their profits through the death of the slaves. Slaves who were alive when they fell in the sea were insured, those who died on board were not. Even in the West Indies, the life of a good, strong slave was reckoned to be no more than ten years in the brutal conditions of the sugar plantations. Thus, apart from new slaves for new plantations where the land had been cleared by slave labour, there was also a 10 per cent attrition and replacement rate each year to satisfy. Merely to replace dead slaves created a demand in Jamaica for 10,000 slaves each year, in the Leeward Islands for 6000, and in Barbados 4000 slaves.

SPAIN AND SLAVERY To exploit the precious-ore and jewel deposits in Mexico, Peru and Colombia needed slaves to work in the mines. However, war, disease, overwork and suicide caused the native Indian population to plummet in one of the worst acts of genocide in history. In the Antilles alone the native population dropped from 300,000 in 1492 to 14,000 in 1514, and millions died on the South American mainland. To save the Indians from extinction, a former explorer, Bartolome de las Casa, proposed that the King of Spain should introduce Negroes as *'the labour of one Negro is more valuable than that of four Indians'*. Thus in 1517, the first *'asiento'* was agreed, enabling 4000 Negroes to be imported into the West Indies over the following eight years. By 1540, an estimated 30,000 men, women and children had been transplanted from Africa to Hispaniola alone. From the 1560s, Hawkins, Drake and others were trafficking slaves to Spanish America, and the slave trade increased until the early 19th century.

TRANSPORTATION Because of the need for labour in the colonies, and the fact that the country's gaols were full to overflowing, a Royal Proclamation of 23 December 1617 allowed any felon, except those convicted of murder, witchcraft, burglary or rape, to be transported to Virginia's tobacco plantations or to the West Indies sugar plantations. Women were particularly required as *'breeders'*. Thousands of children were also rounded up off London's streets and sent on the terrible passage. A 1627 letter notes that 1500 children had been sent to Virginia in 1626 alone. A 17th-century word for

seizing was *'napping'*, and the napping of children *(kids)* to go as servants to America gave rise to the term *'kidnapping'*. Nearly all of the New World's colonists had a criminal background, or were taken against their will. The *Black Act* of 1713 expanded the list of capital offences to over 50, including poaching fish, damaging trees, being caught in a game preserve or stealing a silver spoon. Kidnapping was *not* an offence. In 1717, an Act was passed allowing courts to sentence offenders directly to transportation, so a huge proportion of offenders were transported for periods of seven to 14 years. Capital sentences also could be transmuted to transportation for 14 years or life. From 1720–69, 70 per cent of the Old Bailey's felons were transported, and 16 acts were passed establishing transportation as the sentence for crimes such as perjury. In the 1730s, 10,000 debtors were released to settle the new colony of Georgia. Conditions for transportees were almost as bad as they were on the slave ships.

The Zong Affair

The *Zong* was owned by William Gregson and George Case, well-known merchants in the City of Liverpool, and both former mayors of the city. She sailed from the west coast of Africa on 6 September 1781 with 442 slaves aboard. She was grossly overloaded and did not have sufficient provisions for such a large number. The slaves were chained two by two, right leg and left leg, right hand and left hand, each of them having less room than a man in a coffin. The voyage took nearly two months by which time most of the slaves were malnourished, suffering from sickness and disease. Captain Collingwood lost his way in the Caribbean, which had added to the length of the journey. Sixty slaves and seven crew had already died and Collingwood knew that those who survived, in poor condition, would not fetch a high price on the slave market. He decided to use a shortage of fresh water as a pretext for recording that his *'crew were endangered'*, to justify throwing overboard 133 live slaves. Fifty-five were thrown overboard on 29 November, and another 42 on 30 November. A heavy downfall of rain the following day provided fresh water, but another 26 slaves were thrown overboard on that day, and another ten jumped in voluntarily to defy the captain, embracing each other as they sank. Later, it was claimed that the slaves had been jettisoned *'for the safety of the ship'* as the vessel did not have enough water to keep them alive for the rest of the voyage. This claim was later disproved as the ship had 420 gallons (1910 litres) of water remaining when it arrived in Jamaica on 22 December. If a slave died on board, the insurers would not pay out, deeming it to be *'poor cargo management'*. They would only pay the full insurance if a slave went over the side alive. The owners claimed £30 a head from the insurers which was disputed. The barrister for the owners argued, *'So far from a charge of murder lying against those people, there is not the least imputation…even of impropriety.'* After appeal from the insurers, Lord Chief Justice Mansfield agreed with the ship's owners: *'The matter left to the jury was whether it was necessary that the slaves were thrown into the sea, for they had no doubt that the case of slaves was the same as if horses had been thrown overboard.'* This judgement that the disposal of 'merchandise' was lawful led to a significant turning point in abolitionist campaigns. J.M.W. Turner represented the massacre in his painting *'The Slave Ship'*, and more recently a replica slave ship, named the *Zong*, entered the Pool of London under Royal Navy escort on 29 March 2007.

CHAPTER 4
Death *at* Sea

SEA BATTLES, WARS AND LANDINGS

ACTIUM, BATTLE OF, 31 BCE
In the Roman Civil War Octavian's fleet of 400 ships defeated the larger fleet of Mark Antony and Cleopatra, off the Greek coast. It seems that the oars of Mark Antony's galleys were deliberately targeted. Cleopatra ordered her Egyptian galleys to break off the engagement, Mark Antony followed her, and the rest of the fleet surrendered. Octavian took control of the Roman Empire and is remembered as the Emperor Augustus.

AEGOSPOTAMI, BATTLE OF, 405 BCE The Spartan fleet of 180 ships captured 160 Athenian ships and their crews were executed, so ending the Peloponnesian War and Athenian naval supremacy in the Mediterranean.

ANGLO-DUTCH WARS 1652-4, 1664-7, 1672-4 Wars fought for naval supremacy and trading rights. The second led to the English taking possession of New Amsterdam, renamed New York.

ATLANTIC, BATTLE OF THE, 1939-43 The longest battle of the Second World War was virtually ended when German Admiral Karl Dönitz recalled his wolf-packs of submarines in May 1943. The Allies had lost 3000 merchant ships to submarine attacks alone in 1942, and the Royal Navy was losing 100 ships a year escorting convoys. However, the Allies were now building ships faster than the U-boats could sink them, and developments of the convoy system and in ASDIC submarine-detecting sonar meant that the death-rate of submariners was unsustainable, with almost 800 U-boats being sunk. There were rarely more than 60 U-boats at sea at any one time, of which only 25 were in the North Atlantic. Not only was it the *'longest battle of the Second World War'*, but it gave Churchill his greatest cause for fear concerning British defeat.

AVALANCHE The operational codename for the Allied invasion of Italy in 1943. Initial landings were made at Salerno near Naples on the western coast on 9 September 1943 in the face of severe opposition. It was not until 25 September that the port of Salerno was tenable by ships. The success of the operation was largely due to excellent naval gunnery that kept the Axis forces away from the landing beaches.

BARBARY WARS As a result of the Treaty of Paris in 1783, the USA gained independence, and British troops left America. American merchant ships were now no longer protected by the Royal

Navy, and they became targets for pirate attacks. Muslim corsairs looted American ships in the Mediterranean, and held their crews for ransom. In 1795, as its navy was too involved in fighting France, US Congress decided to pay tribute to the Barbary States to protect American shipping, and a treaty was thus concluded with Algeria, Morocco, Tunisia and Tripolitania (modern Libya). US merchant captains were given a passport that guaranteed no attacks, and their voyages could be insured again. However, the USA paid $2,000,000, only a fifth of the sum expected, so the corsairs eventually resumed their attacks. In 1801, the Pasha of Tripolitania ordered the flagstaff of the US consulate to be cut down. Thomas Jefferson then halted the tribute, as the naval war with France had ended, and took the Pasha's attack as a declaration of war. By 1804, the Pasha's fleet was virtually restricted to Tripoli harbour. This *First Barbary War*, 1801–5, was ended by the US Marines attacking Derna after a six-week march through the Libyan Desert. Their success is commemorated in the Marine Corps hymn '*To the shores of Tripoli*'. The *Second*

Barbary War involved Algiers and the USA, and lasted from 1812–15. When the war with Britain ended in 1815, President James Madison asked the US Navy to attack Algerian shipping. Stephen Decatur's squadron reached Algiers in that year, so the Dey of Algiers sued for peace in the *Third Barbary War*. The British, French and Spanish were also at war with the Barbary States, generally between 1518 and 1830.

CAPE MATAPAN, BATTLE OF, 1717 A Turkish fleet was defeated by a fleet of Papal, Portuguese, Spanish and Venetian ships.

CAPE MATAPAN, BATTLE OF, 28 MARCH 1941 Off the southernmost point of Greece, this was a significant illustration of British superiority in night fighting. Admiral Andrew Cunningham's forces consisted of three battleships and one aircraft carrier. Vice-Admiral Sir Henry Pridham-Wippell in the cruiser *Orion* decoyed the Italian fleet towards the British battle fleet. Admiral Cunningham's dispatch was a masterpiece of understatement – '*Five ships of the enemy fleet were sunk, burnt or*

Boston Tea Party 1773

Samuel Adams led some colonists calling themselves '*The Sons of Liberty*', and disguised as Mohawk Indians, they emptied 342 crates of tea from British cargo ships in Boston Harbour. This protest against English taxes and duties helped to spark the American War of Independence.

destroyed, as per margin. *Except for the loss of one aircraft in action our fleet suffered no damage or casualties. The results of the action cannot be viewed with entire satisfaction since the damaged battleship Vittorio Veneto was allowed to escape.'* The Admiralty had only learned of the Italian fleet's movements as a result of deciphering their codes by the codebreakers at Bletchley Park a few days previously.

CAPES, BATTLE OF THE, 1781

This French defeat of the English in Chesapeake Bay prevented supplies reaching the English troops at Yorktown, Virginia. As a result Lord Cornwallis was forced to surrender to George Washington six weeks later, and the Americans gained independence.

CAPE SAINT VINCENT, BATTLE OF, 1797

Fifteen ships under Sir John Jervis and Horatio Nelson defeated 27 Spanish ships, seriously damaging Napoleon's plans for invading England. Unusually some of the action took place at night.

COD WARS This is the name given to a recent series of difficulties between Iceland and the UK. In the *First Cod War,* 1958, the UK was unable to prevent Iceland extending its fishing limits from 4 to 12 miles (6.4 to 19.3 km). UK trawlers were no longer able to fish within 12 miles (19.3 km) of the Icelandic coast. In the *Second Cod War,* 1972–3, Iceland extended its fishing limits to 50 miles (80 km). In the *Third Cod War,* 1975–6, Iceland extended its limits to 200 miles (322 km), principally over the issue of the amount of cod caught. Icelandic Coastguard vessels cut the nets of British

trawlers within 200 miles (322 km), and there were several dangerous ramming incidents, e.g. when the Hull trawler *Lord Jellicoe* was damaged by the Icelandic Coastguard vessel *Aegir*. NATO interceded, as it was worried about losing its base on Iceland, and an agreement was made limiting British trawlers to 24 ships within the exclusion zone, and an annual catch of 50,000 tons of cod. The agreement caused the loss of jobs of 1500 UK fishermen and 7500 shore-based workers.

COPENHAGEN, BATTLE OF, 1801

Nelson was second-in-command to Admiral Sir Hyde Parker, who signalled to Nelson to withdraw because of the strength of the cannon firing from the shore forts. Nelson famously put his telescope to his blind right eye and continued the battle. Fourteen Danish ships were then captured or destroyed in the English victory.

CORAL SEA, BATTLE OF THE, 1942

Planes from the US aircraft carriers *Lexington* and *Yorktown* inflicted the first major damage of the war on the Japanese fleet. Although *Lexington* and two other ships were lost, the Japanese fleet was prevented from landing troops on New Guinea, and thus Australia was saved from a planned invasion.

D-DAY On 6 June 1944, during the Second World War, seaborne forces landed on five beaches on the coast of Normandy codenamed *Utah, Omaha, Gold, Juno* and *Sword*, beginning *Operation Overlord*, the invasion of German-occupied France. Known as the Normandy Invasion, 127,000 Allied troops were landed in one day, with 11,000 being killed or wounded on the day itself.

DUNKIRK (DUNKERQUE),

26 May–4 JUNE 1940 Around 800 boats of all types ferried 337,100 Allied soldiers from France in the greatest naval evacuation in history, known as *'the miracle of Dunkirk'*. Philip Guedalla wrote in *Mr Churchill* in 1941: *'The little ships, the unforgotten Homeric catalogue of* Mary Jane *and* Peggy IV, *of* Folkestone Belle, Boy Billy, *and* Ethel Maud, *of* Lady Haig *and* Skylark… *the little ships of England brought the Army home.'*

EAST CHINA SEA, BATTLE OF THE, 7 APRIL 1945

This marked the last stand of the Japanese Imperial Navy, when the US Navy sank the battleship *Yamato*, with 2498 crew killed, plus five other capital ships.

GIBRALTAR AND AN EXCUSE FOR A DRINK

Gibraltar's name comes from *'gebel Tarik'* ('mountain of Tarik'), Tarik being the Moorish chief who took the place in 711 and built the castle on the rock. The Moors held Gibraltar till 1309, then Spain took it from 1309 to 1333, then the Moors again from 1333 until they finally lost it to Spain in 1462. Gibraltar was taken for Britain by Sir George Rooke in 1704, and formally assigned to Great Britain by the Treaty of Utrecht in 1713. By the Treaty of Versailles, 1783, Spain agreed to forego her claim to Gibraltar in return for Minorca and Florida (the latter was sold by Spain to the USA in 1809). *'To celebrate the Siege of Gibraltar'* is merely an excuse to have a drink. There were 13 sieges of Gibraltar, including one during the Seond World War, so on any date in the year one can celebrate the anniversary of a siege of Gibraltar.

GLORIOUS FIRST OF JUNE, THE, 1 JUNE 1794

Admiral Lord Howe (then aged 68) in HMS *Queen Charlotte* chased the French fleet for two days until forcing them to action, about 700 miles (1120 km) west of Ushant, northwest France. Seven French ships were captured, and five escaped dismasted and damaged.

GREAT MARIANAS 'TURKEY SHOOT', 1944

In the Battle of the Philippine Sea, ships and planes from aircraft carriers in the US fleet shot down 390 Japanese aircraft.

HELIGOLAND BIGHT, BATTLE OF, 1914

Admiral Beatty's British fleet of battlecruisers defeated a German fleet.

INVASION OF GUAM, 1943

The US amphibious assault on the largest island in the Marianas lasted 20 days, the Japanese losing over 18,250 men compared to the US losses of 1744 killed. Some Japanese fled to the interior of the island and refused to surrender until as late as the 1960s. The measure of Japanese resistance to the American takeover of Pacific islands was demonstrated at Kwajalein in the Marshall Islands in 1944. Of the 8000-man Japanese garrison there was not a single survivor.

IRONBOTTOM SOUND After the Battle of Savo Island (1942) and the Battle of Guadalcanal (1943), this was the name given to the body of water off Guadalcanal in the Solomon Islands, because of the number of wrecks that lay there.

JAVA SEA, BATTLE OF, 1942 In this naval engagement, US, UK, Dutch and Australian ships were annihilated by the Japanese, only four damaged US cruisers managing to escape. The main naval force was almost totally destroyed, with ten ships and 2173 sailors being lost. The Battle of the Java Sea ended significant Allied naval operations in Southeast Asia, and Japanese land forces were now able to invade Java.

JUTLAND, BATTLE OF, 1916 Fought off Denmark, it was possibly the last *'line of battle'* engagement, with both the German and British fleets claiming victory. Britain lost more ships (14 to 11), but the German fleet was forced to retire to its bases for the remainder of the First World War. Germany then began a campaign of unrestricted submarine warfare. It was the largest naval battle in history with over 250 ships engaged, but in reality it marked the end of the battleship's supremacy as a warship. The battle forced the Germans to switch from using surface ships to U-boats for offensive operations at sea. By November 1917, 2932 warships were being employed to combat 170 U-boats.

KAMIKAZE Named after the *'divine wind'* which scattered Kublai Khan's invasion fleet that was directed against Japan in 1281, this was the strategy of suicide flights adopted in the Second

World War. Japanese pilots were given funeral rites and not expected to return. Their mission was to crash with their bomb loads, torpedoes and full fuel tanks into the American fleet. Flights began in October 1944. Pilots were only allowed to return to base if they could not find a target. One who did so on nine occasions was shot for cowardice. Almost 4000 Japanese pilots appear to have been sacrificed in this manner, when the war was obviously being lost. The US Navy admits to losing 34 ships to kamikaze attacks (although the true figure may be as high as 49), with 368 being damaged and 4900 crew killed and 4800 injured.

LA HOGUE, BATTLE OF, 1692 Admiral Edward Russell's fleet of 62 vessels destroyed a French invasion fleet in the English Channel.

LEPANTO, THE BATTLE OF, 1571 A Muslim Turkish fleet was beaten by a smaller allied Christian Holy League fleet of 200 galleys off the west coast of Greece. It was the last great sea battle between galleys and was part of the Wars of the Crusades. The Ottoman commander Ali Pasha is supposed to have told his Christian galley-slaves: *'If I win the battle, I promise you your liberty. If the day is yours, then God has given it to you.'* The allies included vessels from the Papal States, Genoa, Malta, Spain, Sicily, Naples and Venice, around half the fleet being Venetian. Over 30,000 Turks died, 10,000 were taken prisoner and 12,000 Christian slaves were freed. The allies lost just 7500 men. The battle was notable, according to the historian Edward Gibbon, in that it halted the constant march of Islam, and not until the First World War (at Loos in 1916) was such slaughter seen in a battle.

The Spanish author Miguel de Cervantes took part and wrote that it was *'the greatest event witnessed by ages past, present and to come.'* Around 40,000 men died in four hours.

LEYTE GULF, BATTLE OF, BATTLE OF THE PHILIPPINE SEA, 1944 This, the world's greatest

modern naval battle started off Panay, an island in the Philippines, and was unprecedented in terms of ships and aircraft involved. The Japanese had four carriers, two battleship-carriers, seven battleships, 15 cruisers, 33 destroyers and around 473 planes. The United States had 32 carriers, 12 battleships, 23 cruisers, more than 100 destroyers and 1400 planes. The battle included every element of naval power from submarines to aircraft. It sprawled across an area of almost 500,000 square miles (1.3 million km²). During the *Liberation of the Philippines* in 1944, the Japanese attempted to push the US invasion forces from Leyte and destroy the entire US Navy in the Philippines, using virtually all the Japanese Navy. Battle began off Panay Island on 23 October 1944 when the US submarines *Darter* and *Duce* intercepted Admiral Kurita's naval force. The *Darter* hit Kurita's flagship *Atago* and the cruiser *Takao*. After *Atago* was sunk, Kurita transferred to the destroyer *Kishimashi* and still later, to the battleship *Yamato*. Kurita continued fighting and reached Samar in the Philippines, where his fleet suffered much damage and so retired to the China Sea. On the other flank, the Central Group under Nishimura and Shima was almost entirely destroyed in Surigao Strait between Mindanao and Leyte. Japan lost all four aircraft carriers

(and their 473 planes), three battleships, ten cruisers, 11 destroyers and one submarine. The US Navy lost three small carriers, 200 aircraft and three destroyers. The Japanese Navy was defeated, hastening the liberation of the other parts of the Philippines.

LIVE BAIT SQUADRON, 22 SEPTEMBER 1914 Three old

cruisers were commissioned from the Royal Naval Reserve at the beginning of the First World War. Known as the 7th Cruiser Squadron, it was patrolling the Dutch coast at 9 knots (10 mph/16.5 kph), in line abreast, with no destroyer escort. Around 6a.m. the *Aboukir* was torpedoed by the German submarine U-9 and began to sink. In response to her distress call, the other two cruisers stopped to give assistance. The *Hogue* was immediately almost cut in two by two torpedoes, and began to sink. An hour later the *Cressy* was torpedoed through the magazine and she sank almost immediately. The casualties of this passive action – 1400 men, 60 officers and 13 cadets out of a total of 2200 seamen – was more than the losses sustained at the Battle of Trafalgar.

MANILA BAY, BATTLE OF, 1898

In the Spanish-American War, the US Navy captured or destroyed all ten ships in the Spanish fleet, the Americans suffering only eight men wounded.

MEDWAY, BATTLE OF 43 CE

This has been called the second most important battle in British history, after the 1066 landing of the Normans near Hastings. British tribes under Caractacus (Caradog) tried to prevent the Roman invasion in Kent. After being defeated, he retreated to Wales and carried out a

Malta, Siege of, 1565

This island has endured dozens of sieges and battles. In 1565 550 Knights Hospitaller and 5500 other soldiers and civilians defended the island against around 36,000 Ottoman Turks in possibly the most heroic siege in history. The Turkish cannon could be heard in Sicily, 120 miles (200 km) away, over the four-month summer battle. If Suleiman the Great had won, the Ottoman Empire would have controlled the western, as well as eastern, Mediterranean. The outlying fortress of St Elmo eventually fell, and its survivors were tortured to death, mutilated and floated across to the castle of St Angelo nailed to wooden crosses. Jean de Vallette, the commander, then executed all his Turkish prisoners and fired their severed heads over the Ottoman camp. This signalled that there would be no quarter. When relieving forces eventually landed on the island, around half its defenders were dead.

successful guerrilla war until being betrayed by Queen Cartimandua of the Brigantes in Yorkshire.

MIDWAY, BATTLE OF, 1942

This was the turning-point in the battle for the Pacific during the Second World War, when a heavily outgunned US task force sank four Japanese aircraft carriers and a heavy cruiser. US codebreakers had been able to determine details of the Japanese attack, enabling the US Navy to set up an ambush. The badly damaged USS *Yorktown* was sunk by a Japanese submarine after the four-day battle. The Midway Islands are 1134 miles (1825 km) west of Hawaii, midway between American and Asia, and were used as a coaling station after their discovery by the United States in 1859.

MURMANSK RUN Second World War slang for the dangerous convoy route from Britain to Murmansk in Russia. There were very heavy losses because of attacks by U-boats, surface vessels and aircraft, and a man's survival time in the freezing cold water was only likely to be two minutes.

NAVARINO BAY, THE BATTLE OF, 1827

This, the last major battle of the *'Age of Sail'*, took place in the Ionian Sea, off the coast of Greece, when a combined English, French and Russian fleet defeated a Turkish-Egyptian force, heralding Greek independence from the Ottoman Empire of the Turks.

NELSON, DEATH OF In 2008 it was discovered that the plaque on HMS *Victory*'s orlop deck, where Nelson died, was 25 feet (7.5 m) from the true location. Arthur Devis had painted the death scene when the ship returned from Trafalgar, and a study of his preparatory sketches and his *'The Death of Nelson'* painting proved that the place of death was further along the deck, so the 1900 plaque commemorating the spot will be moved.

NEW ORLEANS, BATTLE OF, DECEMBER 1814–JANUARY 1815

The English fleet defeated American warships on the Mississippi River and landed 6000 troops to attack New Orleans. It was successfully defended by General Andrew Jackson, with 2200 English killed, wounded or taken prisoner.

NILE, BATTLE OF THE, ABOUKIR BAY, 1 AUGUST 1798

Thirteen French ships-of-the-line and four large frigates were anchored close inshore in Aboukir Bay, off Alexandria. No attack was expected so close to land, so most of the crews were ashore. Admiral Nelson, with 14 British ships, managed to squeeze inshore of the French and destroyed or took the entire fleet. The French commander Admiral

Brueys kept issuing commands despite having both legs shot off. On another ship, French Admiral Dupetit-Thouars also stayed in command, even after having both arms and one leg shot off. Such heroism was of little use, as there was no time to load the guns because of the element of surprise. The English lost no ships, and the victory put an end to Napoleon's hopes of seizing India from the English. Ships were vital for supplies, and Napoleon's army was then defeated by the British. The explosion of the French flagship *L'Orient* inspired the well-known Felicia Hemans poem *'The Boy Stood on the Burning Deck'*. The captain's ten-year-old son refused to leave the ship without orders from his father, but his father was already dead, and the child died at his post.

NORTH AFRICAN INVASION (OPERATION TORCH), 1942

An amphibious attack was launched by the US and British navies on the Vichy French-held North African ports. Algeria and Morocco had 60,000 French troops friendly to Axis forces. The three ports of Oran, Algiers and Casablanca were mainly targeted, involving almost 74,000 Allied troops. The French army then sided with the Allies and by 1943 the Axis forces had been ousted from North Africa.

OKINAWA INVASION, 1945

The US amphibious assault lasted from 1 April to 21 June, during which time perhaps 25 per cent (150,000) of the Okinawan population were killed. Japanese losses were around 100,000 compared to 12,500 killed and 35,000 wounded Americans. Kamikaze attacks destroyed five ships, and another four were damaged beyond repair. Controversy still rages about the Japanese role in the Okinawan civilian deaths. Okinawa is just one of hundreds of the Ryukyu Islands that lie in a chain over 600 miles (965 km) long, stretching from south of Japan to Taiwan. *'Operation Iceberg'* was the greatest amphibious assault in the Pacific during the Second World War, and the last pitched battle of the war. It lasted 82 days. The battle was called *'Rain of Steel'* by the Japanese because of the intensity of gunfire directed against them. The Allies were pursuing a strategy of 'island-hopping', hoping to seize the large island of Okinawa only 340 miles (550 km) away from Japan, from where they would launch an invasion. They began to convert it for air operations. However, a few weeks after the capture of Okinawa, the atomic bombs dropped at Hiroshima and Nagasaki led to Japanese surrender.

OPIUM WARS The Chinese Government outlawed the use of opium in 1729, but British ships satisfied the widespread Chinese addiction by smuggling opium from India into China, in return for silver, silk, tea and porcelain. The trade went on for decades, and in desperation the Chinese Government seized 20,000 opium chests from British traders in Guangzhou in 1839. Britain went to war to protect its illegal trade, and as a result of the Treaty of Nanking in 1832 it was given Hong Kong plus access to five other Chinese ports. A second Opium War broke out (1856–60), after which the Chinese were forced to legalize the import of opium.

PEARL HARBOR, 7 DECEMBER 1941 Established as a coaling station in 1887, Pearl Harbor was the Hawaiian base of the US Navy's Pacific Fleet. Without declaring war, 191 aircraft from six Japanese carriers attacked the port in December 1941, sinking or damaging 21 US ships including four battleships. There were 2403 American dead, and the Japanese lost 28 planes and three midget submarines. The Japanese commander was reprimanded for not sending in another attack to destroy US fuel supplies. The Japanese subsequently declared war after the attack.

PHILIPPINE SEA, BATTLE OF THE, 19–20 JUNE 1944 This was the last great aircraft carrier battle, between fleets of 112 US and 55 Japanese vessels. Three Japanese aircraft carriers were sunk, and 395 of 430 Japanese aircraft were lost.

POMPEY'S SWEEP OF THE MEDITERRANEAN Gnaeus Pompeius Magnus (Pompey the Great) was given resources by Rome in 67 BCE to rid the Mediterranean of pirates, especially focussing on the region around Cilicia (now southern Turkey). Within 40 days he had virtually accomplished the mission, including destroying over 120 bases and fortresses. His ships were mainly small biremes carrying legionaries and marines. To halt piracy, he gave captured pirates land to farm. He was killed fighting Julius Caesar in 48 BCE. Caesar did not favour an agrarian policy for pirates – he executed them slowly.

PUNIC WARS Carthage, a Phoenician colony in what is now Tunisia, fought wars with Rome in 264–241 BCE,

218–201 BCE and 149–146 BCE, to establish supremacy in the Mediterranean. Rome was driven by jealousy of Carthage's strong fleet and capacity for international trade, and eventually destroyed the city, taking over its maritime trading routes to northern Europe.

QUEEN ANNE'S WAR Better known as *The War of the Spanish Succession*, its end in 1713 caused thousands of experienced European sailors to be discharged, but only into unemployment. There was a massive surge in seamen turning to piracy at this time, because they had few other options ashore. They added to the men who fled the West Country after Monmouth's Rebellion in 1685. Rebels captured were sent to the plantations in Barbados, and many of these escaped to a life of piracy also.

QUIBERON BAY, BATTLE OF, 20 NOVEMBER 1759 In this engagement in the Seven Years War, 11 of 25 French ships were sunk. Admiral Sir Edward Hawke destroyed the French fleet under Marshal de Conflans, between Lorient and St Nazaire. Conflans had not expected the British to pursue him through the dangerous rocky shoals outside Quiberon Bay, and the action removed fears of a French invasion of the British Isles.

RIVER PLATE, BATTLE OF THE, 13 DECEMBER 1939 The British cruisers *Ajax*, *Exeter* and *Achilles*, under Commodore Henry Harwood, forced the German pocket battleship *Admiral Graf Spee* to take refuge in Montevideo in Uruguay after a running fight lasting 14 hours, during which the *Exeter* was severely damaged.

The *Graf Spee* was allowed 72 hours in this neutral port in accordance with international law. She sailed out and scuttled herself on 17 December 1939, six miles (10 km) off Montevideo harbour, thus saving her crew. Her captain committed suicide a day or so later.

RUSSO-JAPANESE WAR 1904–5 The first war at sea involving armoured warships on both sides, ended by the Battle of Tsushima on 27–28 May 1905, a resounding Japanese success.

SAINTES, BATTLE OF THE, 12 APRIL 1782 It was the last major sea battle of the American War of Independence, in the Windward Isles, when Admiral Sir George Rodney defeated Admiral de Grasse. The British inflicted 3000 casualties and captured 8000 French seamen, asserting supremacy in the western hemisphere and regaining its territories in the West Indies.

ST NAZAIRE, RAID ON, 28 MARCH 1942 *Operation Chariot* succeeded admirably in its object of destroying the only large dock outside Germany capable of taking the battleship *Tirpitz*. The centre dock gate was rammed and blown up by HMS *Campbeltown*, and troops landed and demolished the pumping station and dock operating gear. The Victoria Cross for gallantry was awarded to Commander R.E.D. Ryder (in command of the naval forces), to Lieutenant-Commander S.H. Beattie (in command of the *Campbeltown*) and, posthumously, to Able-Bodied Seaman W.A. Savage who was killed at his gun.

SALAMIS, BATTLE OF, 480 BCE Themistocles led a fleet of 370 Athenian galleys, which destroyed the fleet of 1000 ships of Xerxes I, so saving Greece from Persian invasion.

SANTIAGO, BATTLE OF, 3 JULY 1898

In the Spanish-American War, the Spanish fleet tried to run the American blockade and break out from Santiago Harbour in Cuba. In a four-hour battle it was heavily defeated, leading to the US acquisition of Puerto Rico. The war ended on 12 August.

SAVO ISLAND, BATTLE OF, 9 AUGUST 1942

A Japanese fleet sank one Australian and three US heavy cruisers in the South Pacific in Ironbottom Sound off Guadalcanal. It was the US Navy's worst ever defeat at sea, 1000 men were killed while the Japanese suffered no ship casualties and minimal damage.

SCHEVENINGEN, BATTLE OF, 10 AUGUST 1653

The last battle of the Anglo-Dutch War, where Admiral Martin Tromp was killed and the Dutch fleet was defeated off the Netherlands.

SEA BEGGARS AND THE DEFEAT OF THE SPANISH ARMADA

This was the name given to the group of Protestant Calvinist nobles, who from 1567 took to the seas and formed a fleet to fight Catholic Spain. William of Orange had been defeated, and these nobles survived through piracy on both Spanish and neutral shipping, operating from English ports. Under diplomatic pressure, Elizabeth I expelled them, but they captured the important Baltic trading port of Brill. Next they took Flushing, using it as a base for attacks on Spanish forces in Holland and Zeeland. Their bases proved vital in supporting William of Orange's rebellion. The Sea Beggars controlled the few deep water ports in Holland and Zeeland – the future Netherlands, and this doomed the Spanish Armada. The Spanish Armada now had no access to a deep harbour in order to rendezvous with the Army of Flanders to invade Britain in 1588, and its fleet was dispersed by storms. The Sea Beggars' successes spurred William on to greater success in achieving Dutch independence from Spain.

SLUYS, BATTLE OF, 1340

Edward III took 200 merchant ships, with raised 'fighting tops' in their bows and sterns for archers, to Sluys off the coast of Flanders. The fighting was intense and hand-to-hand with axes and swords, and the fleet of Philippe de Valois was beaten. The battle enabled the English to carry on their lucrative wool trade with the markets of Ypres, Bruges and Ghent, and Edward now styled himself *'Lord of the English Sea'*.

SOUTH CHINA SEA, BATTLE OF THE, 10–20 JANUARY 1945

Asserting its dominance, the US fleet sank 15 Japanese Imperial Navy and 29 merchant ships.

SPANISH-AMERICAN WAR, APRIL–AUGUST 1898

The US fleet beat a Spanish naval force at Manila Bay, and gained Puerto Rico, Guam and the Philippines in the resulting peace settlement. Cuba was granted independence. More than any other event, this marked the emergence of the USA as a world power.

Spanish Armada, 21–30 July 1588

An 'armada' of 130 ships with 17,000 soldiers aboard was sent to secure the English Channel, prior to an invasion of England to re-establish Catholicism in that country. They were to ferry Spanish forces from the Netherlands across the Channel. The Duke of Medina Sidonia's fleet was comprehensively scattered by smaller and faster English warships led by Lord Howard, Francis Drake, John Hawkins and Martin Frobisher. The weather forced the fleet eastwards, and it sailed on around the east coast of England, Scotland and back down the west coast of Ireland, losing 28 ships in storms. The English lost one ship, and any real threat of invasion passed until Napoleonic times. The Spanish plan failed because the English ships were too fast. The Spanish sailed into the North Sea to regroup and plan an attack elsewhere. However, the weather worsened and many of the surviving boats were swept against the rocks of the Scottish and Irish coasts. Spanish total losses were over 70 ships. Fewer than 10,000 of Philip's men returned home. Its defeat meant

that much of northern Europe remained Protestant, and from the reign of James I, Elizabeth's successor, Britain began trading with India, China and Africa, and developed colonies in Barbados, Bermuda, New England and Virginia. This rise of British sea power meant the rise of the British Empire. Philip's wars with the United Provinces of Holland and Britain, and his determination to re-establish the Catholic faith across northern Europe, drained his income from the New World. As a result he had to declare four state bankruptcies in 1557, 1560, 1575 and 1596. Spain had become the first sovereign nation to declare bankruptcy. Its immense wealth from the exploitation of the Americas was squandered in wars in Europe.

SURIGAO STRAIT, BATTLE OF, 24–25 OCTOBER, 1944 This was part of the *Battle of Leyte Gulf,* and six Japanese warships were destroyed at the cost of just one US destroyer.

TEXEL, BATTLE OF, 31 JULY 1653 Although the English lost 20 ships and the Dutch only 11, this was in fact a decisive English victory leading to the end of the first Anglo-Dutch War in 1654. Another Battle of Texel, on 11 August 1683, marked the last battle in the third Anglo-Dutch War.

'THERE SEEMS TO BE SOMETHING WRONG WITH OUR BLOODY SHIPS TODAY, CHATFIELD' This remark was made by Vice-Admiral Sir David Beatty to Flag Captain Chatfield on the *Lion* at the Battle of Jutland in 1916. The first near-disaster of the battle had occurred when a 12-inch salvo from the *Lützow* wrecked 'Q' turret of Beatty's *Lion*. Dozens of crewmen were instantly killed, but disaster was averted when the mortally wounded turret commander, Royal Marine Major Harvey, immediately ordered the magazine doors shut and the magazine flooded, thereby preventing the propellant from setting off a massive magazine explosion. Beatty's flagship *Lion* was thus saved by the narrowest of margins. The *Lion* had suffered several more hits when it saw the *Indefatigable* blown up, followed by two other ships of the line, with no German losses. There were only two survivors of the 1019 men on the *Indefatigable*. The next ship to sink was the *Queen Mary*, with only nine of 1275 crew surviving. The *Princess Royal* was next reported lost to Beatty, as she was obscured in smoke and spray. It was then that Beatty made his remark to Chatfield, ordering him to turn more towards the German fleet.

THESSALONIKI, SACKING OF,

1185 When the Normans took this great fortified city-port from Byzantium, the historian Nicetus was less than impressed: *'The barbarians carried their violences to the very foot of the altars in the presence of the holy images…it was thought strange that they would wish to destroy our icons, using them as fuel for the fires on which they cooked. More criminal still, they would dance upon the altars, before which the angels themselves trembled, and sing profane songs, then they would piss all over the church, flooding the altars with urine.'*

TRAFALGAR, BATTLE OF,

21 OCTOBER 1805 Near the Straits of Gibraltar, this defeat of a Franco-Spanish fleet ensured British supremacy of the seas until the 20th century. It is thought that apart from Nelson's tactical genius in breaking the line of battle, a deciding factor was that English naval guns were now fired by flintlock, allowing a shot to be fired every 90 seconds. The French and Spanish cannon had fuses that required twice as long to fire.

TRUK LAGOON, BATTLE OF,

17–18 FEBRUARY 1944 A victory in the southwest Pacific in the Second World War, where the US Navy sank six Japanese capital ships and downed 265 enemy aircraft.

TSUSHIMA, BATTLE OF,

MAY 1905 Bearing in mind the surprise attack on Pearl Harbor some decades later, it is worth noting that the Japanese had also destroyed the Russian Far East Fleet, before declaring war. The Russian Tsar accordingly instructed the Baltic Fleet to steam 18,000 miles (29,000 km) from Kronstadt on the east coast of Russia, around the Cape of Good Hope, to avenge the disaster. The exhausted Russian fleet was annihilated by Admiral Togo's British-built fleet off the southeastern coast of what is now South Korea. In 1934, the Japanese again began a war without an official declaration, announcing a *'co-prosperity sphere'* as its excuse for invading China and committing countless atrocities there.

WAR OF 1812 An inconclusive war between USA and Britain, ended by the Treaty of Ghent, and marking America's real emergence as a global naval power.

WAR OF JENKINS'S EAR

Robert Jenkins (c.1700–45) was a Welsh merchant captain. The Spanish coastguard boarded his brig, the *Rebecca*, in 1731 in the West Indies. They cut off his ear and sacked his cargo. He complained upon his return to England, and the British Commander-in-Chief in the West Indies confirmed this event. He then entered the East India Company as a captain, and became acting Governor of St Helena, a station on the eastern trading route. In 1738, Jenkins told a House of Commons committee about the loss of his ear, producing it in front of them seven years after the event. There was a public outcry, leading to the 'War of Jenkins's Ear' (1739–42), which merged and overlapped with the 'War of the Austrian Succession' (1740–8) also known as the 'War of the Spanish Succession'. Everything was inconclusively concluded with the Treaty of Aix-la-Chapelle in 1748.

WAR SIGNAL, 3 SEPTEMBER 1939

The Admiralty dispatched a signal to all ships, signed by the Head of the Military Branch, timed 11.13, reading: *'Special telegram TOTAL GERMANY repetition TOTAL GERMANY'*. It signified that Britain and Germany were now at war (again).

ZEEBRUGGE, THE RAID ON, 23 APRIL 1918

German submarines were operating from a secure base 8 miles (13 km) inland at Bruges in Belgium, and inflicting heavy losses on Allied shipping. The U-boats were emerging into the North Sea at Zeebrugge, and the Admiralty decided that this exit must be closed. A huge fleet of cruisers, monitors, destroyers, submarines and small craft (162 British and 11 French ships) assembled, and the 4th Battalion Royal Marine Light Infantry and 200 Naval ratings formed storming parties. Under cover of a smoke screen and against heavy odds, the assault parties from the cruiser HMS *Vindictive* stormed ashore on the harbour mole. As they drew the enemy fire, three 'block ships' were sailed into the harbour and, just after midnight, there was a terrific explosion. The submarine C3 had been blown up as planned under the viaduct joining the mole with the mainland, and destroying it. The block ships were also sunk in the approaches to the canal entrance.

Less than three hours after the preliminary bombardment had begun, the signal to withdraw was given. Some 7000 officers, ratings and other ranks were involved in the raid. Casualties were 170 killed and 445 wounded or missing. The following honours were awarded: 11 VCs, 21 DSOs, 29 DSCs, 16 CGMs, 143 DSMs and 283 'mentions in dispatches'. The canal was blocked, which meant that 12 submarines and 23 torpedo craft were bottled up in Bruges for six months until the First World War came to an end.

MARITIME ATTACKING TACTICS

BETWEEN WIND AND WATER
The few feet around the waterline on a sailing ship are alternately exposed to the air or water as the ship rolls through the sea. It was the area aimed at by gunners, as the seas would gush in through the damaged hull as the target rolled.

BOARD AND BOARD Captain John Smith (1627) describes this action when two ships lie alongside each other after a chase: *'when two Ships lie together side by side, but he that knoweth how to defend himself, and work well, will so run his ship, as to force you to enter upon his quarter, which is the highest part of the Ship, and only the Mizzen Shrouds to enter by, from whence he may do you much hurt with little danger, except you set fire to him, which a pirate will never do, neither sink you, if he can choose, unless you force him to defend himself.'*

BOARDING When pirates or privateers *'boarded'* or went aboard a victim's ship, the *'boarding party'* was usually chosen by ballot. Everyone had an equal share of the booty, but being on the 'boarding party' against a ship which had not struck its colours was obviously dangerous. 'Sea-artists' like carpenters and surgeons were never risked. Some pirates volunteered to board, and made up for those on the list who did not wish to board. In the navy, however, boarding parties were usually hand-picked from seamen and officers and took account of their proven effectiveness.

BOARDING HOOKS AND AXES
Hooks were used with lines to haul ships together, and the rails were lashed together for easy boarding. Axes, with two-foot to three-foot-long handles, had a sharp blade on one end of the head and a blunt hammer on the other. The blade was used defensively to cut the ropes of boarding hooks, and the other ship's rigging and spars when attacking, and the hammer was used to break down doors and bulkheads in the mêlée of boarding. The axe could also be used when fire-fighting, to chisel out red-hot cannon balls which might ignite the timbers of a ship.

BREAKING THE LINE For many centuries, naval battles were fought by columns of warships delivering broadsides of cannon fire, and captains were not allowed to fall out of the line unless their ship had been taken and her colours struck. Breaking the line, as a tactic, was discovered accidentally by Admiral Rodney at the Battle of the Saintes in 1782, when a huge gap appeared in the enemy line. Passing through the line, a ship could bring all her cannon on both sides to bear, in relative safety from the enemy's larger cannon, and be presented with a much more extensive target. Passing through the line meant that the gunners could fire at the nearest ship on either side, and a cannon ball might pass through its rigging and hit the next ship, or even the one beyond that. Admiral Duncan at Camperdown in 1797 was forced to use the tactic successfully to get to leeward of the Dutch fleet and prevent it escaping into port for safety, where it would be sheltered by shore batteries. Nelson took full advantage of this new tactic in 1797 at Cape St Vincent. With Collingwood, he risked court-martial by breaking out of the line of battle and cutting out the van of the Spanish fleet, allowing a decisive victory. Luckily Admiral John Jervis saw the benefits of the tactic and the two men were lauded for their actions, instead of being court-martialled. Again with Collingwood as his second-in-command, Nelson also daringly implemented the tactic at Trafalgar in 1805, leading to victory. Admiral Villeneuve had suspected Nelson would try this and evolved a counterplan, but adverse circumstances prevented its effective execution.

Broadside

Firing a broadside meant that every cannon along one side of the ship was fired at once. Some cannon would aim for the waterline, others for the men on decks, others for the gundecks and others for the rigging, depending upon their purpose and how they were loaded. A standard *culverin* could fire one cannon ball a minute, but soon became too hot too operate. The powder charge and its wad were rammed firmly home and set under the touch-hole, the 18-pound (8.2-kg) cannon ball tamped hard, right down the barrel, the priming powder was ignited by a slow-burning match, and everyone stood clear. The 3-ton culverin would recoil, held fast by its breech-rope, and the ship would shake. The modern saying *'deliver a broadside'* means to give someone a real and unpleasant shock. In 1867, Admiral Smyth noted that although a three-decker man-of-war might be rated at 120 guns, in effect she carried more and could deliver a fearful broadside of 1960 pounds (890 kg), almost a ton of cannon balls. Imagine a ton of metal (plus small arms fire and firebombs etc.) hurtling at your ship every minute or so and you get the idea of battles at sea.

BUNKER PORTS, COALING STATIONS

A coaling station is a port built for the purpose of replenishing supplies. The term is usually associated with 19th- and early 20th-century 'blue water' navies, which used coaling stations as a means of extending the range of their warships. In effect, the advent of steam-powered ships led to the strategic importance of remote places such as the Falkland Islands and Midway Islands, as ships needed to refuel on long voyages. Thus many small islands, previously disregarded, were taken by imperial powers to serve this function. The Royal Navy, however, also developed coal ships to refuel their warships at sea.

CHOKE POINT, CHOKEPOINT

In naval strategy, this is a geographical feature which forces a fleet to deploy into a narrower formation (greatly decreasing combat power) in order to pass through it. It allows a numerically inferior fleet to successfully beat off a larger fleet, since the attacker is not able to bring his superior numbers to bear. Important naval choke points first identified by Admiral Fisher (1841–1920) were: Hormuz Strait at the entrance of the Persian Gulf (between Iran and Oman); Strait of Malacca (between Malaysia and Indonesia); Bab-el-Mandeb Passage (from Arabian Sea to Red Sea); Panama Canal (from Atlantic to Pacific); Bosporus (linking Black Sea and Caspian Sea with the Mediterranean), Strait of Gibraltar (linking Mediterranean and Atlantic) and the Cape of Good Hope. It was the suitability of the Caribbean as a 'choke point' that attracted raiders and pirates to lie in wait for Spanish treasure fleets leaving America. Passing through the northerly islands, the Spanish could then pick up strong westerly winds to sail swiftly back to Spain.

DAZZLE-PAINTING

Bold abstract patterns painted on warships during the First World War. Combined with a zigzag course, the camouflage was supposed to make the range, course and speed of a ship difficult for opposing U-boat captains to estimate.

DECOY

From Admiral W. H. Smyth in 1867 we read: *'So to change the aspect of a ship-of-war by striking a top-gallant mast, setting ragged sails, disfiguring the sides with whitewash or gunpowder, yellow & co., as to induce a vessel of inferior force to chase; when, getting within gunshot range, she becomes an easy capture. Similar manoeuvres are sometimes used by a single ship to induce an enemy's squadron to follow her into the view of her own fleet.'*

FLANK SPEED

The fastest speed of which a ship is capable. The term is used exclusively aboard warships to describe an emergency speed, which is employed only in serious situations, disregarding fuel costs or wear and tear on the vessel.

GENERAL QUARTERS

Captain John Wells in *The Royal Navy* states: *'When the bugle or drum sounded for General Quarters every officer and man scrambled to his action station as directed by the quarterbill. The majority of seamen and some marines manned the guns, with officers of quarters in charge of groups; other seamen went to the powder magazines or to steer the ship. With the tradition that sea battles were fought at close range marine marksmen still went aloft to the fighting tops, the steam department raised full power, surgeons prepared first aid posts and a fire brigade of stokers and carpenters connected up the hoses. Supported by the navigator, officer of the watch and signalman the captain fought his ship from the bridge, constructed across and above the upper deck, with voice pipe communication to the engine room.'* Quarterbills are the battle stations assigned to each person on board a warship.

HALF-MUSKET SHOT This is the preferred *'killing range'* for maximum effect of a broadside of cannon. At 100 yards (91 m), this was 'point-blank' range, and the Royal Navy generally aimed at the hull near the waterline to sink the ship. Other navies used different types of cannon to fire at longer range at the masts and yards of British ships, to prevent them from closing in to take advantage of their superior short-range cannon power. Pirates and privateers generally preferred to take the ship, rather than sink it.

HOT CHASE, HOT PURSUIT
This was the principle that a fight on the open seas could be carried on into neutral territory if the enemy tried to escape. Thus, in 1759, Admiral Boscowen chased three French vessels into Portuguese waters and destroyed them.

LINE OF BATTLE Sailing ships could only effectively fire broadsides, so fleets formed lines so that maximum firepower could be brought to bear against an enemy. From this formation we get the term *'ship of the line'*. These ships were not built for manoeuvrability, but for sheer firepower. The strategic objective was to gain and keep advantage of the wind by being windward of the opposing line of ships. This was known as *'keeping the weather gauge'*.

LOCK AND LOAD This means to get ready, and refers to the actions needed to prepare a gun for firing. *Lock* is an archaic term for what is now called the *action* or the *receiver* of a gun. The mechanism locked the hammer back into the cocked position. *Load* is to load the cartridge into the firearm, or the charge and ball in a muzzle-loading musket. The trigger releases the lock to fire the gun.

LONG SHOT Cannon had no sights, and could not be traversed right and left. There was only a small up-down adjustment, which could be negated by the movement of waves. Also each cannon ball was slightly different and the gunpowder charges varied. Cannon balls were most likely to hit and cause real damage with a maximum effective range of 200–500 feet (60–150 m). Thus very few *'long shots'* were effective, and the term came to be used by gamblers.

POINT-BLANK The direction of a gun when levelled horizontally. The shot flies to its target without a curve in its trajectory, so is used from close range. The phrase may have come from the French *'point blanc'*, the white centre of a bull's-eye target in archery, meaning that one would definitely hit the target full-on.

'PRAISE THE LORD AND PASS THE AMMUNITION!'

Serving in the heavy cruiser USS *New Orleans* during the Japanese attack on Pearl Harbor on 7 December 1941, Lieutenant Howell Forgy coined this phrase. Lieutenant Forgy saw the men of an ammunition party tiring as they struggled to bring shells to the anti-aircraft guns. Barred by his non-combatant chaplain status from actively participating in keeping the guns firing, Lieutenant Forgy decided that he could add his moral support to the ammunition bearers. Thus he patted the men on the back and shouted these encouraging words to them as they laboured.

RAKING FIRE This describes the action of directing musket and cannon fire down a ship's length, from the bow or from the stern. The balls can score the whole length of the decks, doing much more damage to men, masts and rigging.

READY TO FIRE Pirate captains ensured that their gunners were always ready for action – they never knew when a prize might appear from around a headland, or if they might be surprised by a naval frigate searching for them. Cannons were kept loaded, with wooden plugs, *'tompions'*, on their muzzles to keep salt spray from spoiling the powder charge. Again, to keep the powder dry, a sheepskin was laid over the touch-hole at the breech, with a lead apron holding it in place.

SHOW YOUR TRUE COLOURS

The national flag was known as *'the colours'*, so we have today the terms *true colours, show your true colours, go down with colours flying, pass with flying colours,*

nail your colours to the mast, etc. It was common practice among all navies to approach enemy ships without disclosing the true colours (national flags) until the very last moment, just before running out the cannon and firing. Even English warships carried flags from other nations to deceive the enemy, but the *'rules of war'* required a ship to show its real colours, or national ensigns, before firing a shot. A pirate ship, however, might hoist its pirate flag when within firing distance, but not before.

A SHOT ACROSS THE BOWS

'A shot across the bows' derives from the practice of firing a cannon shot across the bows of an opponent's ship to show them that you are prepared to do battle. It was hoped that the target would surrender rather than run out its cannon. It has come to mean giving somebody a warning of intent.

SPIKE To prevent a gun or cannon being fired, by knocking a soft nail into the vent or touch-hole with a spike. Therefore the gunpowder could not be ignited.

SPREAD LIKE WILDFIRE

Wildfire was a combustible composition applied to the tips of arrows to set fire to an opposing ship. It was more often used in times of war or emergency by navies, rather than by pirates, who wanted to keep the 'prize' intact and not risk the fire spreading to their own ships.

WHY DID WARSHIPS FLY TWO FLAGS IN ACTION?

This practice of wearing two or more large ensigns was to prevent an enemy from assuming that a ship had struck her colours in surrender, when in fact the ensign might have been shot away.

Warfare at Sea

Roman naval battle during the Punic Wars against Carthage

Deck of a Spanish warship, 16th century

Defeat of privateer Sir Andrew Barton, 1511

Battle between English and Dutch ships in Solebay, 1672

The steam-powered submarine Nordenfeldt, 1888

The Illinois *was a detailed, full-scale replica of an* American Indiana-class battleship

MARITIME WEAPONS

ACOUSTIC TORPEDO Its sensors detect the sound of a ship's propellers, and it then detonates when close to the ship. It was introduced by the German Navy in 1943, and forced ships to begin towing decoy devices which made a louder noise than their own propellers.

APOSTLES A 17th-century term for the charges carried in a bandolier, slung across a pirate's chest when operating on land, because there were usually about a dozen cartridges in this belt.

ARQUEBUS An early handgun, called by Alexandre Exquemelin in 1684 a *'harquebus'*, and also spelt in early sources as: *arkbusshe, hacquebute, hargubush, harquebuz, herquebuze* and *hagabus*.

BAR SHOT Large iron bars, fired by cannon from short range as their trajectory was unpredictable, to smash the ship's rigging and shrouds.

BASTARD Any differently sized cannon, e.g. the government bastard-cannon had a 7-inch (18-cm) bore and fired a 40-pound (18-kg) shot.

BELAYING PINS These thick wooden movable posts held ropes in place, and were also useful in an emergency for hitting someone, if a mariner was *'out of arms'* (his pistols had fired) or his sword was stuck between someone's ribs.

BLUNDERBUSS The *blunderbuss* was a devastating close-range weapon, superseded by the *musketoon* of 1758. This so-called *'thunder gun'* was a huge shotgun with the firepower of a small cannon. There was a 2-inch (5-cm) bore which fanned out to a funnel shape at the end of the barrel, which was designed to help spread the charge of pellets over a wider area. The long handgun, about half the length of a musket, was so powerful that it had to be held away from the body – the recoil would knock a man over. Alternatively, it was held against the hip, and used for boarding parties and personal defence.

BOMBS As well as cast-iron shot, cannon could fire bombs, hollow balls filled with powder and topped with a fuse. The intention was that they should explode on impact, which was timed by the length of the fuse and when it was lit. They could only be fired from 50 to 500 yards (45 to 150 m), whereas a standard cannon ball might reach 1000 yards (915 m).

BUNDLE SHOT Packs of short metal bars fired from cannon as anti-personnel devices, to *clear the deck*.

CALTROPS, CROWSFEET Pirates sometimes tossed these sharp metal implements onto the deck of a ship they were boarding. They were devices with four metal points arranged so that when any three are on the ground, the fourth spike projects upwards. They were originally designed as an effective hazard to the hooves of horses. The word caltrop comes from the Latin *'calcitrapa'* meaning foot trap. Usually a handful of caltrops were tossed at a targeted location to spread the small metal spikes over a large area. Since sailors usually worked barefoot to avoid slipping on wet decks, the spikes could inflict terrible injuries if trodden on.

CARRONADE This was a short-barrelled and wide cannon of heavy calibre, popular in the Royal Navy in the Napoleonic Wars. Its ball smashed into wooden hulls at short range, and it was a decisive factor in many engagements with the French. Although relatively light, it was a devastating cannon firing a 32-pound (14.5-kg) ball or shot.

Carronades were made from around 1779 at the Carron Iron Works foundry in Scotland.

CHAIN SHOT, KNIPPLE SHOT, NIPPLE SHOT A pair of small iron balls joined with a chain or bar, fired from a cannon from medium range. As the shot rotated through the air, it would destroy rigging and sails, and mangle seamen, but not do much damage to the intended prize. The old sea shanty *'Admiral Benbow'* tells the true story of the admiral becoming rather indisposed, i.e. legless, on account of chain shot.

CHASE GUNS Cannons in the bows of the ship used when 'chasing' in the wake of another ship.

CROSS-BAR SHOT, BAR SHOT When folded it took the form of a bar, or complete shot, so could be loaded in the barrel of a cannon. On leaving the muzzle the shot expanded to the shape of a cross to destroy rigging and injure or kill men on deck.

CULVERIN A standard 3-ton cannon, taking 18-pound (8.2-kg) cannon balls.

CUTLASS, CUTLASH, CUTLACE A short curved sword ideal for close-range fighting on deck. The swordsman would lash out to cut the opponent, hence the name *cut-lash*. Rapiers and *'small swords'* had long thin blades to slide between an opponent's ribs to puncture the heart or lungs. The *cutlass* was shorter, thicker and wider and used like a machete for hacking at limbs. A 'basket-guard' covered the handle to protect the hand. However, some Caribbean cutlasses could be up to 3 feet (91 cm) in length. As the curve was slight and the tip was sharpened, a privateer with strong arms could also use it as a rapier when needed. Another possible origin of the name is the medieval French *'coutelace'* or knife. The handles were usually cushioned with leather, strapped on a bone or ivory stock. There was also a 'straight' cutlass called a *'shortsword'* or *'stabbing dagger'*. Another derivation may be from *'curtle-axe'*, a short, broad sword mentioned by Shakespeare and Marlowe. *Cutlass drill* was not introduced into the Royal Navy until 1814, but before that individual officers had devised drills to train their sailors. The Royal Navy retained cutlasses 'officially' until 1936, although there are reports of personnel carrying them in the Second World War. The cutlass was possibly last used by the

Royal Navy when sailors from HMS *Cossack* boarded the *Altmark* in 1940 to liberate British prisoners of war.

DAGGER, DIRK A pirate's dagger was used for eating and for killing. Its straight blade was meant to thrust and puncture, not slash like a cutlass. Its cross-bar or hilt meant that the hand could not slip down onto the blade, and it also deflected the strike of an enemy's cutlass, allowing the pirate to use his own cutlass on his undefended foe in a split second. Pirates usually carried daggers and dirks on their person at all times, just as all seamen carried jack-knives. A dirk was a long thin knife favoured for throwing, fighting and cutting rope.

EXPLODING SHELLS Oak hulls could withstand quite a battering from 'passive' shot, with cannon balls often becoming embedded in their thick hulls. However, exploding shells could penetrate their hulls, and this hastened the use of iron for hull construction. The exploding shell was first fired in battle by Texan brigs against Mexican ships at Yucatán in 1843, during the secession of Texas. In 1853, at the Battle of Sinope in northern Turkey, shellfire from a Russian squadron smashed a Turkish fleet. In the 1840s Britain commenced a huge construction programme of iron-hulled frigates in response to the invention of exploding shells.

FIREBALL Among other weapons, the name given to a cannon ball that has been heated so that it is red-hot. Carefully loaded using wet towels, it would lodge in the enemy's hull or deck and spread fire igniting the combustible pitch and oakum in the seams of planking.

FIREWORKS Devices used to set alight enemy ships, such as flaming arrows or fireballs (q.v.). Fire-pikes were boarding pikes with burning twine or cloth attached and thrown like javelins at the sails and decks.

GRAPESHOT, WHIFF OF GRAPESHOT This missile combined the destructive spread of case-shot with the range and penetrative force of solid shot. It usually consisted of three tiers of cast-iron balls set between four parallel iron discs and held by a central iron pin. They dispersed in flight. It could also be a mass of loosely packed metal balls loaded into a canvas bag, and might also be improvised using chainlinks, shards of glass, rocks, etc. The 'grape' dispersed like buckshot, increasing the likelihood of hitting someone. Napoleon dispersed a Royalist mob on the streets of Paris with a *'whiff of grapeshot'* in 1795 and was rewarded with the command of the Army of Italy.

GRAPNEL, GRAPPLE A light anchor with very sharp flukes, which could be thrown at a ship that was to be boarded. The barbed flukes hooked into the ship and were difficult to extract, so pirates could climb the attached ropes.

GREAT GUNS, GOING GREAT GUNS These were the heaviest cannon that ships carried, and also came to mean the most famous naval officers of the day. The term was later used for heavy weather, as when a wind *'blew great guns'*, probably referring to the crashing and booming of the waves around and against the ship.

GREEK FIRE Fire bombs aimed at sails and rigging from cannon to disable a ship's movement. The Romans used this inextinguishable mixture of naphtha, sulphur and pitch in bombs delivered from catapults.

GRENADE, GRENADO, GRANADO

A square bottle of glass, wood or clay filled with pistol shot, glass, bits of iron and gunpowder. It was a favourite assault weapon of pirates and buccaneers. *'Granado shells'* or *'granadoes'* were in common use from about 1700. The name derived from the Spanish *'granada'* meaning pomegranate. They were also sometimes also called *'powder flasks'*, hollow balls made of iron or wood and filled with gunpowder. With a touch-hole and a fuse, it was thrown at the men on the opposite deck before boarding. No less than 15 grenades were found on the wreck of the pirate ship *Whydah* which sank off Cape Cod in 1717.

GUNPOWDER

This chemical composition, with the application of fire, is converted to gas with vast explosive power. Its general formulation was 75 per cent saltpetre, 15 per cent charcoal and 10 per cent sulphur.

GUN-STONES

The old term for cannon balls, as they were first made of stone rather than iron.

HEAVY METAL, HEAVY ORDNANCE

Cannon of large calibre, not a musical deviation.

HOLLOW SHOT

Cannon used to be aimed at a specific trajectory to drop onto a ship. Hollow balls went further, being two thirds the weight of solid shot, and requiring a smaller charge. Later, when filled with gunpowder, their destructive potential increased.

HOTSHOT

The term dates back to at least the early 17th century, with *'hot-shots'* being men who went to war, perceiving themselves to be excellent at their profession. The nautical term applied to heated cannon balls. On cold days, cannon balls might be heated and each kept in an iron bucket to warm the crew on watch or at rest.

JACK-KNIFE

The sailor's horn-handled clasp knife, worn on a lanyard. A knife first used by 'jack tars', the blade could be retracted (clasped) for safety when climbing rigging to cut ropes etc. It was used off-duty for carving.

LANGRACE, LANGREL

This was possibly the favourite type of cannon shot used by privateers in the 18th and 19th centuries. Also known as *case shot* or *canister shot*, the case was filled with bits of iron, ostensibly to cut through the rigging of a ship and render it inoperable. Buccaneers and pirates, however, preferred to use it as an anti-personnel device. The wide scatter of the shot ripped holes out of defending seamen, while preserving the nautical integrity of the *'prize'* ship. If pieces of iron or grape shot were not available to fill the case, other solid objects were used in an emergency, even stones and gold coins. There is a record of a ship's surgeon cutting up a corpse to extract the gold coins that had penetrated the man's body.

MAGNETIC MINES These were used at the start of the Second World War by the Germans. They were detonated by the magnetic field of a ship passing over them. The Royal Navy dismantled one that was recovered intact and was able to develop countermeasures.

MATCH The slow-burning rope end used to ignite cannons.

MORTAR Very short cannon with a wide mouth, filled with a number of fused bombs, which exploded after hitting the target.

MURDERER (MURTHERER), MURDERING PIECE A swivel gun with a long barrel and a wide mouth for firing nails, spikes, stones and glass. They were known as *'pedreros'* by the Spanish, Anglicized as *'patareros'* or *'perriers'*. The iron pin in the stock was fitted into a socket, and there were sockets at several places on a ship so the gun could be quickly taken to wherever it was needed most. They were used in nearly all merchant ships to repel boarders, up to the early 19th century. In warships they were supplanted by marines, who acted as marksmen, in the early 18th century.

MUSKETOON The musketoon was less accurate than a musket, but had the effect of a small cannon at close range. It was much shorter than the musket, and did not have the flared barrel of a blunderbuss. It was generally used by boarding parties.

PEDRERO This Spanish swivel gun, copied by the English, shot iron balls. The *pedreros pequenos* used 4-pound (1.8-kg) shot, the *esmeriles pedreros* used 3-pound (1.4-kg) shot and the *esmeriles pequenos* used 2-pound (900-gm) shot. In the 18th century, a *pedrero* was a gun that shot stone balls, or a great number of tiny balls, to sweep the deck of enemies, and the *esmeril* was considered the equivalent of a naval *falconet*, a type of light cannon.

PISTOL The pistol, not a rifle, was a pirate's best friend. Blackbeard used to

Musket

The general term for a single-shot firearm of earlier times, the musket was only slightly more accurate than a *blunderbuss*. The musket ball was smaller and designed to shoot straighter, but was less likely to cause the kind of damage that a blunderbuss could inflict. Muskets were used to 'pick off' the helmsman and officers before boarding, and also for hunting. Early muskets were 5–6 feet (1.5– 1.8 m) long, used a double iron bullet, and had to be supported and fired with the aid of a fork rest. For short-range work, barrels were sawn off (like today's sawn-off shotguns), and an effective load of one musket ball and three heavy buckshot pellets was inserted. The handle, or stock, was also sawn off to make it easier to handle and attach to a sash across a pirate's chest. The term comes from the Spanish *'mosquete'* or sparrowhawk.

carry six in his sash, loaded and ready for action. Howel Davis carried four, and Black Bart two. It had a flintlock (presentation) mechanism, with a single shot loaded via the barrel. The *powderbox* or *powder horn* kept powder dry and ready for action – damp powder was useless. A pirate probably did not carry his powder horn with him during combat, but used a smaller container preparatory to action. After loading his pistols and perhaps a musket, he would move into action. In prolonged battles, men were specifically designated to load small arms, ready for the pirates to discharge them.

POLEAXE Short-handled axe or hatchet with a spike or hammer opposite the blade used for slaughtering cattle. The boucaniers, or cattle-killers, began using the variety with the spike and would drive a series of them into the side or stern of a ship. They could then swarm up this *'ladder'* of axes and take their prize. They were also used to slash the rigging and so incapacitate the ship.

POWDER – KEEP YOUR POWDER DRY The saying *'to keep your powder dry'* stems from the need to ensure that gunpowder was not exposed to the damp in the sea air until the time it was needed, otherwise it might not ignite properly.

POWDER BOX, POWDER HORN This was crucial to ensure dry gunpowder, and was generally made of wood, leather or from an ivory horn. In time of battle, the less able, such as the cook, would use powder boxes to reload weapons for the fighting men. All fighting guns were single shot in these times, and a pirate would drop his musket and use his cutlass until

it was reloaded. He would not keep a powder box on his person, as any spark or shot that struck at it would probably kill him. There was also a leather belt, a *'baldrick'*, which held separate measures of powder, which some mariners used, especially the sharpshooters who were stationed in the ship's rigging prior to boarding. A *powder flask* was sometimes another name for a grenade, *flask* being another term for a bottle, which would break on impact.

PRIMING IRON The iron rod forced down the touch-hole of a cannon. It pierced the bag of gunpowder so readying the cannon for firing by applying the match. A *'rammer'* was a wooden cylinder that pushed the powder bag down the barrel of the cannon.

'QUEEN ELIZABETH'S LOST GUNS' This was the title of a BBC TV *Timewatch* programme broadcast in 2009. For 13 years, secret archaeological studies were carried out on an Elizabethan warship wrecked in 1592 off Alderney in the Channel Islands. Ships of that period usually mounted several different sizes of bronze cannon needing different shot. In the mid-16th century an English clergyman had discovered how to cast cannon in iron, instead of in bronze which was in short supply. It seems that Elizabeth's ships were then fitted with sets of smaller, uniform iron cannon, all cast identically and capable of taking the same shot. Their trained gunners could reliably fire a devastating broadside much more precisely than gun crews of the Spanish or French fleets. At the same time, another innovation reduced the risk of fire on the ship. A new design of gun carriage meant that the cannon muzzles could be pushed through the gun holes, instead of being fired from almost within the ship. Their recoil kicked the cannon back far enough for reloading, which could be accomplished up to three times as quickly as with the previous technology.

RED-HOT BALLS Shot was made red-hot in a furnace, loaded using wet wadding, and aimed in order to cause fire when it lodged in the side or decks of the target.

SEAMAN'S KNIFE In the Royal Navy, the seaman's knife, for reasons of safety, is no longer worn except with working dress. There are several reasons for the shape of the blade. It is blunt-ended so it would cause less damage if dropped from aloft. It can be used to cut without damaging clothing or sails, and may be used as a screwdriver.

SHOT Round shot, or cannon balls, were used to destroy masts and rigging, and the splinters of timber could incapacitate or kill crew members. In fact, flying splinters posed the greatest threat of injury. However, they were not as destructive to humans as a *'whiff of grapeshot'*, or *'bar and chain shot'*, which maximized the maiming capacity of cannons. *'Case shot'* was a cylindrical tin full of small shot, stones, musket bullets and small pieces of iron that spread destruction in as wide an area as possible on the crowded decks. The bits of metal were usually enclosed in a wooden case. Sometimes canvas bags were used, but there was a danger that the canvas might snag inside the gun barrel and damage the bore. *'Angel shot'* was slang for chain shot, when two halves of a cannon ball were joined by a short length of chain. It rotated, cutting a

swathe through a ship's rigging, and it was also used to clear a deck of sailors, sending many to join the angels in heaven with one discharge.

STERN CHASER A gun fitted on the stern, often a 9-pounder, to deter chasing ships, and aimed at their rigging and masts. From the 19th century it came to mean either a penis, or a homosexual.

STINKPOTS, STINKBALLS Crockery jars were filled with pitch, rosin, nitre, sulphur, gunpowder and other combustibles, plus a fuse, and used to spread confusion when ships were boarded. They were also sometimes filled with plant gum and rotting fish, and were a crude and early form of tear gas. A popular method was for pirates to suspend them from their yardarms, and when the ships closed together, light and cut them so they dropped onto the deck of the intended prize.

SWIVEL GUN Small cannon set into sockets on the ship's rail at whatever point where pirates or the enemy were attempting to board.

TOMAHAWKS These were throwing axes – commonly used by attacking pirates in their heyday.

TORPEDO The first torpedoes were stationary or drifting floating mines, and were not self-propelled until the invention of the Whitehead torpedo in 1866. The 'torpedo' was named after the electric ray which gives off an electric shock. The term was coined by American inventor Robert Fulton for his underwater mine.

FAMOUS WARSHIPS

CSS *ALABAMA* The most famous and successful of the American Confederate raiders, she was built secretly in England. She sank, burned or captured 64 Union ships between 1862 and 1864, when she was sunk by the USS *Kearsarge* off Cherbourg. A ship of the same name was also the battleship which led the US Navy into Tokyo Bay in 1945 to receive the surrender of Japanese forces at the end of the Second World War. She is now preserved as a memorial and museum in Mobile Bay, Alabama.

USS *ARIZONA* At Pearl Harbor in 1941, *Arizona* sank in less than nine minutes, with the loss of 1177 sailors. She was never decommissioned or salvaged, and the dead seamen were left in situ. A permanent shrine stands above her as a memorial, the site of the US Navy's greatest loss of life aboard a single ship.

BISMARCK The sister-ship to the *Tirpitz*, she sank HMS *Hood* when she went to sea in 1941, but just over two days later was found, pursued and sunk 600 miles (965 km) off the coast of France. The engagement with the *Hood* and *Prince of Wales* became known as *The Battle of Denmark Strait*. The Royal Navy flagship HMS *Hood*, and the battleship *Prince of Wales*, had engaged the *Bismarck* and *Prinz Eugen*. All ships received damage, but the *Hood* sank within three

minutes because a 15-inch shell from *Bismarck* penetrated her magazines. Admiral Holland and 1414 of his crew died, and there were just three survivors. The German ships made for St Nazaire in France to effect repairs, but the *Bismarck* was attacked by Swordfish planes from HMS *Ark Royal*, and a torpedo jammed her steering gear. Her inability to steer made her an easy target for the British fleet, but she fought to the end. Evidence gathered from the dive site at the wreck now points to the fact that the *Bismarck* was scuttled.

USS *CONSTITUTION* The oldest warship afloat in the world, and the US Navy's most celebrated ship, she was launched in 1797. She fought in the Barbary Wars and the War of 1812, when she was nicknamed '*Old Ironsides*' after her defeat of HMS *Guerriere*. She is docked as a memorial in Boston, and is still capable of sea-going.

GOLDEN HIND Formerly called the *Pelican*, this was Francis Drake's flagship on his voyage of circumnavigation of the globe in 1577–80.

HMS *HOOD* Britain's last completed battlecruiser, this Royal Navy flagship was sunk by the *Bismarck* in 1941, with the loss of 1415 of the 1418-man crew. She only took three minutes to sink, and a doomed forward gun turret fired one last salvo just before she went under.

CSS *H.L. HUNLEY* This Confederate submarine was the first underwater vessel to sink another ship in wartime. It was hand-cranked, and carried an explosive charge, attached to a long spar on its bow. Interior illumination was by a solitary candle, which also indicated remaining oxygen supplies. In 1864 it rammed the USS *Housatonic*, a Union blockade ship, in Charleston Harbor. Both ships sank. *H.L. Hunley*'s wreckage was raised in 2000. Its eight crewmen were identified by DNA tests and buried with full military honours in Charleston in 2004.

USS *INDIANAPOLIS* This US heavy cruiser escaped the devastation at Pearl Harbor, being on manoeuvres in Honolulu. She did sustain kamikaze damage in 1945. She was then torpedoed by a Japanese submarine and only 316 of her 1196 crew were rescued. Many survivors, in the water for four days, were subsequently taken by sharks, which inspired a soliloquy by Robert Shaw's character Quint in the film *Jaws*. Her captain was court-martialled for failing to follow a zigzag course. His misplaced guilt troubled him, until he eventually committed suicide in 1968, using his Navy issue revolver. The body of Captain Charles McVay was discovered clasping a toy sailor in one hand. He was posthumously exonerated by a US Congress resolution in 2000.

HMS *JERVIS BAY* In one of the most heroic actions of the Second World War, this armed merchant cruiser, converted from an ocean liner, single-handedly engaged the German pocket battleship *Admiral Scheer* in 1940. Her action allowed 37 merchant ships, in the convoy she was escorting, to escape destruction. The *Jervis Bay* was eventually sunk, with 190 of her 259 crew losing their lives.

MARY ROSE Henry VIII's flagship, a carrack, sank off Portsmouth in 1545. Its hulk and artefacts are on display near HMS *Victory* in Portsmouth. Latest research seems to unlock the riddle of the last words shouted by her captain Lord George Carew, to another English ship in battle against the French. He called out that his men were *'knaves I cannot rule'*. Studies on their skulls seem to prove that 60 per cent were Mediterranean, possibly mercenaries recruited from Spain and Italy. She sank as she performed a sharp turn, when perhaps a fluke breeze helped to heel her over, so her open gun ports took in tons of water. These lay only three feet (91 cm) above the waterline, so possibly Carew's orders to close them, while manoeuvring, had not been understood or acted upon.

USS *NORTH CAROLINA* The most decorated American warship of the Second World War, this battleship was completed in 1941 and won 15 battle stars after Guadalcanal. She is now a National Historic Landmark at Wilmington, North Carolina.

HMS *RATTLER* HMS *Archimedes* had successfully trialled a screw propeller in 1840, but not until 1845 was the Admiralty persuaded to trial the screw-propelled *Rattler* against the paddle steamer HMS *Alecto*. The *Rattler* effectively proved the

HMS *Revenge*

In possibly the most one-sided battle in naval history, Sir Richard Grenville's *Revenge* faced 53 Spanish ships in 1591. A comparatively small vessel of about 500 tons, she was a galleon carrying 46 guns on one gun-deck. Drake had used the *Revenge* as his flagship at the Battle of Gravelines in 1588, and she was again his flagship in a 1591 attack off Portugal. Sir Martin Frobisher had captained her in 1590 to try to intercept the Spanish treasure fleet. Grenville was her captain when the Spanish fleet came upon the English fleet in harbour at the Azores. The ships were being repaired, and due to an epidemic, many of the crews were ashore. Most of the ships managed to slip away, but Grenville decided to wait for his sick crewmen to rejoin him. When he eventually sailed for open waters, he decided to head straight for the Spaniards. For 15 hours the *Revenge* fought off attempts by the Spaniards to board her. By morning on 1 September, the *Revenge* lay with her masts shot away, manned by only 16 survivors out of a crew of 250. When the end looked certain, Grenville ordered *Revenge* to be sunk.

His officers could not agree with this order, and surrender was agreed that guaranteed that the lives of the remaining officers and crew would be spared. After an assurance of proper conduct, *Revenge* then surrendered, becoming the only English ship to be captured by the Spaniards during the Elizabethan period. Grenville died of his wounds two days later aboard the Spanish flagship. The *Revenge* never reached Spain, as she sank with the loss of about 200 Spaniards who had taken over the ship, along with a number of the Spanish fleet in a dreadful storm off the Azores. Alfred, Lord Tennyson immortalized the fight in his poem *'The Revenge: A Ballad of the Fleet'*.

superiority of screw propulsion when the ships were coupled stern to stern and opened up *'full steam ahead'*. The *Rattler* dragged the *Alecto* backwards at 2.8 knots (3.2 mph, 5.2 kph). This historic event is commemorated to this day in Portsmouth Historic Dockyard.

SCHARNHORST This sister ship of the *Gneisenau* was a battlecruiser launched in 1936, which sank 22 merchant ships. She was sunk by torpedoes at the Battle of North Cape in December 1943, with the loss of 1839 seamen.

USS *TAUTOG* This submarine shot down the first Japanese aircraft in the Second World War, at Pearl Harbor. She ultimately sank 26 Japanese ships, the most achieved by any US submarine.

USS *TEXAS* A 1914 US 'dreadnought', she served in both world wars and is now a museum ship in Texas. She is notable in naval design in that she was the first ship to be fitted with anti-aircraft guns, the first battleship to launch an aircraft, the first ship to control gunfire with rangefinders, the first warship fitted with radar, and the first warship to entertain its crew with films.

HMS *VICTORY* – 'THE ENGINE OF WAR'

Nelson's first-rater flagship was launched in 1765, rebuilt in 1801, served in three wars and returned to Portsmouth in 1811. She is now in dry-dock alongside the Royal Naval Museum in Portsmouth, restored to the condition she was in at the time of the Battle of Trafalgar, when Nelson died on her deck. At 2162 tons, when fully commissioned in time of war she carried 45 officers and 800 seamen and marines. It took 60 acres (24 ha) of prime oak forest to build her, 2500 ancient trees having to be felled. Her oak rudder was 38 feet (11.6 m) tall and 6 feet (1.8 m) wide at its base, connected to a 29-foot (8.8-m) oak tiller, and her keel was made of elm because of its length. Her masts were made from fir, because it was flexible (a non-flexible mast would be ripped out of the deck under full sail). The three masts were each constructed in three sections and reached over 200 feet (61 m) above the waterline. There were 5 miles (8 km) of standing (permanent) rigging, which could support 36 sails,

20,000 square yards (16,720 m²) of canvas. Her hull was 226 feet by 51 feet (69 m by 15.5 m), and copper-sheathed below the waterline. Her crew controlled 102 cannon on three gun-decks, capable of firing up to 32-pounder ordnance. Each lower deck cannon weighed 2.5 tons, firing a 32-pound (14.5-kg) shot up to 1.5 miles (2.4 km), requiring a gun crew of 14 men. One broadside could deliver half a ton of round shot more than a mile. Admiral Collingwood rehearsed his men to fire an astonishing three broadsides every two minutes. Her two carronades, used at short range, could deliver 68-pound (30.8-kg) cannon balls. She was stocked with 120 tons of shot and 35 tons of powder, being able to stay operationally at sea for months on end. She is the only 18th-century European ship of the line remaining in the world.

YAMATO A 72,000 ton Japanese battleship fitted with the largest calibre guns ever, nine 18-inch cannon. In the *Battle of Leyte Gulf* she faced attacks by planes from eight carriers. She amazingly received direct hits from seven bombs and 11 torpedoes before sinking.

MUTINY!

The crews of some merchant ship were driven to get rid of their captains because of various reasons, usually extreme cruelty. If they did not shoot the captain, they usually set him and his officers adrift in a pinnace or small boat with a supply of water and biscuits. They often then turned to piracy as they could not return home without facing prosecution. More unusually, some Royal Navy ships did the same, as was the case with Fletcher Christian and Captain Bligh in HMS *Bounty*. Even pirate ships mutinied if they were not successful, and elected another captain. The definition of a mutiny was refusing to obey the legal order of a superior. Mutineers were hanged at the yardarm. If a whole ship's company mutinied, only the ringleaders were executed. The following is a list of some significant naval mutinies:

1747 HMS *Namur*, Portsmouth. Three hanged, 12 men received 50–100 lashes.
1748 HMS *Chesterfield*, West Africa. Two shot, five hanged.
1779 HMS *Defiance*, North America. One hanged, others 'severely flogged'.
1779 HMS *Jackal*, France. Several men hanged.
1781 HMS *Sylph*, Leeward Islands. Six hanged.
1782 HMS *Narcissus*, North America. Six hanged, two flogged.

1795 HMS *Defiance*, home station. Five men hanged, six men 300–600 lashes.
1797 HMS *Beaulieu*, home station. Four men hanged.
1797 HMS *Pompee*, home station. Five men hanged.
1797 HMS *St. George*, Mediterranean. Four men hanged.
1797 HMS *Hermione*, Jamaica. Over the next nine years, 24 men were hanged.
1798 HMS *Amelia*, home station. Two men hanged.
1798 HMS *Renominee*, Jamaica. Four men hanged.
1798 HMS *Marlborough*, Berehaven. One man hanged.
1798 HMS *Princess Royal*, Mediterranean. Four men hanged.
1798 HMS *Adamant*, home station. Two men hanged.
1798 HMS *Defiance*, home station. Eleven men hanged, 13 flogged and/ or transported.
1798 HMS *Queen Charlotte*, home station. Two men 300 lashes.
1798 HMS *Glory*, home station. Eight men hanged, three men flogged.
1798 HMS *Diomede*, home station. One hanged, one man 500 lashes.
1798 HMS *Haughty*, home station. Two men hanged.
1800 HMS *Albanaise*. Two men hanged.
1931 Port of Invergordon, 297 men 'purged from service'.

'BATAVIA'S GRAVEYARD: THE TRUE STORY OF THE MAD HERETIC WHO LED HISTORY'S BLOODIEST MUTINY'

This excellent book by Mike Dash relates the story of the Dutch East India Company flagship *Batavia*, en route from Holland to Batavia (modern Djakarta) to trade in spices. In 1629 she was commanded by Francisco Pelsaert, captained by Ariaen Jacobz, and with Jeronimus Cornelisz in charge of the cargo. There were 341 people onboard, including 38 passengers. As part of a mutiny plot involving an attack on a female passenger, Jacobz steered off-course and the *Batavia* was wrecked. Pelsaert and Jacobz set off for Batavia in an open boat, taking 33 days to get there. Cornelisz took over the mutineers, planning to capture any rescue ship, and to then sail away with the salvaged riches of the *Batavia*. An Anabaptist, he wished to create a new kingdom on Earth, and he decided to kill all the other survivors. As a result 125 men, women and children were murdered. One woman and her six children were axed to death. After a brief fight, Cornelisz and his followers were defeated when the rescue ship arrived, captained by Pelsaert. Cornelisz' hands were chopped off and he was hanged, while his chief accomplice was broken at the wheel. Seven other mutineers were executed, and two were marooned.

THE BENBOW MUTINY 1702

Admiral John Benbow (1653–1702) went to sea when very young, and served in the navy as master's mate and master from 1678 to 1681. When trading in the Mediterranean in 1686 in the *Benbow*, his own frigate, he beat off an attack by a Barbary pirate. In 1701, after numerous promotions, he was sent to the West Indies as the fleet's commander-in-chief. He was cruising with a squadron of seven ships in 1702 when he sighted and gave chase to a French fleet off Santa Marta. However, Admiral Benbow's captains were mutinous, and his flagship *Breda* was only supported by Captain Walton's *Ruby*, which was forced to withdraw. Benbow's right leg was shattered by chain-shot, but he remained on the quarterdeck till morning, when lack of support and the disabled condition of his ship forced him to abandon the chase. On his return to Jamaica, he died of his wounds. At their court-martial, two of the mutinous captains, Kirby and Wade, were convicted and shot, another died awaiting trial, and one was cashiered. Two battleships and a 74-gun ship-of-the-line have since been named HMS *Benbow*, and he was commemorated by Robert Louis Stevenson in *Treasure Island*. The tavern where Jim Hawkins and his mother lived was 'The Admiral Benbow'.

THE *BOUNTY* MUTINEER WHO BECAME A NAVAL CAPTAIN

The 1787 voyage on the HMS *Bounty* was midshipman Peter Heywood's first, and he became friendly with Fletcher Christian. Captain Bligh stated otherwise, but Heywood was not one of the mutiny's ringleaders. When HMS *Pandora* reached Tahiti to track

The *Bounty* Mutiny

Lieutenant William Bligh (1754–1817) had served as sailing master to Captain James Cook on his voyages to the South Pacific. In 1787, he was commissioned by Sir Joseph Banks and the Admiralty to undertake a voyage in a small ship, the 215-ton HMS *Bounty*. Bligh was to obtain breadfruit plants to be taken to the Caribbean, where they would be planted to provide food for the slaves in the colonies. The voyage was difficult, with much ill-feeling among the crew. After a long stay in Tahiti, to enable the gathering and stowing of the breadfruit plants on board the ship, the *Bounty* began its voyage to the Caribbean. On the morning of 28 April 1789, Master's Mate Fletcher Christian led 18 crewmembers in the now famous mutiny, capturing the ship, and setting Bligh and his officers adrift in the ship's launch. Two crew

members took neither side, and 22 sided with Bligh. However, of the loyalists, four were made to stay in Tahiti by the mutineers to help man the *Bounty*. Bligh thus commanded 18 men on the incredible 3618-mile (5822-km) voyage in an open boat to Timor. He later became Governor of New South Wales and a vice-admiral. Because his cargo had been breadfruit plants, his nickname became *'Breadfruit Bligh'*. Some of the mutineers were recaptured by HMS *Pandora* on Tahiti, but others settled on Pitcairn Island.

down the mutineers, 14 were captured. Heywood and five other men asked to see the captain, hoping to make a favourable impression. However, Captain Edwards viewed them all as mutineers and clapped them in irons. Later a wooden jail known as *'Pandora's Box'* was built on the quarterdeck. Heywood and his 13 companions spent four months chained in this cage, hand-cuffed and in leg-irons. The box stood in direct sunlight and was poorly ventilated. When the *Pandora* sank off the Torres Strait, Heywood was among the ten prisoners who survived

both the shipwreck and the 15-day journey to Timor (along with 98 other men) in four open boats. Heywood finally arrived in England in 1792, was court-martialled and sentenced to death. However, he received a Royal Pardon, and upon the recommendation of Lord Hood rejoined the Royal Navy. He served aboard his uncle's ship HMS *Bellerophon* and was eventually made a post-captain, enjoying a distinguished career as a sea-going captain. He nearly achieved the rank of admiral but this was prevented by his death at the age of 58.

HMS *Hermione* 1797

Thanks to the influence of family and family friends, Captain Hugh Pigot was given the captaincy in 1794 of the 32-gun frigate HMS *Success* in the West Indies. Records show that in a period of just 38 weeks, he then inflicted 85 separate floggings, with a total of 1392 lashings (an average of over 16 per man). In 1797, Pigot was moved to command HMS *Hermione*. That summer, news reached the West Indies of the two great mutinies at the Nore and Spithead (q.v.). Such was the disenchantment with naval cruelty that in the West Indies the crew of the schooner HMS *Marie Antoinette* murdered their two officers and sailed her into an enemy port.

The *Hermione* was ordered out for a seven-week patrol of the Mona Passage. Midshipman Casey was in charge of the maintop, and was about to come down when he noticed a carelessly dangling reefpoint. He waited while a sailor went out to secure it. On deck, Captain Pigot began screaming insults at Casey in front of all the crew, demanding that Casey kneel and apologize publicly. Next morning, Casey was stripped to the waist, tied to the grating and given 12 lashes. Midshipmen were hardly ever whipped, as they were officers, and resentment grew as the crew knew of Pigot's earlier record of cruelty on the

Success. Five days later, in a squall, Pigot ordered the topsails to be reefed. He cursed at his men to hurry, especially at three youngsters on the mizzen-topsail yard. In the raging storm, the three teenagers lost their footing and fell to their deaths on the deck. Pigot ordered, *'Throw the lubbers overboard'*. The maintopmen began to protest, and Pigot ordered the bosun's mates to go up and lash at them in this precarious position, and to take their names. Next morning, each of these maintopmen also received a formal lashing. That night, men grabbed the marine guarding the captain's door. Crewmen smashed into his cabin. Captain Pigot grabbed a two-foot dagger, but after a brief fight, Pigot was killed and his body was thrown into the sea through his cabin window.

At the same time, the third lieutenant, who had the watch, was approached by a group of sailors. After slashing him, he fell over the side. Later, he hauled himself through a gunport, as he had fallen into the mizzen chains. He begged to be spared because of his wife and children, but was again thrown overboard. The second lieutenant, a friend of Pigot, ran naked from his cot into the next cabin, and took refuge under the cot of the marine lieutenant, who was ill from fever. The seamen pulled the second lieutenant from under the cot, stabbed him repeatedly, then pushed his body through a porthole. A midshipman whose testimony had caused a sailor to be flogged was also beaten, stabbed and thrown overboard. After those first four deaths the mutineers drank rum, before casting six more victims overboard. The sailor who personally threw the bosun overboard, then appropriated the bosun's wife, the only woman aboard. Nine officers, in addition to the midshipman, were killed. Four other men were spared – Midshipman Casey, the carpenter, the gunner and the ship's master. Next, the mutineers turned the *Hermione* over to the Spanish at La Guaiara in Venezuela. They were allowed to sail away, taking jobs on passing ships.

The Royal Navy instituted an intensive hunt for the culprits, boarding ships at sea and searching for the mutineers. The marines, who had all been loyal, were to serve as witnesses, as were the master and Midshipman Casey. The first court-martial tried four mutineers who had been taken from a captured French privateer. All four men were hanged from the gibbets on Jamaica's Gallows Point. By 1806, when the last mutineer was hanged, 33 of the *Hermione* crew had been brought to trial and 24 had been executed at the yardarm. In the meantime the *Hermione* had come back into British hands through *'one of the bravest, best planned, and most successful operations in British Naval history'*, led by Captain Edward Hamilton, who was subsequently knighted.

SPITHEAD MUTINY 16 April 1797 Every ship in the Channel Fleet refused to put to sea on this day during the Napoleonic Wars. By May, as a result of the mutiny, some of the more hated officers had been removed from their posts, the seamen were pardoned, and food and rates of pay were improved.

NORE MUTINY May 1797 The Nore was a naval anchorage in the Thames Estuary. Following the example of their comrades at Spithead (q.v.), the mutiny at the Nore began when the crew of HMS *Sandwich* seized control of the ship. Other ships followed, but some slipped their moorings. The mutineers had been unable to organize easily, because ships were scattered along the estuary, but they did elect delegates for each ship. A former naval officer and French sympathizer, Richard Parker was elected *'President of the Delegates of the Fleet'*. The mutineers demanded pardons, better pay, and alterations to the *'Articles of War'*. They then increased their demands to require the dissolution of Parliament and an immediate peace to be negotiated with France. The Admiralty offered pardons as at Spithead if the sailors immediately returned to duty. Parker (1767–97) was an intriguing character, a grammar school boy from a good family, who as a midshipman had challenged his Captain Edward Riou to a duel. He had been demoted and because of rheumatism left the sea to become a teacher. In dire financial straits, in 1797 he took the £30 offered by the Royal Navy to serve as it was desperately short of seamen. He was convicted of treason and piracy, one of the jury being Captain Riou, and hanged from the yardarm of HMS *Sandwich*. A total of 29 ringleaders were hanged, with others being flogged, imprisoned or transported to Australia.

THE GOLD STANDARD AND THE INVERGORDON MUTINY

15–16 SEPTEMBER 1931 Around half the Royal Navy went on strike when the Atlantic Fleet, which was anchored at Invergordon on the Cromarty Firth in Scotland, mutinied. Around 12,000 seamen, many of them facing a 25 per cent pay cut, refused to obey orders. The naval pay cuts of 1931 were part of a massive austerity package imposed by Ramsay MacDonald's National Government to save the pound. At 6a.m. on 15 September, the crew of the battleship *Rodney* refused to obey orders

and went on strike. As each ship's company stopped work, they gathered on deck and cheered, passing the message down the line. All radio communications were shut down. Even the marines joined the striking seamen. On the flagship, HMS *Nelson*, the seamen prevented the officers from putting the ship to sea. Within 24 hours the Admiralty capitulated and restored part of the wage cut. The mutiny also terrified the City of London and investors, and created a financial panic. Foreign holders of sterling were alarmed, and an act suspending the *'Gold Standard'* was rushed through Parliament. The pound still dropped in value by over 25 per cent. Later, 397 sailors were disciplined, not just those from the Atlantic fleet, showing that there was widespread support for the action in other ports. In 1932, the *Atlantic Fleet* was renamed the *Home Fleet*, to try to erase the memory of this little-known but historically important mutiny.

PORT CHICAGO MUTINY 1944

An important stepping-stone in the long, long road to American racial equality. In 1944, 320 men were killed and another 390 injured when two ammunition ships blew up at Port Chicago near San Francisco. Over two-thirds of the dead were black navy seamen assigned to bomb loading on the ships. Fifty blacks refused to return to work after the disaster, because whites were given leave before returning, but the leave did not apply to them. They were court-martialled and imprisoned until the end of the war. Their actions led to the end of overt segregation in the US armed forces from 1948, but most of the mutineers were not cleared until the 1990s.

TRAGEDIES AT SEA AND ON RIVERS

These are some of the major disasters that befell individual ships at sea and on rivers in peacetime:

1782 – HMS *Royal George* sank at Spithead while undergoing repairs and over 800 crew and vistors perished.

1822 – The loss of the sailing junk *Tek Sing*, with over 1600 people drowned.

1859 – The *Royal Charter*, homeward bound from Australia, was lost off North Wales with 500 passengers and a cargo of gold.

1865 – The worst ship disaster in American history occurred when the Mississippi River paddle steamer *Sultana* exploded, killing 1547 men. Some 2134 of the 2300 men on board were Union prisoners returning from Confederate prison camps after the American Civil War had ended.

1904 – *General Slocum*, a wooden side-wheel excursion boat caught fire at Hell Gate, New York and 1031 people died, mainly women and children on a Sunday School outing.

1912 –The Japanese steamship *Kiche Maru* sank in a storm off Japan with the loss of more than 1000.

1912 – The most famous sea tragedy is the sinking of steamship RMS *Titanic* on her maiden voyage from Southampton to New York. Despite the most advanced technology of the period, the 'unsinkable' vessel sank after colliding with an iceberg, killing 1503 people. There were not enough lifeboats, and no lifejackets suitable for children.

1947 – The *Grandcamp*, a French Line liberty ship, exploded while loading ammonium nitrate fertilizer in Texas City, Galveston. The blast began fires in nearby chemical plants and ignited two more freighters. At least 581 died, more than 3500 were wounded and the cost of the damage amounted to over $67million. The *Grandcamp*'s 1.5 ton anchor was found two miles (3.2 km) from the blast.

1948 – The *Kiangya* was a Chinese passenger ship carrying refugees fleeing the communist troops of Mao Zedong (Mao Tse-tung), which struck a mine off the port of Shanghai, with the loss of around 3000 lives.

1963 – During deep-diving tests the nuclear reactor shut down on the submarine USS *Thresher*. At a depth of 8400 feet (2560 m) on the floor of the ocean, 240 miles (386 km) east of Boston, all 129 crew were lost inside the crushed submarine. After the accident the US Navy established additional safety procedures including the SUBSAFE quality assurance programme which requires each nuclear submarine to pass a series of safety tests.

1987 – Britain's worst post-war disaster at sea was the sinking of Townsend Thorenson's ferry *Herald of Free Enterprise*, which capsized 100 yards (91 m) off the Belgian port of Zeebrugge en route to Dover. The bow door of the roll-on, roll-off ferry had not been closed properly, and as she gathered speed, water poured into the car deck. Of the 539 on board, 193 people died.

1987 – The worst peacetime maritime tragedy occurred in the Philippines when the ferry *Dona Paz* sank after colliding with the tanker *Vector* in the Sibuyan Sea. A total of 4375 passengers on the liner and 11 crew members from the tanker were killed.

1991 – 464 people were killed when the passenger ship *Salem Express* hit coral outside the Red Sea port of Safaga, the same Egyptian port which the *al-Salam Boccaccio 98* ferry was also destined never to reach (see below).

1994 – Europe witnessed its worst maritime tragedy. The *Estonia* car ferry was carrying 989 passengers and crew from Tallinn, Estonia, to Stockholm, Sweden, when fierce 15-feet (4.5-m) waves in a Force 9 gale smashed open her bow doors. Water rushed into the car deck and the vessel listed and sank. A total of 852 people lost their lives.

2002 – The ferry *Joola* sank with the loss of at least 1863 passengers. Built in Germany in 1990, she was constructed to only hold 580 passengers. She was operated by the Government of Senegal.

2006 – The *al-Salam Boccaccio 98* ferry sank with 1415 people on board in the Red Sea. Only 388 people were rescued.

These are some of the major disasters that befell individual ships at sea and on rivers in wartime:

1914 – HMS *Bulwark*, a 15,000-ton battleship, was loading coal on the estuary of the River Medway when a huge explosion ripped her apart, killing 736 men. This was the greatest number of men lost in any peacetime or wartime Royal Naval incident until 1939.

1915 – RMS *Lusitania* was torpedoed off Ireland by a German submarine, resulting in 1198 deaths, including 128 Americans. Her loss helped draw the USA into the conflict of the First World War.

1917 – In the Narrows of Halifax Harbour, Nova Scotia in 1917, the French munitions freighter *Montblanc* collided with the Norwegian tramp steamer *Imo*. The explosion and fire wrecked many other vessels and buildings. Almost 2000 people afloat and onshore were killed in the accident, 9000 were injured and 25,000 were left homeless.

1939 – HMS *Royal Oak* was sunk by the German submarine U-47 while anchored at Scapa Flow, with the loss of 834 crew.

1940 – The liner RMS *Lancastria* was bombed by German aircraft and went down off the French port of St. Nazaire with 2000 military and civilian deaths. She was evacuating British troops and nationals from France two weeks after the Dunkirk evacuation.

1942 – 777 of 778 Romanian and Russian Jews were killed when the refugee ship *Struma* hit a mine. With its engines inoperable, the Turkish authorities had towed the *Struma* out of Istanbul into the Black Sea and set her adrift.

1944 – The British submarine *Tradewind* sank the Japanese cargo ship *Junyo*

approach and make safe. Her 1400 tons of explosives are becoming more volatile with the passage of time, and if she explodes, it is estimated that almost every window in Sheerness would be broken and many buildings would be damaged.

1945 – At the end of the war, thousands of inmates from the Neuengamme concentration camp near Hamburg were herded aboard the old liner *Cap Arcona*. The 'passengers' were told that they were to be surrendered to the Swedes, but the intended plan was to haul all non-functioning ships like her into the Baltic and sink them. The RAF, believing that the ships were ferrying SS members to Norway, bombed the *Cap Arcona*, along with the *Thielbeck* and the *Deutschland* on 3 May 1945. She burned, and then rolled on to her side and sank in shallow water off Neustadt. Those who did not die aboard the ship, or in the water, were executed by the SS, cadets from a submarine school, and the Home Guard from Neustadt as they reached shore. Around 7000 to 8000 people died and there were only around 350 survivors.

1945 – The *Goya* was torpedoed by a Russian submarine in April. She sank and around 7000 German soldiers and refugees from the Russian advance lost their lives.

1945 – The *Steuben* was sunk, with around 4000 refugees drowning.

1945 – The SS *Wilhelm Gustloff*, was built as a German low-cost cruise liner but was drafted as a hospital ship during the war. She was carrying 10,600 wounded civilians and soldiers when torpedoed by a Russian submarine on 30 January 1945, 20 miles (32 km) off the Polish port of Gdansk. There were 904 survivors – a casualty toll of more than 9600.

Maru off Sumatra. It was carrying 4200 Indonesian slave labourers and 2300 British, American, Dutch and Australian POWs. More than 5620 people died.

1944 – The Allies bombarded the *Ryusei Maru* and *Tangu Maru*, giving rise to combined casualties of over 8000 forced labourers and soldiers.

1944 – The *Toyama Maru* was sunk with the loss of 5600 Japanese soldiers.

1944 – A typhoon hit a US fleet refuelling in the Eastern Philippine Sea, and 790 men were drowned.

1944 – 1540 forced labourers died on the *Koshu Maru*.

1944 – 1529 civilian deaths on the *Tsushima Maru*.

1944 – 1792 prisoners-of-war died on the *Arisan Maru*.

1944 – The cargo-carrying Liberty ship *Richard Montgomery* ran aground off Sheerness, Kent, loaded with munitions. The wreck remains too dangerous to

THE MERCHANT NAVY

MERCHANT NAVY *'We must ensure the maintenance of a large, modern and highly efficient Merchant Navy. This country must never forget the debt she owes to her merchant seamen. The men who sailed the convoys to Britain, to Malta, to Russia and all over the world must be sure of steady employment, ships designed to give them good living conditions, good standards of food, and proper provision for their welfare.'* Winston Churchill, 1945.

Since 1975, the number of UK-owned and registered vessels with a capacity of 500 gross tons or more has slumped from 1600 to less than 300, while the number of British seamen serving on them has dropped from 90,000 to just 16,000. The decline of the service, sometimes known as the *'fourth arm'* for its contribution to the defence of the nation, has weakened Britain strategically and economically, by forcing it to become dependent on foreign shipping, and by reducing its ability to take part in overseas military operations, such as the Falklands War of 1982.

MERCHANT NAVY LOSSES IN THE SECOND WORLD WAR

Of the 61,631 men killed on Allied merchant ships, 34,541 (56 per cent) were on British ships. The following table puts into perspective the merchant losses at sea:

Merchant Seamen	Deaths
British	22,490
Indian lascars on British ships	6093
Chinese on British ships	2023
USA	5662
Norway	4795
Greece	2000 (est)
Holland	1914
Denmark	1886
Canada	1437
Belgium	893
South Africa	182
Australia	109
New Zealand	72
TOTAL	49,556

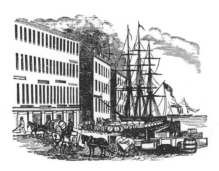

MERCHANT SEAMEN Just like the Royal Navy, many of these had been forcibly 'impressed' into service, and had to endure disgusting food, disease, dysentery, minimal wages, cramped conditions and cruel masters. Dr Samuel Johnson said *'no man will be a sailor who has contrivance enough to get himself into jail; for being in a ship is being in jail with the chance of being drowned...A man in jail has more room, better food, and commonly better company.'* It is little wonder that they were unwilling to fight pirates, and that former merchant seamen formed the vast bulk of the pirate brethren. Punishment was so harsh for trivial offences, as in the Royal Navy, that the popular saying *'You might as well be hung for a sheep as for a lamb'* comes from this time – the punishment was the same for small offences as it was for serious ones. In times of peace, seamen's wages remained unchanged between 1700 and 1750. A merchant captain took about £5–£6 per month, and his first mate and surgeon around £3–£4. Cooks, carpenters and boatswains received around £2, and ordinary crew members around 50p–£1. They were often not allowed to leave the ship in port, especially at home, in case they were tempted to desert, and were often unpaid while a ship was in port or at anchor.

Long stays in port, seeking a cargo, could sometimes lead to mutiny by the unpaid crews. During the First and Second World Wars a merchant seaman's pay was stopped immediately his ship was abandoned. There was no financial relief for his family at home, who often did not know if the lost sailor was dead or alive. Prime Minister Winston Churchill formally stated that the only worry he had in the Second World War concerned the outcome of the Battle of the Atlantic, the war's longest battle. Britain's forces at home and abroad needed merchant ships to supply them, and Britain's population also needed food and supplies. The bravery of the merchant seaman, returning to his local port to sign on for a new voyage time and time again, helped to win the war for Britain.

MERCHANT SHIPS In the 17th and 18th centuries, commercial ships were called merchant ships, but seamen usually reserved this term specifically for the three-masted, square rigged vessel. They could carry passengers or cargo, and a typical ship would measure about 280 tons and 80 feet (24 m) in length, with 20 crew. They might carry 16 cannon, but it is doubtful if the 'short-handed' crew could handle more than four guns at a time. With excellent sail power, they could cross the Atlantic from Britain to America in about four weeks. The largest merchant ships were the East Indiamen, which operated under charter or licence to any of the East India Companies.

CHAPTER 5

Heroes, Heroines, Sea People *and* Navigation

SEA HEROES

ALFRED THE GREAT *c.*849–899
In response to heavy Danish raids from
the seventh century onwards, he planned
a co-ordinated response, creating
England's first Royal Navy.

**BLAKE, ADMIRAL ROBERT,
1599–1657 – FATHER OF THE
ROYAL NAVY** Robert Blake was
General of the Commonwealth forces
in the English Civil War, at the Siege of
Bristol (1643), Siege of Lyme (1644),
Siege of Taunton (1645) and the Siege
of Dunster (1645). At Taunton he had
declared that he would eat four pairs of
boots before surrendering. Cromwell
appointed Blake 'General at Sea' in 1649.
Blake constructed the largest navy
England had ever known, and was the
first admiral to keep a fleet at sea over the
winter. An innovator in tactics, blockades
and landings, his *Sailing Instructions* and
Fighting Instructions remained the
foundation of English naval tactics for
over a century. From 1649 he fought
Prince Rupert's Royalist fleet, helping
Cromwell to secure Ireland, Scotland and
the English colonies in the Americas.
Then, in the First Anglo-Dutch War, he
campaigned against Admiral van Tromp,
defeating and killing him at the Battle of
Scheveningen. He then campaigned
against the Bey of Tunis in 1655, and
from 1656 successfully led the English

fleet in the Anglo-Spanish War. Nelson
ranked Robert Blake as one of the
greatest naval leaders of all time. He was
interred in Westminster Abbey. When
Charles II was restored to the crown, he
inherited a fleet of no fewer than 154
ships from Admiral Blake. In 1661,
Charles had Blake's body dug up and
thrown into a common burial pit. A naval
ship's 'commissioning' or 'masthead
pendant' is said to have originated from
Blake's Whip, that is reputed to have
been nailed to the masthead in grateful
commemoration of his driving the Dutch
from the seas in 1653. Blake had done
this in defiance of the Dutch Admiral van
Tromp, who had the previous year
hoisted a broom to his masthead,
signifying that he had swept the British
from the seas.

BLANE, SIR GILBERT, 1749–1834
He was the physician who helped to
eradicate scurvy from the Royal Navy by
encouraging the consumption of lemon
juice. He also contributed to other
significant improvements in health and
sanitary conditions.

**BROWN, ADMIRAL WILLIAM,
1777–1857** E.F. Knight, in *The Cruise of
the Falcon* (1884) wrote: '*Near the Chico
(lightship) we passed the new Argentine
man-of-war, the* Almirante Brown. *This*

vessel was constructed in England, and recently steamed over the Atlantic with the intention of reaching some port of the Argentine Republic. This she has not done, and will never do, for it is found that this white elephant draws too much water to enter Argentine waters at all, so here she remains at anchor in the high seas, disconsolately rolling about, a constant butt for the caricaturists and comic papers of Montevideo.' The *Almirante Brown* was named in honour of one of the most remarkable seamen of all time, a man barely known outside South America. Brown was born in County Mayo, Ireland and his family emigrated to Philadelphia in 1786, when William was only nine years old. His father died of yellow fever, so William sought employment as a cabin boy, and worked his way up to the captaincy of a merchant vessel. After ten years sailing the Atlantic, he was press-ganged by the Royal Navy.

In 1809 Brown married and emigrated, becoming a merchant in Montevideo, Uruguay, and started a sailing-packet service between Montevideo and Buenos Aires in Argentina. Spanish ships destroyed his schooner, and as a result, Argentina decided to provide ships to protect her coasts and trade. Brown was appointed the first Commander-in-Chief of the Argentine fleet, and he decided to attack the Spanish squadron with his seven small ships. In 1809, the Spanish commander sailed his ships to Montevideo, pursued by Brown who blockaded him. Brown pretended to retreat, and the Spanish fleet came out to sea, beyond the protective range of the fort's cannon. In a battle two days later, Brown's leg was shattered by a cannon

ball, but he continued to command his fleet while stretched on the deck of the *Hercules*. Three Spanish ships were taken, the Spanish blockade of the River Plate was ended forever, and Montevideo fell to the Argentines. Brown's flagship, the *Hercules*, was given to him as a personal reward for his services. Argentina and Brazil went to war in 1825, and Brown took command of a new naval squadron, attacking Brazilian shipping and its coastline. With just seven ships and eight launches he destroyed a 17-ship Brazilian fleet at the Battle of Juncal in 1827. In that same year, with 11 ships, he routed a 31-ship Brazilian fleet off Buenos Aires, leading to peace. In 1842, Brown defeated a Uruguayan fleet on the River Paraná, commanded by Giuseppe Garibaldi. Brown ordered his men to let Garibaldi go, with the words: *'Let him escape, that gringo is a brave man'*. During Admiral Brown's burial, General Mitre in his eulogy said: *'Brown in his lifetime, standing on the quarterdeck of his ship, was worth a fleet to us'*.

BROWN, THE UNSINKABLE MOLLY, 1867–1932 A millionairess from Denver, in 1912 she rallied the *Titanic* survivors on lifeboat number 6 until rescue arrived. She was reputed to have rowed for over seven hours, and was awarded the French Legion d'Honneur. She was a noted philanthropist and prominent suffragette.

CHICHESTER, SIR FRANCIS, 1901–72 In 1960 he won the first solo sailing race across the Atlantic. In 1967, he set a solo speed record for circumnavigation in the 55-feet (16.8-m) *Gipsy Moth IV*, of 274 days.

Brunel, Isambard Kingdom, 1806–59

An engineering genius, who built tunnels and bridges, he also designed steamships. His *Great Britain*, *Great Western* and *Great Eastern* set records for their type of construction, speed, power and size.

COCHRANE, ADMIRAL LORD THOMAS, 10th EARL OF DUNDONALD, 1775–1860 – 'THE SEA WOLF'

He was possibly the most skilful and courageous English naval captain of all time, inspiring the characters and exploits of the heroes in novels by C.S. Forester, Frederick Marryat and Patrick O'Brian. As a lieutenant in command of his first ship, the sloop *Speedy* with 14 guns and a crew of only 92, he captured 50 ships, 122 guns and 534 prisoners in just a year. His most famous engagement was the capture of the 32-gun Spanish frigate *El Gamo* in 1801. Cochrane ordered the hoisting of the American flag to confuse the Spanish. Cochrane stormed the Spanish ship with a boarding party which included the entire crew, except *Speedy*'s surgeon. He ordered one man to climb the mast and haul down the colours, whereupon the Spanish crew of 319 surrendered. Promoted to post-captain and given command of the frigates *Pallas* and later *Imperieuse*, Cochrane terrorized shipping along the French and Spanish coasts so much that Napoleon referred to him as the *Sea Wolf*. In 1808 he attacked

Valencia in Spain and captured several ships. At the Battle of Basque Roads in 1809 Cochrane used fireships to spread terror among the French squadron, most of which was run aground. The gunpowder on the fireships was pressed down with bricks, so that explosive force was directed outwards at the enemy instead of dissipated upwards. After serving with distinction during the Napoleonic Wars, he was wrongly jailed for a stock exchange fraud, and stripped of his naval rank and parliamentary seat. After sensationally escaping from prison in 1815, Cochrane was released. In 1817 he left England and for the next ten years commanded fleets for the Chilean, Brazilian and Greek navies in their wars of independence. The huge Spanish fortress of Valdivia was captured by 300 Chilean troops under Cochrane's command in 1820, and in the same year he cut out the flagship of the Spanish South American fleet, the *Esmeralda*, from the port of Callao in Peru. In charge of the small Brazilian fleet, Cochrane captured the Portuguese garrison of Bahia and accepted the surrender of the fortress at Maranhão. Cochrane was reinstated in the Royal Navy in 1832 under a new King, William IV, and a more sympathetic Whig Government. His final appointment in 1847 was to be Commander-in-Chief of the North American and West Indies Station. Cochrane was buried in Westminster Abbey.

BOY CORNWELL VC, 1900–16
Jack Travers Cornwell, 'Boy first class', is the youngest recipient of the Victoria Cross. He was awarded the VC for remaining at his post as sight-setter at the forward 5.5-inch gun in HMS *Chester* at the Battle of Jutland (31 May 1916), although mortally wounded, with dead and wounded lying all round him,

because '*he thought he might be needed*'. He died of his wounds on 2 June 1916.

DARLING, GRACE, 1815–42
The Grace Darling Museum in Bamburgh, Northumberland, commemorates the rescue of a ship's crew in 1838. Grace Darling and her lighthouse-keeper father rowed out from the Farne Islands Lighthouse, to rescue the stricken crew of the *Warder* at the height of a storm.

DREBBLE, CORNELIUS, 1572–1633 – THE MAKER OF THE FIRST SUBMARINE
William Bourne's design, detailed in his book *Inventions and Devises* of 1578, was one of the first recorded plans for an underwater

Cook, Captain James, 1728–79

Cook was an experienced merchant seaman, being offered his own command, but he wished to join the Royal Navy, signing on as an ordinary seaman. It was extremely rare for a seaman to become an officer, let alone a captain, but this is a partial list of Cook's achievements:

- The first circumnavigation of the world in both directions.
- The discovery of Australia.
- The charting of the South Island of New Zealand.
- A circumnavigation of Antarctica.
- The discovery of Tahiti and the New Hebrides.
- The discovery of the Sandwich Islands and the mapping of the Pacific Islands.

- The charting of the St Lawrence River.
- The drawing of navigational charts still in use today.
- The first man to realize that a properly-fed crew would not catch scurvy.
- The first man to test Harrison's chronometer at sea to establish longitude, thus contributing to the greatest advance in navigation for hundreds of years.

navigation vehicle. Bourne designed an enclosed craft capable of submerging by decreasing the overall volume (rather like flooding chambers found in modern submarines), and being rowed underwater. Bourne designed a ship with a wooden frame, covered in waterproofed leather. Using Bourne's plans, Drebbel manufactured a steerable submarine with a leather-covered wooden frame. He then built the first navigable submarine in 1620 while working for the Royal Navy. Between 1620 and 1624 Drebbel successfully built and tested two more submarines, each one bigger than the last. The third model was demonstrated to King James I in person and several thousand Londoners. It is said that the submarine stayed submerged in the Thames for three hours. It was driven by six oars through sealed holes, and the boat was forced under the water by changing the angle of the blades.

ERICSSON, CAPTAIN JOHN, 1803–89 – THE UNSUNG GENIUS

John Ericsson was a Swedish-born inventor and engineer. When serving in the Swedish army, he was sent to survey northern Sweden, and in his spare time he constructed a 'heat engine' which used fire smoke instead of steam. He moved to England in 1826 to try and capitalize on his invention, but found that it was not as effective with coal as with birch wood. He thus invented other engines based on steam, and added fans to the firebeds to improve their efficiency. In 1829, he built the *Novelty* steam engine, which was the fastest in the 'Rainhill Trials'. However, because of the *Novelty*'s boiler problems, the competition was luckily won by George Stevenson's *Rocket*. Struggling

with poverty, Ericsson now improved ship design with two screw-propellers, which moved in different directions and proved much better than a single screw. Ericsson built the *Francis B. Ogden* with twin screws, and took the Lords of the Admiralty for a trial voyage. Her speed was 10 mph (16 kph), but the Sea Lords were not convinced that the screw was superior to the paddle for steam propulsion. Ericsson then moved to the United States, where he designed a twin screw-propeller steamer, the sloop USS *Princeton*, the most advanced warship of the day. She was also designed to mount a 12-inch muzzle-loading gun on a revolving pedestal and there were other innovations. In 1843, she won a speed competition against the fastest paddle steamer, the SS *Great Western*. At the start of the Civil War in 1861, the Confederacy began developing an ironclad based on the hull of the USS *Merrimac*, following its burning by Union troops. For the Union Ericsson submitted drawings of the USS *Monitor*, a unique design of armoured ship, which progressed from plans to launch in around 100 days. In 1862, the appearance of the *Monitor* saved the Union fleet from defeat, and so influenced Union victory in the war. Ericsson later worked with torpedo inventions, e.g. *'The Destroyer'*, a boat which could launch its torpedoes underwater. In his book *Contributions to the Centennial Exhibition* (1877) he promoted so-called *'sun engines'*, using solar power as propellant for a hot air engine, but financial difficulties prevented the development of many of his inventions. He is regarded as one of the most influential mechanical engineers of all time, inventing and building the surface condenser, hot air engine, torpedo technology, hoop guns, the *Princeton* and *Monitor*, and a solar machine which used concave mirrors to run an engine.

FARRAGUT, DAVID, 1801–70

The US Navy's first admiral, he was the greatest captain in the American Civil War. He commanded the fleet which took New Orleans in 1862, and won the decisive Battle of Mobile Bay for the Union.

FISHER, JOHN ARBUTHNOT (JACKIE), 1841–1920 This British

admiral recognized the German threat before the outbreak of the First World War. Appointed First Sea Lord in 1904, he began the construction of the class-leading HMS *Dreadnought* battleship, promoted submarine developments, and forced through the switch from coal to oil-fired ships.

THE HERO OF CAMPERDOWN (CAMPERDUIN) Jack Crawford

(1775–1831) went to sea aged around 11, and was press-ganged to serve on HMS *Venerable* in 1796. In 1797, at the Battle of Camperdown against the Dutch, part of the mast was felled, and Admiral Duncan's personal flag came down. This was a sign of surrender, so Crawford climbed the remains of the mast under heavy gunfire, and nailed the colours back to the top. He was formally presented to the king after the battle, and granted a government pension of £30 a year.

HOLLAND, JOHN PHILIP,

1841–1914 An Irish-American, he pioneered work on submarines with his boat *Holland*, built in 1898. She proved that submarines could be practical and acted as a prototype for following generations. Holland's firm, the Electric

Boat Company, was taken over by General Dynamics and now builds most of the US Navy's submarines.

HULLS, JONATHAN, 1699–1758

A British inventor from Gloucestershire, he was possibly the first person ever to devise detailed plans for a steam-propelled ship. In 1736 Hulls obtained a patent for a machine to carry *'ships and vessels out of and into any harbour, port, or river against wind and tide or in a calm'*. This steam tugboat was illustrated in a pamphlet published in 1737. Its stern paddle wheel was to be driven by a Newcomen steam engine. The vessel was not a success.

JONES, JOHN PAUL, 1747–92

This Scottish-American sailor commanded the *Bonhomme Richard* when it captured HMS *Serapis* off Flamborough Head in 1799. When asked to surrender, he famously replied *'I have not yet begun to fight!'* He performed great deeds in the American Revolution, but in 1788 accepted a commission as rear-admiral in the Russian Navy fighting the Turks. He died in poverty in Paris, but his remains were later brought to the Naval Academy in Maryland and reburied with military honours.

KNOX-JOHNSTON, SIR ROBIN,

1939– Knox-Johnston was the first yachtsman to complete a non-stop solo circumnavigation of the globe, in *Suhali* in 1968–9, taking 313 days. (Sir Francis Chichester had made one stop, for provisions, during his voyage.)

LINCOLN, ABRAHAM, 1809–65

Probably the most distinguished man to have served as a ship's pilot, covering 4000 miles (6450 km) in flatboats before

Jones, Christopher, c.1570–1622

This mariner was captain of the *Mayflower* on the transatlantic voyage that established the Plymouth Colony settlement. In 1609, he had become the master of the *Mayflower*, owning a quarter of the ship. She was employed transporting goods such as wine, spices and furs, mainly between England and France. In 1620, when he was 50 years old, Christopher Jones and the *Mayflower* were hired to carry the Pilgrim Fathers and their cargo to Northern Virginia. He and the *Mayflower* stayed with the Pilgrims in America through that winter, during which half of the *Mayflower's* crew died. The *Mayflower* left the colony in April, and arrived back in England in May 1621. Jones took the *Mayflower* on another trading run to France later that year, but died shortly after, in March 1622. He was buried at St Mary's Rotherhithe, in southeast London.

he first ran for political office in 1832. Lincoln is also the only President ever to hold a patent, which he received in 1849 for his *'Improved Method of Lifting Vessels over Shoals.'*

LIND, JAMES, 1716–94 This naval surgeon was first to identify the value of using fresh fruit and vegetables to prevent scurvy, and he published *Treatise of the Scurvy* in 1734. He recommended the regular consumption of lemon juice, but nothing was done until 1795 when lime juice was issued by the Royal Navy, as it was much cheaper. Gosport Haslar Hospital reported 1754 cases of scurvy in 1760, but only one in 1806. Scurvy prevailed in the merchant navy until 1844, when lime juice began to be served to crew.

MILLER, CAPTAIN BETSY, 1792–1864 She was born in 1792 to a shipping family at Saltcoats in Ayrshire, and spent her childhood aboard her father's ship. She took over office duties when her brother Hugh took command of the family ship, the 14-man brig *Clytus*. When he drowned, she took over command of the ship, arguing *'Who knows her better than I do?'* For more than three decades she sailed between Ayrshire and Ireland, and was the first woman sea captain to be certificated as a sea captain by the Board of Trade. Known locally as *'the Queen of Saltcoats'*, she was mentioned in the House of Commons during a debate on the Merchant Shipping Act. By expanding from the cargos of timber shipped to Ireland by her father into coal and limestone, Betsy proved herself a highly successful businesswoman. She continued to sail until she was 70, and then handed over command of the *Clytus* to her youngest sister, Hannah, retiring to the family home in Saltcoats. She died there two years later in 1864.

NELSON'S COLUMN – THE MISTAKE

In his signal from his flagship *Victory* at Trafalgar, Nelson asked his Flag Lieutenant to signal *'England confides that every man will do his duty'*, and he added *'You must be quick for I have one more to make, which is for close action'*. Lieutenant Pasco asked if he could substitute *'expects'* for *'confides'* as the signal would be completed more quickly, because the word *'expects'* was in the 'abbreviated flag code vocabulary' while *'confides'* had to be spelt. Nelson replied immediately *'That will do, Pasco, make it directly.'* In the inscription on the base of Nelson's Column in Trafalgar Square, the word

'that' is erroneously omitted, and it reads *'England expects every man will do his duty.'* (Some naval authorities believe that the signal has been much altered from the actual Number 16 in the *'Naval Book'* – *'Engage the enemy more closely'*.)

PELLEW, ADMIRAL SIR EDWARD, VISCOUNT EXMOUTH, 1757–1833 – THE REAL HORNBLOWER

Pellew (aka Pellow) joined the Royal Navy at 13 and quickly showed promise during the American War of Independence, earning promotions through his bravery and qualities of leadership. In 1793, he was captain of the *Nymphe* and during the early stages of the Revolutionary Wars he seized the first French frigate of the struggle, the *Cléopâtre*. In 1796, near Plymouth, Pellew and his men bravely risked themselves to save the crew and passengers of the *Dutton*, a transport that had run aground in a fierce storm. In recognition of his

Nelson, Horatio, 1758–1805

Nelson went to sea aged 12, and led the British fleet that defeated the French at the Battle of the Nile in 1798. His actions led to the British beating the Danish fleet at Copenhagen in 1801. His right arm was shattered and he was blinded in one eye in other battles. In 1805 he died at the Battle of Trafalgar leading his forces against a Franco-Spanish fleet off Cadiz. Dressed conspicuously and remaining on deck, he had been hit by a sniper's bullet.

heroism he was rewarded with a baronetcy. His next command was the 44-gun frigate *Indefatigable*, and against a French ship-of-the-line, the 74-gun *Droits de l'Homme*, he destroyed the much more powerful ship in an all-night duel. He was a popular commander, and he risked his life more than once to dive in and save a drowning man. In 1804 he was made a rear-admiral. While naval chief in the East Indies he destroyed Dutch naval power in the area. From 1808 he was in charge of the North Sea Fleet, and then the Mediterranean Fleet (succeeding Nelson), being promoted to admiral in 1814. After the defeat of Napoleon, Pellew led an allied army assault on horseback against the French revolutionaries. His final campaign included the famous attack on Algiers, after the Dey of Algiers had refused to free Christians held as slaves in his lands. Pellew faced 100 guns and 8000 gunners when he sailed into the harbour at Algiers. The enemy's casualties at Algiers totalled around 7000 men, while the British and Dutch losses were only about 900. The Dey agreed to all of Britain's demands, and a total of 1211 slaves were released. Piracy declined substantially after Pellew's bombardment of Algiers.

'QUICKSILVER BOB' – ROBERT FULTON, 1765–1815 Experiments with

paddle boats driven by man power or horse power had already been tried without success as early as the 17th century. David Ramsay, Dr Grant, and the Marquis of Worcester then each suggested the use of steam to drive ships. A Frenchman called Papin made a steamboat, and in 1736 Jonathan Hulls of Gloucestershire built a large boat which

he tried to drive by a Newcomen steam engine. Robert Fulton was from Pennsylvania, and was popularly known as 'Quicksilver Bob'. He was an architect, painter and an inventor. In 1786 he travelled to England, and while there invented a new machine for spinning flax, another for twisting hemp rope and a third which was a great shovel which scooped up earth to excavate canals. In the 1790s Fulton was commissioned to build his designs for an advanced *'diving boat'* by Napoleon. The intention was to use it to sink English ships. Fulton now built the first submarine, and in 1801 descended to 25 feet (7.6 m) below the surface of Brest harbour in France. On a second trial he travelled for 500 yards (460 m) under water, using compressed air to enable himself and his crew to breathe. On another occasion, he remained under water for 1 hour 40 minutes. However, his *Nautilus* was not successful. Fulton's friend, the Earl of Stanhope, now gave Fulton the idea of propelling boats by steam. Fulton went to Birmingham, and after studying Watt's double-acting steam engine, had a large model built to his own order and shipped to America. He entered into partnership with Chancellor Livingstone, who gave money to fund the building of the *Clermont*. Fulton's English-made engine was installed in it, which was then fitted to drive paddle wheels. On 17 August 1807, Fulton went aboard at New York, started up his engine, and began his historic journey to Albany, the capital of New York State. This was the first practical boat in the world to defy wind and tide. Before he died, aged just 51, Fulton had built 17 steamers which plied up and down the Hudson River.

RUYTER, ADMIRAL MICHIEL DE, 1607–76 In the Anglo-Dutch Wars
he destroyed the English fleet which was anchored on the Medway, and captured its flagship. He was considered to be the leading seaman of his day, and died in the Mediterranean fighting the French.

ST NICHOLAS
The patron saint of sailors is in another guise 'Santa Claus', and he is also the patron saint of prisoners in both Greece and Russia. According to legend, on a trip to Palestine in a terrible storm St Nicholas calmed the waves around the stricken boat in which he was travelling.

SULLIVAN BROTHERS In January
1942 five brothers, the Sullivans, joined the US Navy to avenge a friend who had been killed at Pearl Harbor. They enlisted with the stipulation that they all serve together and all five were assigned to the light cruiser USS *Juneau*. More than 600 crew were killed when the *Juneau* was torpedoed at the Battle of Guadalcanal 13 November 1942, including all five Sullivan brothers. The 'Fighting Sullivan Brothers' became national heroes. As a direct result of the Sullivans' deaths, the US War Department adopted the Sole Survivor Policy, which is a set of regulations in the US military that are designed to protect members of a family from conscription or combat duty if they have already lost family members in the course of military service.

'TAKE HER DOWN!' Commander
Howard Walter Gilmore was desperately wounded and unable to climb down from the bridge into the conning tower of his submarine, USS *Growler* (SS-215). Facing certain death, he issued this command in the face of an approaching Japanese gunboat, 7 February 1943, sacrificing his life so that the boat could submerge and escape. Gilmore was posthumously awarded the Medal of Honor for distinguished gallantry.

THE UNKNOWN HERO In the
merchant navy, when torpedoed, a man's pay was instantly stopped, unlike in the Royal Navy. He received no pay until he signed on for his next voyage. The coastal town of Barry, in South Wales, lost proportionately more men in the merchant navy in the Second World War than any other Allied port. One man was luckier than most, but he is unknown to history. Ernie Haysham survived the war, having been sunk no less than seven times, returning to sea each time. There was no traumatic stress disorder or psychological counselling or compensation in those days of war for soldiers, sailors, airmen and civilians who witnessed the most terrible events. People were just supposed to get on with it – and they did. And without going back to sea, there would be no income for Ernie Haysham's family. The greatest heroes of the war were arguably the mariners of the merchant navy.

THE UNKNOWN SAILOR

The body of an *Unknown Sailor* was found off Christmas Island in the Indian Ocean on 7 February 1942, lying on a Carling raft. There was German shrapnel in his head, the raft was 'riddled with shrapnel' and there was a pair of someone else's boots in it. Many believe him to have been a member of the crew of HMAS *Sydney*, lost at sea on 19 November 1941. No survivor of the 645 crew was ever found. In October 2006 a Royal Australian Navy search team visited the Old European Cemetery on Christmas Island. After an exhaustive search they successfully located the grave of the Unknown Sailor, and exhumed the remains which have been subject to dental, anthropological, pathological, ballistic, metallurgical and DNA analysis at a variety of locations. Identification is as yet unsuccessful.

VAN TROMP, MARTIN, 1597–1653

This great Dutch admiral was killed at the Battle of Scheveningen. After one victory in the Anglo-Dutch Wars, he is said to have tied a broom to the masthead, symbolic of his desire to sweep the English from the seas. His death was not only a severe blow to the Dutch navy, but also to those who sought the defeat of the Commonwealth of England and restoration of the Stuart monarchy.

WALKER, 'JOHNNIE', 1896–1944

Captain Frederic John Walker, CB, DSO and three Bars, served in the destroyers *Mermaid* and *Sarpedon* in 1916 and 1917 respectively. In the Second World War he received a command in October 1941, taking control of the 36th Escort Group and flying his flag in the *Bittern* class sloop *Stork*. His escort group comprised two sloops (including *Stork*) and six corvettes and was based in Liverpool, HQ of Western Approaches Command. In December 1941 his group escorted Convoy HG76 of 32 ships to Gibraltar. During the convoy's voyage five U-boats were sunk in ten days as a result of his innovative tactics. On the return voyage another four U-boats were sunk. In 1942 Walker left the 36th Group, granting him some respite to recuperate from the burden of overwork. Walker begged to be allowed to return to active service, and returned to be commander of the Second Support Group in 1943, consisting of six sloops. Walker flew his flag in *Starling*, a newly commissioned sloop. It was the first hunter-killer group intended to actively hunt and destroy the U-boats that infested in the Atlantic, rather than being restricted to simply escorting convoys. Walker had suggested the idea, and many more U-boats were destroyed in 1943 and 1944 as a result. One successful tactic employed by Walker was for three or more sloops in line to launch depth charges to saturate an area of sea in a manner similar to a rolling barrage by artillery which precedes an infantry attack. During this effort Walker's dedication was terrific, and he took no break from his duties. This would ultimately contribute to his death. Walker suffered a cerebral thrombosis on 7 July 1944 and died two days later aged 48, his death being attributed to overwork and battle fatigue. He was due to be knighted. Walker sank more U-boats during the Battle of the Atlantic than any other British or Allied commander, and was instrumental in the Allied victory of the Battle of the Atlantic, probably the most pivotal campaign of the war.

OTHER INTERESTING
SEA PEOPLE

BEFORE HIS TIME In 1922 retired Admiral Bradley A. Fiske, well-known for his nautical inventions, unveiled a reading machine, the fore-runner of today's 'e-book'. He also invented a device to make reading glasses redundant.

BILLY BLUE and the BLUE PETER Admiral Sir William Cornwallis (1744–1819) was a captain at the Battle of Grenada in 1779. He fought the French twice in the West Indies, and then served at the second relief of Gibraltar and the battles of St Kitts and the Saintes in 1782. After service in the East Indies, he led *'the retreat of Cornwallis'* in 1795, with four ships beating off a French fleet of 12 ships-of-the-line and several frigates. He became a full admiral in 1799 and was very popular with his sailors. His affectionate nicknames included *'Billy go tight'* (possibly because his florid complexion suggested that he was often drunk), *'Coachee'*, *'Mr Whip'* and *'Billy Blue'*. The *'Blue Peter'*, the signal for 'P' in the international code, is a blue flag pierced with a rectangular white centre, and is the universal signal for a ship about to sail, though no longer used in the navy in that sense. The term may to be a corruption of the French *partir* – to leave. The complete expression is attributed to Cornwallis who used to hoist the *Blue Peter* on anchoring to indicate that his fleet would sail again very shortly and so no leave would be granted. For his pains he was nicknamed *'Billy Blue'* by his crews who failed to appreciate his keenness for action.

BYNG, JOHN, 1704–57 During the Seven Years War, this admiral was held responsible for losing Minorca to the French in 1756. In 1757 he was court-martialled and shot on HMS *Monarch*. Voltaire satirically noted the event in *Candide*: *'In this country we find it pays to kill an admiral from time to time to encourage the others'*.

DÖNITZ, ADMIRAL KARL, 1891–1980 He commanded Germany's U-boats from 1939–43, devising and improving their 'wolf-pack' strategy. He succeeded Erich Raeder as Commander-in-Chief of the navy in 1943, and was nominated by Hitler as his successor. The admiral negotiated the surrender of the Third Reich and was subsequently sentenced to ten years imprisonment at the war trials held at Nuremburg.

FUDGE The expression *'Fudging the books'* comes from Captain Fudge, known as *'Lying Fudge'*. He was the captain of the *Black Eagle* which was to transport 55 Quakers in August 1665 from the Newgate to the colonies as a punishment for offences against the Conventicle Act. Delayed at Gravesend, by October 19 prisoners and some crew had died of the plague. He was arrested for debt and his remaining crew mutinied. In February 1666 the ship at last left for the West Indies, but was seized by a Dutch privateer and the Quakers were freed. Israel d'Israeli, the father of the Prime Minister Benjamin D'Israeli, wrote in 1791: *There was, sir, in our time one Captain Fudge, who upon his return from a voyage, how ill-fraught soever his books, always brought home a good cargo of lies, so much that now aboard ship the sailors, when they hear a great lie, cry out "You fudge it!"*

THE GENIUS OF MANAGEMENT

Vice-Admiral Sir George Tryon (1832–93) was commanding the fleet from the brand-new battleship HMS *Victoria* during manoeuvres off Tripoli in 1893. In his flagship he was travelling at 8 knots (9.2 mph/14.8 kph), leading a column of six ships. Rear-Admiral Hastings Markham was in the *Camperdown*, leading the second division of five ships. Tryon discussed his plans for anchoring the fleet with some officers. He wanted the fleet to sail alongside each other 1200 yards (1100 m) apart and then turn inwards in succession by 180 degrees, closing to 400 yards (365 m) and reversing their direction of travel. After travelling a few miles in this formation, the whole fleet would slow. The warships would then simultaneously turn 90 degrees to port and anchor. The officers observed that even 1200 yards between

the two divisions was much too close, let alone 400 yards. They respectfully suggested that the columns should start at least 1600 yards (1460 m) apart, as the combined turning circles of the *Camperdown* and *Victoria* were 1600 yards. Even this would leave insufficient margin for safety. A gap of 2000 yards (1830 m) would be needed for the manoeuvre to be effected safely.

However, Tryon ordered the distance closed to 1300 yards (1190 m), and then reduced it to 1000 yards (915 m). He was again questioned by his officers and angrily shouted that his order was correct. He ordered speed increased to 8.8 knots, making it even more dangerous. Markham, at the head of the other column, was confused by the dangerous order, and delayed raising the flag signal indicating that he had understood it. This caused another flag signal from Tryon – *'What are you waiting for?'* After this rebuke from his commander, Markham immediately ordered his column to start turning. Various officers on the two flagships confirmed later that they had either assumed or hoped that Tryon would order some new manoeuvre at the last minute. Captain Maurice Bourke of the *Victoria* asked Tryon no less than three times for permission to order the engines astern. At the last moment Tryon shouted across to Markham *'Go astern, go astern'*. By the time that both captains had ordered the engines on their ships reversed, it was too late, and *Camperdown's* bow struck the starboard side of *Victoria* about 12 feet (3.6 m) below the waterline. *Victoria* capsized just 13 minutes after the collision, and soon sank. *Camperdown* herself was in a serious condition, but survived, with her crew having to construct a cofferdam across the main deck to stop the flooding. The following ships had more time to take evasive action, and just avoided colliding with each other in turn. A total of 357 crew were rescued but 358 died. Tryon remained on the bridge as the ship sank, and was heard to say, *'It's all my fault'*.

HENRY VII, 1457–1509 Henry Tudor effectively ended the Wars of the Roses (1455–89) and set about making the realm safe from invasion and protecting trade. He used import levies to build his own ships rather than rely on 'borrowing' converted merchantmen. His *'King's Ships'* included the *Mary Fortune, Sweepstake, Regent* and *Sovereign*, and

thus his son Henry VIII inherited a great fleet of warships, Britain's first real navy.

HOUQUA, 1769–1843 The richest Chinese man involved in the China Trade. His *'hong'* or guild controlled all the tea, silk and porcelain that passed through Canton. His personal wealth was estimated at $26 million in 1834, making him a multi-billionaire in today's terms.

KRETCHSMER, OTTO, 1912–88 The most successful U-boat commander of the Second World War, sinking 47 Allied ships and damaging six others. His motto was *'one torpedo, one ship'*. He was trapped by British destroyers in 1941, and scuttled his boat before he and his crew were taken prisoner.

Henry VIII, 1491–1547

Henry VIII increased his father's fleet to form the largest permanent fleet in the world, and was in effect the *'founder of the modern Royal Navy'*. He brought in gun-founders from Flanders, Italian shipwrights and other foreign talent to the naval dockyards. Guns were being developed that needed a new type of ship to carry them. Cannon could now fire a 24-pound (11-kg) stone ball almost a mile, preventing other warships from closing for hand-to-hand fighting. The weight of these cannon meant that they could no longer be secured on the top deck, but had to be placed lower in the ship. The *Mary Rose* was built in 1513, and she was the first

ship to have ports in her sides through which guns would fire. The *Henry Grâce à Dieu* (called at the time the *Great Harry*) was built at Woolwich in 1514, and also had the new gunports. She still carried around 2000 bows and arrows, but from 1568 *broadsides* were used to sink ships and kill men, rather than hand-to-hand fighting.

LAST MESSAGE Richard Haliburton (1900–39), the American writer, swam the Panama Canal (paying a toll of 36 cents) and wrote about his experiences travelling the world. He attempted to sail a Hong Kong junk to San Francisco, and all hands were lost. His prescient last message was: *'Southerly gales, squalls, lee rail under water, wet bunks, hard tack, bully beef, wish you were here – instead of me!'*

LIFEBOAT SURVIVOR Poon Lim (1918–91) was a steward aboard the British merchant navy vessel the SS *Ben Lomond*, torpedoed by the German U-boat U-172 on 23 November 1942, off the coast of Brazil. Poon Lim spotted an empty liferaft to which he swam, and climbed in. With no other survivors in sight he soon realized he was alone and drifting with the ocean swell. Keeping alive for 133 days by eating fish he caught with a crude fishing-line and hook, he was rescued by a fishing boat which took him to Brazil, 700 miles (1125 km) from where his ship sank. There the British consul arranged for him to return to Britain. Poon Lim was the sole survivor of the 54-man crew and holds the world's record as the longest lifeboat survivor. The longest time being adrift at sea in a ship was recorded by Captain Jukichi and one of his crew. Their ship was damaged in a storm off Japan and they drifted for 484 days before being rescued off California in 1815.

LONGEST SERVING SAILOR – 96 YEARS IN SERVICE This was Admiral of the Fleet Sir Provo William Perry Wallis (1791–1892). His father wanted his son to pursue a naval career, and managed to get the four-year-old Provo registered in 1795 as an able

seaman on the 36-gun frigate HMS *Oiseau*. In 1796 Provo became a volunteer in the 40-gun frigate *Prevoyante*, where he remained (on paper at least) for two years before serving in the 64-gun *Asia* until 1800 when he was aged nine. He was then promoted to midshipman on the 32-gun frigate *Cleopatra*. In 1809 he was commissioned as a lieutenant on the *Curieux*. After service in four more ships, in January 1812 aged 20 he was appointed second lieutenant of the 38-gun frigate *Shannon*. The *Shannon* fought with the USS *Chesapeake* off Boston in 1813, an action in which the captain was badly wounded and the first lieutenant was killed. Provo Wallis thus had to captain the *Shannon* as she sailed to Nova Scotia with the captured *Chesapeake*. For this achievement, Wallis was promoted to commander. He served for the rest of the war in command of the 12-gun sloop *Snipe*, and was made captain in 1819. Continually in service, he became naval aide-de-camp to Queen Victoria in 1847. In 1851 he became a rear-admiral, and successively a vice-admiral, admiral, and eventually admiral of the fleet, aged 86. From 1870, the retirement scheme for admirals allowed those who had commanded a ship during the Napoleonic Wars to remain on the active list until death, so his total service amounted to 96 years. He was both the last surviving commanding officer from the Napoleonic Wars and the last veteran of the wars to serve as Admiral of the Fleet.

'NOBBY' OR CAPTAIN EWART Charles J.F. Ewart was in command of HMS *Melpomone* in the Mediterranean and West Indies 1859–63, and was renowned for his strict views on uniformity. Stories related of him include the whitewashing of one of the ship's fowls so that it would match the colour of the others, the securing of fowls to the deck with staples and tacks to ensure their being accurately *'dressed by the right'* for inspection, and even blackening the eyes of the rest of his boat's crew when one member appeared with a black eye. He went on to become an admiral, and his nickname was passed on to all men called Ewart in the navy. At the opera in Malta, it was recorded that he was taking his seat when some sailors on one side of the stalls shouted *'Who whitewashed the goose?'*, and those on the other side responded, *'Why, Nobby Ewart!'*

OCEANOS, CAPTAIN AVRANAS – 'WOMEN AND CHILDREN LAST'

The *Oceanos*, a Greek cruise ship, suffered a machinery explosion off South Africa in 1991 and began to sink. There were 40-knot (46-mph/74-kph) winds and 30-feet (9-m) swells. The supply of power to auxiliary equipment to run the engines had been cut, so the ship was drifting and flooding. Captain Yiannis Avranas and the crew took to the boats, but the lower deck portholes were not closed, which is standard emergency procedure. Nearby vessels responded to the ship's SOS and gave assistance. The South African Navy and Air Force launched a huge seven-hour rescue mission, using 16 helicopters to airlift the remainder of the passengers and crew to nearby island settlements. All 571 people onboard were saved, and entertainers Julian Butler and Moss Hills recorded the efforts to assist the passengers with a home video recorder. Butler, Hills and

Hills' wife Tracy were among the last five passengers to be rescued from the ship. At about 3:30p.m. on the following day, the *Oceanos* sank. The captain was accused by the passengers of leaving hundreds behind, with no one other than the ship's onboard entertainers to help them evacuate. Avranas claimed that he left the ship first in order to arrange for a rescue effort, and that he then supervised the rescue effort from a helicopter. Avranas was quoted in the *New York Times*: *'When I give the order abandon ship, it doesn't matter what time I leave. Abandon is for everybody. If some people want to stay, they can stay.'* Epirotiki Lines had lost the company's flagship *Pegasus* only two months before, and the *Jupiter* three years before.

O'HIGGINS, GENERAL BERNARDO, 1778–1842 – THE LIBERATOR OF CHILE

The son of Ambrosio O'Higgins, Viceroy of Peru, he was Supreme Director of Chile (1817–23) and organized the first Chilean navy, under the command of Lord Thomas Cochrane and Manuel Encalada.

PARKINSON'S LAW AND THE ROYAL NAVY

In 1957, C. Northcote Parkinson wrote a series of essays illustrating what he called *Parkinson's Law*: *'Work expands so as to fill the time available for its completion.'* To offer further elucidation he wrote: *'Granted that work (and especially paperwork) is this elastic in its demands on time, it is manifest that there need be little or no relationship between the work to be done and the size of the staff to which it may be assigned. A lack of real activity does not, of necessity, result in leisure. A lack of occupation is not necessarily revealed by manifest idleness.*

The thing to be done swells in importance and complexity in a direct ratio with the time to be spent ... Politicians and taxpayers have assumed (with occasional phases of doubt) that a rising total in the number of civil servants must reflect a growing volume of work to be done.' To explain further, Parkinson used the fact that although the Royal Navy was in speedy decline, its administrative bureaucracy was ever-expanding in complexity and staff numbers. Using his law, Parkinson wondered why the Royal Navy continued to add more staff, and came up with two axioms: 1) *An official wants to multiply subordinates, not rivals*; and 2) *Officials make work for each other.* Thus, if a person feels overworked, he or she has three simple options: to resign; to share the work with another person; or to request two subordinates to help with the work. Parkinson rightly states, *'There is probably no instance in history, however, of choosing any but the third alternative.'* It would do no good for the person to resign, and sharing the work with another person would be too competitive and bring on board an unwelcome rival. Parkinson used Admiralty data to 'prove' his Law. Incidentally, the 8118 Admiralty and dockyard employees in 1935 rose to number 33,788 by 1954, while the number of ships declined again.

PARKINSON'S LAW UPDATED – LETTER TO THE TIMES 16 May

2008 *'Messrs Falconer and Dias give figures of 30 rear-admirals for the 20 frigates, submarines and other main warships now in commission. I recall that, as one rear-admiral at the height of the Cold War, I was in command of 37 submarines – 4 Polaris missile submarines, 16 fleet*

nuclear submarines and 17 diesel submarines. So one and a half rear-admirals per ship does sound quite a lot. Where are they all going to sleep?' Richard Heaslip, West Parley, Dorset.

Actually it seems Britain has three aircraft carriers (at the end of their commissioning days), eight destroyers, 17 frigates and 13 submarines, making 41 main warships, or 1.3 rear-admirals per ship. This is approximately 1/28th the workload of a rear-admiral of 30 years ago.

PETER I, CZAR OF RUSSIA

1672–1725 'Peter the Great' modernized Russia, turning it into a European power, and is known as *'The Father of the Russian Navy'*. He studied shipbuilding in London and took several eminent shipbuilders back to Russia to build a modern fleet. They were greatly honoured for their work.

PRESIDENT KENNEDY AND THE PRESIDENT'S DESK

The Royal Navy barque *Resolute*, used for Arctic research, was stuck in ice and abandoned. The crew escaped, and the ice floe encasing the ship drifted south. It was found by a US whaler off Cape Mercy. She was brought back to Boston, refitted by the US Government and sent back to England. When the ship eventually came to be broken up, a desk was fashioned from its timbers and sent by Queen Victoria to President Rutherford Hayes in 1880 *'In memory of the courtesy and loving-kindness of the American people.'* Every president since Hayes (except Presidents Johnson, Nixon and Ford) has used the *Resolute* desk. The desk has twice been modified from the original design. Franklin Roosevelt requested that the kneehole should be fitted with a modesty panel carved with the presidential seal. He preferred people not see his leg braces and often placed a waste-paper basket in front of his desks, but he did not live to see it installed. However, President Truman liked the panel's eagle motif and had it installed when he came into office in 1945. Much later, Ronald Reagan requested that the desk should be raised on a 2-inch (5-cm) base to better accommodate him and other tall presidents. The desk was made famous by a photograph of John Kennedy at work while his son, John Jr, peeked out of the front through the kneehole panel. An identical desk was made for Buckingham Palace.

THE REAL McCOY A rum-runner during the Prohibition Era, Captain Bill McCoy's clients always received the finest rum from his ship, rather than stuff of questionable quality, so you could always trust him. Hence the origin of the phrase denoting prime quality goods.

RMS TITANIC, THE SINKING OF, 1912

The President of the White Star Line, Bruce Ismay, was a passenger on the ship, and his decision to save his own life was so widely condemned that he lived as a recluse for the rest of his years, dying in 1937. A total of 1503 lives were lost, simply because the ship was designed to be 'unsinkable', so there were not enough lifeboats. It had watertight bulkheads

athwartships, but the iceberg opened up a long gash all down her side, so they were useless and the ship listed irrecoverably.

VON TRAPP, GEORG, 1880–1947

Born a Croat, this Austrian submarine captain married the granddaughter of the inventor of the Whitehead torpedo. At the end of the First World War, Trapp's wartime record stood at 19 war patrols during which he sank 12 cargo vessels, a French cruiser and an Italian submarine. For his service, Trapp was raised to the nobility and granted the right to use the word *von* before his name. The end of the First World War saw the defeat and collapse of the Austro-Hungarian Empire. According to the peace terms, Austria was reduced in size to its German-speaking core, losing its coastline. Austria now had no need for a navy, leaving von Trapp without a job. However, his wife Agathe's inherited wealth was sufficient to sustain the family. They had seven children. In 1922, Agathe died of scarlet fever contracted from the children. In about 1926, one of the children, Maria, was recovering from an illness and was unable to attend school. Von Trapp hired a tutor, Maria Kutschera, from a local convent. She and Georg married in 1927, and he fathered three more children. In the 1930s von Trapp lost all his wealth. Maria took charge and arranged for concert engagements for the ten children to sing at various events to earn money. In 1938, the family, opposed to Hitler's annexation of Austria and having received offers to perform in the United States, left Austria. They fled to Italy by train (not to Switzerland on foot as in the film) and then to the USA. This story is the factual basis for the musical *The Sound of Music*.

'Screw Smith', 1808–74 – The Inventor of the Screw Marine Propeller

Before the end of the 18th century several patents were taken out for screw propellers, but nothing practical was done until Francis Pettit Smith began to experiment. 'Screw Smith' was a farmer who grazed sheep on Romney Marshes in Kent. His first model was made in 1834, when Smith was 26 years old. The screw in his little boat was worked by a powerful spring. Two years later he took out a patent for propelling vessels by means of a screw revolving beneath the water at the stern, and later that year a small steam vessel of 10 tons with an engine of 6 hp was built to test the invention. The vessel was tried on the Thames, and ran well but slowly. As she sailed up the river the wooden screw struck some floating timber and broke in half, but the boat was propelled forward more rapidly than before. The screw had been in two turns. Smith therefore fitted a new screw with only one turn, with which his vessel worked much better, and the modern screw propeller, with which all ships are fitted, is of this one-turn shape. In 1839 he produced the *Archimedes*, a wooden vessel of 237 tons fitted with his patent screw. Her builders said she would not do more than 5 knots (6 mph/9 kph), but her speed was no less than 9.5 knots (11 mph/17.5 kph). In 1840 she made a tour of all the major ports of Great Britain. After seeing and examining the *Archimedes*, the great engineer Brunel redesigned his ship *Great Britain* and fitted her with a screw. The *Great Britain*, built in 1843, was 274 feet (83.5 m) in length, and much the largest steamer which had been launched up to that date. The first British warship to be fitted with a screw was the *Rattler*, of 888 tons. Trialled against the *Alecto*, a paddle ship of similar power, the *Rattler* easily won. Smith's invention was successful, but by 1856, when his patent expired, he had exhausted all his money by developing and testing it. However, the Institute of Civil Engineers subscribed £2000 as a testimonial, Queen Victoria gave him a Civil List pension of £200 a year and he was made Curator of the Patent Museum at South Kensington. In 1871, three years before he died, he was knighted.

XERXES – NOT A GOOD MAN TO WORK FOR

This Persian emperor attempted to invade Greece in 482 BCE but lost his shipborne supplies as a result of bad weather. A bridge across the Hellespont failed and he ordered the surface of the Hellespont to be whipped 300 times to show his imperial displeasure. When later defeated by the Athenians at Salamis in 480 BCE, all survivors who swam ashore from Xerxes' fleet were executed on his orders. If they swam ashore amongst the Greeks, they were also slaughtered.

ZHENG HE – THE ADMIRAL OF THE WESTERN SEAS

In the 1930s, a stone pillar was discovered in a town in Fujian province, China, with an inscription that described the voyages of a Chinese *'eunuch admiral'* named Zheng He. On it, he described how the emperor of the Ming Dynasty had ordered him to sail to *'the countries beyond the horizon'*, *'all the way to the end of the earth'*. His mission was to display the might of Chinese power and collect tribute from the *'barbarians from beyond the seas'*. The inscription contains the Chinese names for the countries Zheng He visited, 30 nations stretching from Asia to Africa as he voyaged about 35,000 miles (56,300 km). Originally named Ma He, Zheng He was a Muslim from Yunnan Province. When the Ming Dynasty conquered the province in 1378, he was taken to the imperial Chinese capital to serve as a court eunuch. Becoming a great influence in court, he was given command of the Chinese navy. In 1402 Zheng He and Wang Jinghong took a giant fleet to the *Western Ocean* (today's southeast Asia), initiating trade and cultural exchanges.

The number of ships of his fleet ranged from 40 to 63 on his various voyages, and personnel included many soldiers and sailors on each voyage. The total party numbered over 27,000 people. Between 1405 and 1433 he led seven more Chinese expeditions to the Western Ocean, to Java, Jeddah, the Arabian Sea, the Bay of Bengal, probably even rounding Africa's Cape of Good Hope 70 years before the Portuguese did so. His achievements show that China had the ships and navigational skills to explore the world, but China chose not to follow up on these voyages. Instead, the Chinese emperor destroyed their ocean-going ships and halted further expeditions. Thus, a century later, Europeans would 'discover' China, instead of the Chinese 'discovering' Europe. Chinese shipbuilders also developed fore-and-aft sails, the stern post rudder, and boats with paddlewheels. Watertight compartments below decks kept the ship from sinking. Some boats were armour-plated for protection. All these developments made long distance navigation possible. At each country Zheng He visited, he was to present gifts from the emperor and to exact tribute for the glory of the Ming Dynasty. Because China developed its culture in isolation from other great civilizations, it saw itself as the centre of the world. The Chinese therefore called their country *'the Middle Kingdom'*.

NAVIGATORS, NAVIGATION, EXPLORERS AND MAPS

THE ALBERTINUS DE VIRGA WORLD MAP, 1411–15 This Venetian's map (stolen, and lost since 1923) gives a fairly accurate shape of Africa at a time when the continent had not yet been fully explored by European sailors. Around 1415, the Portuguese were just beginning the Age of Discovery, occupying Ceuta on the northern tip of Africa, and none of their sailors had ever voyaged beyond the Canary Islands. (Ceuta is now a Spanish enclave within Morocco.) The source of the information on which the map is based is unknown, although it has been suggested that it could have come from Muslim traders, or possibly from Chinese mapmakers who sailed under Admiral Zheng He.

ANSON, ADMIRAL GEORGE, 1697–1762 This wealthy aristocrat circumnavigated the globe 1740–4, capturing a Spanish treasure galleon, but only one ship of the seven, HMS *Centurion*, completed the voyage. Of his 1955 men 1051 were lost, mainly to scurvy. As First Lord of the Admiralty, he professionalized England's navy.

ANTIKYTHERA MECHANISM – THE WORLD'S OLDEST SCIENTIFIC DEVICE This was discovered with hundreds of valuable artifacts, off the island of Antikythera between Greece and Crete, in 1901. It came from a Greek cargo ship of 150–100 BCE. About a foot (30 cm) high, made of bronze and originally in a wooden frame, 30 of its 37 gear wheels survive. It was used for predicting the positions of the Sun and Moon. Three-dimensional surface-imaging indicates that it could also predict not only planetary motions but also the 18-year Saros, the 54-day Exeligmos, the 19-year Metonic and the 76-year Callippic astronomical cycles. Artefacts of similar complexity did not appear again until well over a millennium later. Although only the size of a shoebox, the mechanism is too valuable to leave its museum in Athens, so a 7.5 ton X-ray tomography machine was transported there from England to examine the device. It has enabled 932 characters to be read on the hidden inscriptions, compared to 180 'almost illegible' characters previously uncovered. Its technical sophistication is a mystery, hinting at an unknown civilization.

BAFFIN, WILLIAM, 1584–1622

He searched for the Northwest Passage, naming Baffin Bay and Baffin Island in Canada in the process, and was the first navigator to measure longitude at sea by the position of the Moon.

BALBOA, VASCO NÚÑEZ DE,

1475–1517 The Spanish navigator and conquistador crossed Panama and was the first European to see the Pacific Ocean from the Americas, naming it the South Sea in 1513. He found gold and pearls and wished to become governor of the region, but was falsely accused of treason and beheaded.

BALLARD, ROBERT DUANE,

1942– This American undersea explorer, marine scientist, and US Naval officer has been on over 65 underwater expeditions in submarines and deep diving submersibles. He found the wreck of the *Titanic* in 1985 and has discovered many other wrecks. The *Titanic* was not his main priority at that time – he was on a secret US Navy mission to locate the lost nuclear submarines *Scorpion* and *Thresher*. Ballard has revolutionized undersea exploring by using remotely controlled submersible robotic devices including *Argo-Jason*. *Argo* is a remotely controlled submersible vehicle with cameras, and *Jason* is a vehicle that is carried in *Argo* and sent from it to collect samples and perform other functions.

BEEBE, WILLIAM, 1877–1962

An American naturalist and undersea explorer. In 1932, Beebe and Otis Barton descended 3000 feet (914 m) in a bathysphere, a pressurized steel sphere which they invented. They made the descent off the coast of Nonsuch Island,

Bermuda, and during the dive they communicated with their team at the surface via telephone.

BELLINGSHAUSEN, FABIAN VON, 1778–1852 Russian naval officer

credited with discovering Antarctica between 1819 and 1821.

BERING, VITUS JONASSEN,

1680–1741 Peter the Great of Russia appointed this Danish navigator to lead an expedition to establish if Asia and Alaska were connected. In 1728 he sailed between the continents, in the waters now known as the Bering Sea and the Bering Strait, without spotting land. In 1741 he repeated the voyage and sighted Alaska. Heavy fog forced him to land on Bering Island, where he died of scurvy.

BIANCO, ANDREA An Italian

sailor-cartographer of the 15th century, his 1436 atlas comprised ten leaves of vellum, with the ninth leaf being a circular world map measuring 10 inches (25 cm) in circumference. The tenth leaf contains a depiction of the Ptolemaic world map on Ptolemy's first projection, with graduation. Some believe that Bianco's maps were the first to correctly portray the coast of Florida, as a large peninsula is attached to a large western island named Antillia. Columbus sailed to the New World over 50 years later, in 1492. Bianco also collaborated with Fra Mauro on the Fra Mauro world map of 1459.

CABOT, JOHN (GIOVANNI CABOTO), c.1450–98

An Italian, he sailed under the English flag from Bristol in 1497 in the *Matthew*, looking for the Northwest Passage to India. He claimed and named Nova Scotia and Newfoundland for England, thinking he had reached Asia. King Henry VII had instructed Cabot to avoid the southern trade routes as the Spanish or Portuguese were likely to seize the *Matthew*, so he had sailed across the Atlantic looking for a route leading to the silk and spice markets of the East. He was thus the first known European to have reached the North American continent. Cabot may have named America after his backer, Richard Amerika. Rewarded with a pension, Cabot set sail again with five ships but died at sea. His son Sebastian (1484–1557) searched for the Northwest and Northeast Passages. A replica of the *Matthew* celebrated the 500th anniversary of the discovery of America by crossing the Atlantic to Newfoundland in 1997. She is now moored in Bristol, alongside the SS *Great Britain*.

CABRILLO, JUAN RODRIGUEZ d.1543

This Portuguese sailor in the service of Spain was the first European to sail the Californian coast, and claimed the west coast of America for Spain in 1542.

CAPE BOJADOR – GIL EANES AND THE FIRST STEP IN EUROPEAN COLONIZATION

Some commentators have argued that the rounding of this cape, on the coast of the Western Sahara, was even more significant for mankind than the voyages of Columbus. It is also known as *'the bulging cape'* and by the Arabs as Abu Khatar *(The Father of Danger)*. The discovery of a passable route around Cape Bojador, in 1434, by the Portuguese explorer Gil Eanes was the main breakthrough for explorers and traders en route to the southern parts of Africa (and later to India.) Eanes had made a previous attempt in 1433 which resulted in failure, but he tried again under the orders of Prince Henry the Navigator. His was the fifteenth expedition made to round this cape. The previous disappearance of numerous European vessels led some to suggest the presence of sea monsters. There are rocky shoals around the coast, but the main problem had been a leeward wind change that forced ships onshore, and an adverse current. Captains were accustomed to sailing close to the land, as they had no knowledge of what lay ahead in the deep oceans. However, Gil Eanes managed to double Cape Bojador by sailing well out to sea, far out of sight of land, until a more favourable wind could be picked up. The region's coastal areas quickly became a very important area for the Portuguese traders, and the first delivery of African slaves to Lisbon occurred in 1434. The event opened up the slave trade for the next 400 years. Winds off the west coast of Africa flow naturally towards Brazil, which facilitated the Triangular Trade route up through the Caribbean and the western seaboard of America and then back across the Atlantic. This led to the establishment of Spanish, Portuguese, French, Dutch and English colonies across the world. It is possible that the Cathaginian Hanno the Navigator first discovered a way round Cape Bojador around 500 BCE, as described in his *Periplus*, but that the knowledge had been lost.

CAVENDISH, SIR THOMAS,

1560–92 This explorer was known as *'the Navigator'* because he led the third expedition to circumnavigate the globe (1586–8), and was the first who had deliberately set out to do so. Magellan and Drake went before him, but circumnavigation had not been their original intention. He was an MP for Shaftesbury, Dorset, 1584, and had sailed with Sir Richard Grenville to Virginia in 1585. Determined to follow Drake's example, Cavendish built a ship named the *Desire*, and his small fleet left Harwich in 1586 and reached the Straits of Magellan in 1587. They then sailed up the western coast of South America, reaching the southern tip of what is now California in October 1587. Along the way Cavendish burned three Spanish towns and 13 ships. In late 1587 he took the 600-ton Spanish galleon *Santa Anna*, looting the ship of its cargo which included over 122,000 silver dollars, at that time the richest Spanish treasure to fall into English hands. His ship was too small to carry all the bullion, and he did not have enough men to sail the Spanish galleon, so he burned it and the remaining treasure sank to the bottom of Cabo San Luca harbour in Mexico. Cavendish luckily captured a Spanish pilot, who knew the way across the Pacific, and he then sailed across that ocean to the Philippines. He eventually reached the coast of Africa and finally returned to England in 1588, completing the circumnavigation nine months faster than Drake. Only the *Desire* survived the voyage. He was now financially secure for life at the age of 28, but nevertheless sailed on a second expedition in 1591 on the *Lester*, accompanied by John Davis on the *Desire*. They looted the Brazilian port of Santos, but he later lost most of his crew in a battle against the Portuguese. Cavendish died of unknown causes, possibly off Ascension Island. John Davis discovered the Falkland Islands, and eventually returned to England although most of his crew were lost to starvation and illness.

CELESTIAL NAVIGATION

Also called 'astro-navigation', computing the position of the ship using time, the position of the stars and by reference to mathematical tables.

CHAMPLAIN, SAMUEL DE,

1567–1635 From 1603 he explored the Atlantic coast from Cape Breton to Cape Cod, founding Quebec City and the colony of New France (Canada).

COUSTEAU, JACQUES-YVES,

1910–97 He was a French undersea explorer, environmentalist and innovator. In 1943, Cousteau and the French-Canadian engineer Emile Gagnan invented the aqualung, a breathing apparatus that supplied oxygen to divers and allowed them to stay underwater for several hours. Cousteau travelled the world's oceans in his research vessel *Calypso*, beginning in 1948. Cousteau's popular TV series, films and many books introduced the general public to the wonders of the sea.

DAVIS, JOHN, **1550–1605** He made

three attempts to find the Northwest Passage, and the Davis Strait between Greenland and North America is named after him. He sailed with Cavendish, discovered the Falkland Islands and fought against the Spanish Armada. Davis also published two treatises on navigation

Columbus, Christopher, 1451–1506

Cristóbal Colón (as he was known to his Spanish sponsors) was an Italian from Genoa in the service of the Spanish crown, who landed in the Bahamas in 1492 during a voyage that was searching for a western route to Asia and the Indies. In 1496 he became the first recorded European to land on the South American mainland, in Venezuela. He made a total of four voyages to the New World, and on his fourth faced famine and mutiny.

and invented the Davis Quadrant. He was killed by pirates in the East Indies.

DERROTERO A book of sailing directions used by the Spanish. The equivalent Portuguese *'roteiro'* evolved into the French *'routier'*, and the English *'rutter'*. These were of incomparable value in the New World and East Indies. A captain could see views of the coast taken from seaward, with instructions added regarding anchorages, fresh water, currents etc. Captain Bartholomew Sharp captured one in the South Pacific from the Spanish ship *Rosario* in 1680. This was most unusual, because they were usually thrown weighted overboard in the face of pirate attack. When Sharp was tried for piracy, he gave Charles II the translation of a priceless derrotero, was acquitted, and made a captain in the Royal Navy. English rutters held details of anchorages, harbours, courses etc., and were continually updated by their owners, often being passed down from

father to son. Famous Spanish derroteros were devoted to the Americas and Spain (1575), and Florida, the Caribbean and Veracruz (1583).

DIAS, BARTHOLOMEU, *c.*1450–1500 In 1478, the Portuguese navigator sailed with three ships, becoming the first man known to round Africa's Cape of Good Hope and thus opening up trade routes to Asia. In 1590 he commanded four ships in Cabral's expedition which discovered Brazil, but died in a storm on the homeward voyage.

ELCANO, JUAN SEBASTIÁN DE, *c.*1476–1526 The first man to circumnavigate the world, taking over command when Magellan died in 1521, and returning to Spain in 1522. The *Victoria* was the only ship of five to complete the expedition.

ERIK THE RED, *c.*950–*c.*1010 After discovering Greenland, Erik Thorvaldsson encouraged Icelandic

settlers to journey there by giving the
island an attractive name. His parents had
been exiled to Iceland for killings, and
Erik himself was then banished from
Iceland after committing seven murders.
He took 500 followers and settled in
Greenland, and after his term of exile was
over, returned to Iceland to encourage
more settlers to join him.

'FATHER OF MODERN OCEANOGRAPHY' – MATTHEW FONTAINE MAURY,

1806–73 From 1825 to 1834, this
American made three extended voyages
– to Europe, around the world, and to the
Pacific coast of South America. During
the years 1834 to 1841, Maury produced
works on sea navigation. In 1842 he began
publishing his research on oceanography
and meteorology, as well as charts and
sailing directions, and by 1853 he had
become internationally recognized for
his work. His system of recording
oceanographic data for naval vessels and
merchant marine ships was adopted
worldwide. In 1855, he published *The
Physical Geography of the Sea*, which is
credited as *'the first textbook of modern
oceanography'*. During the American Civil
War, Maury was successful in acquiring
war vessels for the Confederacy, and
developed harbour defences, experimenting
with electrical mines and torpedoes.

FRA MAURO WORLD MAP,

1457–9 This parchment map is probably
the greatest memorial of medieval
cartography. It was made by the Venetian
monk Fra Mauro. His assistant on the
original map was Andrea Bianco, under a
commission from King Alfonso V of
Portugal. That map was sent to Portugal,
but has not survived. Fra Mauro died the

following year while he was making a
copy of the map for Venice, and the copy
was completed by Andrea Bianco.

GAMA, VASCO DA, c.1460–1524

In 1497–8, this Portuguese mariner
rounded the Cape of Good Hope, leading
the first European seaborne mission to
India. Only two of his four ships made it
back to Lisbon, and half his crews died of
scurvy, but he was given the title *'Admiral
of the Indian Seas'*. His journey underlined
the importance of the east coast of Africa,
Mozambique being colonized, and
Portugal became the first Western nation
to exploit the lucrative spice trade. Vasco
da Gama was the first Portuguese of
non-royal blood to be made a count, after
a second voyage with 20 warships to
India. Utterly ruthless, he was responsible
for the rise of Portugal as a colonizing
power, and the wonderful monastery,
Mosteiro dos Jerónimos, was built in
Belém, Lisbon in his honour.

GOSNOLD, BARTHOLOMEW,

1572–1607 A barely remembered English
navigator who explored the New England
coast in the *Concord*, he was the first
European to sight Cape Cod, Nantucket
and Martha's Vineyard in 1602. In 1607

he was a leader in the English colony at Jamestown but soon died of *'swamp fever'* (leptospirosis or malaria).

GREAT CIRCLE A course plotted on the surface of the globe, which is the shortest distance between two points. Lines of longitude (meridians) are great circles, but lines of latitude (except the equator) are not. The 'course line' on the surface of the Earth thus follows a plane, passing through the centre of the Earth. In practice, a great circle describes the shortest distance between any two points on Earth.

HAKLUYT, RICHARD, 1552–1616 An English geographer whose superb *Principal Navigations, Voyages, Traffics and Discoveries of the English Nation* (1589) recorded accounts of over 200 voyages in different parts of the world over the ages, stimulating both colonization and improvements in navigation.

HANNO THE NAVIGATOR It is believed that this Carthaginian led an expedition of 60 ships around Cape Bojador and down the western coast of Africa in 500 BCE, almost 2000 years before the route was rediscovered by Gil Eanes. His *Periplus*, or sailing document, described the coastline from Morocco to the Gulf of Guinea.

HARRISON, JOHN, 1693–1776 The genius who created precise hand-held timepieces, *chronometers*, which could be used at sea to measure time, thereby enabling accurate plotting of longitude for the first time.

HENRY THE NAVIGATOR, 1394–1460 A Portuguese prince, described as *'The Father of Modern Navigation'*. He sponsored several expeditions and established an observatory at Cape Sagres in southwest Portugal for the study of astronomy, navigation and cartography. There is a wonderful memorial to him in Lisbon harbour, near the World Heritage Site of the Tower of Belém and the Jerónimos Monastery.

HEYERDAHL, THOR, 1914–2002 Norwegian anthropologist who in 1947 sailed the raft *Kon-Tiki*, made from balsa-wood, 4300 miles (6920 km) from Peru to Polynesia, attempting to prove that the Polynesian islanders originally came from South America. In 1970 he sailed the papyrus boat *Ra II* from Africa to the West Indies to demonstrate that Egyptians could have built the pyramids in South America. In 1977 he sailed *Tigris*, a reed boat, from Iraq through the Persian Gulf to Pakistan and the Red Sea, to show that Mesopotamia could have traded with the Indus Valley.

HUDSON, HENRY, d.1611 An English explorer who tried to find the Northeast and Northwest Passages. Hudson Bay and the Hudson River are named after him. After a winter spent bound in ice, his crew mutinied and set him adrift to die in an open boat in Hudson Bay. Little is known about his early life.

HUMBOLDT, BARON ALEXANDER VON, 1769–1859 A naturalist who explored South America from 1799–1804 and who gave his name to the cold current of water which runs up the west coast of the continent. There are many places in the Americas named after him, and his name is given to species of flowers, tree, shrubs, penguin, squid and the Amazon River dolphin.

IBN BATTUTA (1304–1368 or 1377) AND THE CHINESE DISCOVERY OF AMERICA

Abu Abdullah Muhammad Ibn Abdullah Al Lawati Al Tanji Ibn Battuta was a Moroccan Berber scholar and Sunni Islamic judge, best known as a traveller and explorer, who covered 73,000 miles (117,500 km) in his lifetime. His journeys encompassed almost all of the known Islamic world and beyond, including Europe, Africa, India and China. His account was *A Gift to Those Who Contemplate the Wonders of Cities and the Marvels of Travelling*, often simply referred to as the *Rihla* or *Journey*. He tells of a conversation with a Chinese captain in Zanzibar, who told him that he had made in his youth a voyage to *'a land of gold...so many days east of China they were unaccountable'*. The Chinese expedition brought back gold and silver from high mountains and a holy lake. This may refer to Peru – where else east of China could it be?

LEIF ERICSON, LEIFR EIRIKSSON, c.970–c.1020

The son of Erik the Red, he was converted to Christianity in Norway and introduced the religion to Greenland. This Norseman was probably the first European to land in North America (excluding Greenland), almost 500 years before the Spanish, English and French. According to the *Sagas of the Icelanders*, he established a settlement at *Vinland*, which has been identified with the L'Anse aux Meadows Norse site on the northern tip of the island of Newfoundland.

LESSEPS, FERDINAND DE, 1805–94

He constructed the Suez Canal from 1859–69, then tried to build a lockless canal across the Panama Isthmus from 1882–8 until the company went bankrupt. Ensuing financial difficulties led to him being fined and almost imprisoned in 1893, when he was 88 years old. The US bought out the canal rights in 1904 and completed his works.

LODESTAR

A guiding star, from the Middle English *'lode sterre' (leading star)*. In the northern hemisphere, it was usually the North Star (Polaris).

LONGITUDE

Because of the general inability to calculate longitude accurately at sea until the invention of John Harrison's chronometer in the 18th century, merchant ships were forced to cluster upon well-known routes, where they were more at threat from pirate, privateer or enemy attack. Dava Sobel's exposition in her book *Longitude* is an excellent summary. Suitable chronometers were not widely used until the late 18th century, so the earlier navigational feats of pirates and circumnavigators like Roberts, Dampier and Woodes Rogers are truly remarkable. In the 18th century, the English measured longitude west of Greenwich, the French measured west of Paris, and the Spanish west of Tenerife and sometimes Cadiz, until Greenwich in England was adopted globally as the zero meridian.

MAGELLAN, FERDINAND, c.1480–1521

This Portuguese explorer commanded the first expedition to circumnavigate the globe, for Spain (1519–22). When he passed through the Magellan Straits below South America, the new ocean was remarkably calm compared to the Atlantic, so Magellan named it the *Pacific* Ocean. He was killed in the Philippines, and Juan Sebastián de Elcano captained the ship home to Spain.

MAP There is no such word in the vocabulary of a real sailor. One uses a 'chart' at sea.

MARCONI, GUGLIEMO, 1874–1937

In 1895 Marconi developed the first telegraph signals that could be transmitted through the air without the need for wires. From Lavernock in Wales he sent the first radio message over water, to the island of Flat Holm in the Bristol Channel in 1897. In 1901 he transmitted the first transatlantic wireless message, and from then on shipping communications were transformed.

MARINER'S MIRROR

(MIRROUR) Lucius Wagenaer first published this collection of sea charts in Holland in 1583, and it was translated into English in 1588. For the next hundred years or so, it was widely used by seamen across the world.

MARINUS OF TYRE (*c.*70–130) AND THE FORTUNATE ISLES

He was a geographer and mathematician, as well as the founder of mathematical geography. Marinus assigned to each place its proper latitude and longitude with equal spacing for lines, developing a system of nautical charts. Rhodes was his central point of reference. His maps were based on previous maps and the diaries of travellers, and were the first in the Roman Empire to show China. Around 120 CE, Marinus wrote that the habitable world was bounded on the west by the *Fortunate Islands*. Claudius Ptolemy (90–168) adopted the Fortunate Islands as the prime meridian for his *Geographia*, written around 150 CE. This was the most famous classical map of the world, unsurpassed for almost 1500 years, and the sources that Ptolemy cited most consistently were the maps and writings of Marinus. Some 1700 years before the modern discovery of the source of the Nile, Marinus wrote an account of a journey to the Ruwenzori in around 110 CE. A Greek merchant, Diogenes, had made a 25-day journey inland from the African East coast to *'two great lakes and the snowy range of mountains where the Nile draws its twin sources'*.

Ptolemy and Marinus were major authorities used by Columbus in determining the circumference of the globe. The importance of Marinus is that he knew there was a continent on the eastern side of the Pacific Ocean, as his maps (and those of Ptolemy, two generations later) showed the west coast of America, not the east. He mapped three prominent capes, just south of the equator, which are Cape San Lorenzo, Cape Santa Elena and Cabo Blanco. It is unsure how Marinus knew there was an American continent – the fire at the great Library in Alexandria, Egypt destroyed much knowledge of the ancient world.

MERCATOR, GERHARDUS (ORIGINALLY GERHARD KREMER) 1512–94 This Flemish

cartographer was the first man to use the terms North and South America. His world map of 1569 was the first to show a round Earth on a flat map. It was created using his *'Mercator Projection'* of parallel lines of latitude.

The Naming of America

Richard Amerike (Ameryk or ap Meryk, *c.*1445–1503) was a wealthy Welsh merchant trading from Bristol. His original name was Richard ap Meuric or ap Meurig, which he anglicized to Richard Amerike. He was King's Customs Officer three times, becoming the Sheriff of Bristol in 1497. In 1908 a Bristol antiquarian, Alfred Hudd proposed that the word 'America' was originally applied to a destination across the western ocean, possibly an island or a fishing station in Newfoundland. This would have been before the existence of the continent became known to Europeans through the voyages of Columbus. According to *Newfoundland and Labrador Heritage, 'While it has been difficult to pinpoint the exact time frame of these North Atlantic probes, evidence that they were indeed occurring by the 1490s is found in a report sent by Pedro de Ayala, a Spanish envoy located in London. The year after Cabot's successful transatlantic voyage* [which was in 1497, five years after Columbus found the West Indies] *he wrote to Ferdinand and Isabella stating that for the previous seven years the Bristolians had been equipping caravels to look for the islands of Brasile and the Seven Cities. While it is not possible to ascertain whether or not these were large scale ventures and precisely what their motives might have been, Ayala's words seem to supply some proof of westward bound voyages.'* Bristol sent fishing ships to Newfoundland in search of cod before Columbus' first voyage of 1492. Bristol merchants had formerly bought salt cod from Iceland until 1475, but the King of Denmark banned the trade. In 1479 four Bristol merchants received a royal charter to locate another source of fish, and in 1480, 12 years before Columbus, English fishermen may have been processing fish on the Newfoundland coast. In 1960, trading records were discovered that indicated that Richard Amerike was involved in this business. A letter from around 1481 suggests that Amerike shipped salt (for salting fish) to these men at a place they had named *Brassyle*. The letter also states that they had many names for headlands and harbours. The suggestion is that one of these names may have been America. Giovanni Caboto (John Cabot) came to Bristol in 1495 looking for investment in a new project. In 1496 he was authorized by Henry VII to make a voyage of discovery and claim lands on behalf of the king. It is believed that Richard Amerike was one of the principal investors in the building of Cabot's ship, the *Matthew*. Cabot is known to have produced maps of the coast from Maine to Newfoundland, although none has survived. Copies of these maps were sent to Spain by John Day, where Columbus and Amerigo Vespucci may have seen them. It is suggested that Cabot wrote the name America on his maps.

PANAMA CANAL The USA under Theodore Roosevelt undertook the completion of Ferdinand de Lesseps's abandoned project in 1904 and under US control it was completed in 1914. Some 27,500 men died during its entire history of construction, nearly all of diseases and fevers. It is 51 miles (82 km) long, and locks raise and lower ships by 85 feet (26 m). It is the busiest canal in the world, shortening the route between New York and San Francisco by 9000 miles (14,500 km), and has had a massive effect on global shipping routes. Each day around 40 ships use it, taking around nine hours each to make the transit, and around 205 million tons of cargo pass through it every year. A class of ships known as *'Panamax'* have been developed and constructed, which are built to the maximum dimensions that the Canal can accept. The retreat of the ice that has historically blocked the Northwest Passage may weaken its importance.

PICCARD, JACQUES, 1922–2008 This explorer and scientist was the first person to descend to the deepest parts of the Pacific Ocean. On 23 January 1960, he and US Navy Lt. Don Walsh descended over 35,802 feet (10,912 m) or nearly seven miles in a pressured bathyscaphe called *Trieste*. They went to the bottom of the Challenger Deep of the Marianas Trench (200 miles/322 km southwest of Guam in the Marianas), the deepest place on Earth, the trip taking five hours. The bathyscaphe was built by Piccard and his father, Auguste Piccard (1884–1962), a notable Belgian physicist and inventor, who also twice held the world ballooning height record. Jacques Piccard's son Bertrand commanded the first non-stop round-the-world balloon expedition, making three generations of adventurers.

THE PIRI REIS MAP AND THE MYSTERY OF THE LOST PEOPLE In 1929, historians found a map drawn on a gazelle skin. It had been created in 1513 by Piri Reis, a famous admiral of the Turkish fleet. His high rank within the Turkish navy allowed him to have a privileged access to the Imperial Library of Constantinople, so he could have sourced lost maps dating back to the 4th century BCE or even earlier. The Piri Reis map shows the western coast of Africa, the eastern coast of South America and the northern coast of Antarctica. It is the oldest surviving map to show the Americas. We do not know how Piri Reis managed to draw such an accurate map of the Antarctic region 300 years before it was discovered, or how the map shows the actual northern Antarctic coastline under the ice. Geological evidence confirms that the latest date that Queen Maud Land could have been charted in an ice-free state is 4000 BCE. Did he have knowledge from a past civilization? The last period of ice-free conditions in the Antarctic began about 13,000-9000 BCE and ended about 4000 BCE. The first civilization developed in the Middle East around 6500 BCE, to be followed within a millennium by those of the Indus valley and China. Somehow, a map was drawn then that is only now possible by the application of modern technology. In 1953, a Turkish naval officer sent the Piri Reis map to the US Navy Hydrographic Bureau. To evaluate it, the Chief Engineer of the Bureau asked Arlington H. Mallery, an authority on ancient maps, to help. Mallery discovered the projection method used, by making a grid and transferring the Piri Reis map onto a globe. The map was accurate, and Mallery stated that the only way to draw map of such accuracy was by aerial surveying. Also the spheroid trigonometry used to determine longitudes was supposedly a process not known until the mid-18th century. It was seemingly copied from map-makers who knew that the Earth was round, and also had knowledge of its true circumference to within 50 miles (80 km). On 6 July 1960 the US Air Force responded to Prof. Charles H. Hapgood of Keene College, and specifically to his request for an evaluation of the ancient Piri Reis Map:

Dear Professor Hapgood,

Your request of evaluation of certain unusual features of the Piri Reis map of 1513 by this organization has been reviewed. The claim that the lower part of the map portrays the Princess Martha Coast of Queen Maud Land, Antarctic, and the Palmer Peninsula, is reasonable. We find that this is the most logical and in all probability the correct interpretation of the map. The geographical detail shown in the lower part of the map agrees very remarkably with the results of the seismic profile made across the top of the ice-cap by the Swedish-British Antarctic Expedition of 1949.This indicates the coastline had been mapped before it was covered by the ice-cap. The ice-cap in this region is now about a mile thick.We have no idea how the data on this map can be reconciled with the supposed state of geographical knowledge in 1513.

Harold Z. Ohlmeyer Lt. Colonel, USAF Commander

PLAIN SAILING The origin was probably *'plane sailing'*, the method of recording the course and speed of a ship on a plane projection of the spherical earth. It has come to mean sailing that is easy and uncomplicated. Adam Martindale wrote in 1683 *'A Collection of Letters for Improvement of Husbandry & Trade': 'A Token for Ship-Boys, or Plain-Sailing, made more plain.'* The first use of it in a figurative sense, meaning simply *'easy and uncomplicated'*, comes in Fanny Burney's *Camilla*, 1796: *'The rudiments, which would no sooner be run over, than the rest would become plain sailing.'*

PONCE DE LEÓN, JUAN,

1474–1521 A Spanish explorer who sought the *'fountain of youth'* on a voyage that he financed himself. He discovered Florida on Easter Sunday 1513 and named it Pascua Florida, after the Easter Flower celebration in Spain. He also discovered the *Gulf Current*, which became the favoured passage home to Europe for Spanish ships. De León was appointed Governor of the region but killed by Indians in 1521. Taken to Cuba, he died there and is buried in San Juan. The fountain of youth was believed to be a spring that would restore the youth of anyone who drank it. It was thought to be in Florida, or possibly on Bimini in the Bahamas.

PTOLEMY, CLAUDIUS, 90–168

Graeco-Egyptian cartographer, mathematician and astronomer from Alexandria whose *Geographia* included 8000 places across the known world, including their latitude and longitude. Early maps were known as *'ptolemies'* until medieval times.

Portolani and Unnatural Precision

In the Middle Ages sailing charts were called *portolani*. They were accurate maps of the most common sailing routes, showing coastlines, harbours, straits, bays, etc. Most portolani focused on the Mediterranean and the Aegean seas, but there were other known routes, such as the sailing book of Piri Reis. *Dulcert's Portolano* of 1339 gives the perfect latitude of Europe and North Africa, and the longitudinal coordinates of the Mediterranean and of the Black Sea are approximated to half a degree. Even more incredible in accuracy is *'Zeno's Chart'* of 1380. It shows a huge area in the north, as far as Greenland. Professor Charles Hapgood in *Maps of the Ancient Sea Kings* states *'It's impossible that someone in the fourteenth century could* have found the exact latitudes of these places, not to mention the precision of the longitudes...'* Another amazing chart is that of the Turkish Hadji Ahmed, 1559, in which he shows a land strip, about 1000 miles (1600 km) wide, joining Alaska and Siberia. Such a natural bridge was then covered by seawater at the end of the glacial period, so could he have used ancient maps to learn of its position? Oronteus Fineus represented the Antarctic with no ice-cap in 1532, as had Piri Reis in 1513. There are also maps showing Greenland as two separated islands, and this was confirmed in the 20th century by a French polar expedition which found out that there actually is a thick ice cap joining two islands.

PYTHEAS Around 370 BCE this Greek explorer sailed from Marseilles to Britain, noting that the Pole Star does not exactly coincide with the North Pole. Because of the much stronger tides in the Atlantic, compared to the Mediterranean, he also deduced that tidal movements were caused by the Moon.

SEA-CARD A 17th-century term for a nautical chart.

SHELIKOV, GRIGORY, d.1795 This fur trader claimed Alaska for Russia in 1793, and was called *'the Russian Columbus'*. In 1867, the USA paid Russia two cents an acre for Alaska – perhaps the greatest land deal in history.

SLOCUM, JOSHUA, 1844–1909
Canadian-American Slocum was the first man to sail solo around the world, in the 37-feet (11-m) sloop *Spray* (1895–8).

THE SUEZ CANAL AND THE DEATH OF SAILING SHIPS This
canal has connected the Red Sea and the Mediterranean since 1869. It is 119 miles (191.5 km) long, with no locks and it cuts over 4000 miles (6450 km) off the sea

route around Africa between Europe and Asia. It is up to 66 feet (20 m) deep, and is a single passage-way, with only four passing places. Sailing was virtually impossible in the narrow, windless channel, and just before the opening ceremony, a three-masted frigate became stuck in mid-channel. The authorities threatened to blow her up if she could not be moved. Just a year after this, the canal's builder, de Lesseps wrote *'I apologise to the sailing vessels.'* UK control of the canal ended with 'the Suez Crisis' when President Nasser of Egypt nationalized the waterway in 1956. The freeing of the ice that has for centuries blocked the Northeast Passage may well weaken the canal's strategic importance.

SUNSTONES Vikings navigated the oceans with sundials aboard their Norse ships. It is suggested that on overcast or foggy days, Vikings looked towards the sky through rock crystals called sunstones to give them direction. A research team recently sailed the Arctic Ocean aboard the Swedish icebreaker *Oden* and found that sunstones actually could point the way in foggy and cloudy conditions. Crystals such as cordierite, calcite or tourmaline work like polarizing filters, changing in brightness and colour as they detect the angle of sunlight. From these changes, Vikings could have accurately determined where the polarized sky light was coming from, and pinpointed the direction of the Sun.

TAKE SOUNDINGS On today's maritime charts, the depth of water, or *sounding*, at any point is shown as a number indicating depth, with hundreds of soundings pinpointed on any chart.

From the earliest times, sailors took soundings to chart ways through reefs and past sandbanks into ports and to pass through channels. Generally this was carried out by dropping a lead weight on a knotted rope, each knot representing a fathom or foot measurement.

TIME BALL A 19th-century device, consisting of a large black ball mounted prominently at major ports around the world, which was lowered exactly at the stroke of noon, so that ship's navigators could set their chronometers correctly.

VANCOUVER, GEORGE, 1757–98 Aboard the *Discovery* between 1792 and 1794, he explored the coastlines of the western USA and western Canada. He surveyed from San Diego to Alaska and wrote an account of his 1790–5 circumnavigation.

VESPUCCI, AMERIGO, 1454–1512 An Italian navigator in the service of Portugal, in 1501 he found that Columbus had not actually discovered India or Asia, but instead a previously unknown *'New World'*. Vespucci found a *'torrid zone'* where *'both sexes go about naked'*. In this region, the women, *'being very lustful, cause the private parts of their husbands to swell up to such huge size that they appear deformed and disgusting.'* The increase in size was also recorded as being due to *'the biting of certain poisonous animals'*.

VINLAND MAP In 1965 it was announced that this 15th-century map proved that Vikings had explored North America before the arrival of Christopher Columbus. It showed the area known as *Vinland*, west of Greenland. The map seems likely to be counterfeit.

CHAPTER 6

Villains *of* *the* Seas

THE WORLD OF PIRATES
AND BUCCANEERS

ACT FOR THE MORE EFFECTUAL SUPPRESSION OF PIRACY, 1700 This English law allowed for severe punishment without recourse to a jury. If captured upon the ocean, pirates could be immediately hanged at the yardarm, as no legal judgment could be made on a sea voyage. Pirates who attacked a ship belonging to the British Empire could henceforth be executed without any legal procedures, nor any access to a man of religion to repent of their sins.

ACT OF GRACE, ACT OF PARDON This was a general amnesty given to a pirate who promised to reform his ways. The November 1698 proclamation offered a free pardon to all pirates operating east of the Cape of Good Hope, except for Captain Kidd. Nonetheless, nine of his crew that surrendered under this Act of Grace were hanged with him in Execution Dock off Wapping Old Stairs in London. Pirate captains, such as John Bowen, and many crews would not surrender because they did not trust the authorities.

ARMED TO THE TEETH A pirate phrase, it originated in Port Royal in the 1600s. Carrying cutlasses and single-shot muskets, with pistols strapped across their

chests, pirates and buccaneers would often carry a dagger or throwing knife in their teeth when boarding a ship. This gave them maximum operational effectiveness, carrying every weapon they could possibly use. The musket was dropped after being fired, then the pistols were expended, before the pirate was left with his cutlass and dagger.

ARTIST A skilled man, such as a surgeon, carpenter or navigator. Sometimes these men, like musicians, were 'forced' to join the pirates to cover gaps in the crew. Pirate captains then issued them with a notification that they had been 'forced', which might be used at any subsequent trial by the Crown. While most pirates at trial would claim that they had been 'forced', usually only skilled men, 'artists', would be acquitted. All of Black Bart's surgeons were acquitted, except Peter Scudamore who seemed to revel in telling the truth of the matter, revealing to the court that he had joined up voluntarily.

BLOODY FLAG Naval warships used to raise this large flag upon going into battle. When pirates hoisted the red flag, it meant that they would give no quarter after exhausting negotiations to take a ship peaceably.

BUCCANEER The term 'buccaneer' is often used as a synonym for 'pirate'. However, the crews of buccaneer ships were generally more numerous than those of pirate vessels, and more localized to the Caribbean than later pirate crews who sailed to the Indian Ocean in the late 17th century. Some buccaneers had been issued with 'a letter of marque' – an official warrant authorizing the holder to search, seize or destroy specified assets, merchant shipping or personnel belonging to a foreign enemy.

DEFOE, DANIEL, c.1660–1731 – THE MAN WHO TOLD US ABOUT PIRATES

Captain Charles Johnson, the most reliable authority on pirates (much like Esquemeling/Exquemelin on buccaneers) wrote *A General History of the Robberies and Murders of the Most Notorious Pyrates*, which was first published in 1724. Many editions followed, and much information came from the transcripts of pirate trials of the time, and accounts published in the *Daily Post* and *London Gazette*. In 1732 it was claimed that 'Johnson' was none other than Daniel Defoe, who had also written pirate fiction (*Robinson Crusoe* and *Captain Singleton*) and pirate non-fiction (on Captain Avery and John Gow). Defoe often wrote anonymously, both for fear of imprisonment and because he often owed money and was consequently reluctant to part with any new income streams.

ESQUEMELING, JOHN ALEXANDRE EXQUEMELIN, c.1645–c.1707

This French Huguenot, often described as a *'Dutchman'*, wrote the definitive history of the buccaneers, *The Buccaneers of America*. He tells us that he went voluntarily to the West Indies, to Tortuga, in the service of the French West India Company. It sold him on to a cruel landowner, who fell ill, and he sold Esquemeling to a surgeon for 70 pieces of eight. The surgeon treated him humanely, supplying reasonable food and decent clothes, and after a year offered Esquemeling his freedom for indenture, for just 100 pieces of eight, that should be repaid when Esquemeling was *'in a capacity to do so'*. Being an honourable man, he resolved to repay this debt and joined the buccaneers as the quickest way of doing so. He voyaged during these years in the fleet under captains such as Henry Morgan. As he had assisted a surgeon, he travelled as a ship's surgeon until he returned home in 1674, some time after Morgan's assault on Panama. The first edition of his book about his contemporary privateers was entitled *De Americaensche Zee-Roovers* and was published in 1678 in Amsterdam. It was followed by a 1679 Nuremburg edition called *Americanische Seeräuber* and the 1681 Spanish edition *Piratas de la America*. The 1684 English version was translated from the anti-English Spanish version and was therefore libellous to Sir Henry Morgan. It was titled: *'Bucaniers of America; or a true account of the … assaults committed … upon the coasts of the West Indies, by the Bucaniers of Jamaica … especially the … exploits of Sir Henry Morgan … written originally in Dutch by J. Esquemeling … now rendered into English, London 1684'*. A second edition followed within three months, and this was followed shortly by yet another English version in 1684 vindicating Morgan and absolving him of the cruelty and lack of breeding described in the first two editions – the new book was entitled *'The History of the Bucaniers; being an impartial account of all the battels, sieges, and other most eminent assaults committed for several years upon the coasts of the West Indies by the pirates of Jamaica and Tortuga. More especially the unparalleled achievements of Sir Henry Morgan … Very much corrected from the errors of the original, by the relations of some English gentlemen, that then resided in those parts'.* Morgan had instituted the first case of 'libel' in Britain, and the publishers had to retract Esquemeling's claims. The book was amazingly popular, no doubt because it was rewritten to suit different nationalities. In the Spanish version, Henry Morgan was a torturing ogre, but the English and Dutch editions ask the reader to consider how *'God permitted the unrighteousness of the buccaneers to flourish, for the chastisement of the Spaniards'.*

FREEBOOTER From the Dutch *'vrijbuiter'* or pirate.

FROM THE SEAS If a pirate ship was hailed and asked her home port, this could be the answer given. By their articles, pirates forsook their homelands, and thereupon belonged only *'to the seas'.*

GIVE QUARTER Pirates *'gave quarter'* to a ship if it surrendered immediately, so that none of the crew would be hurt. The term dates back to the time when captured knights and nobles would be returned for a ransom of around a quarter of their yearly income.

GO ON THE ACCOUNT

Undertake a privateering or pirate voyage. The term stems from the fact that if actions were illegal, persons would have to *account* for their actions as being

within the law, or else be punished. From the 15th century onwards, craftsmen and professionals worked *'on account'*, and so did pirates and privateers when they signed the ship's articles for a voyage, with *'no prey, no pay'.*

THE GOLDEN AGE OF PIRACY

This lasted from about 1690 until the death of Black Bart Roberts in 1722. After this date the Royal Navy grew in strength in parallel with the expansion of the British Empire and naval ships patrolled the seas. Naval sloops, fast and well-armed with shallow draught, were built specifically to be *'pirate-hunters'.* Britain desperately wanted to protect its growing empire and huge trading connections that relied on the sea.

JAMAICA DISCIPLINE, LAW OF THE PRIVATEERS, CODE OF THE COAST

Customs passed down from the *'boucaniers'* of the 1630s onwards in the Caribbean. There were democratic controls on any type of authority in the *'pirate code'*, or *'code of the coast'*. Under the code, any *'prize'* was divided up evenly, with usually two shares to the captain and one each to all men. Other rules covered the presence of women on board, hours of drinking, the settlement of disputes, and the apportionment of prize money to those maimed and injured. Henry Morgan's last expedition granted his captains eight shares each, while Admiral Morgan took 1 per cent. This was agreed before the outset of the venture.

MATELOTAGE

From this French term we have today's *'mate'*, meaning a close friend/bosom buddy. The *'cow-killers'* or first *'boucaniers'* had no wives

Jolly Roger

An adaptation of the *'black flag'*, commonly a black flag with a *skull and crossbones*, flown towards the end of the Golden Age of piracy. Other versions showed a whole skeleton with a sword on one hand and an hourglass in the other. It was possibly named after Black Bart Roberts, from his habit of dressing up in red silks before battle. He was known as *'le jolie rouge'*, the *'pretty man in red'*. In 1700 we learn of the first recorded use of the black flag, flown by the Breton pirate Emanuel Wynne fighting HMS *Poole*

off Santiago. It had a skull and crossbones and an hourglass. If an intended victim refused to surrender when the black flag was raised, a red flag was hoisted, signifying that blood would flow and that no quarter would be given.

or children, but usually lived with another male who would inherit from him. This custom was called *'matelotage'*. Any arguments between these *'mates'* were usually settled by a duel according to *'la coutume de la côte'* (the custom, or code, of the coast).

MODERN PIRACY There are over 300 known cases of piracy and armed robbery of ships every year, often involving the taking of hostages for ransom. Many incidents are unreported. Some go unreported as a ship's owners wish to avoid long delays in ports due to police investigations. A ship's operating costs can be $15,000 a day, so it simply may not be cost-effective to seek justice. Again, some cargoes might be dubious or illegal in the first place, as maritime law-enforcement is fragmented across the world. Pirate hot-spots today are the South China Sea, the Indian Ocean and

the Malacca Straits. Countries associated with piracy are Indonesia, the Philippines, India, Malaysia, Brazil, Ecuador, Bangladesh and Somalia/Djibouti. Surprise attacks by fast boats upon ships navigating slowly through narrow channels are favoured, and pirates now routinely possess grenade launchers and the ubiquitous Kalashnikov rifle. Most successful attacks take place between the hours of 10p.m. and 6a.m. when most of the crew are asleep. Attacking from the stern, pirates use grappling hooks to board tankers, cargo ships, bulk carriers and container ships, as well as luxury yachts and other vessels. Countries like Brazil cannot attempt to suppress piracy as it has no coastguards, and its police have no boats. In the Far East, much piracy is controlled by crime syndicates which pay bribes to quash investigations. Here, entire cargoes can disappear, along with the ships which can later appear as *'phantom ships'* with fake documents after the crew has been killed or set adrift. Brazilian pirates prefer to take high-tech equipment for sale on the black market, while West African pirates literally strip a ship of everything. Somalia is the most high-profile pirate base today, with around 1500 fishermen who have turned to piracy. They initially armed themelves to fend off foreign trawlers illegally fishing their waters. The fish trade was ruined and the Somalis turned to attacking cruise ships and cargo ships, including those carrying food aid to the millions starving in Somalia. International warships now patrol the Gulf of Aden. At the end of May 2009, 20 ships were being held hostage by pirates around the world, there were 102 pirate attacks in the first quarter of the year, and £50 million had been paid out to pirates in ransoms in the first five months of the year. There had been 114 attacks by pirates, 29 of which had been successful. In 2008 the huge Saudi oil tanker *Sirius Star* was taken, 450 miles (725 km) off Kenya. It had only been launched in that year, at a cost of £65 million, and was carrying two million barrels of crude oil worth £67 million. The price of oil jumped a dollar a barrel on 18 November 2008 as a direct result of its capture. Somalis in two speedboats, armed with AK-47s and rocket-propelled grenades, had launched the attack from a mother-ship, probably a captured Nigerian tug. One speedboat circled the tanker while another fired rockets at the bridge until the captain surrendered. The pirates drew alongside, threw grappling hooks 30 feet (9 m) up to the deck and imprisoned the crew. The pirates wanted £6 million in ransom money, but released the *Sirius Star* on payment of £2 million. Over £80 million has been paid to release hijacked ships.

NO PREY NO PAY OR NO PURCHASE NO PAY Pirate motto, referring to the fact that without capturing (purchasing) other ships, there was no money to be made.

NO QUARTER GIVEN Pirates would threaten no mercy to ships which fought back when they saw the Jolly Roger hoisted. The Red Flag replaced it, signifying that no crew would be spared.

PICAROON, PICKAROON 17th-century term for a pirate, from the Spanish *'picaro'*, meaning rogue or rascal.

PIRACY ACT OF 1721 Pirates were tried in civil courts until 1340, when Edward III destroyed the French fleet at Sluys, and claimed thereafter to be *'Sovereign of the Seas'*. From then on Admiralty Courts were empowered to try piracy cases. Henry VIII passed the first Piracy Act in 1536, creating a Vice-Admiral of the Coast to hold trials and sentence pirates. In 1611, another act authorized Courts of the Admiralty to try cases in the colonies and plantations of North America and the West Indies. The 1721 Act stated that anyone who traded with a pirate, if found guilty, would also be treated as a pirate and charged accordingly. Until then, it was fairly easy to dispose of stolen goods.

Also, anyone who provided a pirate with ammunition, stores or provisions, or who fitted out a ship for piracy, or corresponded with a pirate, was now deemed to be a pirate, felon and robber.

PIRATE ARTICLES These were the rules of the ship that every pirate joining the crew had to sign, or put his thumbprint to. These simple rules helped stop arguments and fights developing. There had to be a form of discipline upon ship, and they were arrived at by a democratic process of agreement among the ship's crew. The Welsh Captains Black Bart Roberts and John Phillips had their articles transcribed by Daniel Defoe (alias Captain Charles Johnson) after speaking to captured and forced men, and condemned pirates. After Walter Kennedy's 'desertion', the despondent *Black Captain* (Roberts) drew up his famous 'articles' to be kept by the crew, and signed by all new members. Each pirate signed the articles, as Black Bart commented *'for the greatest security it is in everyone's interest to observe these articles if he is minded to keep up so abominable a combination* (profession).'

PIRATE ATTACK Buccaneers were superb marksmen, and their favoured method of attack was to sail in fast sloops into musket range of heavy, homeward-bound merchant ships. Most of the crew lay prone on the deck to avoid terrible injuries caused by grapeshot, while the musketeers picked off the helmsman and any sailors in the ship's rigging. As soon as the merchant was unable to manoeuvre, the pirates made for the stern, often in a pinnace, to jam the rudder and swarm up the side of the boat. Homebound ships were preferred as they were slower and

carried cargoes of silver, jewels and easily traded loot, rather than slaves, wine and wheat. Night attacks were popular, as ships had to anchor if sailing in shoal waters, especially off Tortuga.

PIRATE CODE The articles drawn up by privateers and pirates before setting sail, setting out injury compensation, ways of dealing with grievances, and pay. These formed a contract between the brethren which could not be broken.

PIRATE COMPENSATION
In general, the following rules applied amongst pirate crews as the basis for financial compensation for injuries received in battle:

Injury	Compensation
Loss of an eye	100 pieces of eight*
Loss of right arm	600 pieces of eight
Loss of left arm	500 pieces of eight
Loss of a finger	100 pieces of eight
Loss of right leg	500 pieces of eight
Loss of left leg	400 pieces of eight

* see page 264

PIRATE COUNCIL Each crewman was a member, unlike the officers' councils of war in the Royal Navy. The democratically elected council decided where to go, what to do, what punishments to make, who should be the captain and ship's officers, whether the captain should be deposed and so on.

PIRATE FLAGS The *Old Roger* or *Jolly Roger* is the most famous pirate flag, the 'skull and crossbones', but most pirates amended this to their own personal banner. Black Bart Roberts' main flag had

Pirate Articles of Captain Roberts

According to Johnson/Defoe, writing in 1724, *'The following, is the Substance of the Articles* (of Roberts), *as taken from the Pyrates' own Informations'*.

I Every Man has a Vote in Affairs of Moment; has equal Title to the fresh Provisions, or strong Liquors, at any Time seized, and may use them at Pleasure, unless a Scarcity make it necessary, for the Good of all, to vote a Retrenchment.

II Every Man to be called fairly in Turn, by List, on board of Prizes, because, (over and above their proper Share) they were on these occasions allowed a shift of Cloathes [change of clothes]: But if he defrauded the Company to the Value of a Dollar, in Plate, Jewels or Money, Marooning was their punishment. This was a barbarous Custom of putting the Offender on Shore, on some desolate or uninhabited Cape or Island, with a Gun, a few Shot, a Bottle of Water, and a Bottle of Powder, to subsist with, or starve. If the Robbery was only betwixt one another, they contented themselves with slitting the Ears and Nose of Him that was Guilty, and set him on Shore, not in an uninhabited Place, but somewhere, where he was sure to encounter Hardships.

III No Person to Game at Cards or Dice for Money.

IV The Lights and Candles to be put out at eight a-Clock at Night: If any of the Crew, after that Hour, still remained inclined for Drinking, they were to do it on the open Deck; which Roberts believed would give a Check to their Debauches,

for he was a sober Man himself, but found at length, that all his Endeavours to put an End to this Debauch, proved ineffectual.

V To keep their Piece (firearm), Pistols, and Cutlass clean, and fit for Service: In this they were extravagantly nice, endeavouring to outdo one another, in the Beauty and Richness of their Arms, giving sometimes at an Auction (at the Mast) 30 or 40 pounds a pair, for Pistols. These were slung in Time of Service, with different coloured Ribbands, over their Shoulders, in a Way peculiar to these Fellows, in which they took great Delight.

VI No Boy or Woman to be allowed. If any Man is found seducing any of the latter Sex, and carries her to Sea, disguised, he is to suffer Death; so that when any fell into their Hands, as it chanced in the Onslow, they put a Sentinel immediately over her to prevent ill Consequences from so dangerous an Instrument of Division and Quarrel; but here lyes the Roguery; they contend who shall be Sentinel, which happens generally to be one of the greatest Bullies, who, to secure the Lady's Virtue, will let none lie with her but himself.

VI To Desert the Ship, or their Quarters in Battle, is punished with Death or Marooning.

VIII No striking one another on board, but every Man's Quarrels to be ended on Shore, at Sword and Pistol, thus: The Quarter-Master of the Ship, when the Parties will not come to any Reconciliation, accompanies them to Shore with what Assistance he thinks proper, and turns the Disputants Back to Back, at so many Paces

Distant: At the Word of Command they turn and fire immediately, (or else the Piece is knocked out of their Hands:) If both miss, they come to their Cutlashes [cutlasses], and then he is declared Victor who draws the first Blood.

IX No man to talk of breaking up their Way of Living, till each has shares of 1000 Pounds. If in order to do this, any Man should lose a Limb, or become a Cripple in their Service, he is to have 800 Dollars, out of the publick Stock, and for lesser Hurts, proportionately.

X The Captain and Quarter-Master to receive two Shares of a Prize; the Master, Boatswain, and Gunner, one Share and a half, and other Officers one and a quarter.

XI The Musicians to have Rest on the Sabbath Day, but the other six Days and Nights, none without special Favour. These, we are assured, were some of Roberts' Articles, but as they had taken Care to throw over-board the Original they had signed and sworn to, there is a great deal of Room to suspect, the Remainder contained something too horrid to be disclosed to any, except such as were willing to be Sharers in the Iniquity of them; let them be what they will, they were together the Test of all new Comers, who were initiated by an oath taken on a Bible, reserved for that Purpose only, and were subscribed to in the Presence of the worshipful Mr Roberts.'

Defoe also enumerates Captain Phillips' articles on board the *Revenge* as follows:

1. Every Man shall obey civil Command; the Captain shall have one full Share and a half in all Prizes; the Master, carpenter, Boatswain and Gunner shall have one Share and a quarter.

2. If any Man shall offer to run away, or keep any Secret from the Company, he shall be marooned, with one Bottle of Powder, one Bottle of Water, one small Arm and shot.

3. If any Man steal any Thing in the Company, or game to the Value of a Piece of Eight, he shall be marooned or shot.

4. If at any Time we should meet another Marooner (that is, Pyrate) that Man shall sign his Articles without the Consent of our Company, shall suffer such Punishment and the Captain and Company shall think fit.

5. That man that shall strike another whilst these Articles are in force, shall receive Moses' Law (that is, 40 Stripes lacking one) on the bare Back.

6. That man that shall snap his Arms, or smoke Tobacco in the Hold, without a Cap to his Pipe, or carry a Candle lighted without a Lanthorn, shall suffer the same Punishment as the former Article.

7. That Man that shall not keep his Arms clean, fit for an Engagement, or neglect his Business, shall be cut off from his Share, and suffer such other Punishment as the Captain and the Company think fit.

8. If any Man shall lose a Joint in Time of an Engagement, he shall have 400 Pieces of Eight, if a Limb, 800.

9. If at any Time we meet with a prudent Woman, that Man who offers to meddle with her, without her Consent, shall suffer present Death.

him sharing a glass of wine with the skeleton of the devil, who was holding a burning spear. His personal pennant was a picture of him with a raised sword, standing on two skulls, marked ABH and AMH. These signified a Barbadan's head and a Martinican's head, as the governors of these colonies both sent vessels to capture Roberts. Later, he hanged the Governor of Martinique from his yardarm. The flags were meant to strike fear into the enemy's heart, and when a merchant ship saw Roberts' flags being raised, they did not generally wish to fight *'the great pyrate'*.

PIRATE HAVENS – TRADITIONAL

Medieval pirates in Britain favoured Wales and the West Country, where many harbours were protected by hills and difficult to reach by road. They were usually welcomed by local inhabitants and officials, being a welcome source of cheap trade. The majority of British buccaneers and pirates came from the great ports of London, Wales and the West Country. In the 17th century, the buccaneers favoured the island of Tortuga in the Caribbean, as it was hilly and difficult to attack but also near the shipping lanes. However, as the French and English naval presence grew, they moved on to New Providence in the Bahamas, and Madagascar in the Indian Ocean, neither then under control of any government. One of the major problems came when trying to sell contraband as there were few traders in these havens, and those there took a vast profit. As a result, pirates often tried to cut a deal with corrupt governors of settlements and colonies, where there were better prices available from a multitude of traders. Jamaica's Port Royal was a haven in the mid to late 17th century, because of its distance from London.

PIRATE HAVENS – MODERN

The US Government has issued a *'priority watch list of pirate havens'* – countries where the pirating of copyrights, patents and the like are common. They are: Argentina, Brazil, Colombia, Dominican Republic, Egypt, Hungary, India, Indonesia, Israel, Lebanon, Philippines, Russia, Taiwan and Uruguay. The EU is also surprisingly included, which comprises the major trading bloc of European nations including Germany, France and Great Britain. It is surprising that Thailand is omitted from the US list as it is on the UK's list of top ten pirate havens, especially with regard to illicit CD manufacture, along with China and Taiwan. China is omitted from the US list probably because it owns so many US Treasury long-term bonds which support the American economy, which is its largest market. China lends America the money to buy its goods, many of them pirated copies of American originals.

PIRATE HOOKS

This replacement for a hand would have been strapped to the stump of the arm with leather fastenings, but there are no records of pirates surviving amputation and wearing them. Their popularity in fancy-dress costume probably comes from J.M. Barrie's character Captain Hook in *Peter Pan*.

PIRATE ROUND

The route from North America to the Indian Ocean – where pirates could be encountered anywhere along the way.

Pirate Ships

These had to be fast, and easy and quick to careen, so small boats of 30-50 tons were favoured in the Caribbean. If a large boat was taken, it was usually used to store plunder before being destroyed, sold or set adrift. A shallow draught was essential to operate around the cays of the West Indies, and facilitate escape from larger vessels. All deckhouses were cut down to streamline the ship and to leave the deck uncluttered so that it was easier to shift cannon and resources from one side to the other in a fight. The gunwales were raised to give the crew extra protection. An alphabetical list of some of pirate ships with their captains is as follows: *Adventure, Queen Anne's Revenge* (Edward Teach, Blackbeard); *Adventure Galley, Adventure Prize* (William Kidd); *Bachelor's Delight* (William Dampier); *Barbara* (John Phillips); *Black Joke* (Benito de Soto); *Blessing* (Captain Brown); *Bravo* (Captain Power); *Cassandra* (John Taylor); *Charles* (John Halsey); *Childhood* (Captain Carracioli); *Delight* (Francis Spriggs); *Delivery, Happy Delivery, Ranger* (George Lowther); *Desire* (Thomas Cavendish); *Dolphin* (Thomas Booth); *Fancy* (Henry Every); *Flying Dragon* (Edward Condent); *Flying Horse* (Captain Rhoade); *Flying King* (Captain Sample); *Fortune, Royal Fortune, Good Fortune, Royal Fortune, Great Ranger, Little Ranger, Rover, Sea King* (Black Bart Roberts); *Gift* (John Ward); *Golden Chalice* (John Callice); *Happy Delivery* (George Lowther); *Liberty* (Thomas Tew); *Mary Anne, Whydah* (Black Sam Bellamy); *Mayflower* (Captain Cox); *Mocha* (Robert Culliford); *Most Holy Trinity* (Bartholomew Sharp); *New York Revenge* (Captain Cole); *Night Rambler* (Captain Cooper); *Oxford* (Henry Morgan); *Ranger* (George Lowther, Charles Vane); *Revenge* (Cowley, Phillips, Gow, Bonnet, Blackbeard and others); *Rising Sun* (William Moody); *Royal James* (Edward England); *Scowerer* (John Evans); *Sea King* (Captain le Vasseur, Bart Roberts); *Snap Dragon* (Captain Goldsmith); *Speaker, Speedy Return* (John Bowen); *Sudden Death* (Captain Derdrake); *Victory* (Olivier la Bouche).

PRIVATEERS These were 'semi-official' pirates who supplemented a country's navy with *'private'* ships of war. Given *'letters of marque'*, they were allowed to attack enemy shipping in times of war, and to keep a large percentage of any plunder. They cost nothing, and their only reward was what they could take, or *'purchase'*. With the end of the War of Spanish Succession in

1714, there were literally thousands of privateers in the Caribbean and European ports, but their letters of marque had been withdrawn because peace had been declared. Thus many turned to piracy, culminating in a period of almost complete pirate domination of the West Indies and American coasts between 1718 and 1722. In the 16th century, Francis Drake and John Hawkins were noted privateers, and in the 17th century Henry Morgan was the most successful of all privateers. This was also the name given to the privately owned armed vessel with a letter of marque, which enabled it to take *'prizes'* in wartime. From 1589, 10 per cent of the prize value went to the Crown, and 90 per cent to the owner and crews. Privateering was abolished by the Treaty of Paris in 1856.

RED FLAG The red flag as a symbol of socialism was first used in the Merthyr Riots in Wales, when the Welsh miner Dic Penderyn was wrongly executed for stabbing a soldier. However, until around 1700 it was the emblem of a pirate ship, when it was generally replaced by the black flag, and various derivations of the black flag to denote different captains. It then seems to have been run up only if the merchant crew refused to surrender at the sight of the black flag, and its hoisting meant that there would be no mercy shown to her crew.

SEA DOGS, SEA WOLVES *'Sea dogs'* was the term originally used for the privateers of Elizabeth II's reign, and it came to mean any sailor who had been at sea for a long time. The term *'Sea wolves'* was also used to describe privateers.

SEA ROVERS This was applied to pirates, buccaneers and *'sea-robbers'*. The term was used in John Esquemeling's *De Americaensche Zee-Roovers*, published in 1678, and published as *The Buccaneers of America* in London in 1684. Germans referred to a pirate as a *Seeräuber*, which means a sea robber.

SHARES OF PRIZES In 1627, Captain John Smith listed the common apportionment of any prize taken by a privateer as follows: *'The Ship hath one third part, The Victualler the other third. The other third part is for the (ship's) Company, and this is subdivided thus in shares: The Captain 10 in some but 9 in others; Lieutenant 9 or as he agrees with the Captain; Master 8 in some but 7 in others; Mates 7 (or 5); Chyrugion [Surgeon] 6 (or 3); Gunner 6 (or 5); Boatswain 6 (or 5); Carpenter 6 (or 5), Trumpeter 6 (or 5); the 4 Quarter-Masters 5 (or 4); Cooper 5 (or 4); Chyrugion's mate 5 (or 4); Gunner's mate 5 (or 4); Carpenter's Mate 5 (or 4); Corporal 4 (or 3); Quarter-Gunners 4 (or 3); Trumpeter's Mate 3 (or 3 or 1); Steward 4 (or 3); Cook 4 (or 3), Coxwain 4 (or 3), Swabber 4 (or 3)…'*

SWEET TRADE A term describing the act of piracy or buccaneering.

WALKING THE PLANK There is absolutely no evidence of this punishment ever having occurred on pirate ships, except for Plutarch's account of Cilician pirates around 100 CE making their Roman captives *'walk home'*. However, sailors were asked to walk the line of a plank on the quarterdeck if suspected of being drunk aboard ship.

FAMOUS PIRATES AND PIRATE COMMANDERS

ANGRIA DYNASTY A Black African Muslim family, powerful Indian pirate kings from *c.*1704. In the 1720s they repelled three British fleets, until finally defeated in 1756.

THE BARBAROSSA BROTHERS – SULTANS OF ALGIERS – THE GIFT OF GOD *Redbeard (barba rossa)* was the nickname of the Barbary pirate Aruz, who became an admiral in the Turkish fleet, and who spent his life attacking Christian ships and amassing slaves. With his brother Hizir, he twice defeated the Genoese Admiral Andrea Doria. Originally Greek, Barbarossa murdered the Sultan of Algiers and became Sultan himself. When Aruz was killed by the Spanish, Hizir took over and was then known as Khair-el-Din *(the Gift of God)*, being officially granted the Sultanate of Algiers by the Ottoman emperor. This younger Barbarossa brother helped consolidate Ottoman power in the eastern Mediterranean. From Hizir Barbarossa's death in 1547, the Turkish navy remained supreme in the Mediterranean until defeated at the Battle of Lepanto in 1571.

BARBARY PIRATES From the 16th to 19th centuries, these raiders plagued Mediterranean commerce, demanding tributes, taking ships and ransoming or enslaving crews. They raided coastlines across Europe, taking thousands of Christian slaves from as far afield as the West Country of England.

BLACKBEARD, d.1718 Edward Teach, Edward Thatch, also known as Thatch Drummond, was a giant of a man from Bristol. First sailing under the pirate captain Hornigold, by 1718 he was in charge of the 40-gun *Queen Anne's Revenge*. He dressed all in black, had a beard to his waist, and tied coloured ribbons in his pigtails. Blackbeard set fire to slow-burning fuses on his hat in battle to make himself appear more frightening. He shot fellow pirate Israel Hands under his captain's table, crippling him for life. Blackbeard blockaded Charleston, South Carolina, and a reward of £100 was offered for his head. The Governor of Virginia sent Lieutenant Robert Maynard with two sloops to Ocracoke Island off North Carolina. On 22 November 1718, Blackbeard was killed on his ship *Adventure* and beheaded. It took 25 separate wounds to kill him. His sailing-master Israel Hands appears as a character in R.L. Stevenson's *Treasure Island*. He was also known as '*Basilica*' Hands, and was sentenced for piracy in

Virginia in 1718 after being captured. He was pardoned in return for giving evidence against corrupt North Carolina officials (see below). He was last heard of begging in London, but almost certainly joined Black Bart Roberts' crew, being gibbeted at Cape Coast Castle on the Gold Coast of Africa in 1722. Blackbeard took 23 ships in seven months, all in the West Indies, which puts Black Bart Roberts' extraordinary total of over 400 in two years, on both sides of the Atlantic, into perspective.

BLACK PIRATES Black Bart Roberts employed at one time around 140 black crewmen, mainly former slaves, and Samuel Bellamy's *Whydah* had between 30 and 40 aboard. Black pirates had equal shares as white pirates, and some became quartermasters and boatswains during the Golden Age of Piracy. A black man, Diego Grillo, commanded a ship in Henry Morgan's sack of Panama in 1671. A pirate ship was the very essence of social democracy in these times of slavery.

'BLACK' SAM BELLAMY, d.1717
This pirate captain died in the wreck of the *Whydah*, off Cape Cod, and artefacts have been recovered from the wreck since 1894. Daniel Defoe made up a terrific ranting speech for him, as Bellamy shouts at one captured merchant captain: *'They vilify us, the scoundrels do, where there is only the difference (that) they rob the poor under cover of law, forsooth, and we plunder the rich under the protection of*

The Black Captain, The Great Pyrate, 'Black' Bart Roberts, d.1722

Bartholomew Roberts was a very tall man, with a *'swarthy'* demeanour, and therefore a *'black look'* about him. This may have come from the fact that this Welshman first went to sea aged 13, so his skin would have been extremely weathered and tanned. His pirate flags were the most feared on the high seas. His demise was greeted with relief by governors of colonies in the Americas, Caribbean, India and Africa, as he had almost halted transatlantic shipping. This most famous pirate in history was born John Roberts, and was a lifelong teetotaller. It is interesting that in the 19th century, doing *'a John Roberts in Wales'*, was to drink enough to keep drunk from Saturday morning until Sunday night. *Time* magazine called him the *'last and most lethal pirate'*. He took over 400 recorded prizes from the coast of Africa to the Caribbean, and was by far the most successful and most feared Western pirate ever.

our own courage; had you not better make one of us, (rather) than sneak after the arses of those villains for employment?'

BONNET, CAPTAIN STEDE,

d.1718 Bonnet was one of the more unusual pirates, a middle-aged Barbadian plantation-owner, who took to both privateering and piracy to escape a nagging wife. Known as the *'Gentleman Pirate'*, he later sailed with Blackbeard against his will as a *'guest'*. He was captured and hanged with 29 of his crew at Charleston.

BONNY, ANNE AND MARY READ – THE FEMALE PIRATES

These female pirates sailed with *'Calico Jack'* Rackham, and were sentenced to hang in Jamaica in 1720, but reprieved. They had taken part in battle and were convicted to be executed, like the rest of the crew. The judge asked if there was any reason why they should not be hanged, and both answered *'My Lord, we plead our bellies'*, the traditional plea of pregnant women. As it was illegal to kill an unborn child, they were reprieved until they had given birth, and they seem to have escaped subsequent execution.

BRETHREN OF THE COAST, LES FRÈRES DE LA CÔTE

From the 1530s onwards, Europeans had established small settlements on the coasts of Jamaica, Cuba and especially Hispaniola. The surviving Indians, those not wiped out by the Spanish, showed them how to cure long strips of meat on a barbecue over a slow fire, in a hut called a *'boucan'*. They caught wild cattle and pigs, and exchanged the hides, meat and tallow for guns, clothes, provisions and alcohol. Excellent sharpshooters, their favourite food was the warm marrow from the bones of newly slaughtered animals. In retaliation against Spanish attacks on their settlements, they attacked Spanish shipping in *'pirogues'* or *'piraguas'*, hollowed-out tree-trunks that served as canoes. The Spanish tried to massacre their herds, and this turned these *'Brethren of the Coast'* even more to piracy and buccaneering. From 1630 the island of Tortuga became their unofficial headquarters. They evolved a strict code, the *'Custom of the Coast'* whereby they shared booty on an even basis, and did not enquire about each other's pasts or surnames. Crossing the Tropic of Cancer *'drowned'* their former lives, according to their superstition. A *'buccaneer council'* of equals decided where they would get provisions, what shares each would have and where they would attack under an elected captain. Stealing or hiding of plunder was forbidden. Anyone stealing from a 'brother' had his nose sliced off, and a second offence led to marooning with just a jug of water, a musket and some shot.

THE BUCCANEERS

These unruly *'boucaniers'* were usually based in the Caribbean islands of Tortuga and northern Hispaniola from where they attacked ships, but not usually those of their own homeland. They were named after a French term *'boucan'* (from the Indian *'bukan'*) – a hut containing a slow grill of animal dung and green twigs over which meat was smoked or cooked. Their favoured form of attack was in long canoes or small, single-masted barques. They packed the boat with sharpshooters to shoot at anyone trying to fire a cannon at them, and they usually approached from astern of the prize ship, giving a minimal target to aim at. If they attacked an anchored ship at night, there was little time for her to cut the anchor and sheets and get up enough sail to escape. They then jammed the rudder and climbed up the stern of the ship, under cover of a fusillade of musket-fire. Although some called themselves *'privateers'*, they rarely had letters of commission or marque. Sometimes they carried expired commissions, and sometimes forgeries. In the 17th century, they became useful allies for Henry Morgan's privateers, sailing under his commissions.

CALICO JACK – JOHN RACKHAM, d.1720 Nicknamed for his

clothing, made from coarse white 'calico' cotton, he raided the American colonies from 1718 with Mary Read and Anne Bonny in his crew. He was eventually hanged in Jamaica.

CALLICE, JOHN Active from

1574–87, he was the most successful Elizabethan pirate. A Welshman with friends in high places, he was probably killed off the Barbary Coast.

CAPTAIN (PIRATE) A pirate captain

had remarkably few rights or benefits, only being in charge of the vessel when the crew was fighting, chasing or being pursued. In such action, he was allowed to strike, stab or shoot any man who disobeyed his orders. He also had power over prisoners and whether they were ill-used or freed, but no power over the captured vessel or its cargo. He was usually chosen for being *'pistol-proof'*, having a dominating and daring character. He had the right to sole use of the great cabin, but no privacy there. Any man could enter his cabin, drink from his punch bowl, swear at him and take his food with little come-back. He was usually deposed by popular vote, just as he was elected. Most of the day-to-day tasks were delegated to the quartermaster.

CAPTAIN OF THE SEA The name

given to the admiral who commanded the corsairs of Algiers, Tunis and Tripoli (Libya), and who dealt with Christian governments in peacetime.

CONFEDERACY OF THE BUCCANEERS OF AMERICA

The grandiose name that the *'Brethren of the Coast'* gave themselves, when they banded in their ships under Edward Mansveldt and then Henry Morgan in order to go privateering.

CORSAIRES French for pirates, like

the Spanish *'corsarios'* – a term associated with the Mediterranean. The Barbary Corsairs operated from North African states, and they were often 'hired' by Islamic nations to attack Christian ships. In return, the Christian corsairs were known as the Maltese Corsairs, and followed the orders of the Knights of St John to attack the Turks.

DAMPIER, WILLIAM, 1652–1715

Dampier circumnavigated the world three times, exploring Australia and the South Pacific. On his second voyage, he abandoned a crewman called Alexander Selkirk on the Juan Fernández Islands off Chile. Selkirk's marooning was the basis for the plot of *Robinson Crusoe*. Dampier was noted at the time for his extreme cowardice when faced with taking enemy ships. A recent biography lauds this untrustworthy character.

DAVIS, HOWELL, 'THE CAVALIER PRINCE OF PIRATES'

A notable Welsh pirate, renowned for his bravery and cunning, who captured Bart Roberts from a slaver. Roberts succeeded him as captain when Davis was killed in an ambush in 1719.

'DEAD CATS DON'T MEW'

The South American pirate Don Pedro Gibert made this exclamation in 1832, after he captured the American brig *Mexican* off Florida. After stripping the ship, he told his crew to lock the prisoners below decks, slash the rigging and set the ship on fire, observing *'Dead cats don't mew'*. However, the crew managed to free themselves, and let the fire burn until Gibert had vanished, then they extinguished it. After six weeks, they made it back home to Salem, Massachusetts. It was the last recorded act of piracy in American waters. He was captured by the Royal Navy's *Curlew* off West Africa and hanged in 1834 at Boston, Massachusetts.

EVERY, HENRY (LONG JOHN, LONG BEN), *c.1665–97* He was a

successful pirate in the Red Sea, taking £600,000 in gold, silver and jewels in 1694. The British East India Company placed a bounty on his head, but he vanished from the records in Ireland from 1695. His huge booty attracted many other seamen into piracy. It would now be worth £78 million using the Retail Prices Index, but a staggering £921 million using the Average Earnings Index.

FILIBUSTIERS A French term for

buccaneer, in Spanish *'filibusteros'* and in English becoming *'filibusterers'* and *'freebooters'*. The origin is the Dutch *'vrijbuiter'*. It may be that the French could not pronounce vrijbuiter or freebooter, and their attempt, *'filibustier'*, returned into the English language as *filibuster* in the 19th century. A more recent theory is that the origin was the Dutch *'vliebooter'*, the small flyboat used successfully in the fight for independence from Spain in the 16th century. By the end of that century the term had come to mean a fast sailing vessel used for piracy, and by the late 17th century had come to mean seaborne raiders. An American politician described his opponent's tactics in obstructing legislation as *'filibustering against the United States'* so it has now come to be synonymous with this activity in the legislature, such as making an endless speech to prevent a vote on a bill.

HANDS, ISRAEL – HIS REAL

FATE Stevenson's novel *Treasure Island* of 1883 only mentions five 'real' pirates – the Welshmen Black Bart Roberts, Roberts' surgeon Peter Scudamore, Roberts' former captor Howel Davis, the West countryman Captain Edward England, and Israel Hands, who was probably from Bristol or perhaps Aberdeen. Hands served with Blackbeard, and was captured and taken to Virginia for trial. In exchange for immunity, he gave testimony against corrupt North Carolina officials in 1718. Captain Charles Johnson (possibly a pseudonym for Daniel Defoe) then states that Hands died in poverty in London. However, the 29-year-old 'Israel Hynde' joined Black Bart Roberts' crew when the galley *Mercy*

Drake, Sir Francis, *c*.1540–96

Born in Devon, Drake went to sea at an early age, and made one of the first English slaving voyages as part of a fleet led by his cousin John Hawkins, bringing African slaves to the New World. It seems that Hawkins and Drake just wanted to trade, but only two small ships survived when attacked in 1569 by a Spanish squadron at San Juan de Ulúa, Mexico. The Spanish now became a lifelong enemy for Drake, and they in turn considered him a pirate. In 1570 and 1571 Drake made two profitable trading voyages to the West Indies, and in 1572 he commanded two vessels in a privateering expedition against Spanish ports there. He captured Nombre de Dios on the Isthmus of Panama, returning to England with a cargo of Spanish treasure. In 1577, Drake was secretly commissioned by Elizabeth I for another expedition against the Spanish colonies, on the American Pacific coast. He sailed with five ships, but by the time he reached the Pacific Ocean in October 1578 only one was left – his flagship the *Pelican*, renamed the *Golden Hind*. To reach the Pacific, Drake became the first Englishman to navigate the Straits of Magellan. He voyaged up the west coast of South America, plundering Spanish ports. Continuing north, hoping to find a route back across to the Atlantic, he sailed further up the west coast of America than any European. Unable to find a passage, he turned south again and, in July 1579, headed west across the Pacific. He landed at the Moluccas, Celebes, Java and then rounded the Cape of Good Hope. Drake arrived back in England in September 1580 with a rich cargo of spices and Spanish treasure. He had become the second man to circumnavigate the globe. Seven months later, Elizabeth knighted him aboard the *Golden Hind*. In 1585 Drake sailed to the West Indies and the coast of Florida where he again sacked and plundered Spanish cities. On his return voyage, he picked up the unsuccessful colonists of Roanoke Island off the coast of the Carolinas, which had been the first English colony in the New World. In 1587 war with Spain was imminent. Drake daringly entered the port of Cadiz and destroyed 30 of the ships that the Spanish were assembling to invade England, *'singeing the King of Spain's beard'*. In 1588 Drake was second-in-command in the fleet that defeated the Armada. Drake's last expedition, again with John Hawkins, was to the West Indies, but it was a disaster. He died in 1596 of dysentery off the coast of Puerto Rico. Hawkins died at the same time, and their bodies were buried at sea.

was captured in October 1721 on the Calabar River. He was taken into custody from the *Ranger* when Black Bart Roberts was killed on 10 February 1721, and found guilty of piracy and sentenced to be hanged in chains at Cape Corso on 13 April 1722. Of the other three men taken from the *Mercy*, the surgeon was acquitted, and the other two were reprieved to serve seven years in the Royal Africa Company. There were only 18 men sentenced to be hanged in chains of the 52 sentenced to death. They were all experienced pirates, such as the members of the *'House of Lords'* who served under Howel Davis, and the surgeon Scudamore who would not rescind his crimes. It thus appears that Hands did not die a beggar but returned to the sea to just three more months of piracy. In *Treasure Island* Israel Hands becomes the terrifying coxswain of the *Hispaniola*, whom the hero Jim has to shoot dead. His shipmate, the surgeon Peter Scudamore, is mentioned in *Treasure Island* also, and their fate is blamed upon the fact that Captain Bart Roberts changed the name of his ship several times, and so brought bad luck upon it.

HAWKINS, SIR JOHN, 1532–95

In 1562, Hawkins captained a ship making huge profits selling slaves to the Spanish in Hispaniola. He had taken the slaves from two Portuguese ships. In 1564 he sold slaves in Venezuela, and in 1567 again stole slaves off Portuguese ships off Africa to sell in the Caribbean. In 1569, despite a truce, the Spanish fleet attacked the English fleet, and the only two ships to escape were his and that of his cousin Francis Drake. In 1588 he commanded a squadron against the Spanish Armada, and died with Drake off Puerto Rico on another voyage against the Spanish.

HOLY PIRATES To distinguish them from the Muslim *Barbary Corsairs* in the Mediterranean, the *Knights Hospitaller*, the *Knights of St Stephen*, the *Knights of Rhodes* and the *Knights of Malta* were collectively known by this term. The Knights Hospitaller were successively based in Jerusalem from 1070, then Syria, then Cyprus, and eventually were ousted from Rhodes in 1522, moving on to Malta. All these Christian orders were virtually permanently at war with the forces of Islam for hundreds of years.

HOUSE OF LORDS The name that the senior members of Howel Davis's pirates, who then served under Bart Roberts, gave themselves. They addressed each other as *'my Lord'* and treated the other crew members as the *'Commons'*.

JIBBER THE KIBBER The trick of decoying vessels onto shore at night to wreck them. A lantern was attached to a horse's neck. The animal was lamed or hobbled in one leg, so that its movements looked like a lantern on a ship riding at anchor. A ship would make for it, believing that it would be a safe roadstead to anchor in, but be driven on to the shore and then plundered. It was practised on the western coasts of Britain until the 19th century.

KIDD, CAPTAIN WILLIAM,

*c.*1645–1701 William Kidd's fame and reputation is surprising, when you compare his achievements with those of Black Bart Roberts. Kidd only took one significant prize and only made one major voyage. He began privateering in 1695.

After a show trial, he was hanged at Wapping Old Stairs in 1701, leaving behind a legend of hidden treasure buried somewhere between Boston and India. During his execution, the hangman's rope broke and Kidd was hanged on the second attempt. His body was gibbeted and left to hang in chains as a warning to other would-be pirates.

THE KING OF PRUSSIA

John Carter (1770–c.1807) lived with his brother Harry at Prussia Cove under a sheltered headland at Mount's Bay in Cornwall. The cove had slipways for landing goods, and a house with cellars and lofts where they could store the contraband that they had landed. John Carter named the cove Prussia Cove because of his deep admiration for Frederick the Great, King of Prussia. Carter himself became known as the *King of Prussia*, as he engaged in ever more daring encounters with the revenue. Mount's Bay was an area notorious for lawless gangs of wreckers and smugglers. The Carter brothers owned a 19-gun cutter of 160 tons, and a 20-gun lugger, each manned with a crew of around 30 men. Each vessel would be equipped with at least one smaller boat for inshore work. The local Cornish community helped with smuggling, as most saw nothing immoral in it, and there was therefore a network of people to store, transport and sell the goods in distant markets. Inevitably battles broke out with customs men, as both sides were armed to the teeth. Harry Carter records one such battle in 1788 – *'the bone of my nose was cut right in two and two very large cuts in my head that two or three pieces of my skull worked out afterwards'*.

THE KNIGHTS OF MALTA

The Knights Hospitaller were forced to flee their stronghold on the Mediterranean island of Rhodes in 1522 after an Ottoman invasion. They settled in Malta, where they became Christian corsairs. By the 1550s their war galleys were seriously disrupting Ottoman trade in the Mediterranean. Because of their attacks on Venetian vessels, they found it difficult to get Christian aid to fortify the island, and their power had waned by the mid-17th century. They lost Malta in 1798.

LAFITTE, JEAN, 1780–1826

Commissioned by Latin-American countries, this privateer had 50 pirate ships under his command when he helped win the Battle of New Orleans in 1815. For his assistance in the War of 1812, he and his 1000 pirate followers were granted pardons by President James Madison.

L'OLONNAIS, d.1668 – THE FLAIL OF THE SPANISH

One of the most horrible of all buccaneers, Jean David Nau came from Les Sables d'Olonne in western France, hence his nickname. He seems to have never taken prisoners, often cutting heads off instead and licking the blood from his blade. He was known as *'Fleau des Espagnoles' (Flail of the Spanish)*. On the Central American coast, he allegedly cut open the heart of a prisoner and gnawed at it before throwing it on the ground. Captured by native Indians shortly after this, they slowly cut him up into little pieces.

MONTBARS THE EXTERMINATOR

This buccaneer's favourite torture was to slit a man's stomach open, take out his intestines and nail them to a post. Then he pressed burning wood into the victim's buttocks to force him to dance to the furthest extent of his intestines. The Spanish Inquisition practised similar tortures and possibly worse upon their European victims, so the Spanish were *'fair game'* for such horrors.

MORGAN, ADMIRAL SIR HENRY, *c.1635*–88 An accomplished general of troops as well as the most successful buccaneer of all time, the Welshman Morgan almost single-handedly kept Jamaica a British possession until his death in 1688. As *'Admiral of the Brethren of the Coast'* he led the first successful attack upon 'impregnable' Panama, and also took Portobelo and Puerto Principe in his long career. Cleverly, he ensured that he had 'letters of commission' for each attack, and these letters were worded so that all profits from overland raids would accrue to him and his crews, rather than go to the Crown and the ship's owners. Thus all of his six successful expeditions against the Spanish generally ignored ships at sea and concentrated on attacking land targets.

NORTH AFRICAN PIRATES AND THE OTTOMAN EMPIRE

The Mediterranean ports of Tripoli (Libya), Tunis (Tunisia) and Algiers (Algeria) were the main havens of the Barbary Corsairs, who from 1480 to 1630 virtually controlled shipping in the area. These cities lay on the edge of the desert, so the sea was regarded as their main resource. The Ottoman rulers became so reliant upon the corsairs that eventually the ruler came to be elected from the pirates. The corsairs had protected status in the Ottoman Empire, so enjoyed the use of secure bases from which to attack

Christian ships and ports. The Barbarossa brothers were each in turn Sultan of Algiers, and they attacked the Spanish for around 50 years in the early 1500s. After the death of Suleiman the Magnificent in 1566, the Ottoman Empire slowly declined until by the early 1800s it was described as *'the sick man of Europe'* by Tsar Nicholas I of Russia.

O'MALLEY, GRACE, 1530–1603
'The Queen of the Irish Seas' attacked English shipping with a fleet of 20 ships, but was somehow pardoned by Queen Elizabeth I, after a private meeting.

PEG-LEG A nickname for sailors who had lost a leg in battle or accident, the leg being replaced by a wooden stump. François le Clerc and Cornelius Jol were pirate 'peg-legs'. The Dutch equivalent was *'houtebeen'* and the Spanish *'pie de palo'*. Like losing a hand, losing a leg generally meant that most victims would die of gangrene, so relatively few pirates survived to wear a peg-leg. Captain Ahab in *Moby-Dick* had an ivory leg. Nowhere in *Treasure Island* is Long John Silver described as having an artificial leg. He used crutches, and the peg-leg is the addition of film-makers.

Raleigh, Sir Walter, 1554–1618

Part explorer, part courtier and part privateer, he fought against the Spanish Armada. He named a large part of the new American colony Virginia, as a tribute to Elizabeth I, the Virgin Queen. The state of Virginia is a small remnant of this original region. He was said to have made tobacco smoking fashionable, and founded the *'Lost Colony'* of Roanoke Island off North Carolina. His poems were set to music and were the 'pop songs' of his day. Falsely imprisoned for treason by James I, he was found guilty but released to go in quest of the fabled land of *El Dorado*. He failed, but his lieutenant sacked the Spanish settlement at Santo Thomé on the Orinoco River, where Raleigh's son was killed. After a show trial to appease Spain, his death penalty was reinstated and he was beheaded by order of King James I. He left a message for all future leaders of countries, which still appears to be little understood by people in power: *'A man must first govern himself ere he is fit to govern a family; and his family ere he be fit to bear the government of the Commonwealth.'*

ROBINSON CRUSOE, WILLIAM THE MOSQUITO AND ALEXANDER SELKIRK

Buccaneers under Captain Watling were scared off the uninhabited Juan Fernández Island in January 1681, and in their haste left a Mosquito (Miskito) Indian called William there. In March 1684, buccaneers under Captain Cook of the *Batchelor's Delight* and Captain Swan of the *Cygnet* came into sight of Juan Fernández. Some of Cook's men had sailed under Watling, and they wanted to send a boat ashore to look for William. William Dampier related in his journals that he went ashore with another Mosquito (Miskito) Indian named Robin and met him. William had been left on the island with just a musket, knife, some powder and some shot. Dampier tells us that *'when his ammunition was expended, he contrived by notching his knife to saw the barrel of his gun into small pieces, wherewith he made harpoons, lances, hooks and a long knife, heating the pieces of iron first in the fire, and then hammering them out as he pleased with stones.'* Fishing lines were made from the skins of seals cut into thongs and knotted. William had no clothes left, and wore a goatskin around his waist. It seems that William is virtually a perfect model for Daniel Defoe's *Robinson Crusoe*. Dampier's *Journals* were published in 1697 and 1699 and Defoe's book in

1719. However, most people believe that the Robinson Crusoe story was inspired by Alexander Selkirk (1676–1721), a Scot marooned on the same island. Dampier features again in this version. In late summer 1704, he was captain of the privateer *St George*, and Thomas Stradling was captaining the consort ship *Cinque Ports*. In September the *Cinque Ports* needed caulking and put into Juan Fernández for repairs, where the ship's master Selkirk and its captain Stradling had an argument about the seaworthiness of the ship. Selkirk said that the repairs were not good enough and that the ship would leak badly. He shouted that if Stradling insisted on setting sail in her, he could *'go to the bottom alone'*. Angered, Stradling left Selkirk ashore with his sea chest. Selkirk thought that other men would join him, forcing Stradling to change his mind, but as the ship's boat pulled away from the beach, he shouted to Stradling that he had changed his mind. Stradling shouted back that he had not changed his, and Selkirk was marooned. More than four years after Selkirk was marooned, Dampier was sailing under Woodes Rogers after rounding Cape Horn, trying to put into one of the Juan Fernández Islands. A boat was sent ashore and found Selkirk, dressed in goatskins. When Selkirk saw Dampier, he asked to be put ashore again, but was talked out of it.

ROCK THE BRAZILIAN

From Groningen, Holland, this pirate was called Roche Brasiliano from the long time he spent in Brazil, corrupted to *Rock the Brazilian* by the English buccaneers. He had a pathological hatred of the Spanish, as evidenced by his practice of roasting them alive on spits.

ROGERS, WOODES, 1679–1732 – PRIVATEER TURNED POACHER

In 1709 this Bristolian privateer rescued Alexander Selkirk during a circumnavigation of the globe. Rogers was made Governor of the Bahamas in 1718, and more than any other man was responsible for the eradication of piracy in the Caribbean, clearing New Providence (Nassau) of all pirates and privateers.

SHARPE, BARTHOLOMEW, 1650–90 – PARDONED FOR A MAP

This privateer sailed with Henry Morgan, and in the 1680s plundered Spanish settlements. He was pardoned by Charles II because he had captured a valuable Spanish derrotero.

TAMPA BAY BUCCANEERS

Gasparilla was allegedly a Spanish pirate who was active in the Caribbean from 1782 and who supposedly attacked an American warship with Jean Lafitte in 1822. A former admiral, he is said to have stolen an armada's jewels and gold and holed up in western Florida. From the wealth of tangled stories about him, a pamphlet describing his exploits was written and it was given to visitors to the resort of Boca Grande in the early 20th century. The football team was later named in his honour, and Tampa holds an annual Gasparilla Festival.

TEW, THOMAS, d.1695

Known as *'the Rhode Island Pirate'*, he attacked African slave-trading ports, and in 1693 took an Arab sloop filled with gold in the Indian Ocean. The Governor of New York gave him a privateering commission, but he turned to piracy with Henry 'Long John' Every.

ULUJ ALI PASHA, 1520–87 – THE GREATEST BARBARY CORSAIR

Born Giovanni Dionigi Galeri in Italy, he was captured by Barbarossa's men and forced to serve in the galleys. He became a Muslim to survive, and soon bought a 'galiot' – a small galley with one or two masts and about 20 oars. His bravery saw his reputation grow and he rose through the ranks until he was made commander of all the Barbary Corsairs. He fought brilliantly at the massive Battle of Lepanto in 1571. By his death he had secured the Barbary Coast for the Ottoman Empire. His Arabic nickname, *'farta'*, meant *'scurvied'*.

VANE, CHARLES, d.1720

This English pirate raided the eastern seaboard of the American colonies and the Caribbean. He was replaced as captain by Calico Jack Rackham, for cowardice. He was hanged in Jamaica.

WILLIAMS, WILLIAM, 1725–91 – THE PRIVATEER POLYMATH

This Welsh privateer was marooned on the Miskito Coast of Nicaragua, and hid from the Spanish among the Rama Indians. His is an amazing story. He lost two sons in the American Civil War who were fighting for the cause of independence; he built the first theatre in America, at Philadelphia; he was America's first professional scene-painter; he painted America's first known seascape; he taught music and painting; he inspired Benjamin West to paint, and West later became President of the Royal Academy; Williams wrote a *Lives of the Great Painters*, and was also author of America's first novel, *The Journal of Penrose, Seaman*. This mariner-polymath was formative in the first years of American culture, but is virtually unknown today. His *Journal* is a wonderful tale of faction, based upon his time when marooned among the Rama, full of detailed descriptions of flora and fauna of the jungle and seas, with a strong anti-slavery message.

WRECKERS

Because of the poverty that was prevalent in coastal areas, all classes of society benefited from the activities of smugglers. There was no national law agency and little law enforcement in those times. Under a statute of Edward I, no ship was a *'wreck'* if any man, dog or cat escaped alive from it. If all died, it could be legally looted. Thus in the poorer, more lawless parts of the country 'wreckers' operated, trying to lure ships onto the rocks. It was in their interests that no-one survived, so that they could legitimately take a share of the profits or salvage rights. Lighthouses were smashed, and false lights or beacons erected. In Cornwall, prayers were even said asking for ships to be drawn onto the rocks. Men would line the cliffs on stormy nights with false lights to encourage a ship into thinking that there was a safe harbour nearby. If a sailor then managed to struggle to shore, he was killed, as was the case with Admiral Sir Cloudesley Shovell in the Scilly Isles in 1707, who was then stripped of his possessions. Only in 1753 were wrecking and plundering made capital offences, and then mainly because of the damage being caused to British, as well as foreign, shipping. However, customs officers stood little chance against well-armed gangs of wreckers and smugglers, so for decades after the practices continued.

PIRATE HAUNTS AND TARGETS

BARBADOS Until the taking of Jamaica in 1655, Barbados and St Kitts were England's only possessions in the West Indies. It was a lawless, brawling spot, used by Oliver Cromwell as a place to send defeated Irish and Welsh prisoners from the Civil War as indentured servants (slaves). Henry Whistler described it thus: *'This island is the Dunghill whereine England doth cast forth its rubidge* [rubbish]: *Rodgs* [rogues] *and hors* [whores] *and such like people are those who are generally Broght* [brought] *heare. A rodge in England will hardly make a cheatere here; a Baud* [bawd, harlot] *broght over puts on a demuor* [demure] *comportment, a whore if hansum makes a wife for sume rich planter.'* Barbados was full of deported Royalist prisoners, beggars, exiled Huguenots, Quakers and political dissidents such as *'Perrot, the bearded ranter who refused to doff his hat to the Almighty, ended up in Barbadoes'*. A description of Barabados' inhabitants in 1665 is *'convict gaol birds or riotous persons, rotten before they are sent forth, and at best idle and only fit for the mines.'* Its escaped bondsmen, transported criminals and unemployed seamen made a happy breeding-ground for piracy, especially at the end of Queen Anne's War in 1713.

BARBARY COAST From the 14th century, this was the name for the coastal regions ruled from Tripoli, Tunis and Algiers. These were the *Barbary States*, city-states on the edge of desert. *'Barbary'* was derived from the original Berber inhabitants. Later, Morocco was included, although its rulers did not live by piracy. The coast was a real pirate haven from around 1520–1830. In 1538, Andrea Doria led a combined Christian fleet against the ships of Barbarossa off the Albanian coast, but he was defeated by a smaller force, despite leading 80 Venetian, 30 Spanish and 36 Papal galleys with 60,000 men and 2500 guns. In 1541, the Muslim corsairs won another great battle off Algiers against 500 ships of a Christian European fleet, led again by the Italian Andrea Doria. Thousands were taken as slaves, and 8300 men were killed or drowned. In the late 16th century, Elizabethan pirates and captains such as John Callice began cooperating with the Barbary pirates, teaching them sailing skills. In 1622, English towns raised £70,000 to pay the ransom for English captives held on the Barbary Coast.

BATH TOWN, NORTH CAROLINA, 'THE HOME OF BLACKBEARD'

Founded in 1705, this is North Carolina's oldest town, on the Pamlico River, 50 miles (80 km) inland from the Atlantic. Pirates were made welcome here, the shallow waters lending themselves to smuggling and the hiding of shallow-draught pirate ships. Governor Charles Eden even offered Stede Bonnet and Blackbeard pardons, and along with his officials accepted bribes for turning a blind eye to the trade in illegal goods. In 1718, Blackbeard made Bath Town his home, as his activities around Ocracoke in the Outer Banks had made him and Captain Charles Vane targets for Governor Spottiswood of Virginia. After Blackbeard was killed, Captain Maynard took his captured crew, along with those rounded up in Bath Town, to Williamsburg. Thirteen of the crew were tried and hanged in March 1719.

BOSTON

Like New York and the Rhode Island ports, Boston welcomed pirate trade in the 17th century, and even gave pardons to certain pirates. In 1703 Captain Daniel Plowman was sent out to privateer against the Spanish and French, but his crew imprisoned him and voted for John Quelch as captain. The 80-ton *Charles* took many Portuguese prizes off Brazil, but on its return to Boston the crew were investigated and arrested. Quelch and other ring-leaders were hanged outside Boston in June 1704. The despicable Captain Edward Low was also hanged in chains, at Nick's Mate Island off Boston in July 1724.

CARTAGENA, CARTHAGENA

This was the treasure port between Panama and Venezuela, now part of Colombia. It was one of only three treasure ports visited by the annual Spanish *flota*. Pearls were shipped from Margarita Island, as well as precious woods, gold, silver and emeralds. Founded in 1533, it was heavily defended and was the only major Spanish port never taken by the buccaneers, although Henry Morgan had wanted to attack it. The French navy took it in 1689. In *The Incredible Voyage*, Tristan Jones states that slaves were punished by the Spanish for stealing extra food by being thrown into one of the fortress moats, *'which were purposely stocked with sharks'*.

CHARLES TOWN, CHARLESTON

This city was founded on the banks of the Cooper and Ashley Rivers in South Carolina in 1670, and named in honour of Charles II. Pirates like William Lewis raided the port, and Blackbeard blockaded the town in May 1718. The pirate Charles Vane became such a nuisance that Governor Robert Johnson sent Colonel William Rhett commanding the *Henry* and *Sea Nymph* to capture him. Rhett just missed Vane, but instead caught Stede Bonnet up the Cape Fear River in September 1718. Bonnet and 30 crew were hanged in November at Charles Town.

DRY TORTUGAS

A shoal of islands used by British pirates at the western end of the Florida Keys. Turtling was important to pirate diets, and they were possibly called this to distinguish them from Tortuga (Île de la Tortue) off Hispaniola, and Salt Tortuga off Venezuela. Turtles caught at Salt Tortuga were cured using salt from the nearby salt-pans of the Araya Peninsula. Perhaps turtles caught at the Dry Tortugas were dry-cured…

ÎLE-A-VACHE Also called Île-de-Vache (Cow Island), this favourite pirate location off the southwest of Haiti was mispronounced by the British as *Isle of Ash*. It was Henry Morgan's favourite place for gathering his privateers.

JUAN FERNÁNDEZ ISLANDS

This small group of islands was a pirate haven about 400 miles (650 km) west of Valparaiso, Chile. An American, Bernard Keiser, is convinced that *'the lost treasures of the Incas'*, worth over $10 billion, were hidden in a cave there about 20 feet (6 m) deep, by English corsairs in the 18th century. The largest island, Mas-a-Tierra, was renamed Alexander Selkirk Island in 1966.

MADAGASCAR This is the fourth largest island in the world, and it was the most important pirate haunt outside the West Indies and the Barbary Coast. French and English freebooters congregated here in the Indian Ocean just 250 miles (400 km) off the east coast of Africa. The natives were tolerant, there was abundant fresh water and food, locally growing citrus fruits prevented scurvy and there were hundreds of hidden harbours on the main island and its nearby islets. There were easy takings on the nearby Indian Ocean and Red Sea. For instance, each year, a fleet gathered at Mocha to carry Indian pilgrims, with gold and silver, to Mecca and Jeddah. Also

Jamaica

The expedition sent by Cromwell to take possessions in the West Indies was an absolute disaster. During its attack on Hispaniola, the English commander, General Venables, was so frightened that he hid behind a tree *'so possessed with terror that he could hardly spake'*. Captain Butler, sent to recruit Frenchmen on their island of St Kitts, was so drunk that he fell off his horse and vomited over the feet of the delegation of French officers sent to meet him. Jamaica was taken more by accident than design in 1655, and Venables spent some time in the Tower of London on his return to England. After the taking of Jamaica by the English, French, Dutch and English buccaneers flocked to its main port, Port Royal. The French had forced them out of their Tortuga stronghold, and the English authorities saw them as a source of considerable privateering wealth, and a first line of defence against the activities of the Spanish in the West Indies. By 1662, there was so much looted silver and gold in Port Royal that the English government thought about establishing a mint there.

Portuguese carracks carried precious goods from Goa to Europe. The French, British and Dutch East India Companies frequently had ships loaded with silks, spices and jewels. The French attempt to colonize Madagascar ended with the abandonment of Fort Dauphin in 1674. As it had the first usable harbours after passing the Cape, many ships stopped there for fruit, water and provisions, and it became a magnet for piracy. However, with the ending of the French wars in 1697, British men-of-war started patrolling Madagascar and St Mary's Island, capturing the Welsh pirate David Williams in November 1703. The island was a superb base during the Golden Age of Piracy, far less dangerous than the Caribbean. Popular pirate havens in the area were St Mary's Island (Île Sainte Marie), Mathelage, Johanna Island, Ranter Bay, St Augustine's Bay, Fort Dauphin, Réunion Island and Mauritius. The pirate captains Tew, Every, England, Plantain, Condent and Kidd all used the island as a base at some time in their careers.

STRAITS OF MALACCA This stretch of water, linking the Indian Ocean and the South China Sea, lies between Sumatra and the Malay Peninsula. It is 500 miles (800 km) long but narrows to only 30 miles (48 km). A major shipping lane, it has always been a focus for piracy because it is a natural 'choke point'.

MALTA Just south of Sicily, Malta and its smaller islands of Gozo and Comino were excellent and strategically placed pirate havens. They commanded the passage between the east and west Mediterranean, and were used by corsairs and Christian pirates for centuries until the French occupation of 1798.

MARMORA On the Atlantic coast of Morocco, a renowned pirate base until captured in 1614 by the Spanish.

MOROCCO European corsairs used its Atlantic (and sometimes its Mediterranean) ports as Morocco's ruling dynasty was hostile to the Ottoman Empire. Sale and Mamora were its main pirate havens.

MOSQUITO (MISKITO) COAST This is the eastern (Caribbean) coast of Nicaragua, from the San Juan River in Nicaragua to the Aguán River in Honduras. It is named after the Miskito Indians, not insects. Because of its dense mangrove swamps, hundreds of inlets and lack of arable land, it was never settled by the Spanish, and so became a sanctuary for runaway slaves and a pirate hideout. The English controlled it for many years, via a system of *'Miskito Kings'*.

NEW ORLEANS AND JEAN LAFITTE Barataria Bay near New Orleans was a favourite pirate haunt, the most famous being Jean Lafitte, a former New Orleans blacksmith. He commanded, with his brother Pierre, up to ten ships in the Gulf of Mexico, attacking American, British and Spanish shipping. He died in 1820 or 1821 after burning Galveston.

NEW PROVIDENCE ISLAND, 'THE NEST OF PYRATES' This small Bahamian island was used by pirates from the 1680s. In 1716 Governor Spotswood of Virginia called it the *'Nest of Pyrates'*. It was formerly called Providence Island. In the centre of the Bahamas, it was abandoned by the English in 1704 after repeated French and Spanish attacks. However, its port of Charles Town (now called Nassau) was considered the ideal pirate harbour by Captain Henry Jennings after the end of the War of Spanish Succession in 1714. From 1716–18 it was the most important pirate haven in the Caribbean, and pirates were said to *'dream of Heaven being in New Providence'*. The settlement took over as the *'Sodom of the New World'* after the destruction of Jamaica's Port Royal (q.v.) in 1692. Nassau was a prominent pirate port, and was important because ships could be careened in safety there. Near all the trade routes, there was abundant water, meat, wood and fruit. The port of Nassau was too shallow for warships to attack, but could easily accommodate up to 500 smaller vessels. It was divided at its entrance by Hog Island. Thus to be effectively blockaded, two men-of-war were needed. Woodes Rogers arrived in 1718 as Governor of the Bahamas, and its pirate haven days were effectively ended. The exodus of pirates in 1718 included Howell Davis, Thomas Anstis, Olivier Levasseur (La Buze), Blackbeard, Paul Williams, Samuel Bellamy, Thomas Cocklyn, 'Jolly' Jack Rackham, Christopher Winter, Christopher Condent and others. In 1717, Stede Bonnet, Benjamin Hornigold, Charles Vane and John Martel had also used New Providence.

NEW YORK One of its early governors, Colonel Benjamin Fletcher, earned his living by fencing stolen goods from pirates to corrupt officials. Pirate ships were even charged a fee to anchor in New York City's harbour, after which their goods were passed without problems through customs. Pirates roamed free, spending their money in the port's taverns and brothels. Governor Fletcher became a close friend of Captain Thomas Tew, the *'Rhode Island pirate'*. The governor also asked another friend Captain William Kidd, to privateer against the French off the coast. Fletcher was removed from office by the English crown in 1698. New York was at the forefront of attempts to evade the hated Navigation Taxes, and its merchants traded openly with smugglers, and did business extensively with Adam Baldridge, the main pirate 'fence' in Madagascar. However, as the city grew, normal trade became more important, and by the 1730s the great days of New York as a pirate haunt were over.

PANAMA This was one of the three ports used by the Spanish treasure fleets on the Pacific coast. Every year, silver was taken from Panama on mule trains across the Panama Isthmus to Nombre de Dios, and then to Portobelo (Puerto Bello) on the Caribbean coast. If the Chagres River was full, small boats were used instead of mules. Panama City was sacked by Henry Morgan in 1671, just three years after he had taken Portobelo. Panama city was rebuilt, several miles away. There are five UNESCO World Heritage sites in Panama, including impressive Spanish fortifications at Portobelo and Panama Viejo (Old Panama).

PETIT GOAVE A pirate port in the southwest of St Domingue (today's Haiti), which replaced Tortuga as a buccaneering base in the 1670s.

PORTOBELO (PUERTO BELLO)

Because Francis Drake had sacked Cartagena and Santo Domingo, and Nombre de Dios had an inferior natural harbour, the Spanish developed Portobelo in Panama as the their main Caribbean treasure port from 1595. Drake died of fever in the waters off the port. Henry Morgan sacked it in 1668. In the 18th century, at terrible cost, a road linking it to Panama City on the Pacific side of the isthmus was constructed.

PORT ROYAL, 'THE SODOM OF THE NEW WORLD' Known as

Cagway to Captain Christopher Myngs, in Henry Morgan's early days on the island, the original Carib-Spanish name for Port Royal was *'cayagua'* (literally, island of water). Penn and Venables took Jamaica in 1655, and the new port of Cagway was renamed Port Royal in 1660, on the restoration of Charles II. Because of fear of a Spanish invasion, buccaneers were requested to come from Tortuga to bolster its defences, but after the 1660 peace was conducted with Spain, many buccaneers were granted letters of marque allowing them to attack shipping. By the early 1670s, Port Royal even rivalled Boston for wealth. *'Pirate heaven'* with a huge harbour that could take up to 500 ships, it was at the heart of all the West Indies shipping routes. Buccaneering was unofficially sanctioned by the governors of Jamaica, and the lawyer Francis Hanson of Port Royal wrote in 1683 *'The town of Port Royal, being as it were the Store House or Treasury of the West Indies, is always like a continual Mart or fair where all sorts of choice merchandises are daily imported, not only to furnish the island, but vast quantities are thence again transported to supply the Spaniards, Indians and other Nations, who in exchange return us bars and cakes of gold, wedges and pigs of silver, Pistoles, Pieces of Eight and several other coins of both metals, with store of wrought Plate, jewels, rich pearl necklaces, and of Pearl unsorted or undrilled several bushels ... almost every House hath a rich cupboard of Plate, which they carelessly expose, scarce shutting their doors in the night ... In Port Royal there is more plenty of running Cash (proportionately to the number of its inhabitants) than is in London.'* In July 1661 alone the Council issued licences for 40 new grog shops, taverns and punch houses. Around this time Governor Modyford was making a fortune in bribes from Henry Morgan and other buccaneers. By 1680, there were over 100 licensed taverns for a population of 3000. By 1690, one in four of its buildings were *'brothels, gaming houses, taverns and grog shops'*. A 17th-century clergyman returned to England on the same ship as he sailed out on, writing *'This town is the Sodom of the New World and since the majority of its population consists of pirates, cut-throats, whores and some of the vilest persons in the whole of the world, I felt my permanence there was of no use.'* It was heaven for traders, who cheaply bought pirate loot, sold it in London at huge profits, and also profiteered by selling expensive supplies to pirates.

Port Royal lay on a small cay and the tip of the long sandspit called the Palisadoes, which forms Kingston Harbour. On 7 June 1692 a combined earthquake and tidal wave destroyed this privateering capital, probably killing 2000 people, and sweeping Captain Morgan's grave into the sea. Another 2000 died later from wounds, disease and fever. In the tidal wave that followed the earthquake, *'nothing else was seen but the dead and dying, and heard but shrieks and cries.'* The capital of St Jago de la Vega, corrupted to Santiago, now resumed its authority over Jamaica's affairs. Port Royal was rebuilt after the earthquake, only to suffer a great fire in 1703. It is the only sunken town in the New World, and efforts are being made to have it declared a World Heritage Site, *'an underwater Pompeii'.*

PROSPECT OF WHITBY Possibly the most evocative London dockside pub, from 1543 to 1790 it was known as *The Devil's Tavern*, the haunt of thieves and smugglers. On the north shore of the Thames at Wapping, it was renamed after a Yorkshire ship that used to bring stone to the wharf.

PROVIDENCE ISLAND – ISLA DE PROVIDENCIA, SANTA CATALINA A large island and pirate haven 250 miles (400 km) off Portobelo, Panama, it lay on the Cuba to Venezuela

trading route. Its pirates successfully beat off a Spanish attack in 1635, but it was taken in 1640. Henry Morgan used it for his attack on Panama in 1670–1. The islands almost adjoin, Santa Catalina being the smaller. Because of its same name, Providence in the Bahamas was renamed New Providence.

RHODE ISLAND Newport and Providence in Rhode Island were well-known pirate and smuggling haunts in the second half of the 17th century. Until the first decades of the 18th century pirate captains such as Blackbeard, Henry (Long John) Every, Thomas Tew and Blackbeard frequented their harbours. In 1694, Newport's Thomas Tew returned with huge treasure from the Red Sea. He then received a letter of marque from the Governor of New York to sail to Madagascar. However, as merchant shipping increased in importance, pirates were no longer welcome, and early in the 1720s 26 pirates were hanged outside Newport as a warning to others.

Tortuga

The most famous pirate island, just off northwest Hispaniola (Haiti and the Dominican Republic). It resembles a great *'sea-tortoise'* or turtle, so was called by the Spanish Tortuga del Mar. The Spanish in Santo Domingo regularly attacked the buccaneers in western Hispaniola, and Tortuga was more easy to defend and escape from. Thus the early French settlers and hunters fled Hispaniola to settle there. Around 25 miles (40 km) long, it has fresh water and excellent defensive positions. An early French governor, Jean le Vasseur, was an engineer who built a 24-gun fort close by the harbour to repel Spanish attacks. French governors, like their British counterparts at Port Royal, Jamaica, relied upon buccaneers for local defence. In their turn, buccaneers needed such safe havens and would not let them be taken by the Spanish. Louis le Golif complained in his

Memoirs of a Buccaneer about having to fight two duels on Tortuga to keep suitors at bay. It was reported that its French governor finally imported hundreds of prostitutes to try and wean buccaneers away from *matelotage*, sodomy with their *'mates'*. In the early 1670s there was a series of Spanish and French raids, and Petit Goave replaced it as a pirate haven from the late 17th century. Some Tortugans went to French St Dominique and others to Port Royal. The island is now part of Haiti, with a population of 30,000, and is visited by tourists for its beaches, caves and historic ruins.

SAINT MARY'S ISLAND, ÎLE SAINTE-MARIE A pirate haven until 1722, this 35-mile (56-km) long island in the Indian Ocean lies off the northeast of Madagascar. Pirate traders such as Adam Baldridge controlled it as a base for fencing goods looted from shipping in the Indian Ocean and Red Sea.

TRIPOLI Barbary Corsair haven in Libya from 1550 until 1835.

TUNIS Barbary Corsair haven in Tunisia from 1574 to 1830.

SOMETHING ABOUT TREASURE

BURIED TREASURE Very few buccaneers or pirates ever buried plunder. They shared it out and usually spent it within days on women, gambling and alcohol. One of Morgan's privateers is known to have paid a hundred guineas or 500 pieces of eight, just for the sight of a naked prostitute. The Dutchman Roche Brasiliano was known to the English as *'Rock the Brasilian'*. He was captured by the Spanish and was tortured by the Inquisition at Campeche. He told them of his treasure buried on the Isla de Pinos, off Cuba. Spanish soldiers retrieved over 100,000 pieces of eight, after which the Spanish put *'Rock'* out of his misery. Legend persists that Black Bart hid treasure inside a cave on Little Cayman Island, after his pillaging of the Portuguese fleet at Bahia. Stevenson's novel *Treasure Island* of 1883 popularized the concept of treasure maps and buried treasure. In fact the first buried treasure story was acknowledged to be Edgar Allan Poe's *The Gold Bug* in 1843. However, this to some extent plagiarized the buried treasure tale in *The Journal of Penrose, Seaman* by William Williams, published posthumously in 1815, but written around 1760–70.

CACAFUEGO A bully, braggart or *'spitfire'*, meaning literally in Spanish to defecate fire. The Spanish ship *Nuestra Señora de la Concepcion* was pursued by Francis Drake for several days before he took it on 1 March 1579. She was the greatest prize in history, being valued at around 1.5 million ducats at the time, or around half a billion pounds in today's money. She had been given the vulgar name of the *Cacafuego* by the chasing privateers, *'shitfire'*, because she was one of the few Spanish ships of the time to bear cannon on the Pacific Coast of South America. Queen Elizabeth took most of the booty. A Spanish youth on the captured vessel said that his ship *'shall no longer be called the Cacafuego, but the Cacaplata (shit-silver)'* and that Drake's ship the *Golden Hind* should be renamed the *Cacafuego*.

CURRENCY OF SPAIN IN THE 17th CENTURY

8 copper pesos = 1 silver real
8 silver reals (reales) = 1 silver 'piece of eight' (peso)
10 silver 'pieces of eight' = 1 gold escudo
2 gold escudos = gold doubloon

Dubloons, Ducats and Pieces of Eight

Silver real The real was a coin weighing 0.12 ounces (3.43 g) of silver, and there were eight reales to a peso, hence the term 'pieces of eight' for pesos.

Silver piece of eight An early Spanish silver-dollar-sized coin. As Spanish mints issued silver denominations smaller than eight reales relatively infrequently, these coins would sometimes be chopped up into smaller pieces to provide small change. In the 17th and 18th centuries, so many were in circulation that they were accepted almost anywhere in the world. The American dollar sign $ was derived from the figure 8 stamped on the side of the *'piece of eight'*, the silver peso (or piaster). They were minted at Mexico City and Lima in Peru, and were common currency in all of England's colonies, being valued at four shillings and sixpence. Often they were cut into eight pieces for ease of transaction, so that *'two bits'* made a quarter. The origin of the modern American phrase, *'not worth two bits'*, is from the days when the English colonies around Massachusetts used this Spanish money. Pieces of eight were produced for about 300 years, in Mexico, Peru and Colombia, and they became the standard unit of trade between Europe and China. They were legal tender in the USA until 1857. Before the Spanish started exploiting Potosi in Peru (in today's Bolivia), silver was almost as valuable as gold in the Old World. Such were the quantities taken from the New World, that silver dropped to about a fifteenth of the value of gold. The Spanish exported four billion pesos of silver and gold from the New World between 1492 and 1830.

Gold ducat This was the European gold trade coin during the late medieval and early modern period. The name derives from *ducatus*, the Latin form of the title of the Doge of Venice, where the ducat was first issued in 1284. Called the *'ducado'*, it was worth less than a doubloon, about 10-11 silver 'reales', and was known to the British seaman as a ducat. The coin was copied throughout mainland Europe, and coins of the ducat standard were struck in several European countries up to the 20th century. It was worth a little more than an escudo.

Gold doubloon (doblôn) This was an early Spanish gold coin, the name originally applying to the gold *'excelente'* of Ferdinand and Isabella. It was later transferred to the two-escudo coin issued by Spain and the Spanish colonies in the Americas. It was the largest Spanish gold coin, weighing slightly less than an ounce of gold, and originates from the Latin word duplus, or double. A doubloon was worth about seven weeks wages to a sailor. The name is now firmly linked to tales of pirates and buccaneers, this being the gold version of the silver 'piece of eight'.

GOLD Its stable value and the ease with which it could be converted into anything the pirate needed made this the most lucrative of all targets. John Ayres wrote in 1684: *'Gold was the bait that tempted a pack of merry boys of us, near three hundred in number, under command by our own election of Captain John Coxon'*, when they raided Panama and the Pacific coast. Until the Spanish exploited the huge Potosi silver mines in Peru, silver was more valuable than gold, but from this period on, gold was what men sought.

GOLD ROAD The track across the Isthmus of Panama used to transport Spanish gold by trains of pack mules.

NUESTRA SEÑORA DE ATOCHE This Spanish treasure ship was wrecked in 1622, but rediscovered in 1985, with its cargo worth nearly $400 million consisting of gold, silver and other artefacts, some of which are now on display at a museum in Key West, Florida.

NUESTRA SEÑORA DE LAS MERCEDES She was sunk by the British off Portugal in 1804, and Spain is claiming her gold. Spain believes that a claim made by Odyssey, the deep sea exploration company, to have found a galleon loaded with 500,000 gold and silver coins, refers to this ship. However, some of the coins now at Florida were minted in 1803 in Peru, so the Peruvian Government could also stake a claim on the treasure (see Odyssey, page 266).

OAK ISLAND MONEY PIT The most intriguing of all the sites associated with buried pirate treasure, and linked to Captain Henry Morgan and Captain Kidd, it was first discovered in 1795. Just a few years later, digging through layers of logs and clay, a stone tablet was found. It bore an inscription which was decoded to read: *'Forty Feet Below Two Million Pounds Are Buried'*. Over the years, booby traps and an artificial beach have been discovered, along with an extremely complicated drainage system. Four men died in 1965 excavating the site. There is no space here to describe this remarkable site in detail, but several books have been written on the subject, and the most accessible information is to be found on the *'Swashbuckler's Cove'* website, *'The Money Pit of Oak Island'*.

Odyessey Marine Exploration – The Treasure Hunter

Run by the American entrepreneur Greg Stemm, in 2003 Odyessey discovered the American Civil War era SS *Republic*, 100 miles (160 km) off Savannah, Georgia. It has recovered 14,000 objects and 51,000 gold and silver coins, making more than £29 million in fees and sales in the process. In 2002 Odyessey signed a deal with the British Government to dive on the 80-gun HMS *Sussex*, lost in 1664 off Gibraltar. In 2008 *Odyessey Explorer* found HMS *Victory* in a secret location off Alderney in the Channel Islands. The precursor to Nelson's *Victory*, she was lost in a storm in 1764. It comprises the largest collection of bronze Royal Naval guns ever found; 41 of her 110 guns have been discovered, worth £35,000 each. There may be four tons of Portuguese gold and silver worth £700 million also to be recovered. Odyessey has found 267 wrecks in the English Channel, but the interference of trawlers and dredgers are utterly destroying their value as salvage sites by constantly tearing up the sea bed. *Odyessey Explorer* was seized by the Spanish Government as it believes that a 17-ton £253 million hoard of coins from another ship is from the *Nuestra Señora de las Mercedes* (q.v.). Odyessey responsibly shares the proceeds of its activities with governments, makes a proper, recorded archeological excavation and tries to keep locations secret. It believes that all the inshore wrecks off Italy have been stripped by the Mafia.

OIL – MODERN TREASURE

Millions of years ago, trillions of microscopic plants (phytoplankton) and animals (zooplankton) lived in the seas. When they died, their skeletal remains settled to the sea floor, mixed with mud and silt, and eventually they formed organic-rich sedimentary layers. Other sediments continued to be deposited over time and buried the organic-rich sediment layer to depths of thousands of feet, compressing the layers into a rock that became the source of oil. Over the years, as the depth of the burial increased, pressure on the rock layers increased, along with the temperature. Under these conditions, the remains of phytoplankton and zooplankton broke down into simpler substances called hydrocarbons, compounds of hydrogen and carbon.

This process still continues, although it will be millions of years before it is completed. Extracted hydrocarbons in a liquid form are termed petroleum ('rock oil') and in gaseous form are referred to as natural gas. Crude oil is used to make plastics, waxes and solvents, as well as for transport and creating other types of energy. Nearly a third of the world's oil comes from offshore fields, such as in the Arabian Gulf, the North Sea and the Gulf of Mexico. However, refined oil is also responsible for polluting the ocean. Over the past decade, an average of 600,000 barrels of oil a year has been recorded as being accidentally spilled from ships, the equivalent of 12 times the size of the spillage caused by the sinking of the oil tanker *Prestige* in 2002. A large multiple of this figure also reaches the oceans each year, as a result of leaking automobiles and unrecorded discharges. The Global Marine Oil Pollution Information Gateway website states that accidental spillages only account for around 10-15 per cent of marine oil pollution.

PLATE From the Spanish *plata*, this was silver, usually in the form of bars but sometimes in coins. In maritime law it later came to mean jewels and treasure as well as plate.

PLATE FLEET From the 16th century onwards one royal convoy, the *flota*, left Seville every year, stopping at the Canary and Leeward Islands for water and provisions, then sailing across the Caribbean to Veracruz in Mexico. Later in the year, another flota of *'galeones'* left Cadiz for Cartagena, then on to Portobelo in Panama to meet the merchants who brought treasure across the Isthmus from Peru. The plate fleets carried expensive European manufactured goods, and each fleet usually consisted of over a dozen large galleons and smaller ships, accompanied by two men-of-war, the *Capitana* and *Almirante*. The plate fleets returned to Spain with silver, gold, jewels logwood, indigo, hides and cacao.

ULUBURON SHIPWRECK

Probably the greatest maritime Bronze Age discovery, found off the Turkish coast in 1982. She was mainly carrying copper and tin ingots. So far 18,000 Bronze Age artefacts from the late 14th century BCE have been discovered.

WHYDAH Launched in London in 1715, this 100-feet (30-m) three-masted ship was built as a slave ship for the Triangular Trade. With cloth, alcohol, money, hand tools and weapons, 700 slaves were purchased in Ouidah (Whydah) in west Africa, transported to the Caribbean and exchanged for gold, silver, indigo, dye-woods and cinchona, the source of quinine. However, in February 1717 this profitable trade ended as she was captured by Black Sam Bellamy. The treasure-laden *Whydah* was then wrecked in a northeast gale at Wellfleet, Massachusetts. The ship's bell was recovered in 1985, and altogether over 100,000 artefacts including 2000 coins have been raised from her.

The Greatest Pirate Trial of All-time

This began on 28 March 1722 with a Vice-Admiralty Court led by Captain Mungo Herdman presenting the case against the survivors of Black Bart Roberts' crews. The court at Cape Coast Castle, at Cabo Corso, Ghana was filled with 69 prisoners taken from the *Great Ranger*, commanded by Captain James Skyrme, who was barely alive. Then the prisoners from the *Royal Fortune* came into court, of whom 87 were charged with piracy. A total of 91 pirates were found guilty and 74 acquitted. Captain Skyrme and most members of Roberts' *'House of Lords'* were found *'Guilty in the Highest Degree'*, and the President of the Court, Captain Herdman pronounced: *'Ye and each of you are adjudged and sentenced to be carried back to the place from whence you came, from thence to the place of execution without the gates of this castle, and there within the flood marks to be hanged by the neck till you are dead, dead, dead. And the Lord have mercy on your souls … After this ye and each of you shall be taken down, and your bodies hung in chains.'* Herdman sentenced 52 of Bart Roberts' crew to death, another 20 men to an effective death sentence in the Cape Coast mines, and sent another 17 to be imprisoned in London's Marshalsea Prison. Of these 17, 13 died during the passage to London. The four survivors were eventually pardoned while in Newgate Prison. Two 'guilty' sentences

were 'respited'. Of the 52 pirates hanged at Cape Coast, nearly half were Welsh or West Countrymen, and most of the others were indentured servants or poor white colonists. Fifteen pirates had died of their wounds on the passage to Cape Corso Castle, and four in its dungeons. Ten had been killed in the *Ranger*, and three in the *Royal Fortune*. In all, 118 of Roberts' crews died. The 80 blacks on board the pirate ships were returned to a life of slavery.

Surgeon Atkins's account of the hangings is repeated in Defoe's *History of the Pyrates*. The first six to hang were the hardened *'Lords'* Sutton, Simpson, Ashplant, Moody, Magness and Hardy. Atkins offered his services as a priest, but even Sutton, who had been suffering dysentery for days, ignored him. Christopher Moody had been a pirate captain before joining Roberts, notable for his flag being gold on red rather than white on black. They called out for drinking water, and complained that *'We are poor rogues, and so get hanged while others, no less guilty in another way, escaped.'* Loosened from their shackles, they walked carelessly to the gallows. *'Little David'* Simpson spotted poor Elizabeth Trengrove in the huge crowd, who he had ravished when the *Onslow* was taken in August 1721. He shouted *'I have lain with that bitch three times, and now she has come to see* me hanged.' The executioners did not know how to hang men, and tied their hands in front of the 'Lords'. 'Lord' Hardy stated calmly *'I have seen many a man hanged, but this way of having our hands tied behind us I am a stranger to, and I never saw it before in my life.'* Later hangings saw many of the men admit their sins, especially surgeon Scudamore, the only ship's doctor known to have willingly joined any pirate ship. He asked for two days' reprieve to read the scriptures, and was allowed to sing the *31st Psalm* on the gallows before being swung off. Eighteen of the worst offenders were dipped in tar, encased in a frame of iron bands, and hung from gibbets in chains from nearby Lighthouse Hill, Connor's Hill and Catholic Mission Hill, so that they could be seen by passing ships as a warning to pirates. 'Israel Hynde' was thus gibbeted, proving to this author that he was the same Israel Hands who served under Blackbeard. Other pirates were simply left hanging for the birds to eat.

Fate	Numbers of men	Notes
Executed 3 April–20 April	52	Hanged at Cape Coast Castle. The 'worst' 18 were hung in chains
Guilty, and sentenced to **Death**, commuted to seven years' **Servitude** for Royal Africa Company	20	All seem to have died before their seven years were completed
To **Marshalsea** Prison	17	13 died on the voyage, four pardoned when in Newgate Prison
Respited	2	One died, one pardoned
Acquitted	74	Including forced men and musicians
Blacks	52 *Royal Fortune* 28 *Ranger*	All sold into slavery again
Died en route to Cape Corso	15	
Died in Cape Coast Castle	4	
Killed on *Ranger*	10	
Killed on *Royal Fortune*	3	
TOTAL Crew Members	267	

CHAPTER 7

Islands, Ports, Harbours *and* Capes

ISLANDS

ANTILLES The larger Antilles islands in the Caribbean – Cuba, Hispaniola, Puerto Rico and Jamaica – were those first taken by the Spanish, before 1500. From there, they moved on to Mexico and the rest of South America. This left the chain of *'Lesser Antilles'*, that is the Leeward and Windward Isles, open to other European powers to colonize. The Dutch were trading in the West Indies from 1542, and had a toehold in mainland Guyana by 1580. Between 1609 and 1619, various French English and Dutch missions moved onto islands between the mouth of the Orinoco River and that of the Amazon. The English settled in St Kitts from 1623, and Barbados in 1624–5. In 1628, St Kitts settlers moved on to Nevis and Barbuda, then in 1632 to Antigua and Montserrat. In 1625 the Dutch and English jointly took possession of Santa Cruz. The French took Guadeloupe, Martinique and other Windward Islands from 1635 onwards. Between 1632 and 1634 the Dutch established trading stations on St Eustatius, Tobago and Curaçao. There was constant conflict between these European outposts and the Spanish, and then between each other.

BARDSEY ISLAND, AVALON AND THE WORLD'S RAREST APPLE This small island off the Llŷn Peninsula in Wales is known as *'the isle of 20,000 saints'*. In 1820 a tradition was initiated that the eldest resident male should be declared *King of Bardsey Island*. The first 'King', John Williams, was crowned by Lady Newborough. The tradition ceased in 1922 on the death of *'King Love Pritchard'*. His Bardsey crown was recently re-discovered and can be seen in Bangor Museum. The island measures just two miles by one mile (3.2 by 1.6 km) and has just five residents, including a shepherd and a nun. Its Welsh name, Ynys Enlli, *Isle of the Currents*, reflects the difficulty of reaching it, but its former name was Ynys Afallach *(Isle of Apples)* and it was associated with Merlin. The name Afallach has also caused it to become associated with Avalon. Only in 1998 a lone stunted apple tree on the island, known locally as Merlin's Apple, was discovered to be unique, and a company has now successfully propagated it on the mainland.

BIKINI ATOLL The Pacific site of 27 US nuclear tests between 1946 and 1958, it gave its name to the women's swimsuit, which was said to have been invented in 1946, although the ancient Greeks and Romans wore something similar. Bikini vending machines were set up near beaches in the 1950s but were not a commercial success.

CAY, KEY Small islands, often coral formations, in the West Indies, with sparse vegetation and usually no water. The name derives from the word *'cayos'* (Spanish for rocks). In these hundreds of islets pirates could lie low, carouse or clean (careen) their ships. Sometimes men were marooned on them.

CLIPPERTON – THE FORGOTTEN ISLAND A small coral atoll 600 miles (965 km) southwest of Mexico, it was named after the English privateer John Clipperton. Its other name, Île de la Passion (Passion Island), was given to it in 1711 by a French expedition which annexed it for France. The American Guano Mining Company then claimed the island for the USA under the 1856 Guano Islands Act. In 1858 it was back in French hands, then Mexico took it in 1897. By 1914, about 100 people

were living on the island. Every two months, a ship from Acapulco sailed to Clipperton with provisions. However, in the Mexican Revolution, the supply ship was never sent, and by 1917, all but one of the males on the island had died, some in a failed attempt to sail to the mainland and fetch help. The lighthouse keeper, Victoriano Álvarez, found himself the last man on Clipperton, along with 15 women and children. He proclaimed himself 'king' and began a rampaging reign of rape and murder, before being killed by the widow of the dead garrison commander Captain Arnaud. In 1917, immediately after Álvarez's death, four women and six children, the last survivors, were picked up by the US Navy gunship USS *Yorktown*.

DEAD MAN'S CHEST Edward Teach, *'Blackbeard'*, marooned 15 of his crew that he considered *'mutinous'* upon a tiny island off Tortola in the British Virgin Islands. It is now called *Dead Chest*

Cayman Islands

Grand Cayman and Little Cayman were discovered by Columbus in 1503, and he named them *Las Tortugas*, because they resembled turtles in shape. Francis Drake in 1585 noted that there were *'great serpents, large like lizards, which are edible'*, as well as turtles there. The existence of cayman (types of alligator) on the isles was doubted, until archaeological digs in 1993 and 1996 proved that they had been native there. The islands came under Britain's control when captured from Spain, along with Jamaica, by Cromwell's expeditionary force. They were officially ceded to England in 1670 by the Treaty of Madrid.

Island. The rock was known to sailors as '*The Dead Man's Chest*' as nothing could live there except lizards, snakes and mosquitoes. Each mutineer was handed a cutlass and a bottle of rum, in the hope that they would kill each other. However, a month later when Teach visited, the men were all still alive.

DEVIL'S ISLAND Tristan Jones, in *The Incredible Voyage* casts convincing doubt upon the escape from this island by Henri Charrière *(Papillon)*. It is the smallest of the three Îles de Salut off the coast of French Guiana, and all three served as a French penal colony from 1852 until 1952. Many of the 80,000 prisoners died there. The horrors of the penal settlement had become notorious in 1895 with the publicity surrounding the plight of the Jewish French army captain Alfred Dreyfus who was imprisoned there.

EAST INDIES This region includes the Malay archipelago and parts of southeast Asia. Indonesia was formerly named the Netherlands Indies.

EDWARDS' FAMILY CLAIM ON MANHATTAN ISLAND

Probably the most intriguing court-case in the world is the one involving the heirs of the privateer Robert Edwards, and the ownership of a large chunk of Manhattan real estate. He was given land in what is now the heart of Manhattan, by Queen Anne, for his services in disrupting Spanish shipping. His will gave the area to the Cruger brothers, on a 99-year lease, with the understanding that it would revert back to his heirs after that. Somehow the land has ended up in the hands of Trinity Church, one of New York's biggest landowners. The land is valued at $900 billion, and includes '*ground-zero*' (the site of the World Trade Center), Broadway and Wall Street. Legal proceedings have meandered on for over 75 years. There are various websites devoted to this affair – the greatest pirate treasure being in real estate.

ELBA This is 12 miles (19 km) from Italy, the largest island of the Tuscan Archipelago. After the Treaty of Fontainebleu, Napoleon was exiled to Elba in 1814. He was allowed to keep a personal guard of 600 men, but the island was guarded by British naval patrols. Napoleon stayed on Elba for 300 days before he escaped and returned to France in 1815 for the '*Hundred Days*'. After Waterloo he was exiled again, this time to the barren and isolated St Helena in the South Atlantic.

FLORIDA KEYS In the 16th century this meant any portion of the coast of North America, north and east of Mexico. The term was only limited to its current location in the 19th century. To the Spanish, *Banco Florida* was the Florida Keys and coast.

GALÁPAGOS ISLANDS

The Galápagos Islands are volcanic Pacific islands distributed around the equator, 600 miles (970 km) west of Ecuador. There is a vast number of endemic species, and the studies of the flora and fauna found here by Charles Darwin during the voyage of the *Beagle* led to his theory of evolution by natural selection. However introductions of foreign flora and fauna are sadly destroying this amazing habitat, as is the influence of too much tourism.

GORGONA ISLAND Thirty miles (48 km) off the Pacific coast of Colombia, this was the starting point from which Francisco Pizarro and 13 men set out to discover and conquer the Incas of Peru in the 16th century. In the 1970s it was a terrible penal colony, beyond the knowledge of the civilized world. Its political prisoners had no visitors or any chance of freedom. Even now its history is not widely known.

GREENLAND – THE WORLD'S NEXT SUPERPOWER This is the world's largest island (excluding the continent of Australia), about 836,000 square miles (2.17 million km²) in area, with just 57,000 inhabitants. It acquired home rule from Denmark in 1979, and in 1985 left the European Community (as it was then) in a dispute over fish, the only nation so far to have walked out of this bureaucratic non-democracy. It is the 14th largest country in the world and the 24th richest in terms of natural resources. As the ice melts and the waters recede, scientists believe they will uncover massive deposits of gold, platinum, diamonds, lead, zinc, gas and coal. The US Geological Survey believes that Greenland has the greatest unused oil reserves on earth, in the east of the country where its ice is melting fastest. The island's economy is still dependent upon Danish subsidies of £315 million a year and almost everything must be imported at present. Eighty-eight per cent of the population are Inuit or of mixed Danish-Inuit ancestry and its hunters still kill polar bears, walruses, and seals. Despite present widespread poverty, its mineral resources will probably mean an influx of wealth, and eventually full independence from Denmark. The RSPB (Royal Society for the Protection of Birds) has called upon Greenland to stop slaughtering seabirds, as at least 10,000 of the 56,000 Greenlanders hunt birds (as well as whales, polar bears and seals) for sport. Migratory birds and breeding colonies are being slaughtered. An entire colony of 150,000 Brünnich's guillemots have been exterminated from the island, and eider ducks have declined by 80 per cent in 40 years.

HISPANIOLA Columbus called the island that today is shared by Haiti and the Dominican Republic *'Isla Española'* (Little Spain Island) in 1492, and Hispaniola is the Anglicized version of this designation. Under Oliver Cromwell's grandiose *'Western Design'*, he discussed a possible alliance with Spain while sending out a force to seize Hispaniola from them. The 1654–5 expedition was a shambles, and rather than return home to his wrath, the leaders decided to take Jamaica instead, at the heart of the Spanish Caribbean possessions. The name Saint Dominic was afterwards applied to Hispaniola by the French, who were anxious to rid the island of Spanish connections as they vied with Spain for its possession.

ICELAND This is the largest island entirely formed by volcanic eruptions. It is almost 40,000 square miles (103,600 km²) in area, sitting on the mid-Atlantic ridge, and is actually ocean floor exposed above the ocean surface.

KRAKATOA In 1883, a volcanic eruption reduced the size of this island by 50 per cent, with tsunami waves up to 115 feet (35 m) high smashing into Java and Sumatra, killing around 40,000 people. The waves were so powerful that they circled the world twice, and the huge quantities of ash thrown into the air blocked sunlight, lowering temperatures worldwide for a year.

LEEWARD ISLANDS These are a group of 15 islands and many more islets in the West Indies which are sheltered from trade winds by the Westward Isles. They include Anguilla, Antigua, Barbuda, Guadeloupe, St Christopher, St Eustatius,

Largest Islands

Australia (2,941,513 sq miles/ 7,617,930 km²) is widely considered part of a continental landmass, not officially an island. But without doubt it is the largest island, and when combined with Oceania, the smallest continent on Earth.

Greenland (836,000 sq miles/2,166,000 km²)
New Guinea (303,381 sq miles /785,753 km²) – Indonesia and Papua
  New Guinea
Borneo (288,869 sq miles/748,168 km²) – Indonesia, Brunei, Malaysia
Madagascar (226,917 sq miles/587,713 km²)
Baffin Island (195,928 sq miles/507,451 km²) – Canada
Sumatra (171,069 sq miles/443,066 km²) – Indonesia
Honshu (87,182 sq miles/225,800 km²) – Japan
Victoria Island (83,897 sq miles/217,291 km²) – Canada
Great Britain (80,823 sq miles/209,331 km²)
Ellesmere Island (75,767 sq miles/196,236 km²) – Canada
Sulawesi (69,761 sq miles/180,681 km²) – Indonesia (formerly the Celebes)
South Island (56,308 sq miles/145,836 km²) – New Zealand
Java (53,589 sq miles/138,794 km²) – Indonesia
North Island (43,082 sq miles/114,000 km²) – New Zealand
Newfoundland (42,031 sq miles/108,860 km²) – Canada

The next largest islands are: Cuba, Luzon (Philippines), Iceland, Mindanao, Ireland, Hokkaido (Japan), Hispaniola (Haiti and Dominican Republic), Sakhalin (Russia), Banks Island (Canada), Sri Lanka and Devon Island (Canada – the largest uninhabited island in the world).

St Martin, Montserrat, Nevis, Saba, the British Virgin Islands and the US Virgin Islands.

LUNDY Lundy Island, where the Bristol Channel meets the Atlantic, is a wonderfully evocative place, with a maritime reserve, a population of grey seals and a castle. A former owner declared independence from Britain, issuing his own stamps, and a coinage called *'puffins'*. The island is also home to one of the world's rarest plants, the 'Lundy cabbage' *(Coincya wrightii)*, which has beautiful yellow flowers but a repellent smell and taste. It is one of the very few plants endemic to Britain and is only found on one cliff face, but it was being slowly driven out by non-endemic rhododendrons. After 60 years of

Nantucket – the Whaling Capital of the World

This island means 'faraway land' in the language of the native Wampanoag Indians. English settlers landed here from 1659, farming the island, and they began a system of debt servitude to ensure that they had a ready supply of virtual slave labour. The island became over-farmed, and in around 1690 the islanders decided that they needed income from the sea. Hundreds of Right whales congregated in the sea off Nantucket every autumn to spring, so the islanders engaged a Cape Codder named Ichabod Paddock to come over from the mainland to teach them to hunt whales. They used Wampanoag labour, as there were more Indians than white settlers. In 1712, the Nantucket whaler Captain Hussey was blown out to sea and he spotted several strange whales. He managed to kill a sperm whale. The oil from its blubber was better than that from a right whale, giving a cleaner and brighter light. The oil from its huge block-shaped head was even better, and it was given the name spermaceti because of its resemblance to human sperm. Nantucketers now devoted themselves to pursuing this much richer prize, travelling further and further out to sea, and becoming so famous that Emerson referred to their island as *'the nation of Nantucket'*. It became the whaling capital of the world during the 18th and early 19th centuries. The story of *Moby-Dick* was based on the sinking of Nantucket's *Essex* by a sperm whale in 1820.

struggling against them, it appears that the rhododendrons are being at last exterminated, ensuring the survival of the cabbage – it will be the first eradication of an alien plant on such a scale in Europe. Specific genes from the cabbage can be used to help create new varieties. The pest known as the Lundy cabbage weevil *(Ceutorhynchus contractus* var. *pallipes)* is only found on Lundy and in a small part of northwest Spain. It lives alongside the bronze Lundy cabbage flea beetle *(Psylliodes luridipennis Kutschera)*, a species found only on the island. All three species now apparently have a secure future on the island.

NORFOLK ISLAND A small island 1000 miles (1600 km) northeast of Sydney, Australia. It is where 194 of the descendants of the crewmen involved in the *Mutiny on the Bounty* moved in 1856, from Pitcairn Island.

REMOTEST INHABITED ISLAND Tristan da Cunha in the South Atlantic was discovered by the Portuguese in 1506, and is just 38 square miles (98 km²) in area. The nearest inhabited island to it is St Helena, over 1500 miles (2420 km) away.

ROANOKE ISLAND This was the first English settlement in North America, off the coast of what is now North Carolina. It was used by the English and the early settlers as a base from which to attack Spanish shipping, but the settlers mysteriously disappeared in 1590.

ST HELENA, THE EMPEROR AND THE ZULU KING This remote island in the South Atlantic claims to be Britain's second oldest colony, and was for several centuries of vital strategic importance to ships sailing to Europe from Asia and South Africa. The British used the island as a place of exile and incarceration, notably for Napoleon Bonaparte, Dinuzulu kaCetshwayo and for over 5000 Boer prisoners-of-war. Napoleon was exiled here after the Battle of Waterloo in October 1815. He was married to Marie Louise, Archduchess of Austria, in 1810, but she did not join him in his exile. In the early years of exile Napoleon received many visitors, to the anger of the French minister Richelieu. From 1818, however, as the restrictions placed on him grew tighter, he lived the life of a recluse. Napoleon enjoyed the support of Admiral Lord Cochrane, who was closely involved in the struggles of Chile and Brazil for independence. Cochrane's aim was to make Napoleon Emperor of a unified South American state, but Napoleon died from stomach cancer before Cochrane could try to put it into effect. Dinizulu, son of Cetshwayo, was King of the Zulu nation from 1884–1913. In 1890 he was sentenced to ten years imprisonment on St Helena as punishment for leading a Zulu army against the British, and he served eight years in confinement there.

SALT TORTUGAS Name for the Isla la Tortuga which lies off Venezuela.

SAN JUAN DE ULUA An island off the Mexican coast, and the port for Vera Cruz, one of the three treasure ports of the Spanish *flota*. Silver from Mexico was shipped from here, as well as the contents of the Manila galleons which had sailed from the Philippines to the Pacific coast, so that their treasure could be transported across Mexico for shipping to Spain.

SINKING ISLANDS A group of 40 small islands, many in the Pacific and under imminent threat of disappearing beneath the waves because of rising sea levels, has formed *The Alliance of Small Island States*. Its chairman, from Tuvalu, said in 2003 that his country and its 12,000 people would be the first to go under. The main island, its highest point is only 15 feet (4.6 m) above sea level, had been inundated three times that year. Vegetable plots had been washed away and there was no drinking water. Some families had moved to New Zealand, but older people wanted to stay. The Tuvaluans have brokered a deal with New Zealand to resettle the island's entire population. The chairman said that neighbouring Kiribati and the Marshall Islands, with 80,000 people each, were also close to sinking. *'There is no urgency among the big nations,'* he said. *'We sometimes get the feeling they are going to let us die... To survive the dry periods we now need desalination plants run by solar energy, but we have no money for that, we need help from countries that created the emissions and got us into this mess.'*

VIRGIN ISLANDS In the year 238 CE, the legend is that St Ursula took 11,000 British virgins from Britain and France to Rome to protest against oppression in Britain. On their way home, they were all massacred in a village along the Rhine. It was for these virgins that Columbus named the islands in the Caribbean. There is an anecdote that he gave them this name as they reminded him of a *'fat virgin lying on her back'.*

WINDWARD ISLES They stretch from the eastern Caribbean to South America, protecting the Leeward Islands from the northeast trade winds, and include Dominica, Martinique, Saint Lucia, Grenada and Saint Vincent.

Zanzibar and Rock Music

The birthplace of Farokh (or Farookh) Bulsara, aka Freddy Mercury of the rock group Queen, Zanzibar lies off Tanzania and was the major slave centre on the east African coast. It was renowned as a 'spice island' and is still the world leader in clove production, also exporting pepper, cinnamon and nutmeg. The Zanzibar Leopard *(Panthera pardus adersi)* is a subspecies of leopard endemic to Unguja Island in the Zanzibar archipelago. It was still being hunted in the 1990s and is now almost certainly extinct.

PORTS, HARBOURS, BAYS AND CAPES

THE PORT OF BARRY The then national newspaper *Reynold's News* in 1943, ran a headline *'Port That Craves Adventure'*, and stated *'Barry Dock, Wales' famous coal seaport, has lost more merchant seamen in the war than any other seaport of comparable size in Britain. When the war record of the Merchant Navy comes to be written, the seamen of Barry will feature prominently in it. There are few streets in the town and dock area which have not lost men at sea as a result of enemy action. Scores of Barry seamen have figured in dramatic front page stories of the seas since the war began. Several have spent 30, 40 and more days in open boats after the sinking of their vessels by enemy planes or submarines; a number, since rescued by the Eighth Army, have experienced the hardships of Italian prison camps; many have dodged Jap planes and submarines after the fall of Hong Kong, Singapore, etc. Many died in eastern waters not to mention Jap hands. Today it is safe to say that there are Barry seamen in every United Nations' convoy sailing the seas of the world. Heavy losses of life and incredible hardships suffered by Barry men have not dismayed the youth of the port. They are still entering the MN as soon as they are old enough and can be absorbed by the service.'* (reported in *The Barry and District News* 2 July

1943). The Barry DEMS (Defensively Equipped Merchant Ship) gunners lost are not included in the 360 merchant seamen lost in the war, but if we use the total British casualties of 22,490, then 1 in 62 deaths were of Barry men, at a time when Barry accounted for only 1 in 1250 of the UK population. Again, if we reckon that a fifth of the then population of Barry was capable of serving in the war, omitting restricted occupations, females, the elderly, young and infirm, then 1 in 20 Barry men died in the merchant navy (plus of course there were other deaths in the army, DEMS, navy and air force). When this author was growing up in Barry, it was commonly said that every street in the town had lost someone at sea. Ernest and Elsie Stiff of Cadoxton lost three sons at sea. In 1941 they lost 16-year-old Charles, a mess room boy on the *Rose Schiaffino*. In March 1942 they lost his 21-year-old brother Joseph, a cook on the *Baron Newlands*. In October 1942 they lost their third son, the 19-year-old William, on the *Magdalena*.

BAY OF FUNDY Between New Brunswick and Nova Scotia, the upper part of the bay experiences the greatest difference between high and low tides in the world, around 50 feet (15.2 m).

The Bristol Channel between England and Wales has a tidal difference of up to 47 feet (14.3 m), accounting for the celebrated skills of West Country and Welsh seamen in past centuries.

BIGHT OF BENIN It was said that the Royal Africa Company had three governors for each of its Guinea Coast slave trading forts. There was one who had just died, one in the post, and one on his way to replace him:
'Beware and take care of the Bight o' Benin
For one that comes out there were forty
went in.'

BRISTOL Bristol ships carried more than 2,400,000 slaves from Africa to the Americas, and the city grew wealthy as a consequence of this trade. In 1701–2 it was the second major port in Britain after London. At this time there were 3281 English ships using the eight principal English ports, with a combined total of *c.*260,000 tons. London had 560 ships with over 10,000 men. The next busiest in order of shipping were Bristol, Yarmouth, Exeter, Hull, Whitby, Liverpool and Scarborough.

CAPE (CABO) FINISTERRE
This Spanish cape shares the origin of its name (the Latin *'finis terrae'*) with Finistère in northwest Brittany and Land's End, the western tip of Cornwall.

CAPE OF GOOD HOPE The southern peninsula of Africa, discovered by Bartholomew Dias in 1487, who named it *Stormy Cape* (Cabo Tormatoso). King John II of Portugal renamed it *Cape of Good Hope* (Cabo de Buena Esperanza) to encourage sailors to find a sea route from Europe to India. Vasco da Gama achieved this aim in 1498.

CAPE HORN *The Horn* was discovered by Francis Drake in 1578, but the Dutch navigator Willem Schouten named it in 1616 after his birthplace of Hoorn. It is renowned for storms and the difficulty of rounding it, especially when sailing east to west. It was known as *Cape Stiff* to square-rigger sailors because of the stiff winds. *Cape Horners* were the square-rigged traders used to double the Cape, and the epithet was also applied to the crewmen of these vessels.

ROUNDING CAPE HORN
This 1000-mile (1600-km) voyage in a steam ship took 1500 miles (2414 km) under sail, especially when the vessel was tacking into winds when sailing east to west. Generally for windjammers the west to east voyage took a week, and east to west between two and three weeks. However, the French square-rigger *Cambronne* took 92 days to achieve the rounding. One of the best-documented difficult voyages was that of the *Edward Sewall* in spring 1914. She took 67 days, being twice blasted back to a position she had passed weeks earlier, and covered over 5000 miles (8000 km) to complete the 1500-mile voyage.

CARTHAGE A centre of maritime trading in the Mediterranean. Its situation on the north coast of Africa brought it into continuing conflict with the Romans in the 3rd and 2nd centuries BCE, resulting in the Punic Wars fought between 264 and 146 BCE and eventual Roman mastery of the Mediterranean.

CINQUE PORTS The 'five ports' of Hastings, Sandwich, Dover, Romney and Hythe, on the south coast of England, were identified by their Norman-French-speaking monarch Henry III as ideal bases for the defence of the realm. Their charter dates from 1155. The person in charge of their co-ordination was given the title of *'Warden of the Cinque Ports'*, and the Duke of Wellington and Winston Churchill have both held the title. Rye and Winchelsea were later added, the group of ports then being called *'the Cinque Ports and Two Ancient Towns'*. Seven *'limbs'* were then added – Lydd, Folkestone, Faversham, Margate, Deal, Ramsgate and Tenterden. Another 23 places were over time connected to the confederation, eventually making 42 towns and villages in total.

CODFISH CAPITAL OF THE WORLD Gloucester, Massachusetts, is just 120 miles (193 km) from George's Bank, a shallow sandbar covering almost 1000 square miles (2590 km²) and formerly teeming with fish. The loss of a swordfish boat from Gloucester, the *Andrea Gail*, was the subject of the famous book and film, *The Perfect Storm*.

CORAL CITY For around 3000 years, the chief port of eastern Sudan was on the coraline islet of Suakin, which is now connected to the mainland by a causeway. Its traders were protected from attacks by nomadic raiders by a wall built of coral, and all its buildings were also made of coral. When Suakin was replaced by Port Sudan around 1900 it began to fall into

disrepair, as its rich merchants left the walled city. Coral dwellings need constant care and without income from tourism or World Heritage status, this unique city will soon disappear.

FOO CHOO FOO One of the great tea and trading ports of China in the days of clipper ships, along with Canton, Shanghai, Amoy and Ningpo. In 1896, five ships took part in a great tea race from Foo Choo Foo to London. The *Ariel*, *Taeping* and *Serica* sailed at the same time. By nightfall they had lost sight of each other. Off Land's End, the *Ariel* and *Taeping* fell in with each other for the first time after sailing half-way around the world. Both were crowding on extra canvas for a dramatic race up the English Channel when the *Serica* was spotted. All three ships berthed in London on the same tide.

HARWICH The port's Maritime Museum has a treadwheel crane, which was used at the Naval Yard from 1667 to 1927. It was worked by two men walking inside the wheels, much like the spit in the kitchens of great houses was turned by a dog walking in a treadmill. The house of Captain Christopher Jones of the *Mayflower* can still be seen, as can the Redoubt, a large circular fort built in 1808 to protect the harbour against Napoleonic invasion. For centuries, Harwich was the only safe harbour on the east coast of England between the Humber and the Thames in bad weather, so it was important strategically.

JAMESTOWN The first English settlement in America, along with Roanoke, dating from 1607. It lay on the banks of the James River in Virginia.

LIVERPOOL This port grew through trade with Ireland in the medieval period, displacing Chester in importance. Then, like its great rival Bristol, in the 17th and 18th centuries Liverpool grew rich as a result of trade with North America and the Caribbean, especially the slave trade.

LIVORNO (LEGHORN) This pirate haven near Pisa in Italy was used by the Medicis to sponsor piracy and became a *'free port'* open to any nation and religion in 1590. Muslim slaves were sold here by Christian pirates, and Livornese bankers arranged ransoms for Christian captives of the Barbary Corsairs.

MILFORD HAVEN Esteemed by Nelson, this west Wales town used to have the largest deepwater port on the Atlantic, and is one of the largest natural harbours in Europe.

NEWLYN Cornish ports specialized in catching pilchard, with one harbour recording 24 million being landed in the course of 1907. Huge nets surrounded shoals of the fish which were then winched inshore. Newlyn Pilchard Works was the sole survivor of dozens of pilchard processing factories, where one could see the fish being traditionally preserved in salt. It closed in 2009.

POMPEY This is slang for Portsmouth, and there are three theories for the nickname. The 80-gun French warship *Le Pompée* was captured in 1793. She later fought with distinction in the battle of Algeciras in 1801 and then became guard ship of Portsmouth Harbour. Others say it was from a drunken sailor's interruption of a talk by Agnes Weston, the naval temperance worker. He surfaced from a beery sleep during her lecture on

the Roman Empire to hear that the general Pompey had been killed. *'Poor old Pompey'* he is said to have shouted. The most likely reason is that in 1781 some Portsmouth-based English sailors scaled Pompey's Pillar near Alexandria, 98 feet (30 m) up in the air and toasted their ascent in punch. Their feat earned them the Fleet's tribute as *'The Pompey Boys'*.

POOLE, DORSET Because of complicated currents caused by the Solent and the Isle of Wight, Poole experiences 14 hours of high water a day, making it a popular harbour. It is one of the largest natural harbours in the world, with a 100-mile (161-km) shoreline

PORTS – BUSIEST BY VOLUME This is difficult to categorize, but in 2007 one source claimed that the busiest was Singapore, followed by Rotterdam, South Louisiana, Shanghai, Hong Kong, Houston, Chiba (Japan), Nagoya (Japan), Ulsan (South Korea) and Kwangyang (South Korea). In 2005 the list was Shanghai, Singapore, Rotterdam, Ningbo, Tianjin, Guangzhou, Hong Kong, Busan, South Louisiana and Houston.

PORT ARTHUR (LUSHUN) For centuries it was Russia's only ice-free port in the Pacific, and was ceded to Japan after the Russo-Japanese War of 1904–5. The war started with a surprise attack by the Imperial Japanese Navy on the Russian fleet at Port Arthur, but the battle was indecisive. It is now part of China.

PORTHMADOG Over 100 small ports around the coast of Britain built ocean-going ships. Just one example is Porthmadog, a harbour opened in 1824. It built wooden schooners to export North Wales slate. Much of the slate was taken to Germany for roofing. The 81-feet (25-m) topsail schooner *Cadwalader Jones* was constructed of oak and crossed the Atlantic 42 times. Up to 1913 at least 263 ships had been built here but sadly not one survives today.

RED SAILS IN THE SUNSET

The distinctive red sails of Brixham sailing trawlers were said to have inspired this song, written aboard a Brixham trawler called the *Torbay Lass*. However, others say that the 1935 song was written about Portstewart, a port in Northern Ireland.

SCAPA FLOW This British naval base, a sea basin near the Orkneys, was where the German fleet was taken at the end of the First World War. In 1919, in protest at the terms of the Treaty of Versailles, Admiral von Ruyter ordered all 74 warships to be scuttled. The first major

naval loss of the Second World War was when the submarine U-47 sank HMS *Royal Oak* in Scapa Flow, with the loss of 833 men.

SHELL OIL AND HARTLEPOOL

The Samuel family imported shells for decorative purposes, and Marcus Samuel set up a joint venture with shipowner and broker Fred Lane to sell Russian oil in the Far East. Oil tankers were not allowed to use the Suez Canal, so they specified tankers to be built which were acceptable to the Suez Canal Company. The first three ships, all built in West Hartlepool, were the *Murex*, *Conch* and *Clam*. The *Murex* passed through the Suez Canal in 1892, disrupting the virtual monopoly that Standard Oil had enjoyed there. Standard Oil was inevitably referred to as S.O. and the name became Esso.

Shipyards

There is very little shipbuilding carried out in Britain now, but memories of the great shipyards still remain. On the east coast, there was Goole Shipbuilding in Goole and Brooke Marine in Lowestoft. London had Blackwall Engineering and the south coast was represented by Vosper-Thornycroft in Portsmouth and Vosper Shiprepairers in Southampton. In the southwest there were Falmouth Shiprepairers and Appledore Shipbuilders, and in Northern Ireland Harland and Wolff. Cammell-Laird in Birkenhead and Vickers in Barrow were in the northwest. In the

northeast there were Swan-Hunter, Clelands, Clark Hawthorn and Tyne Shiprepair in Newcastle; Austin and Pickersgill, Sunderland Shipbuilders and Doxford Engines in Sunderland; and Smith's Dock in Middlesbrough.

SOUTHAMPTON This great port owes its existence to the fact that the Union Castle, Royal Mail and Cunard shipping lines adopted it as a passenger terminal. The zenith of the time for cruise liners was 1910–60, but most of the trade now consists of container liners for nearby Fawley.

TIGER BAY Such was Cardiff's explosive growth from coal exports that by 1880 it had been transformed from a small town into one of the world's greatest ports, handling more coal than any other port in the world. At the turn of the century, Cardiff's docks were dealing with more traffic than New York. Coal exports reached their zenith in 1913, with over 10,500,000 tons leaving Cardiff Docks. In its Coal Exchange building, the world's first £1 million pound deal was signed. (The nearby ports of Barry and Penarth shipped 11 million and over 4 million tons respectively in 1913, and Newport, Swansea and Port Talbot were also shipping millions of tons of coal). After the First World War, a boom in Cardiff shipping saw 122 shipping companies in existence by 1920, although the growing importance of oil for ship propulsion and cheap German coal then saw demand crash. In the wake of its prosperity, a dockside area developed around Bute Street and James Street. This quickly developed a terrible reputation for its pubs, gambling dens, dance halls, crimping lodging houses and brothels. This area was known as *'Tiger Bay'* and is said to have been named after the fast swirling waters in the Bristol Channel which reminded sailors of 'raging tigers'. In 1908 it was called *'the dumping ground of Europe'*, and over 40

different ethnic groups had settled there. Now the area has been sanitized with expensive apartments around the redeveloped Cardiff Bay area.

VENICE Venice was once a world power. Legend has it that it was founded on 25 March 421 by Romans fleeing barbarian invasions. The industry which established its prosperity was salt-making from sea water, and for hundreds of years Venice had a monopoly on salt making in southern Europe. By the 13th century, Venice had built up a great navy which wiped out pirates and conquered many Adriatic islands and coastal areas. During the Crusades, Venetian ships were used to carry passengers to the Holy Land, and at the time of the Fourth Crusade (1202–4), the Venetians diverted the crusade to take over Constantinople (Istanbul), the capital of the Byzantine Empire. The four famous bronze horses found at Venice's St Mark's Cathedral were looted from there. By the end of the 14th century, the population had grown to over 200,000, making Venice the most populous city of the Middle Ages. Genoa emerged as a rival sea power on the opposite side of northern Italy, and their rivalry led to a series of wars. After a major victory over Genoa in 1380, Venice took control of the trade routes across the Mediterranean,

and soon the Venetian navy was 3000 ships strong. Venice's position as a world power lessened when the Americas were opened up to exploration and trade, as its sea lanes became relatively less valuable. In 1797, Napoleon Bonaparte of France conquered Venice and put an end to its empire. Venice is built on 118 small islands connected by more than 400 bridges. Its wonderful buildings rest on wooden posts driven into the muddy waters of the Adriatic, but motorboats churn the water, damaging the wooden foundations. The city's 130,000 pigeons deposit tons of acidic droppings that eat away at the stonework of the historic buildings. Its greatest threat is flooding, caused by the city sinking and the sea rising. In the past 50 years, more of Venice has been overtaken by the sea than in all its previous history. St Mark's Square is the city's lowest point, and high tides flood it about 90 times a year.

VENICE ARSENALE AND SHIP DESIGN The Arsenale is a huge dockyard, now largely disused, and there has been a dockyard on this site since the 8th century, when Venice was still a client state of the Byzantine Empire. The word Arsenale possibly stems from the Arabic *'Dar-al-sina'* meaning dockyard. From 1320, all of Venice's military ships, and most of its merchant vessels, were built and serviced at the Arsenale. Venetians revolutionized shipbuilding by abandoning the ancient Roman technique of constructing the hull first and then building the rest of the ship around it. Instead they constructed the entire frame of the ship and then moved it along a production line, adding various parts at each stage. By standardizing designs and

employing specialist teams for each process, Arsenale engineers could produce a ship a day by the early 1500s. Arsenale engineers are credited with increasing the velocity of bullets so that firearms could penetrate armour, in the process rendering crossbows obsolete. By the mid-15th century, the Arsenale was also producing lightweight cannon that could be transported on field carriages.

WEYMOUTH – WHERE SEA BATHING WAS INVENTED
In 1763, Ralph Allen of Bath was told by his doctor that bathing in the English Channel would cure his health problems. There were no swim suits. Rather than be seen naked, he devised a changing hut, on wheels, which could be taken to the water. Pleased with his invention, he told his friend the Duke of Gloucester, who told King George III in turn. Against the advice of his doctors, George III used a *'bathing machine'* like Allen's at Weymouth in 1789. It set the fashion for seaside bathing.

WHITBY This port on the mouth of the River Esk grew with the whaling trade and was also the home of collier brigs, some of which were converted into whalers. Whalers sailed out of Whitby from 1753, and the peak of the trade was *c.*1775, when 15 ships were operating. It was once the biggest whaling port in Britain after Hull.

WICK This former Viking settlement is the only major commercial centre on the northeastern extremity of Scotland. During the six-week herring season, some 1700 boats would put into Wick in the 1860s, making it the largest herring port in Europe.

CHAPTER 8

Animals *of* *the* Seas

INTERESTING THINGS
THAT LIVE IN THE SEA

THE BLOOP This is the name given to an ultra-low frequency underwater sound which was detected by the US National Oceanic and Atmospheric Administration several times during 1997. The source of the sound remains unknown, but it was detected repeatedly by the Equatorial Pacific Ocean autonomous hydrophone array, equipment originally designed to detect the presence of Russian submarines. According to the NOAA description, the sound *'rises rapidly in frequency over about one minute and was of sufficient amplitude to be heard on multiple sensors, at a range of over 5000 km'*. While it bears the varying frequency hallmark of marine animals, the sound is far more powerful than the calls made by any creature known on Earth, the *New Scientist* recorded. The listening stations are situated hundreds of yards below the ocean surface, at a depth where sound waves become trapped in a layer of water known as the *'deep sound channel'*. Here water temperature and pressure cause sound waves to continue travelling without being scattered by the ocean surface or the bottom of the sea. Most of the sounds detected obviously emanate from whales, ships or earthquakes, but these very low frequency noises have proved baffling to scientists.

FIRST ANIMAL ON EARTH IDENTIFIED AS HAVING SEX Putting back the history of sex by around 30 million years, *Funisia dorothea* was a long thin rope-like creature standing erect on the ocean floor up to 570 million years ago. Soft-bodied, it grew up to 12 inches (30 cm) in length and was attached to the ocean bed, swaying in the current and taking in nutrients. Any predators did not evolve until millions of years later. The journal *Science* made the announcement in 2008 stating that it reproduced through sexual rather than asexual reproduction, because the Australian fossil specimens were found in groups and all appeared to be the same age. They were thus the result of simultaneous spawning rather than of uncoordinated asexual births.

FLUKES AND SWIMMING – UP AND DOWN, OR SIDE TO SIDE? The tail fins of fish are vertical, and when fish move their fins from side to side they are propelled forward. However, three major groups of mammals left the sea in prehistoric times, then millions of years later returned to it, and they have horizontal tail flukes. These move up and down, not side to side, for efficient propulsion. The mammal groups are

Animals of the Sea

Arthropods (jointed legged animals) – include crustaceans, including lobsters, shrimp, crabs (*c.*10,000 species) and barnacles (*c.*1000). The four species of horseshoe crabs are arthropods but more closely related to spiders than other crabs.

Chordates (animals with a notochord – nearly all are vertebrates) – there are about 30,000 species of fishes including lampreys (*c.*35 species), hagfishes (*c.*20), sharks (*c.*450), rays and skates (*c.*300), bony fish (*c.*25,000) including gobies, flying fish, barracudas, parrot fish, surgeon fish, flounders, soles, eels, scorpion fish and toad fish.

Reptiles include sea snakes (*c.*70 species), and eight sea turtles – green, black, hawksbill, Kemp's ridley, olive ridley, leatherback, loggerhead and flatback. There are also saltwater alligators, caymans and crocodiles.

Mammals include whales (79). There are 68 'toothed whales'. The 11 'baleen whales' are the blue, humpback, bowhead, right (three types), fin, grey, minke, Bryde's and Sei. A separate family of around 20 beaked whales exists. There are 40 species of dolphin, including the orca or killer whale, and the pilot whale. Some other dolphins are the bottlenose, spotted, spinner, common, dusky, Irrawaddy, Fraser's, Risso's and the striped dolphin. There are only six Porpoises – harbour, Dall's, vaquita, finless, spectacled and Burmeister's. The narwhal and beluga whale are unlike any other marine mammals, being of the monodon species. The sea otter thrives in the kelp beds off western North America.

There are 32 species of seals and sea lions and three subspecies of walrus. Three types of manatee exist in the West Indies, West Africa and the Amazon, but there is only one species of dugong, off Australia.

Molluscs (animals with a mantle) include snails, *c.*15,000 bivalves (two-shelled animals), chitons (*c.*500), tusk shells (*c.*350) and around 800 cephalopods (octopuses, squids, etc.).

Echinoderms (spiny skinned animals) – there are about 6000 species, including sea stars (*c.*1500), brittle stars and basket stars (*c.*2000), sea cucumbers (*c.*900), sea urchins and sand dollars (*c.*950) and around 550 crinoids (sea lilies or feather-stars).

Cnidarians (stinging animals) – of the 9000 species we count around 250 true jellyfish, about 6000 corals, and *c.*2700 hydroids and cubomedusa (box jellies).

Sponges – there are around 5000 species, plus comb jellies and worms.

Sirenia (dugongs and manatees), *Cetacea* (whales and dolphins) and *Pinnepedia* (seals, sea lions and walruses).

MASS EXTINCTION

The greatest mass extinction in the Earth's history happened around 251.4 million years ago, wiping out up to 96 per cent of all marine species and 70 per cent of land species. Whether it was caused by a solar flare-up, supernova gamma-rays from outer space, a meteor strike, huge volcanic activity, or earthquakes releasing methane from the ocean floor is still a matter for debate. However, recent evidence points to a meteor strike, as the extinction happened very, very quickly. Earth became much hotter, and full of poisonous gases in a period known as *'The Great Dying'*. To scientists it is known as the *'Permian-Triassic Extinction'*. Another, smaller extinction wiped out the dinosaurs and other groups of animals about 65 million years ago. We are currently going though another mass extinction, this one caused by over-population created by the class of animals called humans.

MIGRATION RECORDS

Green turtles can migrate more than 1400 miles (2250 km) to lay their eggs. The grey whale migrates more than 10,000 miles (16,000 km) each year, the longest migration of any mammal.

NEW TO SCIENCE

One recent study of a deep-sea community revealed 898 species belonging to more than 100 families in an area about half the size of a tennis court. More than half of these were new to science. The deep ocean floor is home to many unknown organisms, and also chemical-based life-forms.

THE PSYCHEDELIC FISH

A colourful frogfish has been found in 2008 by divers off Indonesia. A new species, it moves along the sea floor like a bouncing ball. Its fins have evolved to be leg-like, and every time it touches the seabed it pushes off with these fins and expels water from its gills, propelling itself upwards. Because of its off-centred tail, it bounces erratically, and is almost impossible to catch.

ROYAL FISH, THE KING'S FISH

The first English reference to royal fishery rights seems to be in 1291–2, in the reign of Edward I, when the king laid claim to treasure trove, wrecks, whales, porpoises and sturgeon.

SEA PROTEIN

The world's oceans holds immense quantities of protein. The total annual commercial harvest from the seas exceeds 85 million metric tons with the People's Republic of China being the biggest fish producer. Fish provides the greatest source of wild or domestic protein in the world.

APEX PREDATORS

Apex predators are healthy adult animals, at the top of their respective food chains, generally not preyed upon by other animals. Man is not included, although he is the most dangerous and deadly of all apex predators because of his access to technology. In prehistoric times, *Megalodon* ruled the seas, but now the following species are among the apex predators: billfish, electric ray, leopard seal, North Pacific giant octopus, orca, saltwater crocodile, sperm whale, tiger shark and walrus.

BILLFISH These graceful, fast fish feed on smaller fish and cephalopods (octopus, squid, jellyfish), and include marlin and sailfish (both hunted for sport, in what is known as *'game fishing'*) and swordfish (hunted for sport and food). The swordfish is the single member of the Xiphiidae family. Numbers of all billfish are rapidly declining.

ELECTRIC RAY The torpedo is named after this fish, *'torpidus'* meaning the numbness and incapacity which follows an electric shock. There are over 30 species of which the largest, *Torpedo nobiliana*, lives in subtropical climate zones. This electric ray feeds by stunning fish such as halibut and small sharks, growing up to 200 pounds (91 kg) in weight. It produces a powerful electric shock of up to 220 volts. The Greeks and

Romans used electric rays to cure gout (by standing on one) and headaches (by applying one to the temple.)

LEOPARD SEAL *Hydrurga leptonyx* is named after its spotted coat. Just like the polar bear in the Arctic, it is the top predator in the Antarctic. Females are the larger specimens, growing up to 1300 pounds (590 kg). They eat crabeater seals, Adelie penguins and squid. Their status is not endangered, as their pack ice habitat is so dangerous to shipping that they remain relatively undisturbed. However, as it is generally a solitary hunter, occasionally it can be caught and killed by a pod of killer whales.

NORTH PACIFIC GIANT OCTOPUS *Enteroctopus dofleini* is the largest species of octopus in the world. It lives for three to five years. In 1967 one was found off British Columbia which measured 23 feet (7 m) from tentacle tip to tentacle tip, and weighed 156 pounds (71 kg). They are excellent at camouflage, blending in with the background rocks or

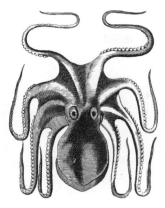

ocean floor. If it is in kelp, it will take on the colour of the seaweed, and also sway in time with it.

ORCA, KILLER WHALE, BLACKFISH, SEAWOLF – THE FASTEST MARINE MAMMAL

Orcinus orca is the largest species of dolphin found across the world. Males weigh up to 8 tons and can reach 32 feet (9.75 m) in length, and attain speeds of over 35 mph (56 kph). They usually hunt in 'pods' and have evolved different hunting methods to take different prey. A pod will attack a young or weak whale, chasing it until its mother is exhausted and unable to defend it. The calf is then prevented from reaching the surface and so drowns. Orca also sometimes kill healthy adult grey and minke whales, and even female sperm whales can be targets. Other prey includes seals, sea lions and even walruses. They kill sea lions by head-butting them, or stunning them with their tail flukes. Seals are sometimes thrown in the air to stun and kill them. They will also eat penguins, gulls, auks, and cormorants. Because herring shoal in vast quantities, some killer whales use the technique of '*carousel feeding*'. The shoal is forced into a tight ball as the killer whales circle them, flashing their white undersides and/or releasing bursts of bubbles into the water. The orca's tail flukes are then slapped into the compressed shoal, stunning or killing between 10–15 fish at once. Killer whales are facing a cull, as their food habits are changing. Because of the continuing decline in numbers of their main prey, such as grey whales and sperm whales, they are targeting rare species such as sea otters, Steller's sea lions and harbour seals. The problem is that there are 100,000–200,000 killer whales around the Earth, and 90 per cent of these feed mainly on fish. It is a separate sub-species which feeds on endangered whales and sea mammals, and it will be almost impossible to differentiate between them if there is a cull.

SALTWATER (ESTUARINE) CROCODILE – THE WORLD'S LARGEST REPTILE

Crocodylus porosus is found on the northern coast of Australia (and inland for up to 60 miles/ 97 km), sometimes growing to a length of 28 feet (8.5 m), and weighing over a ton. The temperature of the egg determines the sex of the crocodile at birth. Aggressive in the breeding season, they will pull humans into the water and drown them before eating them.

SPERM WHALE (THE COMMON CACHALOT)

This is the second largest animal in the world and it has the largest brain of any animal that has ever existed. *Physeter catodon* is one of the deepest diving mammals (up to 3720 feet/1134 m has been recorded), and is the largest toothed whale. Mainly because of the size of its brain, the head accounts for up to a third of its body length. *Cachola* means 'big head' in Portuguese and Spanish, and this whale was known as a *cachalote* by its whalers. The head is filled with spermaceti oil, probably a mechanism to allow the animal to make deep dives, and it was invaluable for lubricating machinery. This led to over-hunting. They were known in the past to grow to 90 feet (27 m) long and 133 tons, but the largest nowadays measure around 60 feet (18 m) and weigh 50 tons. The balance of the sexes was also seriously distorted by hunting, because whalers targeted the larger males. They can live up to 75 years, and are at last listed as 'vulnerable' in conservation lists. There were around 2.4 million sperm whales about a century ago, the population is probably less than 200,000 now. Between 1987 and 2002, 18 sperm whales were killed (and eaten) *'for scientific purposes'*. The sperm whale was the whale hunted in Herman Melville's novel *Moby-Dick*. Calves stay with their mothers for several years. These whales mainly feed on squid, including giant and colossal squid – the largest invertebrates in the world. Octopus, deep-water fish, sharks and skate are also part of their diet.

TIGER SHARK – 'THE DUSTBIN OF THE SEA' *Galeocerdo cuvier* has tiger-like markings on its back, and grows up to 20 feet (6 m) in length. They are found in all warm seas, and are as dangerous as the orca or killer whale is in temperate seas. The tiger shark can reach a speed of 20 mph (32 kph). It preys on fish, turtles, jellyfish, stingrays, clams, crabs, mammals, sea birds, reptiles and other sharks. The tiger shark is usually solitary, unlike the orca, but will attack and eat anything, even a dead animal thrown overboard, which has given rise to its unflattering nickname. Its heavily serrated teeth allow it to slice into the bodies of large sea turtles, as well as seals, sea lions, and cetaceans.

Walrus

The walrus *Odobenus rosmarus* is the only pinniped (comprising the family of seals, sea lions and fur seals) to have tusks, which grow over 3 feet (90 cm) in length. Males can grow to over 1.5 tons and they inhabit Arctic ice-floes, usually feeding on mussels, starfish, sea urchins, sea cucumbers and crabs. Occasionally a walrus will feed on fish, seals and young whales. When it catches one, the walrus holds a seal down on the ice with its flippers and rips it open with its tusks. They live in large herds of up 2000 members, and have been hunted by man for their meat, skin and ivory tusks.

SEA MAMMALS OF INTEREST

BELUGA WHALES – 'THE SEA CANARIES' Characterized by their unique creamy white colour, belugas have an extensive vocal repertoire and have long been called the *'sea canary'* by seamen who heard them. Communicative and emotive calls can be divided between whistles and pulsed calls, and as many as 50 call types have been recognized. Along with the narwhal, it a type of dolphin and the only member (with the narwhal) of the family of Monodontidae.

BLUE WHALE – THE LARGEST ANIMAL EVER TO HAVE LIVED ON EARTH *Balaenoptera musculus* lives on tiny plankton and krill sieved through huge baleen plates in their jaws. The whales live in pods, and grow to be about 80 feet (24 m) long on average, weighing about 120 tons. The largest specimen found was a female 94 feet (28.7 m) long weighing more 174 tons. The females are larger than males, as is the case with all baleen whales. A large blue whale of about 150 tons has a heart that weighs about 1000 pounds (454 kg), while 14,000 pounds (6350 kg) of blood circulate around its body. The heart is about the size of a small car. Blue whales are the loudest animals on Earth, with the volume of their calls reaching levels

up to 188 decibels. This low-frequency whistle can be heard for hundreds of miles. The blue whale is thus louder than a jet, which registers only 140 decibels. Blue whales were hunted by whalers until the International Whaling Commission at last declared them to be a 'protected species' in 1966 because of a huge decrease in their population. It is estimated that there are about 10,000–14,000 blue whales worldwide, down from 350,000 in pre-whaling days. They are an endangered species.

CHINESE RIVER DOLPHIN – THE MOST RECENT MAMMAL TO BECOME EXTINCT After possibly 25 million years of existence *Lipotes vexillifer*, a river-dwelling dolphin known as a baiji and nicknamed *'Goddess of the Yangtze'*, is extinct. It is the first aquatic mammal species to become extinct since the demise of the Japanese sea lion and the Caribbean monk seal in the 1950s. The baiji population declined drastically in recent decades as China industrialized and made heavy use of the Yangtze River for fishing, transportation, and hydroelectricity. The last confirmed sighting of a baiji was in 2004. Historically the baiji occurred along 1000 miles (1600 km) of the middle and lower reaches of the Yangtze from Yichang in the west to the mouth of the river, near Shanghai.

CRABEATER SEAL There are almost 7 billion humans on Earth, and *Lobodon carcinophaga*, the crabeater seal, is probably the second most populous species of large mammal on the globe. There are possibly around 10 million crabeater seals, so humans outnumber them 700 to 1, which gives some indication of man's influence on the planet. Crabeaters live in small family groups on pack ice in Antarctica, and 98 per cent of their diet consists of Atlantic krill, not crabs. The naturalist E.A. Wilson, who was with Scott on the 1910–13 *Terra Nova* Expedition to the South Pole, recorded that the seals, when close to death, would leave the pack ice and clamber up glaciers to die. Dead crabeaters have been found 35 miles (56 km) up the Ferrar Glacier, almost 3500 feet (1067 m) above sea level. The leopard seal is their main predator.

DOLPHINS The Delphinidae family is the largest in the Cetacea order of whales, dolphins and porpoises. Dolphins are amongst the most intelligent of animals. The name derives from the Greek *delphys* (womb), so the origin of their name was possibly *'a fish with a womb'*. Dolphins are closely related to whales and porpoises, and there are almost 40 species divided between 17 genera, varying in size from 4 feet to 30 feet (1.2 m to 9 m) and in weight from 88 pounds (40 kg) to over 10 tons (10.2 tonnes). The biggest dolphin is the orca, also known as the killer whale. Dolphins are found worldwide, mainly in the shallow seas of the continental shelves, and their main diet is fish and squid.

THE DOLPHIN WITH A NEW TAIL In 2006 a two-month-old Atlantic bottlenose dolphin was found floating off Forida, having lost her tail in a crab trap. She was taken to Clearwater Marine Aquarium, where she was named *Winter*, and she recovered from her injuries. One of the world's leading prosthetists constructed a tail of silicone and plastic to fit over her stump, which is engineered to work in every direction of movement.

THE DOLPHINS WHO USE TOOLS Bottlenose dolphins in Shark Bay, Australia, have learned how to protect their noses with a piece of sponge while foraging for fish on the abrasive sea bed. They spend some time looking for the right conically shaped sponges to fit over their noses. The sponge is used to gently scatter the sand and disturb a

buried flatfish. When the fish makes a break, the sponge is dropped and the prey is hunted down.

DUGONGS Dugongs are the only fully plant-eating marine mammal, and the only sea cow to occur in Australian waters where it is found off the north coast.

ELEPHANT SEAL – THE DEEPEST DIVING MAMMAL

It was long thought that the sperm whale was the deepest diving mammal at around 4000 feet (1220 m), but it has been established that the elephant seal can dive to 6500 feet (1980 m). This information has been discovered as a result of a programme to tag seals to study the warming in the Southern Ocean and Antarctic. They have evolved the ability to 'cat-nap' around 1500 feet (450 m) under the surface, because to do so on the surface puts them at risk from sharks and killer whales.

FALKLAND ISLANDS WOLF

Many species of animals native to islands have been lost when man first visits and then colonizes them. One of the most recent extinctions is the Tasmanian wolf, the largest carnivorous marsupial in the world, which happened just 65 years ago. The Falkland Islands wolf probably survived on a diet of seabirds, seal pups, and even on vegetation, and it was one of only two mammals indigenous to the Falkland Islands, the other being a small mouse. Charles Darwin visited the islands during his voyage aboard the *Beagle* in 1833. Commenting on the tameness of the wolves, he feared that this quality might eventually lead to their extinction. Shortly after, American fur traders found them and began their easy and savage

trade. Its scientific name is *Dusicyon australis*, meaning 'foolish dog of the south', alluding to its lack of fear of man. The last Falkland Islands wolf was believed to have been killed in 1876, in West Falkland.

GRAMPUS Risso's dolphin *(Grampus griseus)* is also known as *'the Grampus'*. It is a large, sturdy animal (about 10–12 feet/3–3.7 m long) with a worldwide distribution. It is usually seen offshore and prefers to feed on squid. Risso's dolphin was probably called *'Grand Poisson'* by French sailors, which was corrupted to *'grampus'* by English-speaking crews. Because of their worldwide distribution, and the fact that they usually live far out to sea away from the coast, it has been difficult to estimate how many Risso's dolphins there are. It is on the *Red List of Threatened Species*, and is still hunted in some places, but the main causes of mortality seem to be pollution and accidental entanglement in fishing gear. Like sperm whales, these dolphins usually carry evidence of their fights with squid. It is common to find circular sucker-marks and other scars all over their bodies.

HOODED SEALS AND BIG NOSES

The hooded seal has a large elastic nasal cavity, which when fully inflated resembles a big black rubber ball. They are large aggressive mammals that can exceed 8 feet (2.4 m) in length and weigh up to 900 pounds (400 kg).

MOKO AND THE WHALES

A pigmy sperm whale and its calf were beached off New Zealand's North Island in 2008, and four efforts to push them back into open waters had failed. They

Moby-Dick

In 1820, the *Essex*, a whaler out of Nantucket, was rammed and sunk by a sperm whale 2000 miles (3200 km) off the western coast of South America. Eight men survived and first mate Owen Chase wrote about it in his 1821 *Narrative of the Most Extraordinary and Distressing Shipwreck of the Whale-Ship Essex*. Rare and out-of-print, it was sourced for Herman Melville by his father-in-law. From 1810 to the late 1830s a giant albino sperm whale, *'Mocha Dick'*, was regularly sighted near Mocha Island off Chile. He was riddled with the scars of dozens of harpoons from around 100 attempts to kill him, and was known for ramming ships. The explorer Jeremiah Reynolds wrote of the killing of Mocha Dick in 1838, when the whale had come to the aid of a distraught cow whose calf had just been killed by the whalers. His body was 70 feet (21.3 m) long and yielded 100 barrels of oil, along with some ambergris. The story appeared in the *New York Monthly Magazine* in 1839.

These two whales were the inspiration for the 1851 story of the 'great white whale' *Moby-Dick*. Owen Chase claimed that the whale which sank the *Essex* was 85 feet (26 m) long, an assertion which has been disputed by modern scientists who argue that bulls can not grow past 65 feet (20 m). However, logs of Nantucket whalers prove that bull sperm whales could grow up to 85 feet in length, but 150 years of selective killing of bulls has wiped out larger specimens. In the Nantucket Whaling Museum is an 18-feet (5.5-m) jaw which must have belonged to an adult sperm whale measuring 80 feet (24.4 m) in length. It appears that scientists may be wrong and that sperm whales have still not recovered from the industrialized slaughter that decimated them in the 18th and 19th centuries. Sperm whales communicate in regular 'clicks' at half-second intervals which sound like the blows of a hammer, and which can be heard through the hulls of ships. They were sometimes known as the *'carpenter fish'* because of this.

could not get past a nearby sandbar. The rescuers had given up hope when they heard a local wild bottlenose dolphin, known as *Moko*, respond with its own calls to those of the stranded whales. *Moko* arrived on the scene and the whales followed her in shallow water along the sand bar, 200 yards (182 m) parallel to the beach. She then led them into a sharp right-angled turn through a narrow channel in the sandbar into the open seas. A spokesman from the New Zealand Conservation Service stated that he did not know that dolphins could communicate with pigmy sperm whales. There have been many recorded cases of dolphins saving human lives.

THE MOST ENDANGERED MARINE CETACEAN – THE GULF PORPOISE
The continued existence of the *vaquita* (also known as cochito, Gulf of California porpoise, gulf porpoise) was only confirmed in 1985. The vaquita is unique among porpoises in having such a restricted range, being found only in the upper Gulf of California and in no other sea in the world. It is the world's smallest marine cetacean. Its population has been declining because these porpoises become trapped in gillnets intended for capturing a species of fish endemic to the Gulf, the totoaba. (This type of drum fish is now itself endangered by over-fishing.) It was estimated in 2000 that between 39 and 84 gulf porpoises were killed each year by such gillnets and trawl nets. Less than 600 are probably left, and the vaquita is listed by both the IUCN and the Convention on International Trade in the Endangered Species of Wild Fauna and Flora, in the most critical category at risk of extinction.

Even if the number of vaquita killed by trawlers is reduced to zero, the use of chlorinated pesticides, inbreeding owing to the small population and the reduced flow of freshwater from the Colorado River due to irrigation also have a detrimental effect. The vaquita is one of the top 100 'EDGE Species', the

acronym meaning *'Evolutionarily Distinct, Globally Endangered'*. Evolutionarily distinct animals have no close relatives and represent proportionally more of the tree of life than other species, meaning they are a top priority for conservation campaigns. But it may be too late for the vaquita.

THE MOST POPULAR WHALE IN THE WORLD
In 2009 environmental authorities in Australia declared an exclusion zone for boats, jetskis and aircraft around an albino humpback whale swiming from Antarctica to the Great Barrier Reef. *'Migaloo'* ('white fella' in Aboriginal language) is the only hypo-pigmented, all-white humpback ever documented, and he bears the scars from a collision with a trimaran in 2003. He was first spotted migrating in 1991, and is one of 11,000 humpbacks who migrate each year from feeding grounds in Antactica in order to mate and give birth in warmer waters before returning south. An album featuring his whale songs is to be released.

Narwhal – the Unicorn of the Seas

This mysterious whale with a long spiral tusk (in fact, an incisor tooth that grows out of the upper jaw) is at risk from climate change. It is so narrow in its range of habitat and so specific in its diet that it may be one of the least able of Arctic mammals to adapt to rapid warming. Its population is concentrated in a small area between Baffin Island, Canada and Greenland. With a population of no more than 80,000, narwhals stick closely to established migratory patterns. Any change in the distribution of heavy winter pack ice is likely to adversely affect the whale, which can dive down in excess of 5000 feet (1525 m) in search of its favourite prey, the Greenland halibut. The loss of sea ice is now making narwhal more vulnerable to killer whales, which have in recent years ventured further northwards with the retreat of the ice, but less so to polar bears which hunt narwhal in groups at the edge of the whales' breathing holes. Inuit, which still harvest significant numbers of narwhal, have reported changes in their distribution and condition. During the last significant cooling period between the 12th and 19th centuries ('the Little Ice Age'), narwhals are believed to have ranged farther south, and the last recorded sighting in British waters was in 1588. This was shortly before Queen Elizabeth I valued a narwhal tusk, presented to her by the privateer Martin Frobisher, at ten times its weight in gold.

NORTH ATLANTIC RIGHT WHALE – THE MOST ENDANGERED WHALE

The 'right whale' weighs up to 10 tons and grows up to 56 feet (17 m) long. It is found closer to land than most large whales, especially during the breeding season. Female right whales have a very strong protective maternal instinct, and this characteristic was taken advantage of by early whalers, who captured the calf first, knowing that the mother was then unlikely to try to escape. A relatively slow swimmer, the North Atlantic right whale averages about 6 mph (10 kph). It usually does not fear boats and can be easily approached by them. The species is close to extinction in the eastern North Atlantic, caused by overfishing by the whaling industry. Right whales were so named because they were the 'right' whale to hunt. They were slow, floated when killed and produced a high yield of oil. More than half of the living right whales in the western North Atlantic have experienced at least one ship-strike or net entanglement. Less than 300 are thought to remain.

PELORUS JACK *Pelorus Jack* escorted sailing ships across Admiralty Bay in New Zealand regularly between 1888 and 1912. A Risso's dolphin, Pelorus Jack was first seen when he appeared in front of the schooner *Brindle* when the ship approached French Pass, a channel located between D'Urville Island and the New Zealand mainland. The area is dangerous to ships because of its rocks and strong currents but no shipwrecks occurred when Jack was present to guide them. According to contemporary accounts, Pelorus Jack seemed to want to guide the ships, preferably steamers, through dangerous passages of the French Pass. He might swim alongside a ship for 20 minutes at a time. Sometimes if the crew could not see Jack at first, they would wait for him to appear. At that time, when navigation was difficult, a 'pelorus' was a navigational instrument used to complement compass readings. Jack was so competent at guiding the ships that there was no need of the pelorus, and he became known as Pelorus Jack as a consequence. He was the first sea creature ever to have been recognized and treated as an individual, being given special protection on 26 September 1904. The cause was that a drunken passenger on a ship called the *Penguin* shot and wounded Jack. The crew were extremely unhappy and wanted to lynch him, but both he and Jack survived the incident. A few weeks after this injury Jack returned to his escort work, but he never went near the *Penguin* again, and the ship was wrecked in French Pass a few years after this incident.

PINK DOLPHINS Perhaps these take the place of pink elephants in the Far East. Dolphins have taken on a pink hue in the Pear River delta, between Hong Kong and Macau. It is not known why they are pink in colour but it may be the lack of natural predators, or the by-product of blushing in an effort to regulate body temperature.

POLAR BEAR There are only around 20,000 polar bears left in the Arctic, and scientists from the US Geological Survey predict that up to 70 per cent of these will disappear in the next 50 years because of the loss of sea ice. In northern Canada, the average weight of females is down from 620 pounds to 485 pounds (281 kg to 220 kg), a loss of 21 per cent. Another threat is the billions of dollars scheduled to be spent upon oil exploration in the Arctic in the next few years. Marika Holland of the National Center for Atmospheric Research in Boulder, Colorado, working with scientists from Washington and McGill universities, predicts the end of the Arctic ice cap by 2040, leading to the extinction of the polar bear, narwhal, Arctic fox, walrus and other animals and fish. The extent of the summer ice cap in 2007 was 43 per cent less than it was in 1979, the start of accurate satellite mapping.

PORPOISES AND DOLPHINS These are often confused, and both belong to the cetacean group known as odontocetes (toothed whales). Porpoises are distinguished from dolphins by the shape of their teeth, which are flattened like shovels. Porpoises are smaller in size, have a smaller, triangular shaped dorsal fin, and they lack a long snout. There has been a surge in deaths of porpoises, dolphins and whales reported in Cornwall and the Isles of Scilly, with the numbers of cetaceans found dead up five-fold from 2000 to 2007. The fault probably lies with fishing fleets, especially the practice of *'pair-trawling'* by Irish, French and Spanish fleets. A giant net is strung between two boats, and any air-breathing animals caught in it suffocate and die. Most of the carcasses are swept out to sea, and there is evidence that fishermen attempt to sink the dead mammals to avoid discovery. A Greenpeace UK spokesman, Willie MacKenzie, stated that although cetaceans were protected, they were inevitably a victim of by-catch: *'We have found dead dolphins which were still warm and which had their stomachs slit open so they would sink.'* The United Kingdom has banned its own fishing fleets from a 12-mile (19-km) zone off Cornwall, but the rules of the European Union allow Spanish, French and Irish trawlers to fish there.

The Sea Otter – the Tool User Back From Extinction

The sea otter, *Enhydra lutris*, lives off California, western Alaska and some northern Japanese islands. Growing up to 5 feet (1.5 m) long, they live in beds of giant kelp and eat fish, octopus, sea urchins, crabs and abalones. This otter is unusual in that it has no layer of fat or blubber under the skin. Instead, air trapped inside its thick fur provides insulation and prevents excessive heat loss. In the 18th century these otters were hunted for their thick fur, until specimens became so rare that pelts could fetch $1000 each. In 1910 a law was passed prohibiting the capture of sea otters in American waters, the population then having fallen as low as 1000 otters. The species has recovered to number over 130,000 now, but they only occupy a fifth of their original range. They play a vital role in the kelp beds, as they eat sea urchins, which are voracious feeders on the kelp. The kelp is also useful to sea otters when they sleep at sea, as they wrap it around themselves to prevent drifting in the current. The sea otter is one of a very small group of animals (chimpanzee, bottlenose dolphin, Galápagos woodpecker finch, Egyptian vulture and man) that uses tools. When eating, the animal's chest is used as a table. A flat stone is often placed on the chest and used by the otter as an anvil on which the shells of mussels and other shellfish can be smashed using the forepaws. Killer whales and sharks are their natural predators.

SEAL FUR BAN As of 2009, the EU is banning clothing made of seal fur. White pelts from baby seals were banned in 1986, but seal skin is still used by the fashion industry to make boots, coats, hats, bags and gloves. An import embargo is being drawn up. Of the 200,000 seals killed in Canada in the first half of 2008, 98 per cent were pups between two weeks and three months old. Others were killed in Namibia, Russia and Norway, many dying slowly after being clubbed unconscious by the hunters.

SEALS The greatest concentration of large mammals in the world (apart from man) is a herd of northern fur seals that inhabits two islands off Alaska. There were 2.5 million of them in the late 1950s, but hunting has reduced the numbers to under a million.

WHALE SONGS In 1971 *Science* magazine published a paper detailing the 'songs' of the humpback whale. The US Navy had termed it as 'biological' background noise while working on sonar. In 1952 naval scientists discovered that sound travels five times as fast in water as it does in air, and that in the deepest parts of the oceans sound can also travel very far before being dispersed and lost. Whales were found to have their 'own frequency', a deep channel with a reach of 1000 miles (1600 km). The paper revealed that whales do not emit just noise, but patterned sounds with clear motifs and patterns of development, repeated in chunks of over 30 minutes and sometimes hours in duration. The odd thing is that the songs mutate every season, and all the whales in one area seem to know the same songs. Even odder, it is only males who call and answer, so it is not a mating call. Perhaps the calls supply a sense of social cohesion in the lonely seas. Recent research seems to point to the quality of song depreciating, possibly because of the noise (and other) pollution that increasingly contaminates the waters.

WHAT IS THE ONLY MAMMAL WHICH CANNOT SWIM?
For most quadrupeds swimming is natural, as it involves the same basic motion as walking or running. It is the same to some extent for all two-legged mammals, e.g. monkeys can swim after a fashion. It was always thought that camels were the only mammals not able to swim, but they are trained for racing in swimming pools in the Middle East. Jefferson Davis, when US Secretary of War in 1856, trialled the idea of camels replacing horses and mules for transporting military equipment. In a test crossing of the Colorado River, eight horses and 14 mules drowned, but all the camels crossed safely. However, the body shape of giraffes makes it impossible for them to propel themselves in water.

WHALING

Whales, dolphins and porpoises belong to the family of cetaceans. They are air-breathing, warm-blooded mammals that bear live young, and nurse them on milk. Whales breathe through blowholes on top of their heads, an adaption which allows them to take in air without interrupting their swimming. Unlike fish, which swish their tails from side to side, whales swim by pumping their tails up and down using their flippers to steer. Before the advent of electricity, whale oil was extensively used to light homes and many species were hunted for their blubber and meat. Large-scale whaling began around the 11th century with hunting expeditions organized by the Basques and it gained real momentum in the 19th century with the invention of faster, steam-powered ships and more deadly, explosive harpoons. Whales provided oil for lamps, candles, soaps and perfumes, baleen for whips, corsets and other devices, and meat. In 1819 the British whaler *Syren* found rich whaling grounds off the coast of Japan, and for many years it brought home an estimated 40,000 barrels of whale oil each year. A barrel is *c.*35 British gallons, so the take was some 1,400,000 gallons (6.4 million litres) of whale oil each voyage. The average price per barrel was £8, so each voyage of the *Syren* made about £320,000, around £20 million in today's terms.

From 1850 whaling began to go into decline, but then the invention of artificial butter, 'margarine', called for vast amounts of both animal and vegetable fats, and whale blubber again became valuable. Throughout the 20th century, whale products could be found in everything from women's cosmetics to machine oil, and the meat was also used in petfood. As recently as 1961, 66,000 whales were killed during one season. Whalers took whatever they could, and might be away at sea for up to three years. The *Eclipse* once brought back four whales, 33 belugas, 38 polar bears and one walrus, totalling 49 tons of oil and 3.4 tons of baleen. Baleen whales have huge keratin plates, or combs known as whalebone, in their jaws for filter feeding. This baleen was used to make umbrella stays, buggy whips, and stiffening corsets and dresses, many of its original uses now being displaced by plastics.

In 1986, a moratorium on the commercial whaling industry was at last put in place to allow whale populations in danger of extinction to replenish. The Indian Ocean was declared a whale sanctuary in an effort to stem this trend. However, seven of the 13 great whales remain endangered. Fishing fleets from Japan and Norway profit from the sale of whale meat, which can fetch up to $150 per pound. Hunting figures have constantly been falsified, with the Japanese using the spurious excuse of *'scientific research'* to justify their whaling. Threats also come from entanglement in fishing lines, toxic contamination, ship collisions, gas and oil projects disrupting feeding grounds, climate changes, increased 'noise' at sea and habitat degradation. Environmental pollution in the ocean affects whales in a variety of ways. Chemicals in the water are absorbed and they accumulate in the blubber of baleen whales. These toxins are then slowly released into their milk and so sicken and weaken their calves.

The North Atlantic right whale was hunted to near extinction. The slow-moving whale floats when dead (most whales sink immediately) so it became known as the 'right' whale to hunt, i.e the easiest. After 50 years of protection from hunting, North Atlantic right whale populations have not shown any progress in the past 15 years. Outside natural causes, fatal collisions with ships account for nearly 90 per cent of right whale deaths. Faced with the near extinction of right, blue and sperm whales, the International Whaling Commission imposed a moratorium on commercial whaling from 1986. The IWC, which has 70 member states, allows an exception for subsistence catches of whales for indigenous peoples in places like Greenland, Siberia and Alaska. However, Norway resumed commercial hunts of minke whales in 1993, ignoring the IWC ruling. Norway also resumed whale exports to Iceland and the Faroe Islands in 2002 in defiance of a global trade ban. Iceland also resumed whaling in 2003

when it caught 36 minke whales for so-called 'scientific research'. It cut the quota to 25 in 2004, and caught the same number in 2005. Japan always states officially that it carries out whaling for 'scientific research', but there are never any findings published. It says this is allowed by IWC rules even though opponents call it a cover for commercial whaling. Japan recently caught 850 minke whales in the Antarctic in its annual whaling season and ten fin whales, which are endangered. Japan has also has announced plans that it is going to hunt around 50 fins and humpbacks a year. The meat ends up in restaurants and sushi bars. Norway set itself a huge quota of 1052 whales for 2006.

T.C. Bridges wrote in 1927:
'The destruction of whales is at present so great that the various governments concerned are becoming anxious. Sixteen whales were recently killed in one day off the South African coast and as the whale is a slow-growing creature, taking fifty years to reach its full size, and as the female has only one calf at a time, the numbers are rapidly decreasing. The one safe refuge of the whale is the Antarctic Ocean where the ice is so heavy and weather conditions so bad that whaling ships rarely penetrate far.'

This is the region which the Japanese whalers now target every single year. There are currently seven species of cetaceans in US waters that are protected under the Endangered Species Act. They are the blue whale, the bowhead whale, the fin whale, the humpback whale, the northern right whale, the sei whale and the sperm whale. There are only around 20,000 grey whales, but protection has stabilized this population after it was almost exterminated. The bowhead whale may live to be more than 200 years old, rivalling the claims of longevity for giant tortoises, but we may never discover if this is the case because of declining populations of these creatures. These figures below are only estimates based on available data, as accurate figures are difficult to obtain because of the paucity of cetacean sightings.

Endangered Cetaceans

Species	Population	Status and listings*
Northern right whale	300–800	endangered (ESA, IUCN)
Southern right whale	3000	endangered (ESA); vulnerable (IUCN)
Bowhead whale	8000	endangered (ESA, IUCN)
Blue whale	10,000–14,000	endangered (ESA, IUCN)
Fin whale	120,000–150,000	endangered (ESA); vulnerable (IUCN)
Sei whale	50,000	endangered (ESA)
Humpback whale	10,000+	endangered (ESA, IUCN)
Sperm whale	200,000	endangered (ESA)
Vaquita	a few hundred	endangered (ESA)
Baiji	thought to be extinct	endangered (ESA, IUCN)
Indus susu	500	endangered (ESA, IUCN)
Ganges susu	unknown	vulnerable (IUCN)
Boto	thought to be declining	vulnerable (IUCN)
Franciscana	unknown	not listed
Tucuxi	unknown	not listed
Hector's dolphin	3000–4000	vulnerable (IUCN)
Indo-Pacific humpbacked dolphin	thought to be depleted	not listed
Atlantic humpbacked dolphin	unknown, but depleted	not listed

*ESA denotes listing according to the Endangered Species Act. IUCN denotes listing according to the IUCN/World Conservation Union Red Databook.

BIRDS OF THE SEAS

ALBATROSS It was considered unlucky for a seaman to kill one, as they were supposed to carry the souls of dead sailors. Samuel Coleridge's *'The Rime of the Ancient Mariner'* was inspired by the shooting of a black albatross, which had been described in Captain Shelvocke's *A Voyage Round the World*. The Ancient Mariner is haunted by the ill-luck that shooting an albatross has brought upon his ship:

God save thee, Ancient Mariner!
From the fiends that plague thee thus! –
Why look'st thou so? – "With my crossbow
I shot the Albatross".

Nowadays, anything cumbersome, that makes life very difficult for one, *'hangs round your neck like an albatross'*. With their long, narrow wings, providing maximum lift and minimum drag, these birds are perfectly designed for harnessing the winds and wave-deflected airflows of the world's worst seas. Ornithologists have recorded single feeding trips covering a distance of 9320 miles (15,000 km) by wandering albatrosses.

ALBATROSS EXTINCTION AND FLAGS OF CONVENIENCE

In 1996, just three albatross species were known to be threatened, but today 21 of the 24 species are at risk of extinction in the near future, as a result of longline fishing. Longlining is a fishing method that uses hooks instead of nets. These lines of hooks, which can be 80 miles (130 km) long, are baited for open ocean species like swordfish and tuna. However, seabirds, particularly albatrosses and petrels, regularly grab the baited hooks and are hooked and dragged to their deaths. According to UN estimates pirate fishing vessels now account for up to a quarter of the world's total fish catch. Many of these fishing vessels are registered with 'flag of convenience' countries like Cambodia and Honduras, helping them to avoid fisheries regulations. Such registration only costs about $200 over the internet. The ships then head for the southern oceans, to the major albatross feeding grounds, hunting Patagonian toothfish, also known as Antarctic cod, Chilean sea bass, and mero, which fetches around $6000 a tonne. The Convention on the Conservation of Antarctic Marine Living Resources states that since 1996, pirate longliners have killed over 144,000 albatrosses and 400,000 petrels in Antarctic waters alone. For a bird with an extremely slow rate of reproduction (one chick every two to three years), even relatively small population losses to longlining endangers its survival. Scientists say an increase in adult mortality of just two to four per cent could halve an albatross population in 50 years. Thus the albatross is the most endangered species of any bird in existence and is threatened with extinction. For example, the world's entire population of Amsterdam Island albatrosses now numbers less than 100.

ALBATROSS EMERGENCY SERVICE
In 1887, shipwrecked sailors on the remote Crozet Islands in the Indian Ocean tied their SOS around an albatross's neck. Two weeks later the note was found on a beach in southwest Australia, 3500 miles (5600 km) away.

BOOBY The brown gannet, *Sula cyanops*. This bird was eaten when no other meat at all was available. *'Booby prize'* came to mean something that no-one particularly wanted, but had to have. The word comes from the Spanish *'bobo'* meaning foolish or slow-witted, as the birds were easily caught, perceiving no danger from man.

CORMORANT Cormorants have been trained to help catch fish since possibly 2500 BCE in Mesopotamia and the 5th–6th centuries CE in Japan and China. A ring is attached to their necks to prevent them swallowing larger fish. When the cormorant surfaces with a fish, the fisherman whistles for it to come to the boat and he then takes the catch, rewarding the bird with a small piece of fish in exchange.

GREAT AUKS, BURIAL COSTUMES AND WITCHES
Large breeding colonies of this flightless sea bird, the largest of the auks, once gathered on rocky islands and coasts of the North Atlantic in Canada, Greenland, Iceland, the British Isles and Scandinavia. It was known as a 'penguin', *Pinguinus*

impennis, before the birds we know as penguins were discovered and named. Its extermination began with a slaughter for food and bait by local inhabitants, and continued as hunters used the bird's fat and feathers. As the birds became scarce, they were also collected for their skins and eggs. A body buried at the Maritime Archaic Site at Port au Choix, Newfoundland, dating to about 2000 BCE, seems to have been interred clothed in a suit made from more than 200 great auk skins, with the heads left attached as decoration. On St Kilda Isle, Scotland, in July 1840, the last great auk seen in the British Isles was killed by two St Kildan residents, because they thought it was a witch. The last population in the world was thought to have lived on Geirfuglasker (Great Auk Rock) off Iceland. This island was a volcanic rock surrounded by cliffs which made it inaccessible to humans. However, in 1830 the rock submerged, and the birds moved to the nearby Eldey Island which was accessible from a single side. The last pair of great auks, found incubating an egg, were killed there in 1844, when Jon Brandsson and Sigurdur Islefsson strangled the adults and Ketil Ketilsson smashed the egg with his boot. They had been hired by a collector named Carl Siemsen who wanted auk specimens. However, a later claim that a live individual was sighted in 1852 on the Grand Banks of Newfoundland has been accepted by authorities.

MAN-OF-WAR FOWL The frigate bird, also called the sea-hawk by seamen.

MOTHER CARY'S GOOSE
The great petrel, a brown bird bigger than the mainly white stormy petrel.

NODDY The tern, *Sterna stolida*, sometimes eaten by buccaneers when meat was in short supply.

OLDEST LIVING WILD BIRD The oldest bird recorded is thought to be a Manx shearwater, found on Bardsey Island, Wales. It is a tiny cousin of the albatross. It migrates between Britain (where 90 per cent of its nesting burrows are found) and South America. This particular male had covered over 5 million miles (8 million km) and had returned to breed again in 2004. It was at least 52 years old, and shearwaters may live to be 60 or 70. However, there are rival claims for a Royal albatross in New Zealand which was known to have reached the age of 53, and a Laysan albatross aged over 50. A razorbill on Bardsey Island was known to be 45 years old.

PENGUINS AND POPULATION DECLINE The emperor penguin has to survive temperatures of -4° F (-20° C) and freezing winds when it breeds on the Antarctic sea ice, so its feathers have the highest density of any bird in the world (in common with three other varieties of penguin). Since the beginning of the 20th

Parrots

Many of us remember Captain Flint, Long John Silver's rascally parrot in *Treasure Island*, with its incessant cry *'Pieces of Eight! Pieces of Eight!'* Parrots were very popular on sailing ships, and William Dampier on his second voyage tells us that those near Vera Cruz in the Bay of Campeche were the biggest in the West Indies: *'Their colour was yellow and red, very coarsely mixed; and they would prate very prettily and there was scarce a man but what sent aboard one or two of them. So that with provision, chests, hen-coops and parrot-cages, our ships were full of lumber, with which we intended to sail.'*

Parrots were easier to keep on ship than monkeys, and were sold everywhere. A 1717 advertisement in London's *Post-Man* reads: *'Parrotkeets with red heads from Guinea, and two fine talking Parrotkeets from Buenos Aires, and several young talking Parrots'*, which were for sale at the Leopard and Tiger tavern at Tower Dock. Another 1717 issue offered *'Parrotkeets which talk English, Dutch, French and Spanish, Whistle at command, small parrotkeets with red heads, very tame and pretty'* at the Porter's Lodge, Charing Cross.

century, global numbers of penguins have halved to only 10 million birds. Of the 19 penguin species which live on 43 sites in the southern hemisphere, four are facing extinction and there has been a decline in the population of another six. Of New Zealand penguins, the yellow-eyed and Fiordland crested are down to 1500 and 3000 pairs respectively. The Humboldt penguin population, native to Chile and Peru, has crashed to 12,000 pairs, and South African penguin numbers are falling. There were 1,500,000 African penguin pairs in 1900, but now only 63,000 pairs remain. Magellanic penguins, on Argentina's Atlantic coast now number 200,000 pairs but were 400,000 pairs in the 1960s. Galápagos penguins only number 2500 pairs, down from 10,000 pairs in the 1970s. There has been a 50 per cent collapse in numbers of Adelie and chinstrap penguins in the Antarctic. Causes are complex. Factors include overfishing in some areas, oil drilling and spills, and global warming causing current changes and melting ice. When the ice melts early in the Antarctic, chicks do not have enough fur or fat to survive in freezing waters.

'THE PENGUIN WADDLING GAIT HAS A MORE CONSISTENT STEP WIDTH THAN STEP LENGTH' This is the title of a 2008 research paper from Houston University, which concludes that apparently ungainly penguins are just as stable when they walk as humans. Oh to be a university researcher!

THE PUFFIN AND LENT DIET
In the 40 days of Lent before Easter Sunday, good Christians abstained from eating meat. However, in W.H. Smyth's

The Sailor's Word-Book we read: 'The *fratercula arctica, a sea-bird with a singular bill, formerly supposed to be a bird in show, but a fish in substance, in consequence of which notion the Pope permitted its being eaten in Lent.'* For this reason, the bird being a fish 'in substance', Catholics were allowed to eat puffins on Fridays. Oh to be a theologian!

RAVENS Icelandic sagas and archaeological evidence seem to indicate that the Vikings sailed to Newfoundland, probably using the *'North Atlantic stepping stones'* of the Shetland Isles, the Faroe Islands, Iceland, Greenland, Baffin Island and Labrador. Without compasses or sextants, they generally needed to sail within sight of land, or only briefly to voyage out of sight of land. They used the stars as navigational aids, and also the recognition of cloud patterns which formed over land which could indicate the direction of land even when it was over the horizon. They, along with the Celts, discovered that a raven, when released from a ship, will fly up high enough to see if there is land in the distance, and then fly towards it. If it could not see land, it would return to the ship. Thus ravens were kept on board for longer journeys at sea in their longships.

FISH

THE ARCHERFISH – THE BEST MARINE MARKSMAN

The greatest fish marksman is the archerfish, which lurks just below the surface of the water in marine pools, waiting for an insect to land nearby. When it does, this 'swimming water pistol' fires jet after jet of water, dazing the unlucky bug and knocking it off its perch and into the fish's open mouth. A US submarine, *Archerfish*, sank the largest ship ever destroyed by a submarine, the 68,059-ton Japanese aircraft carrier *Shinano* in November 1944.

BALANCE FISH The old name for the hammerhead shark – its head looks like a double-headed hammer.

BASKING SHARK – THE WORLD'S SECOND LARGEST

FISH *Cetorhinus maximus* is found in all the world's temperate oceans. It is a slow-moving and harmless filter feeder, easy to catch and at risk of extinction due to overfishing to supply the world market for shark fins (for soup), sharkskin (for bags and shoes) and organs such as the liver (for oriental medicines and oil). Body parts such as cartilage are also used in Chinese medicine and as Japanese aphrodisiacs. Until 2008, it was unknown where basking sharks went for eight months of the year, until 25 were electronically tagged. It was thought that

there were four species, but there appears to be just one which migrates constantly from Newfoundland, down through the Caribbean and Brazil across the Atlantic, possibly along western Africa, to Europe and back to the Caribbean. This is against the flow of the currents, probably to facilitate feeding. It can grow up to 40 feet (12.2 m), bigger than a double-decker bus and weigh 10 tons. The author has been in a fishing dinghy off southwest Scotland and seen one in all its majesty just a few feet away. It is a terrible statistic that there are only around 10,000 left in the world. They take 12 to 20 years to reach sexual maturity and there is a one to three year gestation period, so it is unsure if this wonderful fish species can survive the population decline it is experiencing. The fins of a 6-ton basking shark are worth a staggering $50,000 in Asia.

BLUEFIN TUNA AND MERCURY POISONING

The foods with the highest levels of mercury in them are swordfish, marlin, sharks, tuna and shellfish. Mercury is expelled into the atmosphere by coal-fired electricity stations, so the amounts are rising each year because of the increasing pace of Chinese and Indian industrialization. It is used in dental fillings, and thousands of tons were dumped in the Atlantic and

Pacific from sunken Spanish and Portuguese galleons carrying *'quicksilver'*. Most mercury ends up on the bottom of rivers and the seas, and is then absorbed by bacteria and converted to its most deadly form, methylmercury. These toxic bacteria are ingested by larger animals and methylmercury passes through different animals to end up in the apex predators at the top of the food chain, such as tuna. From tuna it passes into man.

Albacore, yellowfin and bigeye tuna all show evidence of significantly dangerous levels of mercury, and the bluefin tuna, the largest of all which has attained a world record size of 1496 pounds (680 kg), naturally has the most. Bluefin tuna are being fished to extinction in the Mediterranean, so large fish are no longer found. As a result, half-grown fish are captured and kept in fish pens to be artificially fattened, killed, frozen and sent to Japan. These fish have not reached sexual maturity, so the species is quickly dying. Mediterranean nations such as Libya, France, Spain, Italy, Greece, Malta, Croatia, Egypt, Morocco and Algeria have all ignored strict fishing quotas established by the International Convention for the Conservation of Atlantic Tunas. As a result, they are killing one of the greatest fish in the sea, and Japanese consumers have a good chance of going mad through mercury poisoning. The reputation of bluefin tuna as *'the king of sushi'* means that in Tokyo's fish market in 2008 £37,400 was paid for a 608-pound (276-kg) fish, around £60 a pound wholesale. From the 1990s onwards, fishing vessels have been able to scoop up 3000 tuna in one catch, and the WWF (World Wide Fund for Nature) estimates that the Atlantic bluefin tuna will be extinct by 2012.

BROWNSNOUT SPOOKFISH – THE UNIQUE VERTEBRATE

Not much was known about these deep-sea creatures until one was caught live in 2007 and studied by researchers. It is the only backboned creature to use mirrors (reflective plates of guanine crystals) rather than lenses to get images into focus. It has two normal red eyes above, and two black eyes below, allowing it to pick out flashes of light in the deep more efficiently. In nearly 500 million years of vertebrate evolution, *Dolichopteryx longipes* is the only known species to solve the fundamental problem faced by all eyes – how to focus an image using a mirror, giving a bright, high contrast image.

CIGUATERA POISONING AND THE FIRST AMERICAN NOVEL

The finfish most commonly implicated in *ciguatera* fish poisoning include groupers, barracudas, snappers, jacks, mackerel, and triggerfish. Global warming and reef disturbance are thought to be the cause of the increased amounts of dinoflagellates that have been observed. Dinoflagellates are microorganisms which cause the formation of ciguatera toxins in the flesh of the fish. Harvesters and divers disturb reefs and cause the coral to die, and dinoflagellate algae species breed on the dead coral. Warmer ocean waters caused by global warming also accelerate the growth of dinoflagellates. Fish feed off the reefs and so ingest the toxins. The fish smells and tastes no different to us, and ciguatera toxins are not destroyed by cooking like most toxins related to food poisoning. Symptoms of this disease usually begin within hours of eating infected fish. Vomiting, diarrhoea and abdominal pains are the first to appear, but gastrointestinal symptoms are not always present. A sufferer can experience pain, sensory and neurological disturbances which may persist for weeks, months or even years. Such cases of poisoning are growing rapidly. In *The Journal of Penrose, Seaman* (*c.*1776), the first American novel, Lewellin Penrose dies of *'red snapper poisoning'*. His daughter America recovers quickly, but Penrose suffers a long and lingering death.

COD – THE FISH THAT CHANGED THE WORLD Cod is
the reason that Europeans first set sail across the Atlantic, and it is the only reason they could survive the journey home. The Vikings ate cod in Greenland and on the five expeditions to America that are recorded in the Icelandic sagas.

It was frozen and dried in the frosty air, then broken into pieces and eaten like hardtack. The staple of the medieval diet was cod, sold salted by the Basques, who did not reveal the source of this unlimited supply of food.

COFFIN FISH – THE WALKING FISH Coffin fish walk along the sea floor
on short stubby fins. They inhabit deep waters around the world. They often come up in nets swollen up into a ball. Like puffer fish, they can swallow large amounts of water to inflate themselves, presumably making it harder for predators to bite into them.

THE COSMOPOLITAN SAILFISH AND THE SPEED LIMIT The
cosmopolitan sailfish is considered one of the world's fastest fish over short distances. In a series of speed trials carried out in Florida, one cosmopolitan sailfish took out 300 feet (91 m) of line in three seconds, equivalent to a velocity of 68 mph (109 kph). Overfishing of this magnificent fish has led to a noticeable decline in their numbers, and they are difficult to study because they are highly migratory and usually encountered many hundreds of miles from shore. They are found in both the Atlantic and Pacific oceans and have been given different scientific names of *Istiophorus albicans* and *Istiophorus platypterus* respectively. However, scientists now believe that these fish are actually the same species. Sailfish usually raise their sails when they are excited or swimming on the surface. The average length is 6 to 8 feet (1.8 to 2.4 m), but the world record holder caught in 1994 weighed 141 pounds (64 kg) and was over 10 feet (3 m) long. It feeds on flying fish and squid, preferring tuna, mackerel, jack and other fish that swim near the ocean's surface. Several sailfish work together to corral their prey, using their high fins to create a barrier that keeps the smaller fish from escaping. They also have long, sharp bills to stun and skewer their prey.

CUCUMBER FISH The cucumber fish
is an elongated, cigar-shaped fish with large green eyes, which are angled to look upward as well as sideways. Pale green above and silvery below, it derives its name from the strange cucumber-like smell it emits.

THE UNKNOWN CYCLOTHONE – THE MOST COMMON VERTEBRATE ON THE PLANET

Bristlemouth fish in the family Gonostomatidae are only a few inches long. Because the deep sea is so vast (about ten times greater than the next-largest habitable volume on Earth), the most common of these fish, *Cyclothone*, is probably the most common vertebrate on the entire planet. Despite its abundance, little is known about it.

THE DEEPEST-LIVING FISH

The world's record holder for deepest-living fish goes to the brotulid family, about which scientists know very little. These fish are benthopelagic, living at depths of over 20,000 feet (6100 m), and their eyes appear to be virtually nonexistent because it is so dark at these depths. The world's deepest known individual fish specimen, *Abyssobrotula galatheae*, was found in the Puerto Rican Trench at a depth of over five miles (8 km).

DOGFISH = CATSHARKS = ROCK SALMON

Catsharks are a family (Scyliorhinidae), with over 110 species recorded. Many of these species are commonly called dogfish. Recent DNA analysis has shown that this group is more closely related to batoids (rays) than to other sharks. They are distinguished by their elongated cat-like eyes. The humpback cat shark can grow up to 13 feet (4 m) in length. The swell sharks of the genus *Cephaloscyllium* can fill their stomachs with water or air when threatened, increasing their girth by a factor of two- or three-fold. The spiny dogfish is the most common shark in the western Atlantic. It hunts both alone and in groups with other dogfish. Dogfish are considered a nuisance by fishermen because they will latch on to almost anything put in the water, including human hands. Rock salmon bought from the fishmonger is the flesh of the dogfish, wolf-fish or catfish, and is also known as hass/huss. It was renamed to make the

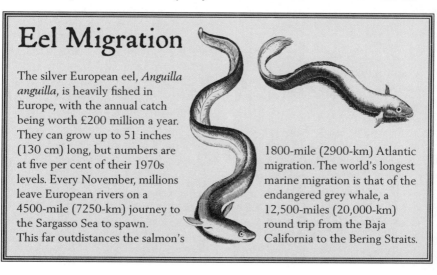

Eel Migration

The silver European eel, *Anguilla anguilla*, is heavily fished in Europe, with the annual catch being worth £200 million a year. They can grow up to 51 inches (130 cm) long, but numbers are at five per cent of their 1970s levels. Every November, millions leave European rivers on a 4500-mile (7250-km) journey to the Sargasso Sea to spawn. This far outdistances the salmon's 1800-mile (2900-km) Atlantic migration. The world's longest marine migration is that of the endangered grey whale, a 12,500-miles (20,000-km) round trip from the Baja California to the Bering Straits.

fish more appealing to consumers, but catches are declining rapidly.

EEL – THE OLDEST FISH

The oldest fish ever recorded was a female European eel which was 88 years old when she died at Halsingborg Museum, Sweden, in 1948.

EUROPE'S RAREST FISH

In February 2007, fishermen caught a sturgeon off the Belgian coast, and landed it alive. It had a French tag. Scientists hoped it could be a European sea sturgeon, *Acipenser sturio*, and contacted the French institute dealing with the protection of this highly endangered species. The fish had been tagged in the French Gironde estuary in August 1996. The European sea sturgeon can grow to over 10 feet (3 m), and is the largest fish to be found in Europe's rivers. It lives in estuaries and shallow parts of the Atlantic Ocean and the North Sea, and in the past reproduced in all the major European river systems. Due to overfishing, river pollution and river construction works, it has all but disappeared. The last place on Earth where it reproduced in the recent past is the Garonne and Dordogne rivers, which converge in the estuary of the Gironde (France). The last reproduction was observed in 1995. The sturgeon caught is presumed to be one of the animals born then. The hope of saving the species from extinction lies with 100 fish, still juveniles, being raised in captivity in two breeding centres in France and Germany.

THE FASTEST FISH The swordfish and marlin may be the fastest fish in the ocean reaching speeds of up to 72 mph (116 kph) in quick bursts. The sailfish has been recorded at 68 mph (109 kph). The bluefin tuna may, however, be capable of 'sustained' speeds of up to 56 mph (90 kph), and can accelerate faster than a sports car. It is being hunted to extinction. Although sharks are generally slow cruisers, the short fin mako is believed to be the fastest with speed bursts of up to 55 mph (88.5 kph).

FISH MIGRATION Many types of fish undertake migrations on a regular basis, covering distances ranging up to thousands of miles. The purpose usually relates to either feeding or breeding, but in some cases the underlying reason is still unknown. Migratory fish are classified according to the following scheme: *diadromous* fish travel between salt and fresh water. There are three types of diadromous fish: *anadromous* fish live in mostly the sea, breeding in fresh water (e.g. salmon); *catadromous* fish live in fresh water, breeding in the sea; and *amphidromous* fish move between fresh and salt water during some part of their life cycle, but not for breeding. *Potamodromous* fish migrate within fresh water only, and *oceanodromous* fish migrate within salt water only. One of the best-known anadromous fish is the salmon, which hatch in small freshwater streams, go to sea for several years, then return to the same streams where they were hatched, spawn there, and die shortly after. The most remarkable catadromous fish are freshwater eels of the genus *Anguilla*, whose larvae drift on the open ocean, sometimes for months or

years, before emerging as adults and travelling thousands of miles back to their original streams. A number of large marine fish, such as tuna, migrate north and south annually, following temperature variations in the ocean. These movements are of great importance to fishing fleets.

THE FISH WITH THE BIGGEST BRAIN

The giant manta ray can measure 25 feet (7.6 m) from wingtip to wingtip and weigh up to 5000 pounds (2268 kg). *Manta birostris* is also known as the devilfish, and it has the biggest brain to body ratio of all sharks and rays. They are filter-feeders and are preyed upon by sharks. With its close cousin, the devil ray, it is also being caught in huge quantities as 'filler' for sharkfin soup, and the gills are used in Chinese medicine. Three-quarters of manta rays show evidence on their bodies of shark attacks, and their wounds are treated at 'cleaning stations' by moonfish and cleaner wrasse. They are usually attacked from behind, their blind spot.

THE FISH WITH THE WORST NAME

The warty frogfish is a shallow water (down to about 30 feet/9 m) tropical reef fish from the Indo-Pacific. It has many wart-like bumps and sports its very own fishing rod as it is a species of anglerfish. The adult warty frogfish is chameleonic and alters its coloration to blend in amongst sponges.

FLATFISH DON'T START OFF FLAT

The newly hatched transparent larvae of flatfish, such as flounder, halibut, plaice and turbot, are shaped like normal fish. Soon after birth one eye 'migrates' to the other side of the head (either the left or the right, depending on the species).

Changes also occur in the skeletal and digestive systems as the body flattens out. Adults have only one dorsal and one anal fin, both without spines. The underside of the flatfish is pale and the top is coloured to match the environment.

GOD'S FISH

This was a nickname for the Gulf of Maine cod – called '*God's fish*' because of the abundant catches that fishermen used to enjoy. However, there are restrictions upon cod fishing today because it has been virtually fished out of existence in the region. The Gulf of Maine stretches from Nova Scotia to Cape Cod, including the Bay of Fundy.

GOLDEN COW-NOSE STINGRAYS

These poisonous rays migrate twice-yearly from the Yucatán Peninsula to western Florida and elsewhere in groups (known as '*fevers*') of up to 10,000 individuals. There are about 70 species of stingrays, and these particularly large rays, up to 6 feet 6 inches (198 cm) across, are named because of their domed heads and bovine appearance. Their liking for crabs and oysters has made them a target for fishermen. They will only attack when cornered, and their 'stinger' is a razor-sharp spine that grows from the rays's whip-like tail. The stinger measures about 15 inches (38 cm) in length and the venom it carries can be fatal to humans. It seems to have evolved as a defence mechanism against sharks, as it can pierce a shark's skin. Steve 'Crocodile Hunter' Irwin (1962–2006) was fatally injured when a bull ray's barb penetrated his heart as he was swimming. In the weeks after, at least ten stingrays were found with their tails cut off on Queensland beaches, apparently as some form of revenge killing.

GREAT WHITE SHARK – THE LARGEST PREDATORY FISH

Adult specimens average 14–15 feet (4.3–4.6 m) in length and generally weigh 1150–1700 pounds (522–771 kg). While few instances have been properly authenticated, there is evidence to suggest that some great whites grow to more than 20 feet (16 m) in length.

GROUNDFISH, GROUND FEEDERS Types of fish which spend

most of their lives on or near the seabed.

HADDOCK AND ST PETER THE FISHERMAN *Melanogrammus*

aeglefinus is a fish found on both sides of the North Atlantic. Its most distinctive feature is a large, black, thumb-print-shaped spot below the lateral line, just behind the head on each side of the body. These spots have been variously described as *'Satan's (or the Devil's) thumb-marks'* or *'St Peter's marks'* (or *thumbprints*). A former French-Canadian name for haddock was *'poisson de St Pierre'*. The spots are reputedly the mark of St Peter's finger and thumb that were imprinted when he drew one of the haddock's ancestors from the Lake of Genneserat. Haddock have never lived in those waters, so this could indeed be regarded as a miracle.

THE HAGFISH (SLIME EEL) AS AN APHRODISIAC The hagfish

'slimes' its enemies, has rows of teeth on its tongue, and feeds on the innards of rotting fish by penetrating any orifice. However, it is considered an aphrodisiac in South Korea, creating a business opportunity for struggling west coast US fishermen who are faced with major restrictions on the catching of salmon and other fish. In existence for 300 million years, it is still debated whether the hagfish is a fish or an eel. It has no jaws and only one nostril. Virtually blind, it dwells in the deep more than 1000 feet (305 m) down. On NBC's TV programme *'Fear Factor'*, two contestants sat in a vat of the creatures and had to push handfuls of them through holes. They described the experience as sticky, stinking and disgusting. Older Korean men take it as an appetizer broiled in sesame oil, sprinkled with salt and accompanied by a shot of liquor. They are caught in five-gallon barrels fitted with trap doors and baited with rotting fish, then loaded live onto jumbo jets and flown to South Korea.

HATCHETFISH The hatchetfish lives

in the midwaters of the ocean. It is so named because it is shaped like an axe blade. Its eyes, which focus like binoculars, point to the surface so it can look for prey or for a mate. They have evolved a defensive strategy called counterillumination (or counter-lighting). This involves the production of bioluminescent light by organs called photophores situated on the fish's belly and flanks. This light helps to camouflage its silhouette from predators lurking in the waters below.

Herrings, Pilchards, Sardines, Sprats, Kippers, Bloaters and Rollmops

The herring family consists of about 200 species, including the *pilchard*. The common herring is *Clupea harengus*. Herrings are found around the seas of western Europe and some are also found in the Pacific. Herring schools consist of millions of fish, near the surface of the water. The pilchard, *Sardinus pilchardus*, is found in European seas, and is only called a pilchard when it is an adult. The young fish (up to one year) are called *sardines*. Sardines were named after the Mediterranean island of Sardinia, where they once shoaled in abundance. A generalization is that if the fish is under 4 inches (10 cm) long it is classed as a sardine, and if larger is classed as a pilchard. The WHO standard for canned sardines cites 21 species that may be classed as sardines, and Fishbase, a comprehensive database of fish, lists at least six species called pilchard and over a dozen called sardine, and many more with the two basic names qualified by various adjectives. As a food, sardines are very rich in minerals, eaten grilled, pickled or smoked, and canned sardines are popular worldwide. The *sprat* is a genus of the herring family. Herring has been important as a food source for 5000 years, and can be eaten raw, fermented, pickled or cured by other techniques. The fish was sometimes known as 'one-eyed steak'. A *kipper* is a split and smoked herring, a *bloater* is a whole smoked herring, a *buckling* is a lightly smoked, dry salted whole herring and *red herring* is heavily smoked and highly salted. *Rollmops* and *bismarcks* are boned herrings marinaded in spiced vinegar. Rollmops are rolled with chopped onions, gherkins and peppercorns. Bismarcks are flat fillets covered with finely sliced onion.

HOLY MACKEREL! Mackerel is caught in huge quantities, but 'goes off' very quickly, especially in its summer '*runs*'. Thus it was the only fish that merchants were allowed to sell in the 17th century on the Holy Day, Sunday.

HOW TO MAKE A FISH SEASICK In 2009 an aquarium containing 49 fish was sent up in an aircraft that went into a steep dive, simulating the absence of gravity that astronauts experience in space flight. Dr Reinhold Hilbig of

Stuttgart stated that eight fish went around and around in circles. They *'lost their orientation. They completely lost their sense of balance, behaving like humans who get seasick.'*

JAWS – THE SHARK

Experts believe that it was a bull shark, not a great white, that was responsible for the attacks off New Jersey in 1916, which were the basis for the novel and film *Jaws*. The Nicaragua bull shark is extremely common in Lake Nicaragua and along Nicaragua's coasts, and is known variously across the world as the Zambesi shark, Van Rooyan's shark, Swan River whaler, square nosed shark, estuary whaler, freshwater whaler, slipway grey shark, shovel nose shark, Ganges River shark and the cub shark. It is the only shark to move from the sea into fresh water, and the males grow up to 7 feet (2.1 m) and weight 200 pounds (91 kg), while the females grow to 11.5 feet (3.5 m) and weigh 500 pounds (227 kg). It is the third most aggressive shark in the world, after the tiger shark and the great white shark.

LIONFISH AND SPECIES EXTINCTION

The lionfish uses a 'net' system to catch other fish, spreading its side fins, and driving the prey into a corner where it can catch them. It lives on coral reefs in the Indian and Pacific oceans, and is a dangerous predator because it has sharp spines that can inflict wounds on other fish and people. It can also inject poison into the wounds, killing or causing excruciating pain to humans. Released from aquaria, it has become an invasive species in the Caribbean and Atlantic in the last 20 years. It has become the only relatively large fish on Bahamian corals. The native fish have gone, failing to recognize it as a predator. It has targeted young fish and wiped out entire ecosystems. It has few natural predators in the Atlantic and has even been seen off Rhode Island in North America.

THE LIVING FOSSIL

The coelacanth is the 410 million-year-old 'living fossil' fish. It predates the dinosaurs by many millions of years and was once thought to have gone extinct with them, 65 million years ago. *Latimeria chalumnae* was rediscovered in 1938 off the coast of Africa. Another species, *Latimeria menadoensis*, was discovered off Indonesia in 1999. The coelacanth is sadly threatened with extinction, with an estimated population of just 500.

MAGNETIC NAVIGATION

Only recently has it been discovered that birds use the Earth's magnetic fields to help them navigate during migration, and even more recently it has been discovered that similar techniques are used by salmon and sharks (and also whales and turtles). The Earth's magnetic field shows slight variations, and each 'ocean' has a different magnetic 'signature'. Baby turtles have an inbuilt 'magnetic map' to guide them in their first trans-Atlantic navigation. It was thought that salmon could locate the place of their birth by 'smelling' the water through their gills, but this can only work over very short distances. Humans also have a 'magnetic' element in their brains, leading to the probability that it was an important sense that has been lost to us over millennia.

MEGALODON – 'BIGTOOTH' – THE MEGATOOTH SHARK

Relatively recent findings of the colossal squid, coelacanth and megamouth shark have led some people to hope that *Megalodon* may still exist in deep waters. The popular press in 1990 claimed that a giant 23-feet (7-m) long Pacific sleeper shark filmed off Japan, was the long-lost megalodon, the giant shark that lived from about 16 to 1.5 million years ago, and was the apex predator of its time. It is the biggest known carnivorous fish to have existed, and a new genus has been proposed for it. Fossil records reveal that the megalodon fed on large animals including the early whales. It is known principally from fossil teeth and a few fossilized vertebrae. As with other sharks, its skeleton was formed of cartilage, not bone, resulting in the poor fossil record. The teeth are in many ways similar to great white shark teeth, but are much larger and can measure more than 7 inches (18 cm) in length. The teeth indicate that this creature could actually have been over 56 feet long. Several whale vertebrae and bones have been found with clear signs of large bite marks made by the teeth that match those of megalodon. The teeth of the megalodon are serrated, which would help in tearing the flesh of prey with great efficiency. It appears that a megalodon would focus its attack on the middle of the body of a whale, crushing the ribs and lungs along with the pectoral fins, in a single attack.

MEGAMOUTH – THE NEW SHARK

The megamouth shark, *Megachasma pelagios*, is an extremely rare and unusual species of deepwater shark. Discovered only in 1976 by the US Navy, only a few have ever been seen, with only 44 specimens known to have been caught or sighted since then. It grows to 18 feet (5.5 m) in length and is distinctive for its large head with rubbery lips. It is so unlike any other type of shark that it is classified in its own family Megachasmidae, though it may belong in the family Cetorhinidae of which the basking shark is currently the sole member. Like the endangered whale shark and basking shark, it is a filter-feeding shark, swimming with its enormous mouth wide open, filtering water for plankton and jellyfish. The 41st specimen found, measuring 13 feet (4m) and weighing 1100 pounds (500 kg), was eaten by Philippine fishermen in 2009.

MUDSKIPPERS AS APHRODISIACS

The Malaysian newspaper *New Straits Times* reported in 2004 that *'the humble mudskipper, a type of fish, is making waves among people in a Kelantan village as an aphrodisiac – but only if swallowed live. Live mudskippers as long as 5cm are now part of the diet for Mr Zulkifli, 45, who eats four or five a day. His late father had 16 children… Every day, he swallows four or five of the little fishes, which he catches from nearby mangrove swamps. "My father must have*

known what he was talking about when he told me that they were good for the libido... Many are now firm believers and they scour the mangrove swamps here for mudskippers after work," he said. Associate Professor Sakri Ibrahim of Kolej Universiti Sains dan Teknologi Malaysia said mudskippers were known to be an aphrodisiac. "The testosterone level increases after live mudskippers are eaten. Higher production of testosterone will increase the male sex drive and improve infertility by increasing blood flow," he said, adding that more research was necessary.'

OARFISH – THE LONGEST BONY FISH
The oarfish, *Regalecus glesne*, is the longest bony fish in the world. It has a snakelike body with a wonderful red fin along its 20–40 feet (6–12 m) length, a horselike face with large saucer-like eyes and blue gills. The oarfish weighs upwards of 400 pounds (181 kg), dwells at depths of around 700 feet (213 m) and only comes to the surface when it is sick or injured. It appears like a prehistoric eel, measuring 4 feet (1.2 m) in circumference.

OCEAN SUNFISH – THE WORLD'S MOST FERTILE FISH
Mola mola is is one of strangest fish in the sea. It has an almost circular, flattened body. It weighs up to 2 tons (2030 kg) and is up to 10 feet (3 m) long, with the head accounting for almost a third of the whole body length. It is the ocean's most fertile fish, producing up to 300 million eggs at one single spawning, each measuring about 0.05 inches (1.3 mm) in diameter. It is the heaviest bony fish. Its name *mola* is Latin for *'millstone'*, which the fish resembles because of its grey color, rough texture, and rounded body.

Its common English name, *sunfish*, refers to the animal's habit of sunbathing at the surface of the water. The Portuguese, French, Spanish and German names all mean *'moon fish'*, in reference to its rounded shape. In German, the fish is also known as *Schwimmender Kopf*, or 'swimming head'.

ORNAMENTAL FISH COLLECTIONS
The Hawaii Division of Aquatic Resources estimates that the number of fish taken from coral reefs is as high as 15 million per year, so numbers of clown fish, yellow tangs, cleaner wrasse, Moorish idols, butterfly fish and all reef fish in the world are dropping. Aquarium harvesters also often destroy reef habitat when they collect bottom-dwelling invertebrates, such as the feather-duster worm, which lives attached to the sea floor. In 1998, the Hawaii state legislature passed a law because of conflicts among aquarium fish harvesters, commercial and subsistence fishers and environmentalists. It declared a minimum of 30 per cent of the west Hawaii Island coastline as Fish Replenishment Areas (FRAs) where aquarium fish collecting is prohibited. It is hoped that the fish will repopulate to past levels, but collectors will probably only move on to harvest other reefs across the world.

PACIFIC SLEEPER SHARK – THE FISH WHICH MAKES YOU DRUNK
Somniosus pacificus generally grows up to 14 feet (4.3 m), although it can possibly reach 23 feet (7 m) in length. It feeds on bottom-dwelling animals such as fish, octopus, squid, crab, carrion and harbour seals. The flesh contains high amounts of urea, so that if it is eaten, symptoms similar to

New Discoveries

Researchers on a joint NZ and Australian voyage aboard the Research Vessel *Tangaroa* in 2003 found new deep-sea sponges and a prickly shark, at depths of up to 1.3 miles (2 km). Many species new to science were recognized, including new sharks and rays, redfish, rattails and a range of invertebrates. The researchers also found a huge fossilized tooth of the extinct shark known as a megalodon (q.v.). The tooth had been lying undisturbed on the sea floor for millions of years. The strange characteristics of the new life-forms are adaptations to completely dark conditions, where the water pressure is hundreds of times greater than at the surface. In total, 500 species of fish and 1300 invertebrates were discovered. Some animals brought up were known only from fossils and had been presumed extinct. A scientist said *'Some animals are just a mouth and a soggy stomach. Whatever they bump into, they eat – even if it's twice their bodyweight – because it may be the only meal they get for months.'* Among the specimens caught were:

The Walking Coffinfish This flabby, bottom-dwelling fish can walk along the seafloor on short leg-like fins, with a glowing lure on its head to attract prey. These fish can swallow large amounts of water to inflate themselves, presumably making it harder for predators to bite into them, and they often come up in trawl nets swollen up into a ball.

Wonky-eyed Jewel Squid The left eye is always much larger than the right, and in some species is telescopic, while the smaller right eye is normal. The eye hangs at a 45° angle and is used to look up for passing prey. The normal right eye looks below for any signs of predators. The name jewel squid, comes from the scattering of small iridescent spots over the undersides of the body, head and limbs. When the squid is hanging at a 45° angle, all the light organs aim down, and produce just enough light to cancel out the silhouette of the squid against the weak light filtering down from the surface above. Jewel squid can float in mid-water by filling their soft flesh with pockets of ammonia solution that is less dense than seawater and cancels out the weight of their muscles. They make these solutions out of their body wastes – urine being used as a buoyancy aid.

The Prickly Shark Among the finds were two male specimens of an undescribed small species of shark. Known as spiked dogfish (genus *Squalus*), these two finds double the known number of specimens in the world. There are poison glands at the base of spines.

Pacific Spookfish *Rhinochimaera pacifica* is a strange cartilaginous fish which uses its long snout just like a metal detector to scan over the seafloor for the electrical impulses of its prey creatures which bury themselves in the muddy seafloor.

Two New Genera of Soft Coral
These are not just new species; they are so different from their nearest relatives that they are new genera as well.

Deep Sea Spiders These sea spiders can grow to 18 inches (46 cm) wide, and cannot fit all their organs in the body. They have hollow legs full of guts and ovaries and they wander around sucking the insides out of anemones. They are not related to terrestrial spiders.

Fangtooth This newly discovered creature has teeth longer than its head, the largest teeth of any fish in the ocean proportionate to body size. To avoid piercing its own brain when it shuts its mouth, its teeth fit into opposing sockets. The fangtooths' oversized teeth and mouths are a common feature among the miniature beasts of the deep (just like viperfishes, daggertooths, bristlemouths, barracudinas and anglerfishes). They are thought to confer a predatory advantage in poorly populated waters where anything encountered (even if it is larger than the fish) must be considered a possible meal.

Viperfish, Sloane's Fangfish
The viperfish has a hinged skull and is one of the most unusual-looking fish. *Chauliodus sloani* is recognized by its large mouth and sharp, fang-like teeth. Its fangs are so large that they will not fit inside the mouth, curving back very close to the fish's eyes. The viperfish is thought to use these sharp teeth to impale its victims by swimming at them at high speeds. The first vertebra, right behind the head, is actually designed to act as a shock absorber. It has a long dorsal spine that is tipped with a light-producing organ to attract its prey through bioluminescence, enabling it to flash the light on and off like a fishing lure to attract smaller fish. The unusually large teeth of the viperfish help it to grab hold of its prey as it hunts in the darkness. They have a hinged skull, which can be rotated up for swallowing unusually large prey, and

also have very large stomachs that allow them to stock up on food whenever it is plentiful. Viperfish have a very low basal metabolic rate, which means they can go for days without food, and this adaptation is probably a result of the scarcity of food in the deep sea.

drunkeness develop. It is one of only two creatures (along with the sperm whale) that feed on giant and colossal squid, as research on stomach contents has shown. Since the shark would have problems catching and devouring a huge squid, it is believed that it may feed on squid carcasses rather than live individuals.

PUFFER FISH, GLOBEFISH, FUGU AND POISONING Its four large teeth are sharp enough to sever a finger. Several species also have spikes sticking out of their skin. When it becomes alarmed, a puffer fish blows itself up into a big balloon using water, and makes a squeaky noise. It pumps water into its stomach, which expands to nearly 100 times its normal size. They can inflate themselves in this way because they have elastic skin and no ribs. The puffer's stomach is formed with pleats, and as it stretches, its spiny armour snaps into an upright position. Nothing can swallow it when it is blown up like a spiny balloon. There are about 120 species of puffer fish or blowfish, which are also called porcupine fish, globefish and fugu. They grow up to 20 inches (51 cm) long. Puffer fish live in the tropical and subtropical regions of the Atlantic, Indian and Pacific Oceans, blending in with the coral. They feed on molluscs and crustaceans. In Japan they are a delicacy after their poison has been removed, but eating them can still be fatal. About 100 Japanese diners die each year after eating puffer fish/fugu.

SALTWATER FISH IN FRESHWATER LAKES AND RIVERS Earthquakes, floods and volcanoes changed the drainage pattern of former saltwater lakes and rivers, so they evolved into freshwater features. Many saltwater fish did not survive the change but some did adapt and continue to thrive, such as the African cichlids in the African Great Lakes. They are considered freshwater fish and they do best in semi-salty water, but not in oceans. Lake Malawi, Lake Tanganyika, Lake Victoria and Lake Edwards were all inland seas about ten million years ago. These seas became landlocked due to the shifting in the Earth's crust which cut them off from the ocean. The cichlids have thus adapted to living with less salt in their habitat.

The source of the Amazon River is located in the Andes Mountains on the west side of South America. Although the Amazon drains into the Atlantic Ocean, it is also very close to the Pacific Ocean. Around 10 to 20 million years ago, a major geological event caused the waters of the Pacific Ocean to rise and flow into the Amazon and its tributaries. During this event, stingrays from the Pacific entered the Amazon. These species survived and adapted to freshwater. Today, the freshwater stingray is only found in the Amazon and its tributaries. When these fish breed, they migrate to the mouth of the Amazon to where the water is more salty.

At one time, Lake Taal was an arm of Balayan Bay in the Philippines. In the late 1600s, Taal volcano erupted and narrowed down the channel that connected Lake Taal to the ocean. The channel was renamed Pansipit River. Over time, the lake changed to freshwater. Lake Taal is known for its venomous black and white sea snake. This lake is also the place where the world's only freshwater sardine is found. Bull sharks were also found in Lake Taal but they became extinct due to overfishing. In Lake Bala in north Wales, the unique gwyniad is found, which is a kind of land-locked herring.

SEA TROUT – THE TASTIEST FISH?

Salmo trutta makes the journey downstream to feed in the sea for a year or so before returning to its river to breed. In Wales, they are called *'sewin'* and prized more than wild salmon. However, some unscrupulous marketers fatten rainbow trout on saltwater fish farms and sell them as sea trout.

SEX CHANGE AND REEF FISH

The majority of reef fish change sex at some point in their lives. Some species will begin life as males and switch to females (protandry), and others switch from female to male (protogyny). Further still, some will change sex in both directions, and others will be both sexes at the same time.

SHARKS AND SHARK ATTACKS

Of the 350 or so shark species, about 80 per cent grow to less than 5 feet (1.5 m), and are unlikely to hurt people. Only 32 species have been documented in attacks on humans, and an additional 36 species are considered potentially dangerous. The chances of being killed by a shark are 1 in 280,000,000, compared to 1 in 6700 of being killed in a car crash. Just three species have been identified repeatedly in attacks on humans: the great white, tiger and bull. All reach large sizes and eat prey such as marine mammals or sea turtles. More attacks on swimmers, free divers, scuba divers, surfers and boats have been reported for the great white shark than for any other species. However, some 80

Sea Horses

With its spiky, curled tail and tiny horse-like head, this fish has always enchanted people. Fishermen in ancient Rome believed that Neptune, the god of the ocean, charged through the water in a horse-drawn chariot. They believed that sea horses were the offspring of Neptune's horses. Today they face an uncertain future as fishermen are catching too many of them, and their undersea habitats are being destroyed. At least 20 million sea horses are taken from the ocean each year. More than 95 per cent of these are used for traditional medicines in Asian countries. They are usually dried and ground up into a powder used to treat such problems as asthma, throat infections, skin diseases and cuts. Sea horses are also bought for aquaria. Sea horse males, not females, give birth. During pregnancy, a pair of sea horses will dance together every day after dawn. They are able to change colours to camouflage themselves and hide from their enemies.

per cent of all shark attacks occur in the tropics and subtropics, where other shark species dominate and great white sharks are relatively rare. There seems to be an increase in shark attacks this millennium, caused possibly because overfishing has taken away food supplies, or because of the boom in seal populations found near tourist areas.

A triathlete was killed off San Diego in 2008, when a shark lifted him out of the water, retreating after a single bite. This is similar to their method of killing seals, and neoprene wetsuits can make human swimmers look like seals. A woman swimming with seals off California was attacked in 2003. Another problem is the rise in shark fishing for 'sport', or the new fashion for people to immerse themselves in metal cages lowered among the sharks. Sharks are drawn to the shores by the lure of baited meat and bloody offal thrown into the sea. This distorts the shark's natural feeding cycle and makes them associate human contact with food. Sharks attack around 50–75 people each year worldwide, causing perhaps 8–12 fatalities according to data compiled in the International Shark Attack File (ISAF). This is far less than the number of people killed each year by donkeys, elephants, bees, crocodiles, lightning or many other natural dangers. (The malaria-carrying mosquito is the deadliest danger to humans.) About 38 million sharks every year are killed through fishing activities. These fish are killed for their meat and fins, which are used for shark fin soup. Fishermen typically catch the sharks, de-fin them while alive and throw the bodies back into the ocean where they either drown or bleed to death.

SLOPEFISH CAMOUFLAGE It lives in the Pacific, and looks like a big pile of floating algae. Tiny crustaceans and fish think it is a safe place to live, but the slopefish eats them.

TELLING THE AGE OF A FISH Scale-less when born, fish grow scales under their outer layer of skin to provide water-proofing. As they age, most species add growth rings. Fish increase the size of their scales to cover their larger bodies. With a very old fish, however, there are fewer additions, making it difficult to pin-point its age. However, some fish, like catfish, do not have scales.

THE TILEFISH MYSTERY In the 1860s a new and valuable food fish was found in huge quantities off New England. A member of the cod family, the tilefish *(Lopholatilus chamaeleonticeps)* grew up to 50 pounds (23 kg) in weight, and was found at a depth of 50–100 fathoms (90–180 m) about 80 miles (130 km) offshore, preferring warm waters with temperatures of around 50° F (10° C). In 1882 ships reported seeing millions of dead tilefish covering the sea – an estimated 256,000 on each square mile of water. It was afterwards found that there had been an increase in the strength of the Arctic current flowing south, which had shifted the warmer Gulf Stream. For over 30 years, not a single tilefish was landed or seen. They eventually returned in 1915, but in nothing like their former numbers.

TOMMY FISH This is the nickname for great white sharks in South Africa. In 1852 the troopship HMS *Birkenhead* sank after hitting an uncharted rock. Only three lifeboats got away, and hundreds of soldiers died, many of them attacked by sharks. British soldiers were known as 'tommies' at this time. In all, 438 of the 693 people on board died. The order *'women and children first'* was given on this ship for the first time ever, and it came to be known as *'Birkenhead drill'*.

WEEDY SEADRAGON *Phyllopteryx taeniolatus*, the weedy seadragon or common seadragon, is a fish related to the seahorse and is found in south Australian waters. They are generally orange/red in colour with whitish spots and have leaf-like appendages so that they resemble seaweed floating on the bottom of the sea floor. Seadragons, sea horses and pipe fish are the only known species where the male carries the eggs.

THE WOLPHIN A false killer whale and a bottlenose dolphin have mated in captivity and produced fertile offspring. The resulting 'wolphin' is supposed to also occur in the wild, but there are certainly two in Hawaii Sea Life Park.

THE WORLD'S LARGEST FISH
The whale shark, *Rhincodon typus*, is a slow filter-feeder that is the largest living fish species. This distinctively marked shark is the only member of its genus *Rhincodon* and is believed to have originated about 60 million years ago. It can live to be 100–150 years old. It was first described in 1828, and is named because it is as large as a whale. A deity in a Vietnamese religion, the whale shark there is called *'Ca Ong'*, ('Sir Fish'). The largest specimen accurately recorded was caught in 1947 off Pakistan. It was 41.5 feet (12.6 m) long, weighed more than 21.2 tons, with a girth of 23 feet (7 m). A 40-feet (12.2-m) long specimen was caught near Bombay in 1983, with a mouth 4 feet (1.2 m) wide and fins over 6 feet (1.8 m) long. They can possibly grow up to 40 tons, and bigger specimens are thought to have existed that measured up to 60 feet (18.3 m) long. The whale shark is not an efficient swimmer since the entire body is used for swimming, which is unusual for a fish – most sharks propel themselves using the tail. Its average speed only measures around 3 mph (5 kph). Not sexually mature until they are 30 years old, they are seriously endangered because of the demand for shark fin soup.

THE WORLD'S SLOWEST FISH
The slowest fish in the world are sea horses. Smaller species like the dwarf sea horse, which is just 1.7 inches (4.3 cm) in length, probably never attain speeds of more than 5 feet (1.5 m) per hour. Instead of escaping from predators, it relies on camouflage to conceal itself. The smallest seahorses are only 1 inch (2.5 cm) from head to tail and the largest is 12 inches (30 cm). The female deposits eggs into a pouch on the male where they are fertilized, and the male gives birth from ten to 25 days later.

THE WORLD'S SMALLEST FISH
The world's smallest marine fish is the carnivorous dwarf goby of the Indo-Pacific, which has an average length of a third of an inch (8 mm).

Curious Ocean Creatures

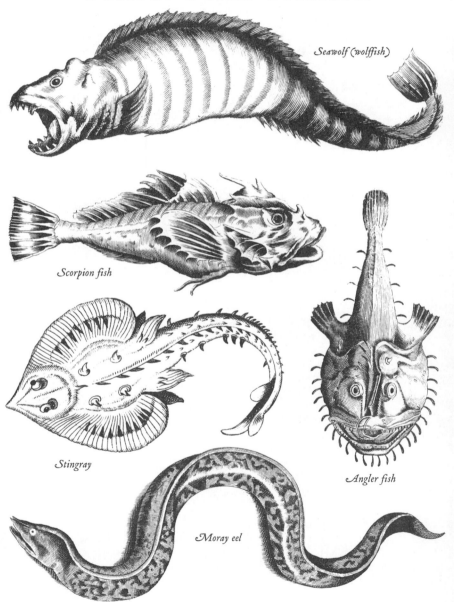

Seawolf (wolffish)

Scorpion fish

Stingray

Angler fish

Moray eel

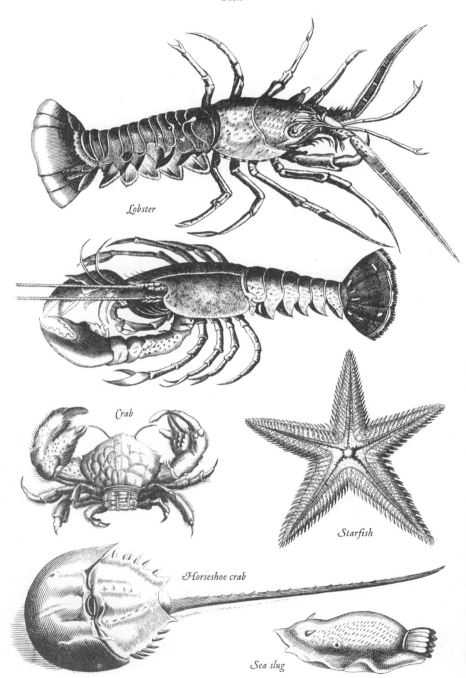

Lobster

Crab

Starfish

Horseshoe crab

Sea slug

MOLLUSCS AND
INVERTEBRATES

**BOX JELLYFISH – THE DEADLY
SEA WASP** *Chironex fleckeri*, the box
jellyfish, is the most venomous marine
creature, probably killing more people
than stonefish, sharks and crocodiles
combined. They are found in shallow
water at the edge of beaches in northern
Australian and in the Indo-Pacific region.
They feed on shrimps and often frequent
beaches that are attractive tourist spots to
humans. They simply wait for their prey
to bump into their tentacles. In each
corner of the box-shaped bell, sometimes
as large as a basketball, there is a bundle
of ten to 60 stinging tentacles, which can
extend for up to 18 feet (5.5 m). They
are armed with thousands of nematocysts,
or stinging cells. Certain chemicals on the
surface of fish, shellfish and humans
activate these, and even minimal contact
with tentacles can prove fatal for an
adult. You may see Australian lifeguards
wearing women's nylon tights over their
arms and on their legs to protect them
from the stings of these *'sea wasps'*. The
poison used to kill their prey works very
quickly in order to prevent a struggling
victim from thrashing at the jellyfish's
delicate tissues. These jellyfish kill four
times as many Australians as sharks do.
It is possible to survive a sting, but if you
have 10 feet (3 m) of tentacle wrapped

around you, you face a certain and
agonizing death. A massive series of stings
is said to cause the most excruciating
pain known to man. The *Chironex* venom
was found to be so strong in tests that,
even diluted 10,000 times, it was
powerful enough to kill small mammals.
The box jellyfish is able to see through
four eyes, one at the centre of each side
of its bell, but it is not known how the
animal processes the visual information
without a brain. Turtles are not affected
by their poisonous sting and eat them.
Good for turtles!

**THE BREADCRUMB SPONGE
AND OVER-COUNTING** In 2008,
it was discovered that almost 33 per cent
of all the named species in the seas had
been 'discovered' at least twice by
naturalists. The new *Census of Marine Life*
now lists 122,559 known species after
discounting a further 55,396 marine
species. The spiny dogfish *(Squalus
acanthias)* had 21 Latin names, a sea
squirt *(Cnemidocarpa verrucosa)* had 19
names and the basking shark *(Cetorhinus
maximus)* had 40 names. However, the
breadcrumb sponge *(Halichondria
panicea)* held the record, having been
named 56 times since its discovery in
1766. They smell 'like gunpowder' and

caused confusion to scientists as they come in many shapes and different colours, such as green and yellow.

COLOSSAL SQUID The giant squid is probably only exceeded in size by the colossal squid, *Mesonychoteuthis hamiltoni*. The colossal squid is sometimes called the Antarctic or giant cranch squid, and is the only member of its genus. Current estimates put its maximum size at 39–46 feet (12–14 m) long, based on analysis of smaller and immature specimens. Unlike the giant squid, whose tentacles are equipped with suckers lined with small teeth, the suckers at the tips of the colossal squid's tentacles have sharp swivelling hooks. Its body is wider and stouter, and therefore heavier, than that of the giant squid. Colossal squid are believed to have a much longer mantle than giant squid, although their tentacles are shorter. The squid is believed to hunt large fish like the Patagonian toothfish and also other squid, using bioluminescence in the deep ocean. The adult squid ranges at least to a depth of 7200 feet (2200 m). Colossal squid are a major prey item for bull sperm whales, and 14 per cent of the squid beaks found in the stomachs of these sperm whales are those of the colossal squid, which indicates that these creatures make up 77 per cent of the biomass consumed by these whales. Many sperm whales carry scars on their backs believed to be caused by the hooks of colossal squid. The species was first discovered in 1925 in the shape of two tentacles found in the stomach of a sperm whale. In 1981 a Russian trawler caught an immature female with a total length of 13 feet (4 m). In 2007 the largest ever specimen, measuring 33 feet (10 m) in length, was captured by a New Zealand fishing boat. It weighed 1091 pounds (495 kg). It was brought to the surface as it was feeding on a Patagonian toothfish that had been caught on a longline. It was enveloped in a net, hauled aboard and frozen in a slurry of ice and sea water. New Zealand scientists are now studying the squid. Its eye is 11 inches (27 cm) in diameter, but would have been 16 inches (40 cm) – beachball size – when alive. It uses six swivelling hooks mounted on the club-like ends of the tentacles to snare prey. Further up the tentacles there are up to 19 fixed points, to hold the victim, which would then be sliced into thumb-sized pieces to feed to the beaked mouth. Beaks discovered in the stomachs of whales have been far larger than this squid's, and so it is believed that they can grow to 1650 pounds (750 kg). A Japanese squid specialist, Tsunemi Kubodera, has tasted colossal squid and states that it is edible, but bitter. Not a lot of people know that squid have three hearts (and whales have three stomachs).

CORAL Coral structure and chemistry is similar to that of human bone. It has, therefore, been used successfully in bone grafts to help human bones to heal quickly and cleanly. There are two types of coral, hard coral and soft coral. Hard

corals (like *brain coral* and *elkhorn coral*) have hard, limestone skeletons which form the basis of coral reefs. Soft corals (like *sea fingers* and *sea whips*) do not build reefs. Coral reefs are found in warm, clear, shallow ocean habitats that are rich in marine life. The reef's massive structure is formed from coral polyps, tiny animals that live in colonies. When these polyps die, they leave behind a hard, stony, branching structure made of limestone. The coral provides shelter for many animals in this complex habitat, including sponges, nudibranchs, fish (like blacktip reef sharks, groupers, clown fish, eels, parrotfish, snapper, and scorpion fish), jellyfish, anemones, sea stars (including the destructive crown of thorns), crustaceans (like crabs, shrimps and lobsters), turtles, sea snakes, snails and molluscs (like octopuses, nautilus and clams). Seabirds also feast on a variety of coral reef animals.

CUTTLEFISH PATTERNS

The cuttlefish is smaller than the octopus, and uses ink dispersal and changing colour and patterns to protect itself. It has four different patterns. The first pattern of zebra stripes makes it harder to see when swimming. Its second pattern of suddenly turning light shades to dark confuses a predator which is not able to figure out where it vanished. Two large dark circular markings – like eyes – also makes the predator think that the cuttlefish is larger and more threatening than it really is. Lastly, its uneven pattern of spots makes the cuttlefish difficult to spot against a background of sand. It was formerly known as the skuttlefish, probably because it 'scuttled' away.

HENRY THE HEXAPUS

Henry, a six-legged octopus, is possibly the first such specimen recorded. He was found in 2008 in a lobster-pot off the island of Anglesey in Wales. Henry is now one of the star attractions of the Blackpool Sea Life aquarium.

OYSTERS AND BONE HEALING

A team at the Muséum National d'Histoire Naturelle in Paris has found that nacre (mother of pearl, found in oyster shells) speeds up the human bone-healing process. Broken human bones and cracked oyster shells both have the capacity for self-repair, and human trials have been conducted.

PISTOL SHRIMPS – LOUDER THAN GUNSHOTS

Native to the Mediterranean, but sometimes found in British waters, rival pistol shrimps compete by seeing who can make the loudest noise. They snap their claws together, with the impact creating a tiny stream of water that spurts out at 60 mph (97 kph). This creates a low pressure bubble in its wake, and when it collapses it makes a bang louder than a rocket launch or jet engine. For a fraction of a second, the temperature in the bubble reaches 8000° F/ 4427° C, and a flash of light lasts a billionth of a second. They are among the loudest marine animals, and the noise created by snapping their claws has been measured at 218 decibels. The level of noise created by the tiny shrimp is comparable to that made by a 40-ton sperm whale. The sudden noise is also used to stun their prey, such as tiny shrimps or plankton, for a second.

Giant Squid – the Mystery

The *Architeuthis dux* is also known as the Atlantic giant squid, and it is debatable as to whether the giant squid or colossal squid is the biggest invertebrate, because the giant squid has longer tentacles but the colossal squid has a bigger mantle. Specimens of the giant squid have measured up to 59 feet (18 m) in length and 1989 pounds (900 kg) in weight. A specimen found washed up in Canada in 1878 had eyes with an estimated diameter of 20 inches (51 cm), the largest eyes of any animal. Less than 50 giant squid have been found in the last 100 years, and it is believed that they live isolated lives. The only enemy of the giant squid seems to be the sperm whale (and possibly the sleeper shark). These whales seek out giant squid and dive to great depths to find them. Dead whales have been found washed up on beaches with large sucker marks on their bodies, apparently caused by squid trying to defend themselves. Scientists are even unsure if there are eight species of the genus *Architeuthis*, or just one. There have been claims reported of specimens measuring up to 66 feet (20 m). In 2004, researchers from the National Science Museum of Japan took the first images of a live giant squid in its natural habitat. Like all squid, a giant squid has a mantle (torso), eight arms and two longer tentacles. Their eyes are very large in order to detect light better (including bioluminescent light) which is scarce in deep water. They catch prey using the two longer tentacles, gripping it with serrated sucker rings on the ends. Then they bring it toward the powerful beak, and shred it with the radula (a tongue with small, file-like teeth) before it reaches the oesophagus.

SEA CUCUMBERS AND BRAIN IMPLANTS A new plastic material mimics a sea cucumber's ability to quickly change the density of its skin as a defence mechanism. When dry, the plastic is very hard and stiff. When it gets wet, it softens and becomes bendable. It is highly capable of switching back and forth very rapidly. Inspired by the chemical make-up of the sea cucumber's skin, the material is composed of a rubber-like base with fibres of cellulose attached to one another by hydrogen bonds which create a rigid surface when dry. When water is added to the system, the hydrogen bonds are broken and the material becomes flexible. One of the possible uses for this new plastic could be for brain implants during brain operations. It could also be used to treat Parkinson's disease or even spinal injuries or even be used in some parts of heart implants like pacemakers. Scientists have already found a gene in the sea cucumber that blocks the parasites that cause malaria.

SQUID ARE BRIGHTER THAN DOGS
This is according to the National Resource Centre for Cephalopods, in Galveston, Texas, which rates squid as the most intelligent of all invertebrates, and cleverer than the average dog. But can a squid return a stick?

TEREDOS WORM Not a worm, but a soft-shelled mollusc, *Teredo navalis* is the most common and dreaded attacker of ships' hulls in warm water. It can enter planks through tiny holes, and lay a million eggs a year. The young molluscs bore parallel to the surface, honeycombing planks with no outward signs of damage. Historically, ships were double-planked, with a layer of felt and pitch between them, to try to keep the teredos out, as well as other molluscs which attached themselves to the hull and proceeded to devour it layer by layer.

If possible, pirates tried to capture brigs and barquentines made from cedar-wood from the Bahamas, which was more resistant to the teredos worm. Vessels were double-hulled and then copper-bottomed to help keep the destructive mollusc at bay.

THE WALKING PLANT – THE SEA LILY
For many years this was thought to be an actual plant, but in fact it is a stalked echinoderm of the class Crinoidea. About 5000 fossil species are known, and about 80 modern species remain. Marine animals, like all echinoderms, they are largely restricted to fairly deep water, from about 35 to 1000 fathoms (64 to 1800 m). The sea lily, *Endoxocrinus parrae*, is closely related to the starfish, sea cucumber and sea urchin. With a ring of feathery fingers and a stalk 20 inches (51 cm) long, it resembles an ocean garden flower. Small organisms and particles are trapped in mucus in grooves located on the feathery, branching arms and are conveyed from there to the mouth. Unlike the free-swimming feather stars to which they are related, sea lilies were thought to remain 'permanently' attached to the ocean bottom by their stems. However, a 2005 video shows, for the first time, a sea lily crawling slowly across the ocean floor on its fingers, dragging its broken stem behind it. It was taken at a depth of 1300 feet (400 m) from a submersible close to Grand Bahama Island. It is thought that the sea lily makes its ocean floor movement to escape the attentions of sea urchins, which have been seen on the sea bed behind the travelling sea lilies, and are known to eat sea lily appendages. Sea lilies can travel hundreds of times more

The World's Largest Jellyfish

The Arctic lion's mane giant jellyfish *(Cyanea capillata)* is among the jellyfish that appeared in the oceans about 650 million years ago, long before the dinosaurs. All jellyfish are made up of 95 per cent water, have no bones or cartilage, no heart or blood, and no brain. Scientists are still unsure how a creature with eyes has no brain, which is where the processing of visual stimuli happens in most higher-order species. Lion's mane jellies can pursue and kill other jellies for food, and its sting can be fatal, causing paralysis of the breathing muscles so that a human would die from suffocation. The largest jellyfish ever found was a lion's mane that washed up dead on a beach – they can reach a diameter of up to 80 inches (200 cm), and their tentacles cover areas of up to 500 square yards (418 m²). To catch its prey the lion's mane slowly sinks with its tentacles spread like a great poisonous net. Nomurai jellyfish, found off Japan and Hawaii, are also claimed as the world's biggest jellyfish, weighing about 450 pounds (204 kg) and measuring about 7 feet (2.1 m) in diameter. During the summer of 2005, about 500 million Nomurai jellyfish floated like bloated white balloons daily into the Sea of Japan. Jellyfish blooms have recently become more common and bigger as a result of the killing of their predators and alterations in the chemical make-up of the seas.

quickly than previously thought possible, faster than a sea urchin. Prior to this recording, the fastest motion of a crinoid was known to be only 2 feet (61 cm) per hour. The 2005 recording showed a sea lily moving at up to an impressive 460 feet (140 m) per hour.

THE WORLD'S OLDEST ANIMAL – PART 1

A quahog clam dredged from icy Arctic waters in 2007 by climate researchers at Bangor University had 405 annual growth rings in its shell. The animal died when the researchers counted its rings. It was found off the coast of Iceland, 260 feet (79 m) down. There are probably many older clams, perhaps even up to 600 years old.

Scientists believe that the secret of the clams' longevity is a slowed cell-replacement process. It may not be the 'oldest animal', which is probably certain corals that grow together to form colonies, but the clam is the oldest non-colonial animal.

THE WORLD'S OLDEST ANIMAL – PART 2

Deep-sea *Leiopathes* black corals and *Gerardia* gold corals have been found at a depth of almost 1000 feet (300 m) in the waters off Hawaii. It is estimated that the black corals are 4000 years old, and the gold corals 2700 years old. Individual polyps can die back, but the stalk remains for the polyps to recolonize.

OTHER MARINE WONDERS

BIOLUMINESCENCE

Bioluminescence is light produced by a chemical reaction which originates in an organism, and can be encountered anytime and in any region or depth in the sea. We can see it often in the brilliantly luminescent bow wave or wake of a ship. The organisms causing this phenomenon are almost always dinoflagellates, single-cell algae, mechanically excited to produce light by the ship's passage or even by the movement of porpoises and smaller fish. Bioluminescent bacteria also occur nearly everywhere, probably most spectacularly as the rare *'milky sea'* phenomenon, particularly in the Indian Ocean, where mariners report steaming for hours through a sea glowing with a soft white light as far as the eye can see. In the deeper depths, the only light is produced by fish themselves. Some of them glow with a coating of luminous slime, and some have luminous bacteria on their bodies. Lantern-eye fishes have eye sockets in which live millions of bacteria that shine with their own light. Other fish have light organs, with lenses and reflectors. Squid communicate with each other using a wide spectrum of colours and postures, signalling at night with luminescent organs. Along with a variety of fish, squid possess luminescent bacteria housed in special sacs called light organs. The bacteria generate light with

an enzyme called luciferase (although not all the time). When the bacteria *Vibrio fischeri* swim free in sea water, their population densities are very low and they do not produce light. When they inhabit the light organs of squid, however, the squid cells nurture the bacteria and their population levels soar. When the bacteria are packed tight, they begin to secrete messenger proteins called autoinducers, which activate a protein to give off light.

'THE BLOB' AND THE BEIJING OLYMPICS

In May 2008, 20 square miles (52 km²)of seawater was covered with thick green algae, nicknamed 'the Blob', at Qindao, the sailing venue for the Olympics. Around 10,000 'volunteers' collected the slime around the clock from May to August with little appreciable improvement. Bulldozers and dump trucks were commandeered to clear beaches. Hundreds of soldiers were seen using their bare hands to gather up the algae, and by the end of July more than 170,000 tons had been cleared. A water pollution expert blamed the algae bloom on sewage and fertilizer.

HORSESHOE CRABS

Horseshoe crabs have existed in essentially the same form for the past 135 million years. Their blood provides a valuable medical test for the presence of toxins that cause septic shock, which previously led to half of all hospital-acquired infections and one-fifth of all hospital deaths.

HOW TO LIVE FOREVER

Become a sea anemone in your next life. With their bright colours and daisy-like shape, sea anemones are the flowers of the sea. Despite their beauty, they are predatory animals, using their stinging tentacles to catch their prey. Sea anemones are grouped in the class Anthozoa, with corals. They form polyps and belong to the same phylum as the jellyfish. There are 6500 species. Sea anemones are anecdotally very long-lived, reaching 60–80 years or more. Like other cnidarians, they do not age, meaning they have the potential to live indefinitely, but most fall foul to predators before old age is reached.

KELP Rockfish and sea otters, among others, find shelter in the rich coastal kelp forests. Giant kelp, a type of algae, is the largest plant in the ocean reaching nearly 200 feet (61 m) in length. Like fungus, kelp is neither plant nor animal. Giant kelp grows at up to 2 feet (61 cm) per day, making it the fastest-growing organism on earth, and it can grow 100 feet (30 m) in a single year. Kelp is used for making textiles, gunpowder, soap, jelly, glass, ice-cream and toothpaste.

'THE NEPTUNE PLANT – A BOTANICAL WONDER OF NATURE'

This is the advertising platform for decorative 'indoor plants' known as 'air ferns', or for underwater decorations for aquaria. The promotional blurb states *'it retains its luminous green hue for years without watering'*. They are actually collected as a by-product by trawlers in the North Sea. The 'plant' is composed of a species of marine animal called *Sertularia argentea*, also known as the *'sea fir'*. The so-called 'ferns' are dead and dried colonies of hydrozoans, colonies of marine hydroids. Hydroids are related to corals and jellyfish. The silvery 'foliage' is often dyed green to make it look more like a conventional houseplant. In the advertising it was claimed that scientists were baffled that there was no name for the 'plant', but as everyone knows the Neptune plant is the species *Sertularia argentea* of the genus *Sertularia* of the family *Sertulariidae* of the order *Leptothecata* of the class *Hydrozoa* of the phylum *Cnideria* of the kingdom *Animalia*.

ORANGE SEASLUG

It lives on coral reefs, and its bright colour serves as a warning to fish. It likes to eat the stinging tentacles of the sea anemone, coating them with special mucus so they can be safely swallowed. Orange seaslugs taste so bad that predators unwise enough to try one spit it out immediately.

RED TIDE – HARMFUL ALGAE BLOOM

Most species of algae or phytoplankton are not harmful and serve as the energy producers at the base of the food chain, without which higher life on this planet would not exist. Sometimes, however, algae grow very fast or 'bloom' and accumulate into dense, visible patches near the surface of the water. *Red tide* is a common name for such a phenomenon, where certain phytoplankton species contain pigments and bloom to discolour seawater. Blooms can appear greenish, brown, and even reddish-orange depending upon the type of organism, the type of water, and the concentration of the organisms. Blooms are not associated with tides and not usually harmful. However, a small number of species of algae produce potent neurotoxins that can be transferred through the food chain, where they affect and can kill the higher forms of life such as zooplankton, shellfish, fish, birds, marine mammals, and even humans that feed either directly or indirectly on them. Scientists now prefer the term HAB (harmful algae bloom) to refer to bloom phenomena that contain toxins or cause negative impacts. When there is a red tide, or other blooms of noxious plankton, or when there are high concentrations of bacteria in the water from sewage run-off, bivalves such as clams and mussels can temporarily become very problematic as a food source. This is because bivalves are filter-feeders, and thus they can concentrate toxins from floating micro-organisms within their tissues.

SARGASSO SEA – THE DUNGEON OF LOST SOULS

East of the Bahamas, an extremely strong eddy causes the Sargasso weed or sargassum *(Fucus natans)* to collect in vast quantities on the surface. Northeast of Bermuda, the sea depth ranges from 1 mile to 4 miles (1.6 to 6.4 km). The 'sea' here is a large pool of very warm water, rotating clockwise very slowly.

Both the Equatorial Current and the Gulf Stream Current push warm water past it, it rarely rains and the weather, like the water, remains very calm. It is also very humid and often extremely hot. It has been likened to a desert in the middle of the ocean, and the lack of rainfall makes the water very saline. There are millions of clumps of sargassum, mainly accumulating towards the centre of the sea, and with little current and little wind, sailing ships could be trapped here for long periods. Becalmed ships ran out of drinking water. Records show that the Spanish threw their war-horses over the side to conserve precious supplies of water. Hence the area became known as the *'Horse Latitudes'*. The ghosts of these horses and lost ships and sailors were thought to inhabit the area. Other names for the area were *'The Doldrums'*, *'The Sea of Berries'* and *'The Dungeon of the Lost Souls'*. Columbus mentioned the difficulty of sailing through these waters as the weeds fouled his ships. He noted strange effects of light on the water (due to its salinity) and that there were extreme compass variations. His sailors implored him to return home. The phenomenon was magnetic variation.

SEA BUTTERFLIES – THE CHIPS OF THE SEA

Thecosomata, or *'flapping snails'*, feed on plankton. Around the size of a lentil, they are eaten by a wide variety of fish, which are in turn consumed. They have been dubbed the *'potato chip'* of the ocean. Half of the carbon dioxide in the Pacific is estimated to have come from human activity. As the ocean thus becomes more acidic and warmer, these snails are not able to survive, as they cannot build up calcium for their shells. It is possible that by 2050 they may not be able to make a shell anymore, and the impact on the food chain will be catastrophic.

THE SEA-FIREFLY A species of chemiluminous myodocopids named *Vargula hilgendorfii* is one of the most famous luminous species. A class of crustacean, they live in the sea around Japan. Nocturnal, by day they hide in the sand. They are not only scavengers on dead meat, but also predators, eating sandworms. Their 'courtship dance' is seen as a spiral rotation of blue light, caused by the chemical reaction of the ejection of enzyme and substrate from their upper lips.

SEAGRASSES Seagrasses are a critical nursery, forming breeding and feeding habitats for many animals including hundreds of fish species, western rock lobsters, green sea turtles and dugongs. Australia has 30 of the world's 58 species of seagrass. The destruction of seagrass by increasing sedimentation and high levels of nutrients is one of the biggest problems facing the Australian marine environment. Across the world seagrasses and coral, the vital shelters for young fish, are being destroyed by being ripped up by giant fishery vessels.

TROPICAL CONE SNAILS – THE HOPE FOR HEALTH? There are around 500 species of the cone snail. They live in warm and tropical climates, and are known for their beauty as well as for their biochemistry, their exquisitely patterned shells being collected and sold as art objects. An £8 million study is ongoing at Strathclyde University into the

Sea Snakes – the Most Deadly Snake Venom

Sea snakes are the most numerous and have the widest distribution of all the Earth's venomous reptiles. They are found in tropical and subtropical marine areas in the Indian Ocean and the Pacific. They frequent shallow waters along the coasts, in rivers and estuaries and around islands. Sea snakes are most closely related to terrestrial elapid snakes, which are some of the most venomous snakes in the world (such as the Australian venomous snakes, cobras, mambas, kraits and coral snakes). There are

scientific descriptions of over 60 species of sea snakes. Scientific research using the measuring unit of 'LD50' shows that sea snakes have the most deadly venom per unit found in any snakes.

Turtles

A common part of sailors' diet in the Americas, they could be kept alive on ships for fairly long periods by flipping them over on their backs, and keeping them covered from the heat and doused with water. They were the most common form of meat for ships in port, Governor Molesworth writing in 1684 of Port Royal, that it *'is what masters of ships chiefly feed their men in port, and I believe that nearly 2000 people, black and white, feed on it daily at Palisadoes Point, to say nothing of what is sent inland.'* The extent of the turtle hunting of the time is revealed by today's maps, with Turtuguero in Costa Rica, Isla la Tortuga off Venezuela (Salt Tortuga), Dry Tortugas off the Florida Keys, Île de la Tortue off Haiti (Tortuga) and Green Turtle Cay in the Bahamas, etc.

strong venom of the tropical cone snail, which it injects into its prey through a harpoon-like tooth. It is believed that the poison, which contains more than 100 different peptides and proteins, may be a source of new antibiotics or anti-inflammatory formulations. Some have already been found to be beneficial to humans, e.g. one is already being marketed as a painkiller, but most have never been investigated. The Cone Snail Genome Project for Health, a European project involving 13 countries, is examining their potential for solving health problems such as obesity, asthma, arthritis, diabetes, hypertension and strokes. Despite the benefits that these snails offer humans, little effort has been spent thus far to protect them. Tropical cone snails face mounting threats and numbers are dropping dramatically. They live in the shallower waters of reefs or mangrove forests, both of which are being destroyed by human activity. Most medical research has focused only on three of the 500 species, so the untapped pharmaceutical potential of the remaining species is immense. Scientists are asking that tropical cone snails should now be protected under the Convention on International Trade in Endangered Species (CITES).

WHALE FALL AND THE WORLD'S NEWEST ANEMONE

When a whale dies, its carcass sinks to the bottom of the ocean. Scientists call this a *'whale fall'*. In May 2007, researchers found a new species of sea anemone living in the carcass of a dead whale, in the depths of the Pacific. It has been named *Anthosactis pearseae*, and is about the size of a human molar tooth. While the flesh of a dead whale decomposes within weeks, their bones can last anywhere from 60 to 100 years.

CHAPTER 9

The Ocean Environment

SEAS AND OCEANS, RACES AND RECORDS

THE ABYSS AND 'BLACK SMOKERS' The abyss is another term for the almost unexplored 'deep sea', away from coastal waters. The abyss is miles deep, beyond the continental shelves which spread out underwater next to continents. Remotely operated submersible vehicles have discovered new species of giant tube worms, clams and shrimp, next to hydrothermal *'black smoker'* vents in this deep sea environment. These species subsist on primitive 'archaea', which are organisms living off dissolved chemicals coming up in these hot vents from the seafloor. A water temperature of 760° F (404° C) has been measured at one hydrothermal vent. Seawater is warmed on the surface of the oceans. It becomes dense with salts and the debris of assorted organisms and sinks, being replaced by upwelling cold water. The heat is trapped in the deep sea, and may take centuries to return again to the surface. This will contribute to global warming in years to come. Furthermore, marine organisms such as plankton account for half of all the carbon dioxide-absorbing photosynthesis on the planet. Much of the carbon trapped by sea life near the surface drops to the seafloor and is buried there, again for centuries. So as well as a heat sink, the abyss acts as a huge carbon dioxide sink. Without the deep seas, CO_2 levels would increase faster in the atmosphere, so accelerating global warming. The more phytoplankton there are, the greater the absorption of this greenhouse gas from the atmosphere, so it is vital that the oceans are kept as a clean environment for plankton.

THE ADMIRAL'S CUP This is the unofficial world championship of offshore yacht racing, sailed at Cowes, Isle of Wight, every other year since 1957.

THE AMAZON AND THE DREADED POROROCA The mighty Amazon is so important a river, draining an area bigger than the USA, and with its source 4000 miles (6440 km) from the ocean, that it must be included in this book. The city of Manaus is 1000 miles (1600 km) from the ocean. There the Amazon is 80 miles (129 km) wide, and at its mouth it is 280 miles (450 km) wide, where Marajo Island is bigger than Switzerland. According to one estimate, the river carries enough mud into the southern Atlantic every year to build an island 480 miles (772 km) by 480 miles in area and 5000 feet (1524 m) high off the seabed. In the dry season its current runs at 6 knots (7 mph/11 kph), but when the Sun moves over the Andes, the ice-melt causes its speed to rise to 15 knots (17 mph/28 kph), and the river level to rise 35 feet (11 m). An area of rainforest bigger than the Mediterranean is flooded. The volume of this yellow water is so great that it holds back the ocean tide until about 15 minutes before the full Moon, or spring, tides. Then the sea overcomes the river, and the *Pororoca*, a vertical wall of water 15 feet (4.6 m) high, roars up the northern mouth of the Amazon. No small boat can survive its overwhelming power.

THE AMERICA'S CUP – THE OLDEST INTERNATIONAL SPORTING EVENT

In 1851, the schooner *America* won the Hundred Guineas Cup, defeating 15 British yachts sailing around the Isle of Wight. The race is held on a 24-mile (39-km) triangular course, off the defending nation's coast. For 132 years it was held by the New York City Yacht Club, and the holders are all from that club unless noted otherwise: 1851 *America*; 1870 *Magic*; 1871 *Columbia*; 1876 *Madeleine*; 1881 *Mischief*; 1885 *Puritan*; 1886 *Mayflower*; 1887 *Volunteer*; 1893 *Vigilant*; 1895 *Defender*; 1899 *Columbia*; 1901 *Columbia*; 1903 *Reliance*; 1920 *Resolute*; 1930 *Enterprise*; 1934 *Rainbow*; 1937 *Ranger*; 1958 *Columbia*; 1962 *Weatherly*; 1964 *Constellation*; 1967 *Intrepid*; 1970

Intrepid; 1974 *Courageous*; 1977 *Courageous*; 1980 *Freedom*; 1983 *Liberty*; 1987 *Kookaburra III* (Perth, Australia); 1988 *Stars and Stripes* (San Diego); 1992 *America* (San Diego); 1995 *Young America* (San Diego); 2000 *Team New Zealand* (NZ); 2003 *Team New Zealand* (NZ); 2007 *Alinghi* (Geneva, Switzerland). Switzerland is land-locked, but has naval patrol boats on Lake Geneva.

THE ANTARCTIC OCEAN

Its ice cap contains 7.1 million cubic miles (30 million km³) of water, about 70 per cent of the world's total of fresh water, and about 90 per cent of its ice. The average thickness of its ice is 1.5 miles (2.4 km), and 3 miles (4.8 km) as its thickest. Antarctica has as much ice as the Atlantic Ocean has water. The Antarctic ice sheet that forms and melts over the ocean each year is nearly twice the size of the United States. The continent is made up of 98 per cent ice and 2 per cent barren rock. If the West Antarctic Ice Sheet melted, global sea levels would rise 15–20 feet (4.6–6 m). If the East melted as well, levels would rise 200 feet (60 m).

ARCHAEA – THE 'ANCIENT THINGS'

These single-celled micro-organisms evolved differently to bacteria, and they are found in extremely cold places like the black ocean depths and also in waters with temperatures of up to 212° F (100° C). Their Greek name means 'ancient things'. Some can live in acids and in other extreme environments next to 'black smokers'.

THE ARCTIC OCEAN

The Arctic is the smallest ocean, containing only 1 per cent of the Earth's seawater. The average thickness of its ice sheet is about 9 to 10 feet (c.3 m), rising in some places to 65 feet (20 m). Seventy-one per cent of the Earth's surface is covered by the seas, but if all ice in the Arctic and Antarctic melted, the sea level would rise by over 500 feet (150 m). Then, up to 90 per cent of the Earth's surface would be inundated. Arctic waters are frozen for ten months of the year, with up to 19 inches (48 cm) of ice covering the ocean. The Arctic produces 10,000 to 50,000 icebergs annually.

'AROUND ALONE' This was formerly the 'BOC Challenge', and now the 'Velux 5 Oceans Challenge', a single-handed round-the-world sailing race held every four years. In 2006 Bernard Stamm of Switzerland smashed the record by circumnavigating in 103 days. The course is 30,140 nautical miles (55,820 km) long.

THE ATLANTIC OCEAN – HEAVY WATER The average depth of the Atlantic Ocean, without its adjacent seas, is 12,880 feet (3743 m). Its greatest depth, 28,231 feet (8605 m) – over five miles – is in the Puerto Rico Trench. It is the world's second largest ocean after the Pacific, bigger that the Indian, Southern and Arctic. According to the CIA, its important strategic access waterways are: the Kiel Canal (Germany), Oresund (Denmark–Sweden), Bosporus (Turkey), Strait of Gibraltar (Morocco–Spain), and the Saint Lawrence Seaway (Canada–US). Atlantic sea water is heavier than Pacific Ocean sea water due to its higher salt content.

BAR This is shallow water caused by wave and tide action, usually parallel to the shore, where the mud or sand is higher than usual. Bars are sometimes exposed at low tides, and marked with buoys in navigational waters.

THE BERING SEA AND CLIMATE CHANGE In comparison to other oceans, the Bering Sea is showing the most dramatic effects of climate changes. It produces 50 per cent of all fish caught in America, and 33 per cent of all fish caught worldwide. Studies and experiments are suggesting that the ecosystem will in future support less fish than what is currently being harvested, such as pollock and hake. As the sea warms, marine mammals and birds here are experiencing mass 'die offs', and there are many invasive species. The Bering Sea has been so productive thanks to diatoms, a large type of phytoplankton. Diatoms are eaten by large zooplankton, which in turn are eaten by large fish. As phytoplankton becomes scarcer, the zooplankton also becomes scarcer, and all the sea creatures that eat the diatoms and zooplankton (and their predators) are suffering from lack of food.

THE BLUE RIBAND This is the title given to the fastest passenger liner in the North Atlantic. It was first bestowed on the English ship *Sirius* in 1838, sailing at 8.03 knots. Other notable westbound passage holders are: 1843 *Great Western* (10.03 knots); 1850 *Asia* (12.25); 1872 *Adriatic* (14.53); 1883 *Alaska* (17.05); 1892 *City of Paris* (20.70); 1909 *Lusitania* (25.65); 1933 *Europa* (27.92); 1937 *Normandie* (30.58); 1938 *Queen Mary* (30.99) and 1952 *United States* (34.51). In 1856 the SS *Persia*, a Cunard ship, held the record of 9 days, 1 hour, and 45 minutes, consuming no less than 143 tons of coal a day.

THE CASPIAN SEA – THE INLAND LAKE WITH SALT WATER

This is the world's largest lake, between Iran and Russia, with 18,713 cubic miles (80,000 km³) of fresh water. Its water is slightly saline, with a third of the salt content of oceanic water. It is a remnant of an ancient ocean, named Tethys, which for about 50–60 million years connected the Atlantic and the Pacific.

CHANNEL Water deep enough for navigation, today usually indicated by buoys. A channel is also the deepest part of a strait or bay through which the main current flows.

CHANNEL FEVER The sense of euphoria felt by English seamen when entering the English Channel after a long voyage. Nowadays the term is used to describe the state of the crew when on any homeward stretch.

THE DEAD SEA This inland sea lies 1312 feet (400 m) below sea level, and its shores are the lowest land point in the world. Only bacteria can survive in its waters. It is the saltiest sea in the world, but is rapidly shrinking because its source waters are being used for agriculture and drinking. The average ocean water is 6 per cent salts, compared to the Dead Sea's 25 per cent. Its water feels oily to the skin because of the calcium content, and one tablespoon will make the drinker violently sick because of its high concentration of chloride of magnesium. It used to stretch another 120 miles (193 km) north, and was higher than the Mediterranean, supporting all types of life, but earthquakes and gradual silting have filled it up. The ruins of Sodom and Gomorrah are near its shores. To the Israelis, it is 'The Sea of Lot', and to the Arabs 'The Stinking Sea'.

Coastlines

COASTLINES The total length of the world's coastlines is about 315,000 miles (507,000 km), enough to circle the equator 12 times. Canada has the longest coastline, at 125,600 miles (202,128 km), with its islands dramatically increasing the length. The next longest coastlines are those of Indonesia (approximately 34,000 miles/54,700 km), Japan (18,500 miles/30,000 km), Australia (16,000 miles/25,700 km) and the USA (12,400 miles/20,000 km). As coastal zones become more and more crowded, the quality of coastal water is generally getting poorer, wildlife is being displaced and the shorelines are eroding. Around 60 per cent of the Pacific and 35 per cent of the Atlantic Coast shoreline are vanishing at a rate of around 3 feet (1 m) every year. More than half the world's population, over 3 billion people, live within 60 miles (100 km) of the coast, and rapid urbanization is leading to the creation of coastal mega-cities. (Thirteen of the world's 15 largest cities are located on or near the coast.)

THE DEEPEST OCEAN The lowest known point on Earth, called the Challenger Deep, is 35,802 feet (10,912 m/6.86 miles) deep, in the Marianas Trench in the western Pacific. If Mount Everest was placed at the bottom of the trench, there would still be over a mile of sea above its peak. The pressure there is over 8 tons per square inch.

THE FASTNET RACE This is one of the classic offshore races, taking place every two years over a course of 608 miles (978 km). The race starts off Cowes on the Isle of Wight, rounds the Fastnet Rock off the southwest coast of Ireland and then finishes at Plymouth after passing south of the Isles of Scilly. The first Fastnet Race, with only seven entries, was held in 1925. A severe storm during 1979 resulted in the deaths of 15 competitors. This led to a major overhaul of the rules and the equipment required for the competition. The start of the 2007 race was postponed by 25 hours due to a severe weather warning. During the race, 207 boats of the 271-strong field retired and five men died. Despite the conditions, Mike Slade's *Icap Leopard 3* set a new elapsed time record of 44 hours 18 minutes, taking almost nine hours off the previous record set in 1999. Ger O'Rourke's *Chieftain* was the overall winner on corrected time.

FOUR OCEANS The four large bodies of water covering most of the surface of the planet: the Atlantic Ocean, the Pacific Ocean, the Indian Ocean and the Arctic Ocean. The Southern Ocean is now usually classed as the 'Fifth Ocean' and in 2005 the International Hydrographic Survey assigned some of the southern Atlantic Ocean into the Southern Ocean.

GOLD AND POISON GAS Apart from the millions of tons of gold suspended in seawater, there are huge gold deposits in the sea bed, for instance off Tonga. However, they are about 1 mile (1.6 km) underwater. To help pay the German reparations after the First World War, Fritz Haber, Head of the Kaiser Wilhelm Institute in Berlin, tried for six years to obtain gold from seawater. Previously, in 1910, he had invented a process for producing ammonia from nitrogen and hydrogen, effectively killing off the guano trade. He then was in charge of the production of poison gas and oversaw its use at the battlefield at Ypres, where thousands died or were maimed. His wife, distraught, killed herself with his revolver. In 1918, the Allies wanted him tried as a war criminal, but later in that year he was awarded the Nobel Prize for Chemistry.

GOLD CONTENT OF THE OCEANS Estimates of the weight of the gold suspended in the world's seawater vary from 20 million tons to 40 times as much. If the latter figure is correct, each of the 6.6 billion people on Earth could theoretically be allotted about 270 pounds (122 kg) of gold, which at $8000 per pound = over $2 million each. So everyone is a millionaire!

THE GRAND BANKS These are the shallow fishing grounds under Canadian jurisdiction, southeast of Newfoundland, around 300 miles (480 km) long by 300 miles (480 km) wide. Overfishing from the 1990s has led to a serious decline in fish stocks in what were one of the most productive fishing grounds in the world.

GREEN WATER Not a pleasant experience on a boat. It is when water on a deck is so deep that it appears green, as the sea is not broken up into spray when it comes over the deck in foul weather.

GROUNDSWELL This name for a build-up of public opinion has a maritime origin. The ground was always the lowest point, so at sea this meant the bottom of ocean. A groundswell was used to describe deep ocean wave movement caused by a distant storm or underwater earthquake or tremor. It often, therefore, preceded a storm.

THE HIGH SEAS These are legally the seas beyond any nation's declared territorial waters (usually 12 nautical miles/22 km) and exclusive economic zone (EEZ, usually 200 nautical miles/ 370 km). They cover almost 50 per cent of the Earth's surface, but are the least protected part of the world. Although there are some treaties that protect ocean-going species such as whales, as well as some fisheries agreements, there are no protected areas in the high seas. In fact, less than 0.5 per cent of marine habitats are protected, compared with 11.5 per cent of global land area.

LANDLOCKED NATIONS Only 40 of the world's 200 nations are landlocked, the largest being Mongolia, whose capital Ulan Bator is 900 miles (1450 km) from the coast. However, there are around 300 ships flying Mongolian flags. Ships used for drug smuggling previously sailed under the North Korean, then under Cambodian flags, but when associated with cocaine, they were re-flagged under Mongolian Maritime Law. You could not make this up.

LARGEST ECONOMIC EXCLUSION ZONE Although Canada has the longest coastline, Australia has the largest EEZ. It is responsible for 4.2 million square miles (11 million km^2) of ocean within its Exclusive Economic Zone of 200 nautical miles (370 km). (It shares maritime borders with five other nations: Indonesia, Papua New Guinea, Solomon Islands, New Zealand and France.)

THE MAGNETIC OCEANS
In 2009, Professor Gregory Ryskin of Northwestern University, Illinois published research suggesting that Earth's magnetism is linked to ocean currents. Salt in seawater allows it to conduct electricity, meaning it generates electrical and magnetic energy as it moves. Thus he posits that Earth's magnetic field is generated by oceanic currents, rather than molten metals at its core. Without a magnetic field, electronics would be damaged and solar radiation would wipe away the atmosphere, so if he is correct any significant changes in ocean currents could prove disastrous to the health of the planet.

MASS EXTINCTION IN THE SEAS

More than 250 million years ago the greatest extinction in the Earth's history occurred, which wiped out up to 96 per cent of all marine species and 70 per cent of land species. Many scientists believe that we are currently in the grip of a 'Sixth Mass Extinction' based on evidence of the accelerating loss of flora and fauna in the last 100 years.

MEAN SEA LEVEL

A tidal observatory in Newlyn, Cornwall, was established to determine the mean sea level to be used to calculate sea level measurements across the UK. This mean (the arithmetic average of a set of values) sea level was calculated between 1915 and 1921, when the height of the water was measured every 15 minutes on every day and night during these six years. The mean sea level was thus established and marked by a brass bolt set into the ground.

MOUNTAINS OF THE SEAS

The tallest mountain in the world is not Mt Everest (29,029 feet/8848 m), but Mauna Kea (White Mountain) volcano on the island of Hawaii. It rises 33,480 feet (10,205 m) from the ocean floor, but only 13,796 feet (4205 m) is above sea level. The Earth's longest mountain range is the Mid-Ocean Ridge which is more than 31,000 miles (50,000 km) in length, circling the Earth from the Arctic Ocean to the Atlantic, skirting Africa, Asia and Australia, and traversing the Pacific to the west coast of North America. It is four times longer than the Andes, Rockies, and Himalayas combined.

NARROW SEAS

This term is usually employed for restricted waters such as the English Channel or St George's (Irish) Channel. In the last 50 years, particularly with reference to the Second World War, it has meant the English Channel and the southern half of the North Sea.

NEAP TIDES

Tides when the Moon is in the second and last quarter. They are not so high, low or swift as Spring tides. *'A ship is beneaped'* when the water does not flow high enough to bring it off the sea ground, or out of a dock, or over a bar.

OCEAN WATER FACTS

The oceans cover about 71 per cent of Earth's surface, 140 million square miles (363 million km^2), and about 97 per cent of all of the Earth's water is saltwater. (Less than 1 per cent is fresh water, and 2–3 per cent is contained in glaciers and ice caps.) The top 10 feet (3 m) of the ocean hold as much heat as our entire atmosphere, and more than 90 per cent of the volume of the oceans is the 'deep sea', also known as the abyss. The average depth is 12,200 feet (3718 m/2.5 miles). Oxygen and hydrogen make up 96.5 per cent of ocean water. The rest consists of dissolved elements, such as chlorine, sodium and other salts. The oceans contain 99 per cent of the living space on the planet, and around 80 per cent of all life on Earth is found under the surface. A wine glass of seawater may contain tens of thousands of zooplankton, hundreds of thousands of phytoplankton and millions of bacteria. The seas absorb up to 50 per

Oceans and Seas of the World

Ocean/Sea	Area in square miles (km²)	Average depth in feet (m)	Greatest depth in feet (m)
Pacific Ocean	60,060,700 (155,556,500)	13,215 (4028)	36,198 (11,033)
Atlantic Ocean	29,637,900 (76,761,800)	12,880 (3926)	30,246 (9219)
Indian Ocean	26,469,500 (68,555,690)	13,002 (3963)	24,460 (7455)
Southern Ocean	7,848,300 (20,327,000)	14,400 (4500)	23,736 (7235)
Arctic Ocean	5,427,000 (14,056,000)	3953 (1205)	18,456 (5625)
Mediterranean Sea	1,144,800 (2,965,000)	4688 (1430)	15,197 (4632)
Caribbean Sea	1,049,500 (2,718,000)	8685 (2647)	22,788 (6946)
South China Sea	895,400 (2,319,000)	5419 (1652)	16,456 (5016)
Bering Sea	884,900 (2,291,900)	5075 (1547)	15,659 (4773)
Gulf of Mexico	615,000 (1,592,850)	4874 (1485)	12,425 (3787)
Okhotsk Sea	613,800 (1,590,000)	2749 (838)	12,001 (3658)
East China Sea	482,300 (1,249,150)	617 (188)	9126 (2782)
Hudson Bay	475,800 (1,232,300)	420 (128)	600 (183)
Japan Sea	389,100 (1,007,800)	4429 (1350)	12,276 (3742)
Andaman Sea	308,000 (798,000)	2854 (870)	12,392 (3777)
North Sea	222,100 (575,200)	308 (94)	2165 (660)
Red Sea	169,100 (438,000)	1611 (491)	7254 (2211)
Baltic Sea	163,000 (422,200)	180 (55)	1380 (421)

cent of the carbon dioxide produced by burning fossil fuel, with CO_2 being transported downwards by plankton. Changes in the temperature of the sea influence the ability of plankton to take up carbon dioxide. If plankton decrease in numbers, the whole food chain is affected. Sea water becomes denser as it becomes colder, down to its freezing point of 28.5° F (-1.9° C). (This is unlike fresh water, which is most dense at 39.2° F/4° C, well above its freezing point.) The average temperature of all ocean water is about 38° F (3.5° C). Life began in the seas 3.1 billion to 3.4 billion years ago, whereas land dwellers only appeared 400 million years ago.

OCEAN ZONES Each layer of the ocean is usually distinguished by the amount of sunlight it receives, the depths it occupies, and the degree of hydrostatic pressure found there. The *Sunlight Zone* extends from the surface to about 600 feet (183 m) down, and it teems with life forms of every sort, from microscopic plankton and diatoms that give the ocean its opaque colour and limit visibility to fish of every shape and size, molluscs, corals and warm-blooded, oxygen-breathing mammals. Colours are spectacular near the surface, but water scatters and absorbs some of the Sun's light, filtering out colours below certain depths. The first colours to go are reds, then oranges, yellows, greens, and then finally blues. At around 60 feet (18 m), it appears that everything is a shade of brown, black, grey and white, unless a bright dive light is used to see the actual colours. At 100 feet (30 m) there is pressure against every square inch of one's body, and the size and volume of the lungs will have been reduced to one third of their capacity at sea level. It is far colder, and a depth of about 180 feet (55 m) is the limit of safe diving for a human breathing compressed air, without a pressurized diving suit.

The *Twilight Zone* (Mesopelagic zone) is known as the mid-water range. It experiences very low levels of sunlight, and appears as virtual darkness to human eyes. This layer ranges from 600 feet (183 m) to about 2600 feet (792 m) down. Plankton, which occupies the sunlight layer in profusion and provides a food source for most of the creatures living in that region, either directly or indirectly, does not live here as plankton need adequate sunlight levels to thrive. The type of foods available to creatures living at these depths tend to be energy-poor and are generally detritus and bacteria, the things that drift down from the sunnier layer. Here, many organisms' body tissues are capable of emitting their

own light, a phenomenon which is known as bioluminescence – they glow in the dark. The colours range from blues to greens and some fish even emit red light as a form of infrared vision to help them see their prey in darkness. Some creatures, such as squid and octopuses, emit clouds of glowing ink to evade predators. Others, such as jellyfish and some bony fish, use light to attract prey. The *Midnight Zone* is the deepest, darkest region of the ocean, from about 3000 feet (900 m) down to the sea floor. Organic 'rainfall' includes dead microscopic organisms, such as phytoplankton and dinoflagellates, sinking downward, fecal pellets of fish and mammals, and carcasses of larger organisms sinking down to the sea bed. Those creatures that do not feed directly on the detritus raining down from above usually prey upon those that do. In a few places on the ocean floor there exist unusually deep zones. *Deep Sea Trenches* are nearly three times deeper than the average depth of the sea floor, with pressures of up to 16,000 pounds per square inch. New life forms, capable of surviving these tremendous pressures, are being discovered there as science begins to uncover this most secret world.

THE PACIFIC OCEAN AND THE SIZE OF THE MOON
The volume of the Moon is about the same as the volume of the Pacific Ocean. The world's largest body of water occupies a third of the Earth's surface. The Pacific contains about 25,000 islands (more than the total number in the rest of the world's oceans combined), almost all of which are found south of the equator. It is the oldest ocean, with the earliest rocks on its floor being 200 million years old. It also

contains the thinnest part of the Earth's crust, about 3.7 miles (5.9 km) thick, in parts of its seabed.

PANTHALASSA – THE SUPER-OCEAN AROUND PANGAEA
In the Permian period, the continents were pushed together by the forces of plate tectonics into one single super-continent known as Pangaea. It stretched from the North Pole to the South Pole. The surrounding super-ocean of Panthalassa was full of sponges, corals, starfish, clams, sea scorpions and bony fish. Around 251 million years ago there was a mass extinction. In a time span of just 80,000 years, 95 per cent of all life became extinct.

REVERSING CLIMATE CHANGE?
Minute iron particles are released by melting icebergs, causing vast blooms of algae. It rises to the surface, absorbs carbon dioxide through the process of photosynthesis, then sinks to the ocean floor, so trapping the greenhouse gas and preventing its release back to the atmosphere. In 2009 an experiment took place near the Falkland Islands, 'seeding' the Southern Ocean with several tons of iron sulphate to create an artifical bloom of algae. If successful, it is claimed that 15 tankers dropping iron particles non-stop, could absorb all CO_2 emissions for a decade.

SALINITY AND QUADRILLIONS
Some scientists estimate that the oceans contain as much as 50 quadrillion tons (= 50 million billion tons = 50,000,000,000,000,000 tons) of dissolved solids. These solids are mainly sodium salts (sodium chloride or common salt), calcium salts (calcium

carbonate or lime, and calcium sulphate), potassium salts (potassium sulphate), and magnesium salts (magnesium chloride, magnesium sulphate, and magnesium bromide). If all these sea salts could be spread evenly over the Earth's land surface, they would create a layer more than 500 feet (150 m) deep.

SEA WATER QUANTITY Sea water constitutes 96.5 per cent of the world's water, followed in quantity by glaciers and snow (1.74 per cent), groundwater (1.69 per cent), permafrost (0.02 per cent), lakes and ponds (0.01 per cent), then fogs and clouds, marshes and swamps, and rivers.

Sea Levels

In 1988 the UN established the Intergovernmental Panel on Climate and Change (IPCC), which has collated sea level data over the last 100 years. In general the level has risen by 4.8 to 8.8 inches (12.2 to 22.4 cm). It is measured relative to a land-based tide-gauge benchmark, but there are also vertical movements in the land surface, e.g. Scotland is rising at 0.12 inches (3 mm) a year, and England is sinking at 0.08 inches (2 mm) a year. This is caused by the land settling towards its original position after the loss of weight of the ice cover of the last ('little') Ice Age. This is despite the fact that the last Scottish ice sheet melted 10,000 years ago. In 'full' Ice Ages, ice lay at a depth of up to 2 miles (3.2 km) across Europe and North America. Possibly the biggest unknown regarding global warming is whether the Greenland and Antarctic ice sheets will melt. Contraction of the ice sheets would cause the sea level to rise, and there is thinning of the polar ice caps. *Sea-ice draft* is the term for the thickness of the ice that is submerged under the sea. Data

acquired by submarines shows that its average thickness fell from 8.6 feet (2.6 m) in most of the deep-water parts of the Arctic Ocean to 5 feet (1.5 m) in the period from 1958–76 to 1993–7. (Measurements are taken at the end of the *'melt season'*). This is a fall in average depth and volume of 40 per cent. For the first time in recorded history, in 2000 a hole appeared in the sea ice above the North Pole, large enough to be seen from space. In 2007, the Arctic Sea ice retreat was the most pronounced ever recorded. Also measurements show that the size of Greenland is shrinking at its coastal margins.

THE SEVEN SEAS These were traditionally the Arctic, Antarctic, North Atlantic, South Atlantic, North Pacific, South Pacific and Indian Oceans. However, from around 1450 to 1650, the *'seven navigated seas'* of the world were deemed to be the Atlantic, Pacific, Indian and Pacific Oceans, the Mediterranean Sea, the Caribbean and the Gulf of Mexico. The Antarctic is not an ocean, but the southern extension of the Pacific, Atlantic (now Southern) and Indian Oceans. However, the largest sea is given in some encyclopaedias as the Bering Sea at 884,900 square miles (2,291,900 km²). The warmest sea in the world is the Red Sea, where temperatures range from 68° F to 87.8° F (20° C to 31° C).

THE SOUTH SEAS Sometimes this referred to the area around the Caribbean, including the Gulf of Mexico, the Florida Coast, Cuba, Jamaica and Hispaniola. It was also the name originally given to the Pacific Ocean, and came to mean the Central and South Pacific.

THE STRAIT OF GIBRALTAR
This strait is 36 miles (13 km) across, narrowing to 8 miles (13 km), linking the calmer Mediterranean Sea and the wilder Atlantic Ocean.

THE STRAIT OF MAGELLAN
This important channel is 320 miles (515 km) long, between Tierra del Fuego and the South American mainland.

THE SYDNEY-HOBART RACE
Every Boxing Day since 1945 this 630-mile (1014-km) race has attracted the best yachtsmen in the world. However, in 1998, the fleet was hit by a massive area of high pressure, known as a *'bomb'*, during the crossing. The storm

created waves as high as 33 feet (10 m) and 78 mph (125 kph) winds. Only 44 of the 115 yachts made it to Tasmania. Seven yachts had to be abandoned and six men died.

THE THERMOCLINE
The thermocline is an ocean zone in which the temperature drops very rapidly, usually found between 1000 to 2600 feet (300 to 800 m) deep, between the relatively warm surface zone and the cold deep zone. As the thermocline blocks sonar, it is a favourite hiding place for military submarines.

THE THREE MILE LIMIT This was originally agreed as the limit of a nation's jurisdiction at sea, for reasons of pragmatism. It was suggested by the Dutch legal authority Cornelius van Bynkershoek in 1702 in *De Domino Maris*. It was able to be enforced because 3 nautical miles (5.5 km) was the range limit of the cannon of shore batteries. Not until 1988 with the Territorial Sea Proclamation Act issued by President Reagan was there a *'high seas'* limit of 12 nautical miles (22 km) established.

THE UNDERSEA RIVER
Monterey Submarine Canyon lies off California, and runs around 95 miles (153 km) into the Pacific, reaching depths of up to 11,800 feet (3600 m) below sea level at its deepest. The canyon's bottom is about 2 miles (3.2 km) below the surface, and the actual canyon itself is about 1 mile (1.6 km) deep, making it of comparable depth to the Grand Canyon.

UPWELLING AND FISHERIES
The ocean is warmer at its top levels and cold at the bottom. Organisms move from one layer to another, and plant and

animal remains containing nutrients 'rain' down, but the layers stay fairly separate in all but a few places. However, the rotation of the Earth, and strong seasonal offshore winds, push surface water away from some western coasts. Water then rises on the western edges of continents to replace it. This 'upwelling' brings cold, nutrient-rich water from the ocean depths up to the surface, and marine life thrives as a consequence. Coastal upwelling occurs along the western edges of continents in the Atlantic, Indian and Pacific Oceans. Upwelling supports about 50 per cent of the world's fishing, although the cool waters where it occurs account for only 10 per cent of the surface area of the global oceans.

VOLCANIC ACTIVITY UNDER THE SEA About 90 per cent of all
volcanic activity on Earth occurs in the ocean, and the largest known concentration of these active volcanoes (over 1100) is in the South Pacific. This area was only located by scientists in 1993, and is the size of New York State. Any major eruption undersea could cause a tsunami. Under the enormous pressures of the deep ocean, sea water can reach very high temperatures without boiling.

THE WATER CYCLE The Sun's
heat provides energy which evaporates water from the Earth's surface, from oceans, lakes, etc. Plants also lose water to the air through transpiration. This water vapour eventually condenses, forming clouds of tiny droplets. When these clouds meet cool air over land, there is precipitation in the form of rain, sleet or snow, and the water returns to the land or seas. Some of the rain soaks into the ground. Other underground water is

trapped between rock or clay layers, and this is called 'groundwater'. However, most of the water flows downhill as runoff (either above ground or underground), and eventually returns to the seas as slightly salty water. The cycle was first described by the Greek philosopher Xenophanes of Colophon (570–480 BCE): *'The Sea is the source of the waters, and the source of the winds. Without the great sea, heaven's rain and flowing rivers could not come from the clouds; for the great Sea is the father of clouds, of rivers and of winds.'*

WATERFALL – THE LARGEST ON EARTH This is actually
underwater, in the Denmark Strait, and slowly cascades downward for 2.2 miles (3.5 km). This is over three times as tall as Angel Falls in Venezuela, which is the tallest land-based waterfall.

WATER PRESSURE The water
pressure at the bottom of the Challenger Deep is over 8 tons per square inch, equal to a human trying to hold 50 jumbo jets in their arms. Organisms do live here, which may help advances in science as we discover more about them.

THE WEDDELL SEA – THE WORLD'S CLEAREST SEAWATER This sea off Antarctica is
the world's clearest. In 1986 scientists lowered a 1-foot (30-cm) disc into the water and it was visible until it reached a depth of 262 feet (80 m). It is as clear as distilled water.

WHAT IS THE DIFFERENCE BETWEEN AN OCEAN AND THE SEA? An ocean is one of the
massive bodies of interconnecting salt water which covers 71 per cent of the

Earth. The four major oceans are the Arctic, Atlantic, Indian and Pacific. However, some sources do not include the Arctic Ocean, defining it as a marginal sea. Others include the Southern Ocean, which has taken over part of the South Atlantic. A sea usually describes saltwater areas on the margins of these oceans, such as the Mediterranean Sea situated along the Atlantic Ocean, and accessed via the Strait of Gibraltar.

WHY ARE THE OCEANS SALTY?

As water flows through rivers, it picks up small amounts of mineral salts from the rocks and soil of the river beds. This eventually flows into the seas. The water only leaves the oceans through evaporation (and the freezing of polar ice), but the salt remains dissolved in the ocean – it does not evaporate. Thus the remaining water gets saltier and saltier as time passes.

WHY ARE THE RED SEA AND BLACK SEA SO NAMED?

The Red Sea often looks red because of red algae that live in this body of water. The Black Sea looks almost black because it has a high concentration of hydrogen sulphide, which appears black.

WHY IS THE SEA BLUE?

Sunlight is made up of the colours of the rainbow: red, orange, yellow, green, blue, indigo and violet. Some sunlight is reflected off the surface of the sea, reflecting the colour of the blue sky. When the day is overcast, the sea does not appear so blue, as it is not reflecting the blue sky. Some sunlight penetrates the water and is scattered by ripples and particles in the water (giving the appearance that the ocean is the colour of these particles).

In deep water, much of the sunlight is scattered by the oxygen in the water, and this scatters more of the blue light. Water absorbs more of the red light in sunlight, but enhances the scattering of blue light, as blue light is more easily bent, or refracted, than red light. If you are underwater, the water around you appears blue, because more blue light is scattered back to your eye than red light.

WORLD OCEANS DAY

This was commemorated on 8 June 2009 by the release of the film *The End of the Line*. It highlights the fact that 90 per cent of ocean predators have disappeared, being replaced by jellyfish and squid. At current rates, fish stocks will be commercially exhausted by 2050. The continuing extinction of Mediterranean bluefin tuna is revealed, and the example of the collapse of the Newfoundland fishing industry in the 1990s, once the biggest in the world, is instructive to some of us. The world's largest fishery is now Alaska, which has seen a 50 per cent decline in its pollock population in the last five years. More than 2 million tons of blue whiting were caught each year, but its population is close to collapse.

ARE WE DOOMED?

THE EIGHT THREATS TO SEAFOOD SUPPLIES Up to 30 per cent of the world's fish and seafood species have almost disappeared from the oceans in our lifetime. If current consumption trends continue, within 40 years all fish and seafood supplies will have virtually vanished. Fish stocks in lakes, rivers, bays and marshlands are also quickly vanishing.

1: Global Warming This warming pattern is causing greater shore and habitat erosion. It is also increasing the salinity of estuaries and freshwater aquifers, altering tidal patterns in rivers and bays, and causing increased coastal flooding. Particularly at risk will be saltwater marshes, mangrove ecosystems, coastal wetlands, coral reefs, coral atolls, river deltas and the marine species that they support.

2: Chemical Pollution and Eutrophication Seventy-five per cent of ocean pollution originates from land sources, reaching the ocean as runoff or discharge into streams and rivers, or through the air. Pollution kills marine life, stunts growth, impairs reproduction, and can even effect genetic mutations. Pollution also encourages eutrophication, the excessive proliferation of plant life, especially algae. These excess plants and the resultant decaying algae reduce the

water's oxygen content, killing off marine life. For example, runoff from farm fertilizers has created a massive 'dead zone' at the mouth of the Mississippi River. In the northern Gulf of Mexico, toxic 'red tide' infestations of algae contaminate oyster beds and other seafood species. Ecologists have estimated that in 1880, there were sufficient oysters filtering the water in Maryland's Chesapeake Bay to filter all the water in the bay in just three days. In 2009, the oyster population in the bay has fallen to a point where it takes them over a year to filter the bay's water.

3: The Alteration of Habitats Over half of the world's population lives within 40 miles (64 km) of a shoreline, but by 2020, 75 per cent will be living less than an hour's drive from the sea. This will mean more coastal erosion and more pollution of the natural habitats of ocean species. Mangroves are being removed to make way for large-scale shrimp aquaculture. Coastal salt marshes are being destroyed by dredging and filling to make room for new housing projects. Mining will further destroy marine habitats.

4: Global Fisheries Operations Major fishing countries have greatly boosted their catching efficiency, to a level at least 30 per cent greater than what is needed to harvest the world catch. The seafood industry has been over-harvesting fish and throwing back (dead and dying) by-catch, quickly depleting stocks.

5: Competition from Non-native Species These are often discharged from ballast water, and the local species is not equipped to compete with the incomers. For example, the American comb jellyfish's appearance in the Black Sea has devastated its anchovy fishery.

6: The Demand for 'Healthy' Food Health-conscious individuals are eating more seafood. Over five years, per-capita annual consumption in the USA rose 9 per cent, to 16.8 pounds (7.6 kg) per person in 2007. Meanwhile, worldwide fish consumption rose from 40 million tons in 1970 to more than 86 million tons in 1998. It is predicted that by 2030, there will be a global seafood shortage of 20 million tons per annum.

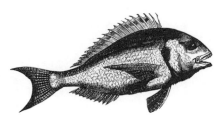

7: High Prices Have Encouraged Overfishing Seafood prices rose 10 per cent in 2008, and continue to rise strongly, replicating what is going on with the demand for other natural resources, making fishing an increasingly valuable industry for investment.

8: World Population Growth By 2030, another two billion people will be living on the planet, eating more and more

seafood, requiring an additional 37 million tons of seafood supplies. Added to this problem is the fact that China and India, with rapidly rising personal disposable incomes, will be able to afford more and better seafood, again placing extreme pressure on limited resources.

THE ALBEDO Albedo is the term for the difference between the proportion of the Sun's energy that strikes the Earth and the proportion of the energy which is reflected back into space. This balance is incredibly important in regulating the world's climate. The average albedo is 0.3, meaning that just under a third of *'incident light'* bounces off. The albedo varies across the world, however. Snow-covered ice has an albedo of up to 0.8–0.9, meaning that 80–90 per cent of energy is being bounced off. However, the open seas have an albedo of under 0.1 (10 per cent). Therefore, ice and snow help keep the Earth cool because they strongly reflect the Sun's rays back into space. As global warming is melting glaciers, as well as ice in Greenland, the Arctic and Antarctic, land and water is being exposed. These darker surfaces reflect less solar heat back into space, allowing the Earth's atmosphere to absorb more warmth. In 1976, the average thickness of Arctic sea ice was 10 feet (3 m), but by 1993–7 it was about 6 feet (1.8 m). It is now around 4 feet (6.4 m) and researchers say that the thinning is continuing at a rate of 4 inches (10 cm) per year. Melting ice will lead to even faster global warming, as the ice caps are warmed from beneath by rising sea temperatures and from above by rising air temperatures. A Russian survey vessel reported a thickness of just

3 feet (90 cm) in some areas in 2008. In a *Washington Post* article (3 December 1999) it was noted that Arctic sea ice is shrinking at a rate of 14,000 square miles (36,250 km²) annually, an area larger than Maryland and Delaware combined. In September 2007, the *Scientific American* stated: *'Covering 1.59 million square miles (4.12 million km²), this summer's sea ice shattered the previous record for the smallest ice cap of 2.05 million square miles (5.31 million km²) in 2005—a further loss of sea ice area equivalent to the states of California and Texas combined.'*

The Antarctic Peninsula has also seen an increase in average temperatures of almost 5° F (2.8° C) in the last 50 years. Heavy sea ice has been the norm in the Antarctic, but in the 1990s sea ice disintegration began. During 1998, the Antarctic had a record low in winter sea ice. NASA has determined that of the warming during the 20th century, the greater warming, about 0.36° F (0.2° C) each decade, has occurred since 1975. Another NASA study in September, 2006, found that the world's temperature is reaching a level that has not been seen in thousands of years. Because of the rapid warming trend over the past 30 years, the Earth is now reaching and passing through the warmest levels in the current interglacial period, which has lasted nearly 12,000 years.

THE CHIMNEYS OF THE GREENLAND SEA
Scientists have evidence that extreme changes are occurring in the Gulf Stream. Without the influence of the Gulf Stream, the weather in Britain and parts of Europe could be as severe as that of Siberia or Labrador which lie on the same latitude. Cambridge University Professor Peter Wadhams has noted these changes. Historically, large columns *('chimneys')* of very cold, dense water in the Greenland Sea sink about 9000 feet (2750 m) from the surface to the seabed. As that water sinks, it allows the warm Gulf Stream current (flowing from the south) to pass over and move westwards to Europe. Wadhams says the number of these chimneys has dropped from about 12 to two. This can cause a severe weakening of the Gulf Stream, with much less heat reaching northern Europe as a consequence. This interaction in the Greenland Sea is part of a global pattern of ocean movement, known as *'thermohaline circulation'*, or more commonly the *'global conveyor belt'*. Wadhams said at a meeting of the European Geosciences Union in Vienna that the slowing of the Gulf Stream could contribute to other severe effects on the planet. If not diverted as usual across the Atlantic, it could cause the complete melting of the Arctic ice cap in the summer months. Current predictions indicate that could happen as early as 2020 or as late as 2080, which could lead to another Ice Age across Europe. The causes of Ice Ages are complex, but the last one lasted 60,000 years, only ending in 10,000 BCE.

GULF STREAM REVERSAL
Scientists from Cambridge University have confirmed that the Gulf Stream is weakening, and this is likely to bring much colder temperatures to Europe within a few years. This is happening because the gigantic *'Greenland Chimneys'* (see above) have all but

Ice Loss in Antarctica

The Times (14 January 2008) reported that the Antarctic is losing ice *'nearly twice as fast as ten years ago'*, with the rate of annual ice loss in the Antarctic increasing by almost 80 billion tons. The total annual loss was estimated at 196 billion tons, and the most extensive ice loss was found to be taking place in west Antarctica, where an estimated 132 billion tons disappeared in 2006. In 1996, only about 83 billion tons was calculated to have slipped into the water, mainly as icebergs. A scientist stated *'This is another observation that confirms the trend in what's happening around the world. We've seen the same thing in mountain glaciers, in Greenland, Patagonia and the same thing in Alaska. We are seeing the same thing everywhere we look.'* The loss is thought to be partly attributable to processes that take place over thousands of years. Ecologically, the warmer seas will mean species extinction of some of the most unusual creatures on the planet. Freezing temperatures have kept predators away, so Antarctica is home to some extraordinary animals, such as giant sea spiders the size of dinner plates, isopod crustaceans that

resemble aquatic woodlice, and sea snails. None of these species has evolved alongside swifter competitors, such as crabs and bony fish, so they have few defences against them. The Antarctic's native fish, which make antifreeze proteins so that their bodily fluids do not freeze, eat small, shrimp-like crustaceans and other soft foods. The main predators on the sea floor are slow-moving sea stars and giant, floppy ribbon-worms. Predators such as crabs, rays and sharks will devastate the continent's fragile and unique marine ecosystem if they are able to move into them. Research at the National Oceanography Centre at Southampton found that warming sea temperatures had allowed crabs to approach closer than ever to the Antarctic continental shelf, suggesting an imminent invasion.

disappeared. The chimneys have been a key to world climate as we know it today, and for many scientists their disappearance signals a catastrophe. The 2004 film *The Day After Tomorrow* has been based on this hypothesis. Cambridge scientists

predicted that there will be clear water at the North Pole as early as 2020, and that temperatures in Britain are likely to drop by 9–14° F (5–8° C), from an average of 72° F (22° C) at present to 58 to 63° F (14 to 17° C) in the future. This will mean that the summer crop (and animal) growing season will be drastically shortened in Europe, and that winters similar to those in Finland will extend far south into France. A series of 'no-melt' summers across the northern latitudes will also alter the *albedo* balance. This weakening of the Gulf Stream is destabilizing currents worldwide, and it is probable that the eastern US and eastern Canada will experience climate change as radical as that in Europe, as the Gulf Stream drops south, away from the colder northern waters.

SEA ICE – THE THREAT OF CLIMATE CHANGE

In the winter, 6.5–7.5 million square miles (17–19.5 million km²) of the Southern Ocean are covered with sea ice, decreasing to 1.1–1.5 million square miles (2.8–3.9 million km²) in summer. The Arctic Ocean has 5–6 million square miles (13–15.5 million km²) in winter and 2.7–3.5 million square miles (7–9 million km²) in summer. Icebergs are not considered sea ice because they are composed of ice that originated from glaciers. Sea ice is frozen seawater that floats on the ocean surface, and forms and melts with the polar seasons. In the Arctic, some sea ice is almost permanent, whereas almost all Southern Ocean or Antarctic sea ice is 'seasonal ice'. Sea ice in the Arctic has a more crucial role in regulating global climate. The September decline trend in Arctic sea ice is at record levels. Not only have over 386,000 square miles (1 million km²) disappeared permanently since 1900, but the ice is losing its bulk, with thinning of up to 40 per cent in parts of the Arctic sea ice. The

increasing substitution of highly-reflective ice by heat-absorbent sea has accelerated global warming, with warmer seas leading to more intense storms. The total power dissipated by hurricanes in the North Atlantic and West Pacific has nearly doubled in the last 30 years. Five-day rainfall events, the main causes of flooding, have also increased. The melting of sea ice does not seriously affect rising sea levels, but it has led to an enormous loss of plankton. Krill feed on plankton, and their numbers have declined massively. Further up the food chain there has been a serious effect on whales, Arctic cod, seals and penguins that feed on krill. The population of Adelie penguins has fallen by 70 per cent in 30 years, and that of Emperor penguins by half. Polar bears feed on seals, so their numbers are also declining. The ability of the oceans to absorb carbon dioxide is also at risk. They absorb about 2 billion tons of carbon annually, but a report in *Nature*, August 1995, suggested that the oceans may be losing fixed nitrogen, the essential fertilizer that allows phytoplankton to grow. Phytoplankton absorb and fix carbon dioxide via photosynthesis. This carbon is eventually then transferred to the '*carbon sink*' of the deep ocean. Plankton take in about half of all the world's CO_2, using the carbon for growth, while releasing oxygen during the process of photosynthesis. Loss of plankton means more greenhouse gases are released into the atmosphere and more global warming. The greatest loss of phytoplankton has occurred in areas where ocean temperatures have risen most significantly.

SEA LEVELS During the most recent Ice Age the world's mean sea level was about 330 feet (100 m) lower than it is today. Sea water had evaporated and been deposited as ice and snow in glaciers. Most of these glaciers had melted by about 10,000 years ago, and melting of the remaining glaciers has caused rising sea levels ever since. However, we are now experiencing acceleration in rising seas. The sea level has risen at around an average of 4–10 inches (10–25 cm) in the last century, and the rate of rise is increasing. Because the oceans react relatively slowly to change, levels will continue to rise even if our climate is stabilized. Loss of ice on Antarctica has the potential to be the biggest cause of rising sea levels in coming decades. If it all melted, which scientists consider highly unlikely by 2100, it is estimated that sea level would rise 200 feet (61 m), compared with 22 feet (7 m) if all of Greenland's glaciers were to melt.

Tipping Points

Since 2005 scientists have been trying to identify 'tipping points' which may propel the Earth into danger. Of these, two significant ones are the destruction of the Amazonian rainforest and the death of cold-adapted trees in Siberia and Canada because of global warming. All the other seven points listed in the *Journal Proceedings of the National Academy of Sciences*, 2008, concern our oceans. They are:

Arctic Sea Ice – the tipping point for total loss of summer sea ice is considered to be imminent.

Greenland Ice Sheet – total melting may take 300 years, but the tipping point to irreversible change could occur within a few decades.

West Antarctic Ice Sheet – this may collapse because of warming.

West African Monsoon – likely to alter and cause droughts.

Indian Monsoon – relies on temperature differential between land and sea, but environmental pollutants are unbalancing the system by causing localized cooling.

El Niño – the Southern Pacific current is being affected by warmer seas, resulting in climate change.

Gulf Stream – this may collapse as it has done in the past, causing a colder climate in Britain and parts of Europe. The Gulf Stream moves 100 times as much water as all the rivers on Earth.

ENVIRONMENTAL ISSUES

BY-CATCH AND DEAD DOLPHINS

This is unintended destruction of marine life caused by the use of non-selective fishing gear, such as trawl nets, longlines and gillnets. It amounts to a known 20 million tons a year. Around 300,000 small whales, dolphins and porpoises die as a result. Fishing for wild shrimp accounts for 2 per cent of global seafood but 33 per cent of global by-catch. Even if we use the low estimate of 20 million tons, this means that almost 7 million tons of marine life is destroyed every year while fishing for shrimp. According to the Worldwide Fund for Nature, in the Gulf of Thailand there can be 14 pounds (6.4 kg) of dead and dying by-catch per pound (0.45 kg) of shrimp landed. Shrimp trawl nets are known to kill thousands of endangered turtles every year, but such by-catch is usually not recorded. By-catch includes species caught and thrown away when other species are targeted, and also the reproductively immature juveniles of the target species. It also includes unwanted invertebrate species, such as echinoderms and non-commercial crustaceans. Dolphins are caught in tuna nets and are drowned, leading to some tuna cans being labelled *'Dolphin Friendly'*. However, this does not mean that dolphins were not killed in the process of catching the tuna, but simply that the fishing fleet did not specifically target a feeding pod of dolphins. It has relied on other methods to find a school of tuna, but still could kill dolphins when netting the tuna.

CARBON DIOXIDE AND NOISY SEAS

Rising levels of CO_2 have made the seas noisier, making it more difficult for whales and dolphins to communicate. When air dissolves in water, carbonic acid is formed, making the seas more acidic. Sound waves are absorbed by certain types of charged molecules that stick together in the water. As the seas become more acidic, the charged molecules absorb less sound, so sound waves travel further, by up to 10 per cent in the Atlantic and Pacific. By 2050, it is estimated that they will travel 70 per cent further, creating an underwater noise making it more difficult for mammals and reef fish that also use sound. The acidification is also hurting diatoms and corals, corroding their carbonate shells.

RACHEL CARSON 1907–64 – THE PIONEER OF ECOLOGY

Born near Springdale, Pennsylvania, in 1936, she was appointed as a junior aquatic biologist with the US Bureau of Fisheries, becoming one of only two women then employed with the Bureau at a professional level. Her first book, *Under the Sea-Wind* (published 1941), demonstrated her ability to present complicated scientific material clearly. In 1943, she was promoted to the position of aquatic biologist in the newly created US Fish and Wildlife Service, where she began writing wildlife bulletins aimed at the American public, such as the series *'Conservation in Action'*. In 1951 her second book, *The Sea Around Us*, was published and translated into 32 languages. It was on *The New York Times'* bestseller list for 81 weeks. This book, along with *The Edge of the Sea*, her third book published in 1956, opened the public's eyes to environmentalism. She popularized the term *'ecology'*, the study of *'our living place'*. Her final book, *Silent Spring* (1962), documented the dangers to the ecosystem caused by pesticides. Her marine studies had provided her with early documentation of the effects of DDT on marine life. Abnormalities show up first in fish and wildlife, so biologists were the first to see the effects of the impending threat to the overall environment. Her books provoked bitter personal attacks on her, with the pesticide industry mounting a massive negative publicity campaign. However, DDT was later banned. This marine biologist had launched the environmental movement. Carson once stated that *'man's endeavors to control nature, by his powers to alter and to destroy, would inevitably evolve into a war against himself, a war he would lose unless he came to terms with nature.'*

CORAL BLEACHING This is the loss of colour in coral caused by the destruction of symbiotic unicellular algae. High sea surface temperature coupled with greater sunshine is the main factor in summer coral bleaching. However, wind, weather conditions and exposure at low tide and can also contribute to it. The most extensive coral bleaching ever reported was in 1997–8, with extensive mortality of fast-growing, as well as some slow-growing, corals. Probably 10 per cent of the world's corals were killed, with as much as 16 per cent in the Great Barrier Reef. The Philippines, the Seychelles, Tanzania and Jamaica reported that 70 per cent or more of their corals had bleached. Bleaching was observed at depths down to 60 feet (18 m), and some coral colonies that were hundreds of years old died. As well as the hard corals that typically suffer bleaching, soft corals, anemones, sponges and giant clams were also adversely affected.

The region that suffered most from the bleaching was the Indian Ocean, where reefs from Sri Lanka to Kenya and the Seychelles whitened and died. Surveys revealed an overall decline in live coral cover from 80 per cent in 1997 to 64 per cent in 1998. Likely impacts of the coral mortality are declining tourism, fisheries changing and perhaps declining considerably, and increased coastal erosion if reefs disintegrate. Mass bleaching events had not been recorded before 1979, since when they have become almost commonplace, being generally linked to higher than normal water temperatures. The Great Barrier Reef has suffered eight mass bleachings in the last 18 years, leading some scientists to predict its demise within 20–30 years. The most widespread and intense events occurred in the summers of 1998 and 2002. Some locations suffered severe damage, with up to 90 per cent of corals killed. The effects from thermal stress are likely to worsen owing to the gradual acidification of the world's oceans.

CORAL REEFS AND SPECIES DEPENDENCY Coral reefs develop in shallow, warm water, usually near land, preferring temperatures between 70 and 85° F (21–30° C). Tropical coral reefs border the shores of 109 countries, many of which are among the world's least developed, and serious degradation of reefs has happened in over 90 countries. Coral reefs comprise less than 0.5 per cent of the ocean floor, but it is estimated that *more than 90 per cent of marine species are directly or indirectly dependent on them*. Nearly 60 per cent of the world's remaining reefs are at significant risk of being lost in the next three decades. The major causes of coral reef decline are coastal development, sewage, sedimentation, destructive fishing practices, pollution, tourism (divers taking chunks of coral), the commercial harvesting of coral for aquaria and global warming (see above). The anchor from one cruise ship can destroy a sea bed area the size of half a football field, and there are hundreds of large cruise ships constantly touring reef zones. Global Coral Monitoring Network states that currently 27 per cent of all coral reefs worldwide have disappeared, and by around 2050 only 30 per cent will be left.

DEAD ZONES IN THE OCEANS These are areas where the water at the sea floor is *'anoxic'* – it has a very low (and sometimes zero) concentration of dissolved oxygen. They are situated along the coasts of major continents, and are rapidly spreading over large areas of the sea floor. Most sea-floor-dependent organisms need oxygen to survive. The sea-floor water becomes anoxic because the organic matter produced by phytoplankton at the surface of the ocean sinks to the bottom. Here it is broken down by bacteria. However, while phytoplankton take in carbon dioxide and produce oxygen during photosynthesis, bacteria survive by absorbing oxygen dissolved in the water, giving off carbon dioxide in the process. Other oxygen-respiring animals on the bottom, such as crabs, clams, shrimp, zooplankton and fish, also need oxygenated water to survive. There are now *'creeping dead zones'* which are areas in the seas where greater numbers of phytoplankton are creating more organic matter, which is respired by bacteria and thus more oxygen is taken from the water. Bottom water anoxia is particularly problematic near the mouths of major river systems, especially China's. Fertilizer is necessary to increase the yields of agricultural crops, but eventually it runs off the fields into the streams and rivers of a watershed. The nutrients in the fertilizer reach the open seas, leading to a phytoplankton population explosion. This in turn leads to more anoxic bottom water and potential ecological disaster. Hundreds of millions of gallons of oil enter the seas from industrial waste and automobiles, to which are added household cleaning products, gardening, and industrial waste as water pollutants. The Mississippi drains more than 40 per cent of the United States, carrying excess nutrients into the

Gulf of Mexico. This causes 'algae blooms' which consume oxygen, kill shellfish and displace fish in a 4000-square-mile (10,000-km²) dead zone off the coast of Louisiana and Texas.

DESALINATION PLANTS In the Arabian Gulf, during every day reverse osmosis plants heat 500 million gallons (2273 million litres) of sea water to high temperatures. This produces 100 million gallons (455 million litres) of fresh water to sustain tourism, golf-courses and the like. The seawater has to be mixed with toxic chemicals, and then injected under high pressure through a series of membrane filters. The balance of 400 million gallons (1818 million litres) of untreated water is returned to the sea each day, but it is at a significantly higher temperature than the Gulf seawater. This superheated brine discharge also contains higher levels of dissolved solids and toxic chemicals, causing a wide range of environmental problems.

THE GREAT PACIFIC GARBAGE PATCH Also known as the *'trash vortex'*, this is in effect *the world's largest rubbish dump*. It is an area twice the size of Texas and is set to double in the next ten years. The *'western garbage patch'* off Hawaii, and the *'eastern garbage patch'* off Japan, are areas where plastic garbage is trapped by giant underwater swirling currents. A fifth of the rubbish comes from ships and oil platforms, and the rest from land. Usually sailors avoid the area of the 'western garbage patch', which is also known as the *'North Pacific gyre'* because it experiences little wind and extreme high pressure systems, so it was only found by accident. Modern plastics are so durable that objects more than 50 years old have been found there. In 2002, the concentration of rubbish in the centre of the patch was estimated at 13 pounds (6 kg) of waste for every 2.2 pounds (1 kg) of plankton, a ratio of 6:1. Plastic now accounts for 90 per cent of rubbish floating in the oceans. In the North Pacific

Great Barrier Reef

The Great Barrier Reef is the largest complex of coral reefs in the world, consisting of 2900 separate reefs and 1000 islands. It is 1550 miles (2500 km) in length. It could instead be called *'the great barrier of reefs'*. It can even be seen from space. Its reefs are made up of 400 species of coral, supporting over 2000 different fish,

4000 species of mollusc and countless other invertebrates. Other huge barrier reefs include the barrier reefs of New Caledonia, the Mesoamerican (Belize) barrier reef, and the large barrier reefs of Fiji. The largest coral atoll complexes occur around the Maldives in the Indian Ocean, and in Micronesia.

gyre, there are over 100 million tons of mostly plastic debris floating just underneath the surface. Because the sea of rubbish is translucent and lies just below the water's surface, it cannot be seen from space, only from the bows of ships. This problem is now so immense that no individual country could afford to clear up the Pacific plastic gyre.

MISUSE OF THE OCEANS In 1993, United States beaches were closed, or swimmers advised not to get in the water, more than 2400 times because of sewage contamination. However, there are worse problems than untreated sewage. The US Coast Guard estimates that in United States waters, sewage treatment plants discharge twice as much oil each year as is released through tanker spills. Sea animals perish when the oil slicks their downy feathers or fur, decreasing the surface area and cutting off their insulation from cold water. Animals also ingest the oil when trying to clean their feathers or fur, and then die or become sick and unable to reproduce properly. Nitrogen and phosphorus from sources such as fertilizer, sewage and detergents also enter coastal waters, causing oxygen depletion and 'dead zones'. The most frequently found item in beach cleanups are pieces of plastic. The main items are plastic foam, plastic utensils, pieces of glass and cigarette butts. Lost or discarded fishing nets are washed up on shores throughout the world. Called *'ghost nets'*, this unforgiving gear entangles fish, marine mammals, and sea birds, preventing them from feeding or causing them to drown. As many as 20,000 northern fur seals may die each year from becoming entangled in netting.

Egypt's High Aswan Dam, built in the 1960s to provide electricity and irrigation water, diverts up to 95 per cent of the Nile River's normal flow. It has since trapped more than one million tons of nutrient-rich silt and caused a sharp decline in Mediterranean sardine and shrimp fisheries. Commercial marine fisheries in the United States discard up to 20 billion pounds (9 billion kg) of non-target fish each year, which is twice the catch of desired commercial and recreational fishing combined. Worldwide, this adds up to well over 26 million tons of discarded fish each year. The United Nations estimates that of the 17 major fisheries areas in the world, four are depleted and the other 13 are either fished to capacity or overfished. It is a bleak picture.

PASSENGER SHIP EMISSIONS Ships have been pumping carbon dioxide into the atmosphere since at least 1870. However, attempts to reduce sulphur emissions have caused the disappearance of the low clouds which used to form over busy shipping lanes and radiated the Sun's heat back into space, helping to keep the planet cool. Big cruise liners produce 0.95 pounds (0.43 kg) of carbon dioxide every passenger mile, compared to only 0.57 pounds (0.26 kg) for flying.

PLASTIC The Mediterranean is the most polluted sea in the world, with 2000 pieces of plastic per square kilometre. Plastic is very slow to degrade and may last for hundreds of years. The sea protects plastic from ultraviolet light, which would otherwise break it down. The plastic waste includes kayaks, Lego blocks, footballs, fishing lines and plastic bags, and causes the deaths of over

Plankton – the Source of All Life

The word comes from the Greek word *planktos* meaning *'wandering'* or *'drifting'*. Plankton consists of both animals and plants that float in the well-lit surface layers of the oceans. It comes in all sizes, from invisible microbes to huge jellyfish. It is the most abundant life form on Earth (apart from bacteria) and is the base of the marine food chain. Planktonic organisms feed barnacles, sea squirts, fish and even whales. (The world's largest fish, the whale shark, is a plankton feeder, as is the world's largest mammal, the blue whale). Almost everything that lives off the oceans owes its existence to *phytoplankton*, the single-celled plants that live at the ocean surface. Phytoplankton need energy from the Sun and nutrients from the water to power their photosynthesis, and *half of the world's oxygen is produced via phytoplankton photosynthesis*. The other half is produced via photosynthesis from trees, shrubs, grasses and plants. Through photosynthesis, the atmosphere over millions of years has become favourable for humans to flourish. However, the concentration of oxygen in the sea is dropping across the world, from Hong Kong to the deeper waters in the Gulf of St Lawrence. This is one of the factors underlying the failure of cod to 'recover' from population decline as their eggs are sensitive to oxygen levels. With fewer phytoplankton, their rate of CO_2–O_2 gas exchange has decreased, and there is rising level of CO_2 and declining level of O_2 in the atmosphere. Ocean acidification is not only slowing the growth of coral, but also affecting the ability of phytoplankton (and lobsters and oysters) to build a shell from calcium carbonate. Oceans are 30 per cent more acidic than in pre-Industrial Revolution times, and if phytoplankton cannot build shells, the food chain ends where it begins.

1 million seabirds a year and more than 100,000 marine mammals. A dead Laysian albatross chick found on a remote Pacific island had dozens of plastic objects in its stomach, including a cigarette lighter, a tampon applicator and a toy robot. European fulmars only eat at sea, and nine out of ten die with plastic rubbish, such as syringes, in their stomachs. A study of 560 fulmars found an average of 44 items in each, and one fulmar had 1603 scraps of plastic inside it. Turtles, whales, seals and sea lions also suffer. Tiny plastic pellets, *'plastic soup'*, also end up in the food chain, polluting it with PCBs and other dangerous compounds.

PLASTIC BAGS The British *Daily Mail* newspaper carried a story on its entire front page and across the following eight pages upon 27 February 2008. It was headlined *'Banish The Bags'*, and the following facts are taken from the newspaper. A plastic bag is typically in use for 20 minutes, but can last up to 1000 years. Around 13 billion a year are given away free in the UK, and 5 trillion are made across the world, most in China. Endangered turtles are suffering as they mistake floating plastic bags for jellyfish. All species of (already endangered) turtle are affected, and the stomachs of up to 80 per cent of all dead turtles washed ashore contain plastics. A minke whale was recently washed up in Normandy. Two pounds (1 kg) of plastic bags were found in her stomach, which had caused her death. Bags also get stuck on coral reefs and start to cover them. Layer upon layer of plastic prevents light from reaching the coral, and so kills it. Some 100,000 sea animals are killed every year because of plastic bags. The victims include whales, dolphins, seals, sea lions and turtles. Beaked whales are particularly vulnerable as they suck in plastics while feeding. Once the animal's body has rotted, the bag is released back into the sea, potentially to kill other species. Seals die from strangulation, drowning, suffocation and starvation because of the bags. Seabirds such as gannets are also affected, and well over 1,000,000 seabirds every year die from these bags. It is impossible to assess the effect upon fish, but the numbers must run into many millions of deaths. In the English Channel, there are at least 300 plastic bags or floating objects in every square mile of water. In one survey, 300,000 pieces of plastic were found in a square mile of ocean floor. Beaches across the world are also littered. In the UK there are 3200 pieces of litter on every mile of beach, of which half are non-biodegradable plastic. *There are 46,000 pieces of floating plastic on the surface of every square mile of ocean.*

SEA AIR IS BAD FOR YOU

Smoke from vessels at sea or in port is affecting air quality in coastal cities, with an extremely high proportion of tiny solid sulphur-rich particles called primary sulphate entering the atmosphere. The pollution is caused when ships burn a cheap sulphur-rich fuel called 'bunker oil', and it is estimated that ship pollution is responsible for 60,000 deaths a year worldwide. It is believed to cause lung cancer, as the particles lodge deep in the lungs. Air samples in coastal California showed that 44 per cent of primary sulphate came from ship smoke. Some giant cargo ships have engines so large that they emit the same quantity of pollutants as 50 million cars in a year. A University of Delaware professor, James Corbett, believes that 39,000 people in the EU die prematurely each year from breathing in ship-origin pollutants. Ship fuel is bought from the cheapest and most contaminated sources, and it may contain 2000 times the levels of sulphur found in the diesel fuels sold for cars, plus heavy metals and other contaminants.

SEA STRUCTURES

THE COLOSSUS OF RHODES

The island of Rhodes had an important strategic harbour in ancient times, and it was conquered by Mausolus of Halicarnassus in 357 BCE (his tomb or 'mausoleum' was one of the Seven Wonders of the World). The Persians took it in 340 BCE, and then it was conquered by Alexander the Great in 332 BCE. The city was next attacked by Demetrius, king of Macedon, in 305 BCE, but held out with support from Egypt. In celebration the Rhodians built a statue of their sun-god Helios, using bronze melted down from the war machines of Demetrius. It possibly took 12 years to build, being completed in 292 BCE. It was 110 feet (33.5 m) high, and was situated on a 50-feet (15-m) pedestal near the harbour entrance. The statue was nude, wearing a spiked crown, shading its eyes from the rising sun with its right hand, and holding a cloak over its left shoulder. It was similar in size to the Statue of Liberty, but the Statue of Liberty is higher because of its taller pedestal and upraised torch. The Colossus was made of bronze over an iron framework. Its designer was Charos of Lindos. After only 56 years an earthquake hit Rhodes and destroyed the statue. Pliny wrote around 300 years later of its remains: *'Even as it lies, it excites our wonder and admiration. Few men can clasp the thumb in their arms,*

and its fingers are larger than most statues. Where the limbs are broken asunder, vast caverns are to be seen yawning in the interior. Within it, too, are to be seen large masses of rock, by the weight of which the artist steadied it while erecting it.' The Rhodians believed that the statue had offended Helios. In the 7th century CE the island was taken by Arabs. One of the most remarkable of the Seven Wonders of the Ancient World was then cut up into smaller pieces and sold as scrap metal.

DUBAI – THE ISLAND-BUILDING STATE

Not content with building the world's first underwater hotel, the emirate has constructed dozens of artificial islands in the shape of a palm tree and also of the world just off the coast of Dubai. They are intended as residential resorts.

DUBAI – THE LARGEST MARINA IN THE WORLD

Dubai not only has the largest marina in the world, but the largest man-made harbour (Jebel Ali), the biggest artificial island, the largest motorway intersection, and it also has the world's tallest hotel, the 1053-feet (321-m) high Burj-al-Arab. Shaped like the billowing sail of an Arab dhow, it is built on its own man-made island. Access to the 7-Star marketed hotel is via a causeway, courtesy of a Rolls-Royce or by helicopter.

EDDYSTONE LIGHT – THE MOST FAMOUS LIGHTHOUSE IN THE WORLD This lighthouse stands on the treacherous Eddystone Rocks off the coast of Devon. It was destroyed (and then rebuilt) in 1703, 1755 and 1877. The present lighthouse was completed in 1883. The folk song *'The Keeper of the Eddystone Light'* begins: *'Me father was the keeper of Eddystone Light/And slept with a mermaid one fine night/From this union there came three/ A porpoise and a porgy and the other was me!'* The first structure was built in 1698 by Henry Winstanley after he had seen two of his ships wrecked on the 23 jagged rocks, 14 miles (22.5 km) south of Plymouth. He spent one year drilling holes in the rocks and the next year he fixed iron bars into the holes with molten

Lighthouse Keepers and the First Message in a Bottle

The Smalls Lighthouse stands on a small rock 20 miles (32 km) off Pembrokeshire, Wales. The first lighthouse had been erected in 1775–6. It was based on nine pillars of oak which allowed the raging seas to pass through. This original design for dispersing the power of the waves was copied in other sea structures. Although subject to rocking and swaying, the lighthouse held together for 80 years. The *first known message in a bottle* was successfully sent from the lighthouse, reaching its addressee through the miles of sea, and allowing a rescue of stranded repair workers including its builder, Henry Whiteside.

An incident on the Smalls Lighthouse resulted in a change in lighthouse policy in 1801. The two keepers, Thomas Howell and Thomas Griffith,

were known to argue, and so when Griffith died in a freak accident, Howell feared that he might be suspected of his murder if he discarded the body into the sea, which was the usual policy. As the body began to decompose, Howell built a makeshift coffin for the corpse and lashed it to an outside shelf. Stiff winds blew the box apart, however, and the body was visible in a macabre, beckoning pose with one arm stretched out of the box. By the time the regular service boat arrived, several months later, Howell was white-haired and had been driven mad. Lighthouse teams were changed to rosters of three from this time until the automation of all British lighthouses in the 1980s. In 1861 Smalls Lighthouse was rebuilt, but the oak stumps of Whiteside's original lighthouse can still be seen.

lead. He lit the first light, which was watched by a crowd that had gathered on Plymouth Hoe, but he was then trapped for five weeks on the lighthouse by a gale. A gale in 1703, during which 8000 seamen drowned, destroyed the stone structure. Another structure was destroyed in 1755 by a fire which began in the keepers' quarters. Recommended by the Royal Society, John Smeaton, the inventor of quick-drying cement, designed the third lighthouse. It took three years to build and was completed in 1759. The rock foundations proved unstable, however, and it was taken down in 1877. The people of Plymouth were so grateful for its service that it was re-erected on Plymouth Hoe, where it stands today.

LILYPAD CITIES These are the invention of Belgian architect Vincent Callebaut. They are intended to accommodate displaced populations facing rising sea levels. Each self-sufficient 'floating city' would house 50,000 people, be fully sustainable, and have a central lake to collect and process rainwater. Power would come from renewable energy sources – solar panels, wind turbines and wave power. The design is based on the huge lilypad that grows on the waterlily *Victoria amazonica*. The city would be covered with plants growing in suspended gardens.

OIL AND GAS PRODUCTION
PLATFORMS When oil or gas is found at an exploration site, the drilling rig is replaced with a drilling platform, generally assembled at the site using a huge barge with heavy-lift cranes. Platforms will vary in size depending on the depth of the water, distance from

shore and size of the oil/gas field. They are generally made of steel and are fixed to the seabed with steel piles. They house an average of 80 workers who usually work a 12-hour day. Bigger platforms are larger than football fields, accommodate 500 workers and they can rise out of the sea to the height of a 25-storey office block. The world's largest platform is the Hibernia off Newfoundland, with ballast weighing 1.2 million tons while the platform is 734 feet (224 m) high.

THE PHAROS – THE WORLD'S
FIRST LIGHTHOUSE Alexandria in Egypt was founded by Alexander the Great in 323 BCE. He situated it 20 miles (32 km) west of the Nile Delta, with separate harbours for Nile and Mediterranean trade. The pharaoh Ptolemy Soter needed a landmark to guide ships into his prosperous city, and he authorized the building of the Pharos in 290 BCE. It took 20 years to build this first lighthouse in the world, the tallest building of the time except for the Great Pyramid. Ptolemy's son, Ptolemy II, wanted only his name on the building. The designer of the Pharos, however, had his name chiselled into the foundation: *'SOSTRATES, SON OF DEXIPHANES OF KNIDOS, ON BEHALF OF ALL MARINERS TO THE SAVIOUR GODS'*. The inscription was covered with plaster, in which was chiselled Ptolemy's name. Centuries later, the plaster aged and was chipped away, revealing Sostrates as the builder. The lighthouse was built on the island of Pharos, and its name became the root of the word for lighthouse in Romance languages, e.g. *'phare'* in French. From 10th century Moorish descriptions the Pharos was 300 cubits high, i.e.

between 450 and 600 feet (137 and 183 m), and designed like a modern skyscraper. It could be seen from up to 100 miles (160 km) away. The Pharos was clad in white marble, and it seems that a large polished metal mirror directed the light of a fire into a beam. It was important for shipping for almost 900 years, and was one of the Seven Wonders of the World. It was damaged by two earthquakes in the 14th century, and a castle was built from some of its stones in the 15th century. Its underwater remains were found in 1994.

RUBBER ANACONDA Hopefully this invention will harness wave power and lead to cleaner power supplies with minimal ecological damage. A rubber tube 600 feet (183 m) long and 20 feet (6 m) wide, it utilizes wave power while it is anchored to the sea bed. It appears that each anaconda will produce 1 megawatt, enough power for 100 homes. The sealed rubber 'snake' is anchored a couple of miles offshore, and as its front end is lifted by the sea, a pulse of water (a 'bulge wave') is created inside the tube. As the peak of the wave moves along the tube, it pushes the bulge wave along the inside of the tube. The continual 'squeezing' makes the bulge bigger and it is eventually squeezed past a turbine which turns to generate electricity. The project is currently in testing.

THE WORLD'S LONGEST SEA-CROSSING BRIDGE

The Hangzhou Bay Bridge links Shanghai to the industrial city of Ningbo across Hangzhou Bay, cutting the driving distance between them by 75 miles (120 km). The 22-mile (35-km), six-lane

bridge opened in May 2008, construction having started in November 2003. It is a cable-stayed structure built at a cost of $1.7 billion. Some of the financing for the bridge came from private sources, a first for such a large infrastructure project in China. The challenging project was completed on time. Hangzhou Bay is a gulf in the East China Sea, and its massive tides were both a bridge construction obstacle and a major project-related tourism draw. The Qiantang River Tide had to be accounted for, being one of China's 'natural wonders' with waves of up to 25 feet (8 m) and tidal speeds of 15–18 mph (24–29 kph). *'It is the greatest construction project the Chinese government has ever undertaken'*, said Liu Ting, deputy director of the Hangzhou Bay Bridge project, *'not only because of the technical aspects but also because it is so important to the economic development of the whole province.'* (The world's longest bridge is Louisiana's 23.8-mile (38.3-km) Lake Pontchartrain Causeway.)

THE WORLD'S WORST OFFSHORE OIL DISASTER

Production at the Piper Alpha North Sea oil platform, once the world's single largest oil producer, had yielded 317,000 barrels of oil a day at its peak. By 1988, production had declined a great deal, however. There had been a small explosion caused by a gas leak in 1984, causing an evacuation. In the 1988 explosion, the flames could be seen 70 miles (113 km) away, after a fireball had risen 700 feet (213 m) in the air. Workers had to jump 170 feet (52 m) into the cold waters to escape the fire, and only relatively few of them survived. Of the 226 men on board, 61 survived.

SEA FISHING

THE FISHERMAN In the *Idylls* of the pastoral poet Theocritus (c.300–250 BCE) we read: *'There were two old fishermen lodged together; in their wattled hut they had spread dry sea-moss for a bed, and there they lay, against the wall of leaves. Besides them were the tools of their trade – creels, rods, hooks, buckets of bait and weeds, lines, baskets, lobster-pots, seine-nets, a pair of oars and an elderly boat on legs. Under their heads was a bit of matting, with their jackets and caps. Such was all their wealth, all their resources. The hut had no door, no watch-dog. What need of such superfluity, when poverty kept watch for them?'*

Fisherman's Prayer

God grant that I may live to fish,
Until my dying day.
And when it comes to my last cast,
I then most humbly pray,
When in the Lord's safe landing net,
I'm peacefully asleep,
That in His Mercy I be judged,
As big enough to keep.

FISH FARMING Salmon is cheap because most of what we eat is farmed in pens. As a result the texture and taste is not that of a muscled fish which has crossed the Atlantic. Half of all fish consumed by humans may now come from aquaculture, but this requires a global supply of small fish for fishmeal. As a result, fish farms consume five tons of wild fish for every ton of fish they sell. Sourcing this sustainably is difficult.

FISHING AS AN INDUSTRY About 70 to 75 million tons of fish are caught in the ocean every year, 29 million tons being for human consumption. Fish supply the greatest percentage of the world's protein consumed by humans. More than 3.5 billion people depend on the ocean for their primary source of food, and in 20 years, this number could double to 7 billion. Fish can be caught, or farmed by aquaculture, and the total production has grown 34 per cent over the last decade. The largest numbers of fish are located in the southern hemisphere as these waters are as yet less exploited. Unless we protect critical marine habitats – warm and cold water coral reefs, seagrass beds and mangroves – fish size and quantity will keep decreasing. Populations of commercially attractive large fish, such as tuna, cod, swordfish and marlin, have declined by as much as 90 per cent in the past century. Each year, illegal longline fishing involving lines up to 80 miles (130 km) long with thousands of baited hooks, kills over 300,000 seabirds, including 100,000 albatrosses. Fifteen out of 17 of the world's largest fisheries are now so heavily exploited that fish reproduction cannot keep up. As a result many fish populations are decreasing rapidly, such as tuna, salmon, haddock, halibut and cod. In the 19th century, cod weighing up to 200 pounds (91 kg) used to be caught. Nowadays, a 40-pound (18-kg) cod is considered a giant.

FISH NOT FOR EATING

Haddock are being fished close to extinction, following the unhappy example of cod. Other fish to avoid if you want to behave ethically, to help reduce demand and allow stocks to rebuild are: eel, tuna, plaice, hake, halibut, swordfish, flounder and shark. Also the intensive fishing of shrimps, prawns and king prawns is destroying mangrove forests. Even farmed salmon causes an ethical problem as they are fed by-catch from the fishing industry. Fish stocks which are ethically reasonable to eat include wild salmon, herring, mackerel and pollock.

SHARK FIN SOUP AND SPECIES EXTINCTION

This 'delicacy' is often served at weddings and banquets as part of a Chinese feast, as a symbol of prestige, being consumed in Thailand, Japan, China and other Far Eastern nations. Especially because of the growing wealth of China, there has been a massive rise in demand for shark fins (along with other costly delicacies such as sea cucumber and bird's nest soup.) The high price of these items is meant to impress guests, as the foods themselves have little flavour. In an on-line survey, 83 per cent of the Chinese participants stated that they had tasted the soup, and in a separate 2006 survey 35per cent said they had tasted it in 2005. Shark fins from even the once common spiny dogfish (sold as 'rock salmon' for marketing purposes) are also used along with shark cartilage in the manufacture of health supplements to strengthen bones, and shark oil is used by the multinational cosmetics industry. Shark meat is eaten across the world, and global catches of sharks have risen from 600,000 tons a year to 800,000 tons, so there is huge pressure upon shark, dogfish and ray populations, even without the shark fin soup problem.

It seems that the vast majority of these fins are cut from living sharks, a process known as 'finning'. The dying sharks are thrown back into the ocean, to make room in the boat for more valuable catches, such as tuna. A 2006 study estimated that between 26 million and 73 million sharks are killed each year, three times higher than the statistics cited in a UN report. Another estimate claims that 100 million sharks are killed annually. Finning is a major cause of shark

Fish Marketing and the Strange Case of the Patagonian Toothfish

Some of us are aware of the tradition of dogfish/catfish/wolfish/huss being marketed as *'rock salmon'* and of bass being sold as *'fresh sea bass'* at inflated restaurant prices. One of the latest marketing efforts concerns the remarkably ugly Patagonian toothfish. It is sold as *Chilean* (or *Antarctic*) *sea bass*. It is an incredibly important fish. Of the 20,000 known species of fish in the world, just 120 live in the Southern Ocean. Over the past 40 million years they have adapted to the freezing conditions by developing a special 'antifreeze' component in their body fluids. All of these Antarctic fish are especially vulnerable to overfishing because most of them take a long time to become sexually mature. The toothfish grows slowly to over 6 feet 6 inches (200 cm) in length, lives as long as 50 years and does not breed until it is at least 10 years old. It lives in deep waters and is part of the diet of the sperm whale, killer whale and colossal squid. It probably comprises up to 98 per cent of the elephant seal's fish diet. This rapidly disappearing Patagonian toothfish is now worth so much money in the marketplace that the fishing industry has dubbed it the *'white gold of the Southern Ocean'*. The price of toothfish in the markets has increased steadily in line with its declining numbers, doubling in price to $11 per kilo between 1998 and 1999.

By the mid-1980s, overfishing had forced many Spanish, South Korean and Japanese fishing fleets out of their national waters. In Chilean waters they caught fish such as Austral hake and golden kingclip, but by the early 1990s overfishing had caused the collapse of these Chilean fisheries. The fishing fleets then targeted the Patagonian toothfish. The population of Patagonian toothfish became depleted in South American waters, so the illegal fishers moved eastwards to the southern Indian Ocean. Industrialized fishing vessels are still poaching thousands of tons of Patagonian toothfish around South America, plus off the sub-Antarctic islands belonging to South Africa, Australia, New Zealand, France as well as in international waters. It is

estimated that in some areas up to 90 per cent of the total Patagonian toothfish catch is taken by illegal and unregulated longliners. In general, illegal catches may be up to five times the legal catch limit, and the toothfish population may collapse within two to five years. Catches are unloaded in countries like Mauritius and Namibia, then sold on the black market, with a single sashimi grade fish (high grade fish that may be served in sushi restaurants) fetching up to $1000.

depopulation, and CITES names three sharks in danger of extinction on its Red List: the great white shark, the basking shark and the whale shark, the latter two being the world's biggest fish. Other shark species need protection to maintain their populations. Oceanic white-tip sharks have declined 99 per cent in the last five years. The main cause of shark numbers dropping is also that by-catch probably accounts for 50 per cent of sharks taken. Fishermen around the world state that sharks are now more difficult to find and they are much smaller in size than ten years ago. WildAid co-director Steven Galster has stated: *'In Costa Rica, the shark population has declined 80 per cent in the past 10 years, while the rate in North America is as high as 90 per cent in the past 15 years.'*

A TEMPORARY SOLUTION TO OVERFISHING? In 1950s research conducted at Aberdeen's Marine Research Laboratories the data showed that the ideal minimum size of mesh for trawl nets was around 4 inches (10 cm). Immature fish slipped unharmed through the mesh to mature for another year or more and hopefully breed. Mesh size is dedcided by fishermen, and is unregulated across the oceans.

TRAWLERS These boats drag 'trawls', a type of fishing net, along the bottom of the sea. Trawlers range up to 3000 tons in size. With refrigerated holds, they can stay at sea until they complete their catch. Brixham was the biggest fishing port in England in the Middle Ages, and the fishing trawler was invented there in the 19th century. The wooden vessels were copied all over the world. Brixham was known as *'the Mother of Deep-Sea*

Fisheries', and in the 1890s 300 trawlers operated from there. Its boats helped to establish the major fishing ports of Grimsby, Hull and Lowestoft operating in the North Sea. The largest fishing port in Europe in the 1980s was Peterhead in northeast Scotland, with 500 trawlers each staying around a week at sea. However, quotas and over-fishing have reduced the fleet's size. In both world wars, many trawlers were converted to serve as minesweepers.

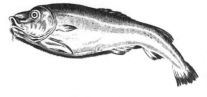

TRAWLING Many parts of Britain's sea bed are trawled up to 20 times a year. Giant weighted nets drag across the sea bed scooping up most life forms down there. It can take years for them to become re-established. Most of the sea bed around Britain is trawled at least twice a year, leading to desertification. Common skate that once grew as big as doors are now almost extinct. Pink seafans, closely related to tropical corals, are vanishing. Anemones are being wiped out during scallop dredging. Oyster beds once covered thousands of square miles but they have vanished. Sharks were once so common in the North Sea that fishermen risked attack. In 1956 the British distant-water fishing fleet brought back 8.36 million tons of fish. In 1997 the entire UK fleet brought back 816,000 tons, despite more efficient trawlers. In 2007 this figure dropped to 600,000 tons. The ripping up of the sea bed means a reduction in fish stocks across the world.

TRAWLERMEN The bravery of trawlermen was eloquently summed up by Alan Villiers in *Posted Missing* (1959): *'Trawlermen have the heart of lions. There was the case of the timber steamer* Fred Borchard, *for example, which foundered off the coast of Norway in 1951 in a dreadful fury of the sea, littered with great baulks of timber broken from the* Borchard's *decks. A little trawler, by name the* Boston Fury, *steamed among these baulks in that wild gale and literally fished twenty-seven of the twenty-nine men in the* Borchard's *crew out of the sea, though the* Boston Fury *could launch no boats. Boats would be smashed up by the timber. But what about men? She put her men in the water, gale or no gale, and they swam among those murdering baulks, which were crashing, rolling and plunging in the violent turmoil of the sea. They got lines to the twenty-seven men, and they saved them. Men said afterwards that only fishermen could have carried out a rescue like that. The* Borchard *went down north of the Arctic Circle, too, and the month was October.'*

The World's 'Greatest Fisherman'

Zyg Gregorek of Devon has travelled 150,000 miles (241,000 km) over 18 years to catch all ten game species of billfish, nine of shark and eight of tuna. In the world of 'big game fishing', catching a specimen of each target species is called a *'Grand Slam'*, and he is the first person known to have achieved a *'Full House'* of grand slams. He caught a great white (an endangered species) using a whaler shark as bait. He is only the second man in history to have caught all nine species of shark, and the only person to have caught three different species of shark weighing over 1000 pounds (454 kg). His shark grand slam included great white, blue, hammerhead, mako, thresher, tiger, tope, whaler and porbeagle. Billfish include swordfish, sailfish and marlin. The President of the International Game Fishing Federation, Rob Kramer, described Gregorek as *'totally unique'* and *'the world's greatest fisherman'*. Others with knowledge of species extinction, carbon footprints and man's inhumanity to animals may have a different perspective. Nearly all of the species caught, such as marlin, are nearing non-sustainable levels in the oceans. The journal *Science* in 2007 claimed that since 1972 the number of blacktip sharks fell by 93 per cent, tiger sharks by 97 per cent and bull sharks, dusky sharks and smooth hammerheads by 99 per cent, warning that the great sharks were on the edge of extinction. In 2004 *Nature* showed that populations of large predators, such as marlin and swordfish, had declined by 90 per cent.

THE WORLD'S LARGEST MARINE RESERVE

The tiny Pacific island nation of Kiribati has created the new *Phoenix Islands Protected Area* of 164,200 square miles (425,000 km²), around the size of California. The islands comprising Kiribati total only about 313 square miles (810 km²). The protected area is home to sea turtles, more than 120 species of coral, 520 species of fish, and it also contains important sea-bird nesting sites. The impoverished nation will be giving up millions of dollars in relinquished commercial fishing licences every year, but hopes to make up for some of the lost revenue through increased tourism. Previously the world's largest marine protected area was the northwestern Hawaiian Islands, set aside by the USA in 2006.

THE WORLD'S LARGEST TUNA-FISHING VESSEL

The Spanish-owned and flagged tuna purse seiner *Albatun Tres* (a purse seine is a large fishing net that hangs vertically in the water) is known as a *'super, super seiner'* which can net 3000 tons of tuna in a single fishing trip. This is almost double the entire annual catch of some Pacific island countries. Purse seine vessels surround schools of fish with curtain-like nets to catch tuna. A rope along the bottom of the net is pulled like a drawstring and the whole catch is hauled onboard. In the process 150 tons of tuna, a whole school, can be exterminated. These vessels have increased their efficiency enormously in the last decade through a variety of technological innovations. While targeting skipjack tuna, these boats also catch juvenile bigeye and yellowfin tuna, seriously threatening their already vulnerable stocks. Foreign fishing nations (including those of the European Union) are fishing unsustainably, while Pacific island countries depend on tuna for income and food. The *Albatun Tres* arrived in the Pacific from the Indian Ocean in 2009.

The western and central Pacific tuna fishery, the world's biggest, has been subjected to intense fishing by fleets from Asia and the United States since the 1960s. With declining tuna stocks in the Atlantic and Indian Ocean, the European Union has gained access to this Pacific fishing ground as a reciprocal benefit for giving aid to Pacific countries. With their own waters fished out, the EU and other foreign fishing fleets including Japan, Korea, Taiwan and the US, are sailing across the world to take vital fish and income from people whose lives depend on it, according to Greenpeace, which has been monitoring the *Albatun Tres*.

References

Ashley, Clifford, *The Ashley Book of Knots*, Doubleday 1944, New York

Atkins, Roy and Leslie, *Jack Tar: Life in Nelson's Navy*, Little, Brown 2008, London

Breverton, T.D. (editor), *The Illustrated Pirate Diaries: A Remarkable Eyewitness Account of Captain Morgan and the Buccaneers by Alexandre Exquemelin*, Harper Collins 2008, New York

Breverton, T.D., *The Pirate Handbook* (*The Pirate Dictionary* USA), Glyndwr Publishing 2004, Glamorgan; *The Pirate Dictionary*, Pelican 2004, New Orleans

Breverton, T.D., *The First American Novel: Part I The Journal of Penrose, Seaman; Part II The Author, the Book and the letters in the Lilly Library*, Glyndwr Publishing 2007, Glamorgan

Breverton, T.D., *Black Bart Roberts: The Greatest Pirate of Them All*, Glyndwr Publishing 2004, Glamorgan; Pelican 2004, New Orleans

Breverton, T.D., *Admiral Sir Henry Morgan: The Greatest Buccaneer of Them All*, Glyndwr Publishing 2005, Glamorgan; Pelican 2005, New Orleans

Breverton, T.D. and Carradice Phil, *Welsh Sailors of the Second World War*, Glyndwr Publishing 2007, Glamorgan

Breverton T.D., *The Book of Welsh Pirates and Buccaneers*, Glyndwr Publishing 2003, Glamorgan

Bridges, T.C., *The Book of the Sea*, Geo. Winderley 1927, Cape Town

Dana, R.H., *The Seaman's Manual, Containing a Treatise of Practical Seamanship*, Moxon 1844, London

Exquemelin, Alexandre Olivier (or Esquemeling John), *The Buccaneers of America*, 1684, London

Falconer, William, *A Marine Dictionary*, 1769, modernized and enlarged Burney, William: as *A New Universal Dictionary of the Marine...*, T. Caldell & W. Davies 1815, London

Johnson, Captain Charles/Defoe, Daniel, *A General History of the Robberies and Murders of the Most Notorious Pyrates...*, 1724, London (available in many editions since)

Mainwaring, Henry, *The Seaman's Glossary*, also known as *The Seaman's Dictionary*, 1623, London

Philbrick, Nathaniel, *In the Heart of the Sea: The Epic True Story that Inspired Moby Dick*, Harper Collins 2000, London

Jones, Tristan, *The Incredible Voyage: A Personal Odyssey*, The Bodley Head 1978, London

Smith, Captain John, *A Sea Grammar*, 1627, London

Smyth, Admiral W.H., *The Sailor's Word-Book*, 1867, republished Conway Maritime Press 1991, London

Index

To buy books in quantity for corporate use or incenti es, call **(800) 962–0973** or e-mail **premiums@GlobePequot.com.**

Text by Terry Breverton
Edited by Philip de Ste. Croix
Designed by Paul Turner and Sue Pressley,
Stonecastle Graphics Ltd
Index by Philip de Ste. Croix

Copyright © Quercus Publishing Plc 2010

First Lyons Press edition, 2010

ALL RIGHTS RESERVED. No part of this book may be reproduced or transmitted in any form by any means, electronic or mechanical, including photocopying and recording, or by any information storage and retrieval system, except as may be expressly permitted in writing from the publisher. Requests for permission should be addressed to The Globe Pequot Press, Attn: Rights and Permissions Department, P.O. Box 480, Guilford, CT 06437.

The Lyons Press is an imprint of The Globe Pequot Press.

Library of Congress Cataloging-in-Publication Data is available on file.

ISBN 978-1-59921-979-0

Printed and bound in China

10 9 8 7 6 5 4 3

Picture credits:
© Dover Publications Inc.: 1, 4, 6, 8, 9, 14 (above), 19, 22, 23, 24, 26, 28, 32, 33, 34, 37 (above), 37 (below), 40, 41, 43, 54, 60, 61, 63, 64, 67, 68–9 (all), 70, 72, 77, 80, 84, 87, 88, 90, 91 (above), 92, 93, 94, 95, 96–7 (all), 99, 104, 107, 108, 109, 111, 115 (above), 116, 117, 118, 119 (above), 119 (below), 127, 130 (above), 130 (below), 131, 133, 137, 138, 139, 140, 141, 142, 145, 146 (above), 146 (below), 152, 153, 159, 164 (above), 167, 170, 172–3 (all), 174, 175, 177, 178, 181, 182, 183, 184, 185, 191, 193, 194 (above), 194 (below), 195, 197, 198, 199, 203, 208, 210, 214, 215, 216, 217 (above), 217 (below), 218, 221, 222, 225, 229, 231, 232, 235, 236, 239, 240, 241, 242, 243, 244, 247, 251, 255 (above), 255 (below), 257, 259, 260, 262 (above), 262 (below), 263, 265 (above), 266, 267, 268, 269, 270, 271 (above), 271 (below), 272, 276, 279, 280, 283, 284, 286, 287, 288, 289 (above), 289 (below), 290 (above), 290 (below), 291, 292, 293, 294, 296, 297, 298, 300, 301, 302, 307, 309, 311, 312, 313, 314, 315, 316, 317, 318, 320, 321, 323, 325, 326–7 (all), 328, 329, 330, 331, 332, 334, 335, 337, 338, 339, 340, 341, 344, 345, 346, 347, 348, 350, 353, 354, 355, 357, 358, 359, 360, 361, 363, 367, 368, 371 (above), 371 (below), 372, 373, 374, 375, 376.

Library of Ornament (Nautical Ornaments): 2, 11 (above), 11 (below), 13, 14 (below), 15, 16, 17, 18, 20, 21, 31, 36, 39, 45, 47, 49, 50, 51, 53, 55, 57, 58, 59, 74, 78, 79, 83, 91 (below), 100, 105, 113, 144, 149, 156, 160, 163, 164 (below), 166, 168, 180, 189, 206, 226, 230, 238, 265 (below), 278.

All other images are in the public domain.